KENTUCKIANS IN GRAY

KENTUCKIANS IN GRAY

Confederate Generals and Field Officers of the Bluegrass State

EDITED BY
BRUCE S. ALLARDICE AND
LAWRENCE LEE HEWITT

THE UNIVERSITY PRESS OF KENTUCKY

Scholarly publisher for the Commonwealth,
serving Bellarmine University, Berea College, Centre
College of Kentucky, Eastern Kentucky University,
The Filson Historical Society, Georgetown College,
Kentucky Historical Society, Kentucky State University,
Morehead State University, Murray State University,
Northern Kentucky University, Transylvania University,
University of Kentucky, University of Louisville,
and Western Kentucky University.
All rights reserved.

Editorial and Sales Offices: The University Press of Kentucky
663 South Limestone Street, Lexington, Kentucky 40508-4008
www.kentuckypress.com

12 11 10 09 08   5 4 3 2 1

Library of Congress Cataloging-in-Publication Data

Kentuckians in gray : Confederate generals and field officers of the
Bluegrass State / edited by Bruce S. Allardice and Lawrence Lee Hewitt.
      p.   cm.
   Includes bibliographical references and index.
   ISBN 978-0-8131-2475-9 (hardcover : alk. paper)
   1. Kentucky—History—Civil War, 1861–1865—Biography. 2. Generals—
Confederate States of America—Biography. 3. Confederate States of America.
Army—Officers—Biography. 4. United States—History—Civil War,
1861–1865—Biography. 5. Soldiers—Kentucky—Biography. I. Allardice,
Bruce S. II. Hewitt, Lawrence L.
   E564.4.K37   2008
   973.7'82092—dc22
   [B]
                                    2008031752

This book is printed on acid-free recycled paper meeting
the requirements of the American National Standard
for Permanence in Paper for Printed Library Materials.

Manufactured in the United States of America.

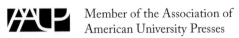   Member of the Association of
American University Presses

CONTENTS

ACKNOWLEDGMENTS

Kentuckians in Gray was truly a collaborative effort. Foremost among the many who assisted us in creating this volume are our coauthors. Though their names appear elsewhere in this volume, it would be remiss of us not to acknowledge their contributions here. We have a better understanding of Kentucky's Confederate generals because of the contributions of Lindsey Apple, Arthur W. Bergeron Jr., C. David Dalton, Stephen Davis, William C. "Jack" Davis, Charles Elliott, John D. Fowler, Robert I. Girardi, Charles D. Grear, Lowell H. Harrison, Nathaniel C. Hughes, M. Jane Johansson, Marshall D. Krolick, Mary Gorton McBride, Brian D. McKnight, Alexander Mendoza, Raymond Mulesky, James M. Prichard, Jeffery S. Prushankin, James A. Ramage, Charles P. Roland, Stuart W. Sanders, Thomas E. Schott, Peter J. Sehlinger, Brian Steel Wills, and Terrence J. Winschel. The credit is due to them; any errors are ours.

Several members of the staff at the University Press of Kentucky were instrumental in shepherding this project through the publication process: Director Stephen M. Wrinn and former acquisitions editor Joyce Harrison, who enthusiastically accepted our proposal; readers Charlie Roland and Jim Ramage, who not only endorsed the manuscript but also enhanced it by their insightful comments and the essays they contributed; advertising, direct mail, and exhibits manager Allison Webster; marketing director Leila Salisbury; and especially editorial assistant Ann M. Malcolm, who labored extensively on selecting the illustrations (which provided more headaches than one could ever imagine) and helped with numerous other things; production manager and image guru Richard Farkas; editing supervisor David Cobb; and Cheryl Hoffman of Hoffman-Paulson Associates, who transformed the work of twenty-eight authors into a uniform style.

Numerous individuals assisted us in ferreting out the illustrations: Jack Davis; Steve Mullinax; Waite Rawls, John Coski, and Melinda Gales of the Museum of the Confederacy; Art Bergeron at the U.S. Army Military History Institute, Carlisle Barracks; Lawrence T. Jones of Confederate Calendar Works; Kevin Johnson, Stuart Sanders, and Charlene Smith of the Kentucky Historical Society; Judy Bolton at Special Collections, Louisiana State University Libraries; Steve Bounds of the Mansfield (Louisiana) State Historic Site; Jeff Rogers and Michael Wright at the Museum of Mississippi History; Jody Cary at the New York Historical Society; Stephen J. Fletcher and Matthew Turi at the Manuscripts Department, Wilson Library, the University of North Carolina at Chapel Hill; Lynn Deal and Kyle McGrogan of the Samuel Bell Maxey House (Texas) State Historic Site; Terry Winschel and Virginia DuBowy at the Vicksburg National Military Park; Meg Glass and Beth Petty of the Valentine Richmond History Center; Alicia Mauldin-Ware of the Special Collections and Archives Division, U.S. Military Academy; Jeffrey Ruggles of the Virginia Historical Society; and especially Mikel Uriguen, the person behind the Web site The Generals of the American Civil War (http://generalsandbrevets.com).

Others who provided recommendations regarding contributors, illustrations, or information regarding the subjects of *Kentuckians in Gray* or assisted with the indexing include Leslie Goddard Allardice, Kent Masterson Brown, Donni Case, Antonio de la Cova, Bob Davis, Larry and Debbie Hicklen, James Klotter, Robert E. L. Krick, Glenn W. LaFantasie, Gary Matthews, Greg Miller, Timothy B. Smith, and Cindy Tyson.

Authors know how much their work depends on the help of other authors, editors, archivists, experts, family members, and friends. Our sincerest thanks to all of you.

Bruce S. Allardice
Lawrence Lee Hewitt

INTRODUCTION

I hope to have God on my side, but I must have Kentucky.
—*attributed to Abraham Lincoln, 1861*

Early in the conflict, President Abraham Lincoln told Sen. Orville Browning of Illinois, "I think to lose Kentucky is nearly the same as to lose the whole game. Kentucky gone, we can not hold Missouri, nor, as I think, Maryland. These all against us, and the job on our hands is too large for us. We would as well consent to separation at once, including the surrender of this capitol." With Kentucky in Confederate hands, the boundary between Union and Confederacy lay along the northern bank of the Ohio River, with the Confederacy threatening the bordering free states of Ohio, Indiana, and Illinois. The Confederates could recruit soldiers in the Bluegrass State while denying volunteers to the Union army and at the same time harvest Kentucky's famed horse and mule production for the South. Control of Kentucky was vital to both sides.

By 1860, Kentucky had an overall population of 1,155,651, of whom 919, 484 (79.6 percent) were white, 225,483 (19.5 percent) were slaves, and 10,684 (1 percent) were free Negroes. Kentucky had a larger white population than all but one of the seceding states, and more than twice as great a free white population as seceding states such as Mississippi or Texas. Kentucky stood third in total population among the slave states, and of these, only seceding Virginia and nonseceding Missouri had a larger white population. Those two states were deeply divided between unionists and secessionists, but not so much as Kentucky.

Following the Confederate attack on Fort Sumter, President Lincoln called on the states to furnish seventy-five thousand volunteer militia to suppress the rebellion. Effectively a declaration of war against the seven seceded states, his action pushed four border slave states, including Virginia and Tennessee, to join the new Confederacy. Lincoln asked Kentucky's state government to provide approximately four thousand troops. At the time, Kentucky's political leaders hoped to keep the state neutral in the conflict so that the Bluegrass State could once again lead the way in forging a compromise between the warring sections. In response to Lincoln's request for soldiers, Gov. Beriah Magoffin, a Democrat friendly to the South, refused, stating, "Kentucky will furnish no troops for the wicked purpose of subduing her sister Southern states." Magoffin's firm stance in favor of neutrality satisfied activists on neither side. The pro-Confederates in the state forced the election of a state convention to consider secession. However, pro-Union voters elected a solid majority to that convention, which blocked any attempt to take Kentucky out of the Union. At the same time, the pro-Union majority in the state legislature prevented Governor Magoffin from taking any active steps to align the commonwealth with the Confederacy. This political deadlock resulted in the state's brief, doomed attempt to keep out of the war beginning to rage around it.

Kentucky's neutral stance quickly crumbled as both the Union and Confederate governments opened recruiting offices in the state. Kentucky's citizens, eager for the conflict, donned the blue or the gray, the state government being powerless to prevent it. In September of 1861, a Confederate army entered Kentucky, violating the state's neutrality and forcing the state to make a choice. The majority of Kentuckians chose to remain loyal to the Union. In a complex series of maneuvers, Governor Magoffin was in essence deprived of power, with the Unionist majority in the legislature taking over his executive powers, and Kentucky officially allied itself with its northern neighbors.

More than any other state in the nation, Kentucky felt the personal holocaust that was the American Civil War. A state of Southern traditions, largely settled by Virginians with all the cultural, political, and social heritage that implies, Kentucky was nonetheless a border state, largely pro-slavery but with an economy that tied it as much to the North as to the South. In the decades prior to the war Kentuckians such as Henry Clay and John J. Crittenden had labored to preserve the Union, promoting compromises that papered over sectional differences but never settled the underlying dilemmas resultant from a country that was, in Abraham Lincoln's famous words, "half slave and half free." Pro-slavery but also pro-Union, Kentuckians were among the last to have to make a choice between North and South. When forced to make that decision, Kentuckians made the choice as individuals, not as part of a group or class, and in the process often ignored the wishes of family, the influence of friends, and the dictates of economic self-interest. Thus brother quite literally fought against brother, and father against son.

President Lincoln's own family illustrates the tragic personal choices Kentuckians made. Lincoln, a proud son of Kentucky and married to a Kentucky belle, saw four of Mary Todd Lincoln's brothers fight for the Confederacy. The husband of Mary's favorite sister and a friend of the president, Benjamin Hardin Helm turned down Lincoln's personal offer of a U.S. army command in order to "go South." The West Point–educated Helm rose to brigadier general in the Confederate army only to be killed at the battle of Chickamauga in 1863. It is said that when Lincoln heard of Helm's death, he wept. It was no different for Kentucky's three leading political families. Four of the grandsons of the "great compromiser" Henry Clay backed the Confederacy, while three others remained loyal. Sons of Senator Crittenden became major generals in opposing armies. Though former vice president and senator John C. Breckinridge joined the Confederacy, his cousin Rev. Robert Breckinridge remained loyal and gave the keynote address at the 1864 Union Party Convention.

As the Civil War slips further into our past and things associated with the Confederacy are increasingly renamed or removed from sight, even the most famous of Kentucky's gray-clad warriors may one day be forgotten, as some of them already have been. This volume is an attempt to stem that tide. The larger portion of the present work is a biographical dictionary of Kentucky's "generals in gray," the Bluegrass State's native sons or, in the cases of John Hunt Morgan and Lloyd Tilghman, longtime Kentucky residents who became generals in the Confederate army.

Confederate army law provided for four different grades of general. A rank of brigadier general was designed for officers commanding—not surprisingly—a brigade, a unit of two or more regiments numbering anywhere from one thousand to three thousand men. A division, composed of two or more brigades, was slated as a command for a major general. A lieutenant general generally commanded a corps of two or more divisions, while a full general usually commanded an army of two or more corps.

The president of the Confederacy, Kentucky native Jefferson Davis, had the sole legal power to create generals. Laws provided that the president appoint the general, after which appointment the new general had to be confirmed by the Confederate Senate in his new rank. Upon confirmation, the officer would rank from the date of appointment or other date designated by the president.

In all, 426 officers of the Confederate army achieved the rank of general. Kentucky claimed 39 of them (9.2 percent) as native sons or wartime residents. These 39 generals are the primary subjects of this book. Following the biographies of the generals are briefer biographical sketches of the men who became field officers of these regiments and battalions.

A disproportionate number of Kentuckians rose to high military rank considering that the state provided only 4 percent of Confederate soldiers. Two Kentucky natives (Albert Sidney Johnston and John Bell Hood) were among the 8 men who achieved the highest Confederate army rank, that of full general. Two more (Simon Bolivar Buckner and Richard Taylor) were among only 19 who rose to lieutenant general. Gustavus W. Smith, a major general, preceded Robert E. Lee in command of what was to become the Army of Northern Virginia. Another major general and corps commander, politician John C. Breckinridge, became the secretary of war in February of 1865 when President Davis was pressured by the Congress to reform the War Department.

Nowhere was the adage of the Civil War "brother against brother" more poignantly illustrated than with Kentucky's Confederate generals. George Crittenden's brother Thomas became a major general and corps commander in the Union army. Abraham H. Buford's two Buford cousins (John, the hero of Gettysburg, and Napoleon) also became Union generals. Jo Shelby's cousin Frank Blair led the Union cause in Missouri, later rising to corps commander under William T. Sherman. John B. Grayson's half brother Peter B. Porter, a colonel in the Union army, was killed at the battle of Cold Harbor. Roger Hanson's brother Charles became colonel of the Union army's Twentieth Kentucky Infantry,

As with all armies, there were many more enlisted men than officers. More than 100,000 Kentuckians served in the war, with approximately 51,000 white and 25,000 black men fighting for the Union and 25,000–30,000 whites serving the Confederacy. An additional 75,000 white males of suitable age to have served in the army maintained their individual neutrality by staying home. Though divided and predominantly pro-Union, Kentucky provided the Confederate army with nine infantry and fifteen cavalry regiments, several battalions and artillery batteries, as well as partisan ranger bands.

The regiment of infantry or cavalry was the basic component unit of Civil War–era armies, and the unit with which the common soldier most often identified himself. Briefly, regiments in either army were to consist of ten companies, each with a minimum of 64 and a maximum of 100 privates, plus a few staff officers for each regiment. Each regiment was to be commanded by a colonel who would be assisted by two other "field officers," a lieutenant colonel and a major. The lieutenant colonel and the major were charged with assisting the colonel in the drill and command of the regiment. In battle the lieutenant colonel and the major were to command the right and left wings of the deployed regiment, with the colonel in overall command.

In practice, at any given moment at least one of these field officers would be absent from the regiment. Accordingly, a regiment might go into a battle commanded by its major, with a senior captain as second in command. Numerous colonels, lieutenant colonels, and majors commanded a brigade at one time or another due to the absence of their superiors.

Approximately 17 percent (more than one in six) of Confederate army full colonels went on to become generals. Three-fourths of the Confederate generals were full colonels at one point in their careers, with others being promoted to brigadier general direct from lieutenant colonel or even major.

Due to battle casualties, disease, and details, it was rare for a Civil War regiment to muster anything near the thousand-man strength the regulations called for. By the third year of the war, a combat regiment was lucky to muster "present for duty" even one-third of its thousand-man nominal strength.

Kentucky's Confederate field officers included a number of officers on the fast track to promotion to general but who never achieved that star. Col. Thomas Hunt of the Ninth Kentucky, John Hunt Morgan's uncle, resigned to take care of his family before the promotion to brigadier came through. Hunt had often led a brigade as senior colonel and won universal admiration for his courage and "superior natural intellect." Another colonel who almost won promotion was Robert P. Trabue of the Fourth Kentucky, who led a brigade at Shiloh but died of disease soon after. Col. J. Warren Grigsby of the Sixth Kentucky Cavalry often led a brigade and was termed "general" in a number of postwar memoirs. Maj. John B. Castleman, an undercover Confederate agent in the North, finally won his generalship—in the U.S. Army during the Spanish-American War!

Many of the officers described within these pages are remembered for reasons other than their rank in the Confederate army. Among the more colorful generals was Abraham H. Buford, reputedly three hundred pounds and the heaviest Confederate general. A hard-drinking, hard-fighting, temperamental officer and one of Nathan Bedford Forrest's favorite subordinates, Buford celebrated the capturing of a Union supply ship by seizing the only jug of whiskey on board the vessel, proclaiming,

"Plenty of meat, boys, plenty of hard-tack, shoes, and clothes for the boys, but just enough whisky for the general." The droop-eyed Kentuckian and adopted Texan, John Bell Hood, may have been the bravest man in the Confederate army. Hood was literally shot to pieces during the war, losing a leg and the use of an arm, yet soldiered on, having to be strapped into the saddle in order to lead his army into battle. After the war Hood fathered no fewer than eleven children in ten years, proving beyond doubt that at least some parts of his body weren't injured in the war. Joseph Shelby, the "Forrest of the Trans-Mississippi," employed a former newspaper editor and aspiring poet to write his official reports, reports that were sprinkled with poetry, Latin doggerel, and classical allusions. When the Confederacy collapsed, Shelby led a large contingent of his men into Mexico and established a Confederate colony there. The loud-voiced and valiant "Cerro Gordo" Williams loved liquor as much as fighting and in 1863 was relieved of his command on charges of drunkenness. Maj. Jacob W. Griffith is little known, but his son, D. W. Griffith, became the world-famous movie director of *Birth of a Nation* and other classics. Col. "Ap" Shacklett is better known as the great-granduncle of Hall of Fame shortstop Harold "Pee Wee" Reese. Simon Bolivar Buckner's son of the same name commanded the U.S. Tenth Army at the battle of Okinawa, where in 1945 he lost his life—the highest-ranking U.S. officer killed in action in World War II. Col. Joseph Morehead saw more fighting in Arizona and Mexico prior to the Civil War than he did before his death in the latter conflict. Lt. Col. Clarence Prentice, who disappointed his unionist father by "going South" (and by owning a whorehouse), was said to be the best shot in the Confederate army, able to mark a card with a pistol bullet while astride a galloping horse.

A number of Kentucky's Confederate officers achieved high political rank after the war. In Kentucky's postwar politics, service in the Confederate army became one's ticket to high political office. Perhaps the most distinguished, Buckner, became governor of Kentucky, and ran for vice president in 1896 on a breakaway Democratic ticket. Other governors include Lt. Col. James B. McCreary and Arkansas governor Thomas J. Churchill. Generals Williams, Samuel B. Maxey, and Randall L. Gibson, as well as Lieutenant Colonel McCreary, won seats in the U.S. Senate. Among the postwar members of the U.S. House of Representatives were Cols. Edward Crossland, William C. P. Breckinridge, and John W. Caldwell. In the Confederate Congress were Gens. Humphrey Marshall and George B. Hodge, along with Maj. Benjamin F. Bradley, Lt. Col. William E. Simms, and Cols. R. J. Breckinridge and Henry C. Burnett.

Generals Marshall and Breckinridge both served in the prewar U.S. House, with Breckinridge being elected vice president in 1856. Col. Martin H. Cofer became justice of the Kentucky Supreme Court, and other officers filled a host of pre- and postwar elected offices.

A number of Kentucky's Confederate leaders suffered unusual ends. Col. Benjamin Anderson quit the Confederate army and took a loyalty oath to the Union but later became involved in the Northwest Conspiracy to free rebel prisoners at Camp Douglas, in Chicago. During his trial for treason, the morose Anderson grabbed a gun from one of his guards and shot himself. The once wealthy General Buford lost his fortune after the war. Racked with pain, reduced to penury and reliance on the charity of relatives, Buford killed himself. The brilliant but mercurial Col. Henry Clay King fell in love with the widow of Maj. Gen. Gideon Pillow and, when a fellow lawyer insulted Mrs. Pillow, murdered the insulter. King barely escaped a lynch mob and died in the Tennessee State Penitentiary. A Union bullet late in the war took out Brig. Gen. Adam R. "Stovepipe" Johnson's eyesight, but the indomitable Johnson, ignoring his blindness, earned a fortune in real estate after the war. Near the end of the war Col. William Faulkner was killed, not by a Union army bullet, but by a shot from a Confederate army deserter he had hunted down. Col. Albert P. Thompson had his head blown off by a cannon shell within sight of his Paducah home. Maj. Robert Alston, a lawyer, was murdered in the Georgia capitol by a man angered at Alston's handling of his property, and another lawyer, Lt. Col. William D. Lannom, was killed by a client who owed Lannom money. In 1881, Lt. Col. Andrew R. Hynes committed suicide in a San Francisco bathhouse. In 1888, Brig. Gen. William Wirt Adams "shot it out" with a newspaper editor in the streets of Jackson, Mississippi, both contestants dying on the spot. In 1907, Lt. Col. David J. Caudill hanged himself in his farm's smokehouse. Maj. Peter Everett spent the last twenty-six years of his life in an insane asylum after being bitten by a rabid dog.

The Bluegrass State's contributions to the Confederate cause have rarely, if ever, been fully appreciated. As Ed Porter Thompson, historian of the Orphan Brigade, wrote in 1898:

Almost the sole representatives . . . of a State renowned of old for the gallantry of her sons, displayed on almost every field since the Revolution; completely isolated from home, and for the time in direct antagonism to the authority of their Commonwealth, without the comforts and encouragements that others enjoyed—the soldierly qualities exhibited in battling so manfully, suffering so patiently, bearing themselves so loftily under all, were such as would have attracted the attention of the county under any circumstances, and would seem to deserve special notice at the hands of the historians.

The authors fondly hope that this volume is part of that "special notice" they deserve.

Brig. Gen. Daniel Weisiger Adams

SOMETIME IN THE spring of 1821, Anna Weisiger Adams, a native Kentuckian, gave birth to Daniel Weisiger Adams in Frankfort, Kentucky. Anna's husband, George Adams, practiced law and according to a later biographical sketch "was admitted to the bar about the same time as Henry Clay, and the two were intimate friends and correspondents through life." The couple already had one son, William Wirt Adams, who later also became a Confederate general. In 1825 the family moved to Natchez, Mississippi, and voters elected George Adams as the state attorney general in 1828. This marked the beginning of a rapid professional ascent for George, as President Andrew Jackson first appointed him as a district attorney for the U.S. Court in 1830 and 1834 and then appointed him as "District Judge of the United States Court for Mississippi" in 1836. While his father achieved success, Daniel Adams returned to his home state of Kentucky and attended college in Bardstown in 1837. Although some sources state that he attended the University of Virginia, there is no record of his attendance at that university.

Sometime in the early 1840s, officials admitted Daniel Adams to the Mississippi state bar, and he began his career as an attorney. Near the beginning of his professional career, Adams became entangled in a sensational event, the killing of James Hagan, a Vicksburg newspaper editor. In 1843, state officials conducted an investigation into the alleged embezzlement by former Mississippi state treasurer R. S. Graves. Under the title of "More Thieving at Jackson," James Hagan stated that Gov. Tilghman Mayfield Tucker had given Judge George Adams $500; editor Hagan implied that the payment was for unknown and possibly unethical services. In the editor's opinion Adams's activities were just as tainted as those of treasurer Graves. On June 7, 1843, soon after the publication of the article,

Daniel Adams traveled to Vicksburg to ask Hagan to retract his allegation. Friends in Vicksburg encouraged the young Adams to arm himself in case Hagan had a weapon. Adams acquired a pistol and approached Hagan. After a scuffle Hagan and Adams fell to the ground, and Hagan put his hand around Adams's throat. Adams drew his pistol from a pocket, shot, and killed Hagan. Adams surrendered to authorities and was soon tried on murder charges. With the able legal assistance of Henry S. Foote and two other attorneys, the jury acquitted him of the charges.

A year later, Judge Adams died and his son embarked on a political career, initially as an alderman in Jackson, Mississippi. On September 16, 1844, he married Anna M. Bullis in her native Tennessee. She was a sister-in-law to Charles Scott, a prominent judge. The couple eventually had two sons, Daniel and Charles. In 1852, Hinds County voters elected Adams to the Mississippi state senate, a position he held until 1856. According to an obituary, "he made his mark as a leader of his party at a time of high political excitement." Following his service as a state senator, Adams moved to New Orleans and entered the business world. For a time Adams joined with William Raphael Miles as a cotton factor and commission merchant, and in 1860, apparently in connection with this work, Adams either owned or was employed at a coffee house. In either 1859 or 1860, Adams partnered with Harry T. Hays in a law firm and cut his ties with Miles in 1860.

In January 1861, Louisiana seceded from the Union and cast its fortunes with a new country, the Confederate States of America. In the weeks following, Gov. Thomas O. Moore appointed Adams to a three-member board to prepare Louisiana for war. Adams's appointment to this important post is somewhat mysterious, as he had no military experience; perhaps his political connections or his background as an attorney and businessman won him the appointment. On February 5, 1861, Moore appointed him lieutenant colonel of the First Louisiana Regulars infantry regiment. Transferred to Confederate service on March 13, the regiment was ordered to Pensacola, Florida, where it joined other units under the overall command of Brig. Gen. Braxton Bragg. While the First Louisiana Regulars was stationed in Florida, President Jefferson Davis promoted its colonel, Adley H. Gladden, to brigadier general on October 30, 1861, and Adams became the new colonel of the regiment. One month later, Colonel Adams listened from about a mile away as Union forces bombarded Fort McRee, near Pensacola. The end of the year found Adams serving on a court of inquiry in Mobile, Alabama, investigating charges against a quartermaster. His military unit joined him near Mobile in February

1862, and later that month the regiment traveled to Corinth, Mississippi. Here, Confederate military leaders busily worked on concentrating thousands of troops as a prelude for the attempt to drive the enemy from the Tennessee River Valley. Stationed near Purdy, Tennessee, Adams first came under enemy fire during two scouting expeditions.

The First Louisiana Regulars entered the battle of Shiloh on April 6, 1862, as part of Brigadier General Gladden's brigade. While advancing near Spain Field, Gladden fell mortally wounded, and Colonel Adams took command of the brigade. At one point, he seized the colors of the First Louisiana Regulars, rode to the front of the brigade, and led the men against the enemy. Later in the morning, while he continued to push the enemy, a Union soldier shot Adams above the left eye, the bullet exiting his skull above his left ear. This wound destroyed the sight in Adams's left eye. According to a New Orleans obituary written when Adams died in 1872, soldiers evacuated Adams from the battlefield in a wagon "in a helpless, senseless condition." While traveling toward Corinth, the wagon driver threw Adams onto the side of the road believing him dead. However, passing soldiers of the Tenth Mississippi Infantry recognized him and transported him to Corinth, where Adams spent several weeks recovering. In mid-May, Bragg offered him the command of a brigade and stated that he had recommended him for promotion to brigadier general. At the time, Adams was medically unready to return to field command, and he spent several more weeks recovering in Columbus, Mississippi.

In August 1862, Bragg reorganized his army, now stationed near Chattanooga, Tennessee. Adams, who had been promoted to brigadier general to rank from May 23, 1862, was given command of a new brigade consisting of the Eleventh, Thirteenth, Sixteenth, Twentieth, and Twenty-fifth Louisiana infantry regiments as well as the crack Fifth Company of the Washington Artillery. The units in this all-Louisiana brigade, with the exception of the Twenty-fifth, were veterans of Shiloh. Soon after the creation of the brigade, authorities disbanded the Eleventh Louisiana. About two hundred of its soldiers became members of a new unit in the brigade, the Fourteenth Louisiana Sharpshooters infantry battalion, commanded by Maj. John E. Austin. Adams and his veteran brigade soon began a march northward through Tennessee and then invaded Kentucky. Adams served for several weeks in his native Kentucky and played an active combat role during the battle near the small town of Perryville.

Soon after crossing the state line into Kentucky, Adams made his first speech to his command, a rousing address that resulted in his soldiers' shouting for miles on the march. On the confusing field of Perryville,

Adams's brigade advanced on the left flank of the Confederate army. While approaching Union forces near the vicinity of Squire Bottom's house, Adams believed they were actually approaching Confederate troops. It was not until Adams was fired upon by Union troops that he admitted his error and ordered his men to fire. Taking control of a portion of Brig. Gen. Bushrod R. Johnson's brigade and aided by Brig. Gen. Patrick R. Cleburne's men, Adams forced out the enemy near Squire Bottom's house. Unfortunately for Confederate soldiers, the gains won at Perryville were temporary, as the army soon retreated to Tennessee.

Sometime after the retreat, Adams traveled to Richmond, Virginia, for now unknown reasons. While visiting he "met there many of [his] old friends and acquaintances." Rejoining his brigade in November 1862, Adams and the rest of the army began preparing for a campaign in Middle Tennessee. On December 31, 1862, Gen. Braxton Bragg ordered his Army of Tennessee to attack Federal troops camped near Stones River, which flowed close to the town of Murfreesboro. Assigned almost on the far right flank of the army as part of Maj. Gen. John C. Breckinridge's division, Adams's brigade saw no action until the afternoon. As the battle developed and Union troops were pushed back on their right flank, a Union stronghold developed in the Round Forest, a plot of land near the Nashville Turnpike and the Nashville and Chattanooga Railroad. Beginning that morning, Bragg ordered a series of fruitless brigade attacks on the Round Forest. At approximately 2:00 P.M., Adams, or "Old Pelican," as his soldiers were starting to call him, was ordered to attack the position with his brigade. Writing after the battle, Adams stated that he believed the order was "a very imprudent & unwise one," and indeed it proved to be. Maneuvering across the Cowan farm with its fenced fields was challenging, and the men were faced with heavy fire from the enemy. While Adams was encouraging the brigade forward, a piece of shell struck his left arm, forcing him to leave the field and turn brigade command over to Col. Randall L. Gibson of the Thirteenth Louisiana. Before departing, Adams was heard to utter by Lt. Ezekiel John Ellis of the Sixteenth Louisiana, "Boys we fall back but D—n it, we are *not* whipped." Although the Louisiana brigade joined the Orphan Brigade in its famous charge on January 2, 1863, 544 of its 703 total casualties occurred in its attack on the Round Forest. Adams was once again knocked out of the war. For several months he recuperated in Marietta, Georgia, and then rejoined his command in May in Tennessee.

By this time, Adams hoped for a promotion to major general, a promotion that he felt he deserved. However, he would not be promoted again. Officials soon ordered Breckinridge's Division to Mississippi where Gen. Joseph E. Johnston hoped to launch an attack that would relieve the besieged city of Vicksburg. This relief effort failed. After the fall of Vicksburg, Maj. Gen. William T. Sherman's army advanced on Johnston, and he and his men were attacked in the entrenchments around Jackson, Mississippi. Here, Adams personally helped defend the city where he had once served as a state senator by climbing on the breastworks and firing two shots at the enemy. His Louisianans helped turn back a Union attack, but the Confederates evacuated the city shortly thereafter.

Adams's final service with the Army of Tennessee occurred during the Chickamauga campaign in September 1863. Maj. Gen. William S. Rosecrans maneuvered his army into Georgia with the goal of capturing the strategic city of Chattanooga. The Army of Tennessee attacked Union forces near Chickamauga Creek in northern Georgia on September 19. As Adams's Brigade marched from the left to the right flank of the Confederate army on that day, they were involved in no significant combat. On September 20, Adams's Brigade, in conjunction with another brigade, advanced behind the Union rear and initially brushed aside enemy units. Putting together a hasty defense, Union soldiers suddenly staggered the advancing Louisianans with a tremendous volley. Col. Randall L. Gibson noticed Adams "on foot and looking at his arm as we were advancing." A bullet had fractured the general's left arm, and Union troops captured him after the Confederate retreat. Several Union soldiers claimed the capture of Adams, and apparently Federal soldiers robbed him of various personal possessions. He was transported to a hospital in Murfreesboro, Tennessee, and surgeons successfully operated on his arm on September 23. After about one month, officials exchanged Adams, and he continued his recuperation in Georgia.

Following his recovery in the spring of 1864, Adams became both a cavalry commander and a district commander. In May 1864, the Confederate high command gave him control of the District of North Alabama, and in the fall he also became the commander of the District of Central Alabama. He and his men, primarily state troops, were engaged in mostly small, defensive operations, although his command gave support to the Army of Tennessee as it moved through northern Alabama into Tennessee in the fall of 1864. In March 1865, Adams became commander of the new District of Alabama that comprised much of the state. His men aided Lt. Gen. Nathan Bedford Forrest in fighting Brig. Gen. James H. Wilson's invaders, and in April Adams fought in the battle of Selma and at Columbus, Georgia. His military career ended on May 9, 1865, at Meridian, Mississippi, when he received his parole.

After the war, Adams visited Europe and then returned to New Orleans and reentered his law partnership with Harry T. Hays, also a former Confederate general. Some accounts state that he left his first wife; shortly after the war he married Mary Virginia Calloway of North Carolina and had two children, Mary and Daniel. In the late 1860s, Adams and his family moved to New York City, where he engaged, according to an obituary, "in a Southern land business." Adams also corresponded with Braxton Bragg and attempted to interest him in a position in the Egyptian army. Sometime in the spring of 1872, Adams returned again to New Orleans, reentered his law practice, and actively engaged in Reconstruction politics.

Adams "was struck down suddenly as if by a red bolt from the skies" on June 13, 1872, in his law office at 15 Carondelet Street in New Orleans. His sudden death came after several days of complaints of ill health. While writing a brief, Adams suddenly slumped forward, and his spectacles clattered onto his desk. His assistant, T. W. Boland, and former Confederate brigadier general and Louisiana governor Paul Octave Hébert rushed to his aid "and bathed his head and temples." By the time Dr. Bricknell arrived, Adams had somewhat revived and spoke with his "usual clearness . . . [and] complained of a terrible pain in the back of his head." The doctor wrote a prescription, suggested rest, and left. Several minutes later, Adams complained, "I feel very badly, send for the Doctor quick!" By the time Bricknell returned, Adams had died, at approximately 4:15 P.M. So ended the life of Daniel W. Adams at age fifty-one, ending a career as attorney, businessman, politician, and soldier. Press stories labeled him as "gallant," "a sterling gentleman," "the beau ideal of intrepid chivalry . . . lion-hearted,'" and "tender as a woman to the sufferings of his comrades in arms.'" He was buried in Greenwood Cemetery in Jackson, Mississippi, in an unmarked grave. Sixteen years later his brother, William Wirt Adams, was laid to rest next to him. With no previous military experience, Adams achieved a worthy record as a defender of the Confederacy.

BIBLIOGRAPHY

Daniel W. Adams Papers, Louisiana Historical Association Collection, Manuscripts Division, Howard-Tilton Memorial Library, Tulane University, New Orleans.

Davis, William C., ed. *The Confederate General.* 6 vols. Harrisburg, PA: National Historical Society, 1991.
U.S. War Department. *The War of the Rebellion: A Compilation of the Official Records of the Union and Confederate Armies.* 70 vols. in 128 pts. Washington, DC: Government Printing Office, 1880–1901.

—M. Jane Johansson

Brig. Gen. William Wirt Adams

WIRT ADAMS'S LIFE was one of service. He was born in Kentucky; his family relocated to Mississippi when he was a child. Throughout his youth, he moved between Kentucky, Mississippi, and Texas, while receiving his education and serving in the military. Before the Civil War, he began his political career and parlayed it into a Confederate commission once fighting began. He spent much of the Civil War operating in Tennessee and Mississippi. After the war, he worked in the banking business and secured political appointments before his tragic death in 1888.

Born to George and Anna Weisiger Adams in Frankfort, Kentucky, on March 22, 1819, William Wirt Adams was still small when his brother, future Confederate general Daniel Weisiger Adams, was born in 1821. In 1825, George Adams moved his family to Natchez, Mississippi, where he became politically prominent. Wirt returned to Kentucky in 1839 and attended college in Bardstown. Apparently, his stay in Kentucky was a short one, since he enlisted in the service of the Republic of Texas that same year. Joining Col. Edward Burleson's command as a private, Adams quickly rose to the position of adjutant and fought against the Cherokee and Comanche in northeastern Texas.

During the early 1840s, Adams returned to Mississippi upon his father's death. He spent the next several years in Iberville, Louisiana, establishing himself as a sugar planter. With his financial success assured, he married Sallie Huger Mayrant in 1850 and moved back to Mississippi, where he began to work in banking and expanded his planting interests. By the middle 1850s, he managed businesses in both Jackson and Vicksburg.

With his finances thriving, Adams ran for and won a seat in the Mississippi legislature in 1858 and was reelected in 1860. During the secession crisis of 1860–1861, he worked for the secession of his adopted state of Mississippi and then crossed the river to campaign for Louisiana to follow suit. In February, the Confederacy was established and newly inaugurated President Jefferson Davis offered him the position of postmaster general. Adams declined the offer of a cabinet seat but did join the army, being commissioned a colonel on October 15, 1861. The forty-two-year-old raised the First Mississippi Cavalry, which became officially known as Wirt Adams's Regiment of Cavalry by the end of 1861.

By late October 1861, Adams was at Camp Hardee in Bowling Green, Kentucky, where his cavalry busied itself by striking at Union strongholds in the region. Allowed to operate independently, Adams's men remained in that border state throughout the winter watching river crossings, pursuing small enemy bands, and providing valuable reconnaissance services to Maj. Gen. William J. Hardee, commander of the Army of Central Kentucky.

Following the fall of Forts Henry and Donelson in February 1862, Adams's cavalry was ordered to Nashville. Later that month it hooked up with Gen. Albert Sidney Johnston at Murfreesboro. From there, Adams's Mississippians served as rear guard to Johnston's force on its march to Corinth, Mississippi. By late March, Johnston's men were spread throughout northern Mississippi and Alabama, with the Union's Maj. Gen. Ulysses S. Grant showing no sign of slowing his advance. Adams's men occupied the north bank of the Tennessee River at Decatur, Alabama, awaiting the coming conflict. Ordered westward to Corinth, the Mississippians arrived in time to move out with Johnston's army on the afternoon of April 3 toward the battle that would become known as Shiloh. During the fight on April 6, Adams and his men held the far right end of the Confederate line. However, upon the Confederate order to retreat, Adams sprang to action along with other cavalry units to provide cover for the Confederate withdrawal back to Corinth.

By May, Adams was working closely with Gen. Braxton Bragg and fell back to Baldwin, Mississippi, with the rest of Gen. P. G. T. Beauregard's army on May 29, before withdrawing farther south to Tupelo. Through the long summer of 1862, Adams's regiment waited anxiously for an opportunity to strike back at the Federals. That chance came in September. While Southern forces were moving into Tennessee and Kentucky, Maj. Gen. Sterling Price, with Wirt Adams's Mississippians in tow, moved north toward the Memphis and Charleston Railroad running through Corinth and Iuka. At Iuka, Price's men found the town recently abandoned by the Union, but Grant ordered forces back to the town and succeeded in forcing Price out on September 19. Two weeks later, Price and

Maj. Gen. Earl Van Dorn struck Corinth in an attempt to retake that pivotal junction, but they were again forced back. Adams's cavalry earned much distinction during the campaign, particularly at Hatchie Bridge, where the Mississippians are credited with keeping open Van Dorn's only remaining avenue of escape.

From northern Mississippi, Adams and his men were ordered west to watch the Mississippi River for Lt. Gen. John C. Pemberton. In late February, Adams supported the Confederate expedition to Greenville, Mississippi, by detaching part of his force, which fought at Deer Creek and Fish Lake Bridge. Although sources indicate that Adams's cavalry was worn and weak by the winter of 1863, it played a major role in the capture of the Federal steamer *Indianola*. When the Confederates took the vessel, they found that its commander had drilled holes in its hull in an attempt to scuttle the steamer. Towing her to shore the Confederates celebrated capturing such a prize, particularly one filled with valuable stores. However, the approach of a dummy Federal gunboat tricked the Southerners into completing the scuttling, thereby destroying nearly all of the captured booty. Within days, Adams's invigorated men were lined up against Rear Adm. David Dixon Porter's gunships at Rolling Fork during the Steele's Bayou Expedition.

A month later, a daring Union raid captured Adams's attention. Col. Benjamin H. Grierson left La Grange, Tennessee, on April 17, 1863, with 1,700 cavalrymen. For the next two weeks, the raiders traversed the state of Mississippi tearing up railroads, destroying supplies, terrifying the civilian population, and, most importantly, drawing Confederate attention away from Vicksburg. After more than five hundred miles in the saddle, on May 2, Grierson reached Union lines at Baton Rouge, Louisiana.

As Grierson's raiders rode south through Mississippi, Confederate cavalrymen tried in vain to catch the colonel. On April 28, Grierson's column was on the Natchez road near Union Church when Confederate skirmishers began harassing the Union pickets. The Federal cavalrymen handily pushed the enemy through the town of Union Church and remained there through the night, engaged in sporadic fighting. By the time night fell, Wirt Adams was aware of the day's action and was planning to spring a trap on Grierson's raiders. Ordering five companies to Fayette and personally leading two others, Adams hoped to put part of his cavalry behind Grierson to drive the Union colonel out of his camp and into the teeth of an ambush. However, a loose-lipped lieutenant bragging about the details to a lone Federal spy single-handedly undid

Adams's perfectly laid trap. The next morning, instead of bagging the raiders, Adams resumed the chase.

As Grierson was frustrating his Confederate pursuers, Grant's army moved into position for an assault on Vicksburg. At Champion Hill on the night of May 15, Adams, whose ability to gather and deliver intelligence was impressive, scouted through the darkness and occasionally skirmished with the enemy. The bullets that flew toward Adams and his men were the first of the coming battle of Champion Hill. After the May 16 fight, Adams was again called on to provide rearguard support for the retreating Confederates, an activity he and his men performed frequently and well during the war. In the wake of Champion Hill, Adams's troopers set about to slow Grant's advance toward Vicksburg as much as possible. Skirmishing whenever advantageous, Adams's Mississippians fought bravely in the face of overwhelming odds. Hoping to further delay Grant's army, Pemberton ordered Adams to abandon his position at the head of the enemy force and begin disrupting Grant's supply and communication lines in his rear. After the fall of Vicksburg on July 4, Wirt Adams joined forces with his brother Daniel, now a brigadier general, near Midway, Mississippi, to defend against Union cavalry raids. Because he had earned an excellent reputation as a cavalry commander, particularly during the siege of Vicksburg, Jefferson Davis promoted Wirt Adams to the rank of brigadier general on September 28, 1863. In a testament to his tenacity, that same day Grant lamented, "[Col. John] Logan and Wirt Adams infest the country from about Rodney to Port Hudson."

As the Union's Anaconda Plan slowly strangled the Confederacy, Wirt Adams's Mississippians provided much resistance in their home state. Remaining outside Vicksburg as a harassing force, the regiment proved itself a considerable nuisance to the Union's Maj. Gen. James B. McPherson and bolstered the hopes of Confederates in Mississippi. Near Natchez on the morning of December 7, understanding that a considerable Union cavalry force was standing nearby awaiting infantry support, Adams attacked the horsemen and within minutes sent the Federals fleeing back toward the city. A secondary duty of Adams's during late 1863 was to locate good crossings on the Mississippi River to allow for the transport of weaponry to Lt. Gen. Edmund Kirby Smith in the Trans-Mississippi, where it could be used in the war rather than fall into Union hands. By the latter part of December, Kirby Smith had his guns, thanks to Adams.

In early February 1864, Adams continued his troubling of McPherson by alternately skirmishing and withdrawing all the way from Vicksburg through Jackson. With the state capital in the hands of the Federals, Maj. Gen. William Tecumseh Sherman proceeded on to Meridian, fully expecting Adams to continue his attempts to stop the Union tide. Sherman was not surprised as Confederate cavalry under Adams, Peter Starke, Samuel Ferguson, and Sul Ross repeatedly struck his advancing columns during their trek east until Meridian finally fell in late February.

Like all great leaders, Wirt Adams stood tall when events were most grim. In the wake of Sherman's march across Mississippi, Adams volunteered to personally supervise the repair of the badly damaged Mississippi Central Railroad. Lt. Gen. Leonidas Polk happily agreed and authorized Adams to "take complete control of that road and make all impressments necessary to drive the work through in the shortest time possible." Almost immediately upon Adams's moving to Canton, Mississippi, to begin work on the railroad, Union forces moved out of Vicksburg intent on driving Adams off and further damaging the rails. Over the course of the next two weeks, Adams fought hard to hold the enemy in check as they made the most of every opportunity to burn trestles and draw Adams away from his rail line. By May 15, the Federals withdrew to Vicksburg.

With the Confederacy reeling, Adams remained one of the shining examples of Confederate success. By July 1864 he was working closely with Maj. Gen. Nathan Bedford Forrest, and on July 31 he became the Confederate commander of the military district lying between Natchez and Grenada, Mississippi. In that position, Adams exercised considerable control over the region's administration. However, his confiscation of Enfield rifles and subsequent giving of some of them over to the state militia got him into trouble with Confederate authorities.

Throughout the remainder of 1864 and early 1865, Adams, still in command of the Central District of Mississippi, was revisited by Benjamin Grierson. Brigadier General Grierson's second raid lasted for more than two weeks and through the destruction of railroad tracks, trestles, cars, locomotives, telegraph lines, and the defeat of Adams and his men at Franklin, Mississippi, effectively cut off Gen. John Bell Hood's expectation of support from the west.

As the last months of the war passed, Adams took command of the newly formed District of South Mississippi and East Louisiana and harassed Union forces between Vicksburg and Meridian. Adams and Forrest also spent considerable time capturing deserters and enlisting willing men into their cause. In early April, events spiraled out of control throughout Mississippi and Alabama. Ordered out of Mississippi and to Florence,

Alabama, Adams had to know that the Confederate cause was breathing its last. Bvt. Maj. Gen. James Wilson's raid on Elyton and Selma had split that state in half while also providing subordinate commanders like Col. John Croxton ample opportunities to attack points such as Tuscaloosa. Wirt Adams, on his way north, was warned by superiors that he might be forced to stop in Tuscaloosa to help deal with Croxton; but Adams's orders were changed, now calling for him to move south toward Selma, where he could support Forrest. By the time Wilson's raid ended on April 20, 1865, the war was drawing to a close. On May 4, Adams surrendered near Ramsey Station, in Sumter County, Alabama, and received his parole on May 12.

As he aged through the Reconstruction era, Adams grew high-strung, particularly in regard to politics. In 1880, he became state revenue agent and left that position in 1883 to accept President Grover Cleveland's offer of the position of postmaster of Jackson, Mississippi. A strong supporter of the Democratic Party, in 1887 Adams authored the "Red Manifesto," which was distributed throughout Jackson and promised to have blacks who attempted to vote in the coming election "wiped out." On May 5, 1887, an event took place that further inflamed Adams's political sentiments. A young editor of a prohibitionist newspaper was chased and shot down in cold blood by a former Confederate officer. Adams, by then the city's postmaster and a political ally of the perpetrator, became an editorial target of J. H. Martin, the editor of the *New Mississippian*. On May 1, 1888, Adams and Martin met on the street. After a brief exchange of words, Adams drew his pistol and fired at Martin. Taking cover behind a tree, Martin pulled his gun and fired six shots at Adams. Although Adams only shot three times, he hit his opponent in the thigh and chest, inflicting a mortal wound. As Martin fell, Adams stood up straight but collapsed with a single bullet through his heart. The entire fight had taken only a few seconds, and the men were within ten feet of each other the whole time. Adams was buried in Greenwood Cemetery in Jackson.

Wirt Adams's inglorious end belied the life he had built for himself. He had parlayed his self-confidence into successful business ventures and then had taken that accomplishment-oriented attitude into the Civil War as one of the Confederacy's most trusted cavalry commanders. With his success in business, military experience, and innate leadership ability, Adams epitomized the antebellum Southern ideal. However, Adams, like countless other former Confederates living in the wake of defeat, had difficulty adapting to the new world thrust upon him.

Bibliography

Davis, William C., ed. *The Confederate General.* 6 vols. Harrisburg, PA: National Historical Society, 1991.

Frazier, Rodney Randolph. *Broken Swords: The Lives, Times, and Deaths of Eight Former Confederate Generals Murdered after the Smoke of Battle Had Cleared.* New York: Vantage Press, 2003.

U.S. War Department. *The War of the Rebellion: A Compilation of the Official Records of the Union and Confederate Armies.* 70 vols. in 128 pts. Washington, DC: Government Printing Office, 1880–1901.

—Brian D. McKnight

Brig. Gen. William Nelson Rector Beall

WILLIAM NELSON RECTOR
BEALL, brigadier general, prisoner of war, and Confederate agent,
was born to Samuel Tannehill
and Sally Rector Beall on March
20, 1825, in Bardstown, Kentucky. In 1840, the family moved
to Little Rock, Arkansas, where
his mother's relatives held high
elective office. Tragically, both
parents died shortly after their
arrival, leaving behind five children. Four years later, Beall entered the U.S. Military Academy,
graduating thirtieth of thirty-eight cadets in 1848, too late to
see any military action in the
Mexican War.

Commissioned as a brevet second lieutenant with the Fourth Infantry
Regiment, Beall served initially on the northwestern frontier. In April
1849, he was promoted to second lieutenant and assigned to the Fifth
Infantry, serving until 1855 in the Indian Territory and Texas. He made
first lieutenant on March 3, 1855, and then captain in the First Cavalry on
March 27, 1855. Beall scouted and skirmished against various Indian
tribes in the West, most notably at the Walnut Creek Crossing, Kansas
Territory, along the Santa Fe Trail in 1859.

As the sectional controversy divided the country in 1860, Beall remained stationed on the frontier, where he participated in raids against
the Kiowa and Comanche. Even after his adopted state of Arkansas seceded from the Union in May of 1861, Beall remained loyal to the federal
government, and his company was one of two units ordered to Fort Kearney, Nebraska, to hold hostile Indians in check. Perhaps Beall had more
in common with his native state of Kentucky, whose halfway house of
armed neutrality seemed to suit most in the Bluegrass State. Eventually,
though, Beall resigned his commission on August 20, 1861, casting his lot
with the Confederacy, being one of the last U.S. Army officers to do so.

He was commissioned a captain in the Confederate army to rank from March 16, 1861.

As a West Point graduate and career military officer, Beall didn't have to wait long for assignment. On September 12, 1861, Special Orders No. 151 instructed him to report to Gen. Albert Sidney Johnston at Memphis, Tennessee. Beall made an immediate impression on Johnston, who mentioned him for possible promotion to colonel of the Third Kentucky Regiment the following month. Instead, Beall used his reputation and state ties to help raise troops from Arkansas. From his headquarters in Little Rock, on January 29, 1862, Confederate major general Earl Van Dorn announced several changes to his staff, including adding Beall as his assistant adjutant general. Due to Beall's good work, Van Dorn recommended that Beall be advanced in rank to colonel in March and brigadier general on April 11, 1862, to command Confederate cavalry at Corinth, Mississippi.

By midsummer, a reorganization of western armies meant that Beall found himself on the move to Jackson, Mississippi, where Van Dorn placed him in command of the Second District of the Department of Southern Mississippi and East Louisiana and, later, the District of East Louisiana. In both situations, however, his command was temporary, lasting less than a month. This should not be viewed as a lack of confidence in Beall by his superiors; instead, it was simply a matter of additional troops arriving in the area, necessitating a higher-ranking officer to command.

The Mississippi River was vital to Confederate operations, and the Union Anaconda Plan targeted that waterway in the hope of controlling it and thereby dividing the Confederacy. In the spring of 1862, the Union took possession of New Orleans. In response, the South fortified Port Hudson, Louisiana, a small village located on a bend of the Mississippi River, twenty-five miles upriver from Baton Rouge, and the site of Beall's next appointment.

On August 29, 1862, he took command of 2,500 men at Port Hudson and immediately realized that a previous plan of defense would require ten times that number to implement, men that neither he nor the Confederacy had available. Therefore, Beall began work on a new, more concentrated line of defense requiring far fewer men. He called for substantial entrenchments along all roads leading into Port Hudson, but progress was slow due to a lack of local volunteers. Beall then applied for and received permission from President Jefferson Davis to issue a call to the surrounding area for slave labor. But before he could complete the new defensive line, on December 27, 1862, Beall was superseded in command of the Third Military District, Department of Mississippi and East Louisiana, a position he had held since October 21. He remained at Port Hudson in command of his brigade until the garrison surrendered on July 9, 1863.

Port Hudson was situated on the eastern bank in a substantial bend of the Mississippi River, with its highest point eighty-five feet above the river. Any movement by Union naval forces would, out of geographic necessity, be a slow one, making them easy targets for the heavy Confederate siege guns trained down upon the river. Infantry would find the going no easier, as the eastern bank of the river was carved up by deep ravines and the recently constructed parapets averaged nearly twenty feet in thickness, rising nearly the same height above the base of the ditch. With such adequate earthworks, Port Hudson was as formidable an obstacle to the Federal plan of controlling the Mississippi River as its northern neighbor, Vicksburg.

The Union's plan of dividing the Confederacy was in its final stages by the spring of 1863, with Union major general Ulysses S. Grant laying siege to Vicksburg, while Maj. Gen. Nathaniel P. Banks operated against Port Hudson. Banks's army, numbering between thirty thousand and forty thousand men, hoped for a quick victory over the vastly outnumbered Confederates, less than eight thousand strong, commanded by Maj. Gen. Franklin Gardner, so that they could then be in a position to assist Grant. In April, Lt. Gen. John Pemberton suggested Gardner lead five thousand troops to Vicksburg, leaving Beall in command at Port Hudson with sufficient artillery for its defense. As the proposal was only a suggestion, Gardner rejected the idea. Then just days before the Union assault on Port Hudson, Gen. Joseph E. Johnston ordered Gardner to evacuate the position and join him at Jackson, Mississippi, but the correspondence did not reach Port Hudson before Banks's army had advanced toward that bastion.

Banks's plan called for three divisions to move down the Red and Mississippi rivers, attacking from the north, while two other divisions would move up the Mississippi from Baton Rouge. By May 22, Banks had the Confederates trapped behind four and a half miles of earthen fortifications. He issued orders for a simultaneous attack all along the Confederate perimeter for May 27. Shortly before sunrise, the Union artillery opened up on the defenders' left flank, which guarded the northern approaches to Port Hudson. But a tangle of trees and dense underbrush, as well as swamplands and deep ravines, slowed the Union advance. The natural barriers were quite formidable, especially since the Confederate rifle pits were atop bluffs overlooking the swamps and ravines. Timely reinforcements from the center allowed the Confederates to repulse several assaults. Interior lines afforded them the ability to move men from their right flank to reinforce the center because the coordinated attacks Banks planned did not occur. In fact, it was well into the afternoon before the Union division attacked the center, defended by Beall. With diminished fire on their left, Beall's men poured down a heavy fire upon the Federals, driving them back. The day was a complete disaster for Banks. Union casualties were nearly two thousand men to fewer than five hundred for the Confederates. Union losses included some six hundred black troops of the First and Third Louisiana Native Guards, composed of free, educated men of color as well as former slaves.

During the next two weeks, both sides engaged in skirmishing and heavy shelling, with Banks attempting to advance his artillery as close as possible for another assault. On June 13, he demanded that Gardner surrender the garrison. When Gardner refused, Banks ordered another attack for the following morning. This time, the main Union assault was against Beall's troops in the center. His men repulsed several charges, despite running low on percussion caps, and his loss of men was slight as compared to that of the enemy. This attempt cost the Union nearly two thousand casualties to fewer than two hundred Confederates. Other than running low on ammunition, Beall's only concern was that most of his artillery had been disabled by the constant Union bombardment.

Even as Port Hudson evidenced some of the most horrific fighting of the Civil War, civility was also displayed as Beall and Union brigadier general William Dwight agreed to a cease-fire in order to remove the dead and wounded from the field. Having failed on two occasions with attacks, Banks settled into a siege of the Confederate garrison. Over the next several weeks, the Confederates nearly exhausted their ammunition and were reduced to eating mules, horses, and rats. But when word reached Port Hudson that Pemberton had surrendered at Vicksburg, Gardner realized that his situation was hopeless and nothing could be gained by continuing the battle. Surrender terms were negotiated, and on July 9, 1863, after forty-eight days, the longest true siege in American military history, and thousands of casualties, the Union army entered Port Hudson.

By the terms agreed upon, all Confederate soldiers became prisoners of war. On July 16, Union brigadier general Charles Stone wrote Grant that he had sent a large number (189) of Confederate officers, including Beall, to Vicksburg aboard the steamboat *Planet*. A week later, Beall was admitted to the Union officers' general hospital in Memphis, Tennessee, with anemia and remittent fever. Once recovered, he was sent north to be imprisoned with other Confederate officers at Johnson's Island on Lake Erie near Sandusky, Ohio.

Union records indicate that only about two hundred prisoners died as a result of the harsh Ohio winters, food and fuel shortages, and disease, making Johnson's Island one of the safer Civil War prisons. Nonetheless, Beall recognized the suffering of his fellow Confederates and on September 12, 1864, asked for permission to buy several items: candles and oil to bring light into the hospital, and brooms to help keep the facility clean. This talent for recognizing the needs of others and speaking up for them proved to be the next path in Beall's Civil War service record.

As the conflict entered its fourth year, conditions in many prison camps had deteriorated, prompting an agreement between Grant and Judge Robert Ould, Confederate agent for exchange of prisoners, on November 12, 1864, whereby both North and South could supply essential items to their prisoners. Ould nominated Confederate major general Isaac Trimble, prisoner in Boston's Fort Warren, to be the chief receiving agent, with Beall listed as alternate. But Union secretary of war Edwin Stanton objected to Trimble, thus elevating Beall to a new, and arguably his most important, responsibility: selling Confederate cotton that was allowed to pass through the Union blockade and using the proceeds to purchase critical food and supplies for Confederate prisoners. By terms of the agreement, Beall was paroled on December 6, 1864, in order to begin his work. He was bound by oath to give no aid, assistance, or information to the enemy beyond the limits of his new position.

Beall's first act was to send a circular letter, dated December 9, 1864, to Confederate prisoners of war: "I therefore desire that you will at once determine, by a committee or otherwise, the supplies (clothing, blankets, and provisions) you most need." Replies placed food and blankets at the top of the list. Beall then rented a store at 75 Murray Street in New York City and invited local vendors to submit samples for possible purchase. He also placed a sign in his window that read, "Brig. Gen. W. N. R. Beall, C.S. Army, agent to supply prisoners of war," which drew the attention of the *New York Tribune* and a negative public reaction. Realizing his status was tenuous at best, Beall proposed to change his sign, deleting the reference to the Confederacy, but the damage was already done.

On January 3, 1865, Union major general Henry Halleck wrote Grant regarding Beall: "Since commencing this letter I learn that General Beall's course of conduct in New York has been so conspicuous and offensive that the Secretary of War has ordered his sign to be taken down. General

[Halbert] Paine has also been directed to suspend his parole and take him into custody till the cotton arrives."

Secretary of War Edwin Stanton suspended Beall's parole and placed him in Fort Lafayette in New York Harbor as a prisoner of war until the anticipated thousand bales of cotton arrived from Mobile Bay. When they did, he went back to work, and by the end of February Beall had made over two dozen shipments of clothes and food to various Union facilities for imprisoned Confederates. But with the war's end, Beall's efforts came to a close. He was finally released from custody on August 2, 1865.

After the war, he moved to St. Louis, Missouri, married Felicia Eakin Bass, a woman twenty years younger than he, and became a general commission merchant. On June 10, 1879, the U.S. Senate approved a resolution removing all "political disabilities" from Beall, essentially restoring his citizenship. A "well liked Christian soldier," Beall moved to Tennessee for his health. He died on July 26, 1883, in McMinnville, and he is buried in the Confederate Circle, Mount Olivet Cemetery, in Nashville.

BIBLIOGRAPHY

Davis, William C., ed. *The Confederate General.* 6 vols. Harrisburg, PA: National Historical Society, 1991.
Harrington, Fred Harvey. "Arkansas Defends the Mississippi." *Arkansas Historical Quarterly* 4 (Summer 1945): 109–17.
Hewitt, Lawrence Lee. *Port Hudson, Confederate Bastion on the Mississippi.* Baton Rouge: Louisiana State University Press, 1987.
Powell, Morgan Allen. "Cotton for the Relief of Confederate Prisoners." *Civil War History* 9 (March 1963): 24–35.

—C. DAVID DALTON

Brig. Gen. Tyree Harris Bell

TEN DAYS AFTER Fort Sumter the good citizens of Newbern, Tennessee, rallied at Albert Harris's store and raised the secession pole. They organized themselves into a company, decided on a name—Newbern Blues—and asked Albert's cousin, Tyree Bell, to become their captain. Tyree had no military experience, but he was a community leader, and he shared the vision of Gov. Isham G. Harris and Gideon J. Pillow, who had been building a state military organization since March 1861. Pillow called Captain Bell to his headquarters in  Memphis that summer and offered him command of a regiment of West Tennesseans, yet to be recruited.

Why Bell? He was a faithful Democrat, good friend of West Tennessee congressman John C. D. Atkins, and a well-known Methodist layman with church and business associates across several counties. He had carved a plantation out of the Dyer County wilderness and gained a reputation as a shrewd livestock breeder. Granted, for a soldier he was green, and old—forty-six—but he was powerful physically, blessed with common sense, and exuded a quiet confidence. Unlike many with leadership ambitions, Bell did not require a steady ration of attention.

Tyree Bell knew Kentucky almost as well as he knew Tennessee. He was born September 5, 1815, in southeastern Kentucky, just northeast of Lancaster, in Garrard County. He would grow up, however, 150 miles south in Sumner County, Tennessee. There he would be educated in the "English School" of William Price Thomas, but he was his mother's son, and the two of them returned often to the old brick home place in Garrard. Bell always felt comfortable there among the sprawling Harris family. His grandfather Tyree Rodes Harris had held about every office in Garrard, even represented his fellow citizens in the Kentucky General

Assembly. Another positive influence was Tyree's father-in-law, Squire Josiah Walton of Sumner County, Andrew Jackson's private secretary in the First Seminole War, Methodist leader and prosperous, influential Sumner County farmer. Squire Walton had given Tyree and his bride, Mary Ann Walton, land on which to build a home. He treated Tyree as a son.

The Bell clan was different. Tough, bristling people, they descended from the notorious Reivers, Scots of the borderland of questionable reputation who fought constantly with the English. Among the fighting Bells, legends persisted of seven-foot Ninian Beall and Thomas Allen Beall, direct forebears of Tyree from Maryland and Virginia. So did stories of raiding, revolution, repression, and deportation. Not that these tales came from Tyree's father. Failure stalked Absalom B. Bell. A plasterer by trade, he followed the fortunes of his wife, Susannah, and her family.

Tyree waited until age twenty-seven to marry. He had established himself in Sumner County and prospered. He kept buying additional tracts of land and built an impressive brick home at Cottontown. He grew a variety of crops, however, and developed an enviable herd of livestock, not to speak of raising a large family. He and Mary Ann were consumed by the demands of the farm, so much so that Tyree watched friends and kinsmen head off to Mexico in 1847 while he remained at home. In 1857, however, Tyree heard the call of West Tennessee and left Sumner for the Mississippi River county of Dyer. He and his oldest sons and "[his] family of negros" journeyed west and carved a 160-acre farm from the deep woods, traveling back and forth between Newbern and Cottontown until 1859, when Bell brought out the entire family. Newbern, Mary Ann found, consisted of ten families, "a fine school and two stores." Bell again diversified his crops, growing wheat, corn, and tobacco. The farm bountifully supported their family of eleven as well as sixteen slaves.

On May 26, 1861, the Newbern Blues with Bell at their head marched to Jackson, Tennessee, to enter state service. They were designated as Company G, Twelfth Tennessee Infantry, and a week later the Twelfth elected Bell lieutenant colonel. His election was notable since the Twelfth was predominantly a Gibson County regiment, with eight of the ten companies from that county. Moreover, the regiment contained two prominent political figures, better known certainly than Tyree, who shunned speech making. A former professional soldier, Robert Milton Russell, would lead the Twelfth. So short was experienced leadership, however, that Col. Milton Russell was soon called away to command the Second Brigade, Pillow's division. Lieutenant Colonel Bell, farmer turned soldier, would command the regiment for the next nine months. The Twelfth trained at Jackson, then moved up to Union City, and from there they rode north to Columbus, Kentucky, to secure the great chalk bluffs that dominated the Mississippi.

The Twelfth trained hard under Russell and Bell. The two got along famously as both adjusted to unfamiliar roles. In the process they became close friends for life and were tested two months after reaching Columbus. A Union steamboat fleet loaded with a strong expeditionary force landed above Columbus on the Missouri shore. Russell's brigade quickly boarded small steamers and crossed to the Confederate camp on the west bank at Belmont. Pillow formed his men in line of battle and gave Bell and his Twelfth the right-flank position. Worried about his inexperience and being separated from the brigade, Bell protested to Pillow, but to no avail.

The Confederates, deployed amateurishly, took heavy fire from the advancing Union troops under Ulysses S. Grant. After an abortive bayonet charge, Pillow's troops fell back, and the Twelfth found itself confronting Grant's strongest regiment reinforced by a second regiment and a section of artillery. Bell's men fought well from a good position but were outflanked and abandoned by the troops on their left. They fled to the riverbank. Bell gathered a portion of his men, however, and, reinforced by fresh troops from Columbus, moved to the rear of the attackers using the cover of the woods and formed a blocking position. The Yankees had to pay a high price to punch a hole through Bell's line and escape back to their boats.

Bell performed creditably in this bloody little battle in the tangled river bottom. Separated from Russell and his brigade, undersupplied with ammunition, attacked by a superior force, Bell lost control of his regiment, but he proved he could lead men and gained important but painful experience. "I suffered more that day," he stated, "than I ever did on any battle field during the whole war."

More suffering came at Shiloh. Although Bell and his men drove the enemy to the banks of the Tennessee River, Bell was shot in the chest as the Twelfth fought off a furious Union counterattack. The second day, in great pain and unable to perform his duties, he was carried back to Corinth, then to Newbern to begin six weeks of convalescence. Almost as soon as he could walk again, Bell set out to rejoin the army.

In Mississippi Bell found the Twelfth, badly depleted by casualties, consolidated with the Twenty-second Tennessee Infantry and himself named as colonel in May. His friend Russell had been relegated to supernumerary status, replaced by Preston Smith as brigade commander. In the late summer 1862, Bell participated in the invasion of Kentucky, being detailed to Edmund Kirby Smith's army, Patrick Cleburne's division. "At that time I was considered a great invalid." Bell recalled. "My lower limbs had swollen so that I had to be bandaged from my waist to my toes every morning before I could get into my saddle." Nevertheless Kirby Smith appreciated Bell and used him on several independent missions. At Richmond, Kentucky, Bell fought effectively, winning the confidence of Preston Smith.

Upon his return to Tennessee, Bell learned of the pending consolidation of the Twelfth and Twenty-second Tennessee Regiment with the Forty-seventh Tennessee Regiment, which would reduce the former to a battalion in the proposed Twelfth, Twenty-second, and Forty-seventh Regiment. Bell would command the new regiment, but half of his former officers and noncommissioned officers would be left without commands. The Twelfth as he had known it would be gone. Bell was unhappy and let it be known. Gen. Frank Cheatham sent him and a party of leaders from the old regiment to West Tennessee to recruit a regiment. This effort accomplished nothing for Nathan Bedford Forrest, whom they planned to join. Forrest had been defeated, and the west bank of the Tennessee River now swarmed with Federals. Bell's party returned, and General Polk gave him and what remained of the regiment (56 percent had been killed or wounded at Murfreesboro) the duty of garrisoning Shelbyville, Tennessee. Bell took leave during this quiet time and met with Pillow and Forrest at Columbia, Tennessee. The three agreed that opportunity beckoned in West Tennessee, and on June 21, 1863, Bell rode out of camp "for the purpose of recruiting our Army." His association with the Twelfth and the Army of Tennessee had ended. He had become a subordinate of Gideon Pillow.

Pillow gave Bell control of the Volunteer and Conscript Bureau in West Tennessee, including command of half a dozen small partisan organizations, and directed him to raise a regiment, a brigade if possible. Bell worked hard and, aided by Milton Russell, assembled 2,500 "recruits" at Jackson by the end of September 1863. Bragg was ecstatic and provided arms, equipment, and money, but Forrest pulled Bell to his side, asking Bell to help him build "Forrest's Cavalry" in north Mississippi.

Until Christmas 1863, Forrest and Bell gathered individuals and small bands at Jackson, Tennessee, then marched south, a ponderous column, mostly unarmed, with some forty commissary wagons and a large herd of beef cattle. In a show of audacity Bell attacked an advancing Union force and drove it back from the head of the column and continued driving it until sundown.

Bell then guided the heavy column across the Memphis and Charleston Railroad to Como, Mississippi. There he and Forrest set about organizing and training their little army. Bell had a brigade of cavalry now, consisting of five regiments, one of which was Milton Russell's Twentieth Tennessee Cavalry.

In March 1864 Abraham Buford appeared in camp with a tiny brigade of Kentucky infantry and became Bell's division commander. To mount and equip the Kentuckians and to season his new army, Forrest ventured north to the Ohio. They attacked Paducah, Kentucky, capturing prisoners, hundreds of mounts, and a wagon train of provisions and equipment, then turned south to Trenton, Tennessee, recruiting and conscripting, swelling Bell's ranks by a thousand men. Buford learned of another cache of horses and returned about April 8 for a second strike at Paducah.

Forrest had Bell move south instead, to unite with Robert "Black Bob" McCullough's smaller brigade and march on Fort Pillow. Bell's Brigade left Eaton, Tennessee, at midnight April 11, found a crossing of the Forked Deer River, waded half a mile in knee-deep water, pulling two of Forrest's precious fieldpieces, marched all night, all the next day, rendezvoused with McCullough ahead of schedule, and arrived before Fort Pillow in the rain and darkness, a seventy-mile forced march in thirty hours.

The enemy abandoned their two-mile front and fell back to a prepared second line, then into the earthen fort itself. As Forrest's cavalrymen approached, about six hundred Federals awaited them: four companies of the Sixth U.S. Heavy Artillery (Colored) and a section from the Second U.S. Light Artillery (Colored), plus Bradford's West Tennessee cavalry battalion. The five Union fieldpieces opened, supported by fire from the gunboat *New Era*. The Confederates moved in still closer before calling for the surrender of the garrison. This was refused, and after reconnoitering the defenses and testing the Federals' reactions, Forrest again demanded surrender. The Federal commander refused. Forrest then ordered the assault. It lasted five minutes, perhaps less. Among the first over the top was Bell's son Isaac. He yanked down the enemy colors and raised the Confederate flag above the earthworks. The enemy broke for the river and the protection of the gunboats. Forrest's men raced in pursuit and fired upon the Federals as they fled down the bluff. Soon many of them stood helpless in the river. Forrest and Bell atop the bluff worried more, it appears, about the enemy boats. They manned one of the fort's Parrott rifles, rolled it up to the bluff, turned it about and opened on one of the gunboats, having a great time serving the piece.

Bell's performance at Fort Pillow was energetic, brave, and resourceful, but the "Fort Pillow massacre," as it is known, blighted his name. Bell denied the deliberate killings in a sworn statement, although he admitted in his memoir that "promiscuous shooting for some time" occurred during the assault.

Colonel Bell returned to sweeping upper West Tennessee for deserters and conscripts and strengthened the brigade by three hundred, just in time to join in the attack on Sam Sturgis's advancing column from Memphis at Brices Cross Roads on June 10. This proved to be Bell's and Forrest's best fight. Bell confronted Federal infantry in strength and fought them not in skirmisher fashion but in line of battle, Twelfth Tennessee style. They drove back the enemy and broke their lines, sending the Federals fleeing from the field. Bell and Forrest led the pursuit back toward Memphis.

Bell's big brigade had been badly hurt, however, suffering about half of Forrest's losses. Even sharper losses would follow at Harrisburg July 14–15. Piecemeal frontal attacks against a strongly posted veteran enemy led to bad defeat. The startling raid on Memphis in August 1864 was followed by a larger raid into Middle Tennessee in late September and the spectacular Johnsonville raid in October.

November and December 1864 brought a killing march to join John B. Hood's army at Florence, Alabama. Six weeks of constant fighting, highlighted by the battles of Franklin and Nashville, followed. Bell played a crucial role covering the retreat of Hood's demoralized army from Tennessee. In a heavy fight at Richland Creek a shell burst over Bell and shrapnel tore into his face, destroying his right eye. He remounted, fled to high ground bordering the creek, then turned about with his escort and fired a volley into a "stream of Federal cavalry," confusing his pursuers and allowing time for Bell and his troopers to swim their horses across the creek then slip across the Tennessee River. Except for his promotion to brigadier general February 28, 1865, the war for Tyree Bell was over.

The prototype American citizen-soldier, Bell proved Forrest's most reliable lieutenant, his "right arm." He commanded the largest brigade, and Forrest employed him much as Sherman used George Thomas as his base of maneuver. Kirby Smith, Leonidas Polk, and Forrest realized Bell's gift for moving large bodies of troops and trains over difficult country. He was responsible, prompt, loyal, and a fearsome fighter and drew men to him. As recruiter he was peerless. Bell knew Forrest very well and shared his campfire. He interpreted Forrest to the troops and field-grade officers to their chief. They made a splendid team.

Bell returned to his Dyer County farm after the surrender, yet in 1878 he left the South and moved to California. He died in New Orleans on September 1, 1902, and is buried in Bethel Cemetery, Sanger, California.

BIBLIOGRAPHY

Davis, William C., ed. *The Confederate General.* 6 vols. Harrisburg, PA: National Historical Society, 1991.

Hughes, Nathaniel Cheairs, Jr., Connie Walton Moretti, and James Michael Browne. *Brigadier General Tyree H. Bell, C.S.A., Forrest's Fighting Lieutenant.* Knoxville: University of Tennessee Press, 2004.

U.S. War Department. *The War of the Rebellion: A Compilation of the Official Records of the Union and Confederate Armies.* 70 vols. in 128 pts. Washington, DC: Government Printing Office, 1880–1901.

—NATHANIEL C. HUGHES

Maj. Gen. John Cabell Breckinridge

KENTUCKIANS SEEMED ALWAYS to be caught in the middle. Maybe it was the Bluegrass State's geographical position on the border between North and South, or perhaps it was the towering presence of her greatest statesman, Henry Clay, the great compromiser. Whatever accounted for it, Kentucky and her sons faced dilemmas in the 1860s that strained families, loyalties, and hearts in ways endured by few other Americans. Certainly that was the case with John Cabell Breckinridge, the man many thought inherited Clay's mantle. The sectional controversy helped to make him, and it tried mightily to destroy him.

He came of a distinguished bloodline. His grandfather John Breckinridge moved the family from Virginia to Kentucky in 1793, settling an estate called Cabell's Dale outside Lexington. This Breckinridge made a place for himself in the sectional controversy by securing in the state legislature adoption of the Kentucky Resolutions of 1798. Though Thomas Jefferson was their author, myth attributed the resolves to Breckinridge, with their assertion of the right of state nullification of federal laws, one of the foundation stones of secession doctrine. John Breckinridge went on to serve in the U.S. Senate and then briefly as Jefferson's first attorney general before his untimely death in 1806. John Breckinridge's son Joseph Cabell Breckinridge tried to emulate his father's example, but he, too, died young while serving as speaker of the house in Kentucky's legislature in 1823.

A few years before, Joseph Cabell Breckinridge had married Mary Clay Smith, daughter of the president of the College of New Jersey (now Princeton University) and granddaughter of the college's founder, Rev. John Witherspoon, a signer of the Declaration of Independence. On January 16, 1821, she gave him his first and only son, John Cabell Breckinridge, born at their home Thorn Hill in Lexington. It was on this infant boy that the family pinned its expectations of someone to continue the heritage of the first John Breckinridge.

John C. Breckinridge grew up in Lexington, fatherless but much influenced by his several uncles, particularly Robert Jefferson Breckinridge. The family were almost all Jeffersonian Republicans, devout Presbyterians opposed in principle to slavery, but also opposed to any form of abolition other than voluntary emancipation, believing as they did that the central government could not interfere in the individual states' institutions. Young Breckinridge and his widowed mother moved to Cabell's Dale, and he attended the Kentucky Academy at Pisgah and then in 1834 entered Centre College at Danville, a Presbyterian school run by his uncle John Young. After four years at Centre, Breckinridge went east to the College of New Jersey for six months of prelaw study, after which he returned home and read law under Judge William Owsley, a prominent jurist and leader in the new Whig Party, which arose in opposition to Andrew Jackson's Democrats. Most of the Breckinridges adhered to the new party, but at about this time young John C. Breckinridge began to find Democratic ideas more persuasive. When he finished reading law, Breckinridge spent a year at Lexington's Transylvania University and graduated in 1841 with an LL.B. degree and an almost perfect academic record. One day after graduation he was admitted to the Kentucky bar.

While Breckinridge immediately commenced a law practice in Frankfort, he did not prosper, and that plus an unrequited love affair persuaded him to start anew in the Iowa Territory. After two years there he came back to Lexington, established what would become a flourishing practice, and met Mary Cyrene Burch, whom he married on December 12, 1843. For the next several years he practiced successfully, began to raise a family, and shocked some of his family by becoming more and more a confirmed Democrat. He did not rush to enlist when war broke out with Mexico in 1846, but a year later he delivered such an impressive oration over Kentucky dead brought home from the war that he was commissioned major of the Third Kentucky Volunteers without seeking the position, and soon left for a year in Mexico. He saw no combat but learned a lot about management of men and materiel, and moreover became acquainted with some of the leading younger soldiers of the day, men he would work with intimately in a different uniform some years hence.

Being a Breckinridge, it was almost inevitable that he would be drawn into active politics, and the time came on his return from Mexico when he won a seat in the legislature. Then in October 1850, when Henry Clay came home to Lexington after passage of the Omnibus Bill better known as the Compromise of 1850, Breckinridge was selected to give a welcoming speech, and it was so eloquent that Clay all but endorsed young Breckinridge for higher office. The next year Breckinridge won Clay's old seat in Congress and was reelected in 1853. He quickly became one of the more dynamic young statesmen in Washington, often linked with Stephen A. Douglas of Illinois, and Breckinridge himself acquired unusual influence with President Franklin Pierce, using it to get Pierce to sign off on the Kansas-Nebraska legislation that essentially repealed the Missouri Compromise.

In 1855 Breckinridge did not seek reelection, needing to repair his personal finances and attend to his law practice, but in 1856 the Democratic convention nominated him for the vice presidency, and in the fall of that year he and James Buchanan were elected. Theirs was not a happy partnership. Buchanan was weak, indecisive, and vacillating. Moreover, he was jealous of his more popular running mate and probably harbored distrust as a result of Breckinridge's close association with Buchanan's rival Douglas. As a result, Breckinridge played almost no role in their administration, did not have Buchanan's confidence, and was not consulted or involved in the administration's fumbling handling of the sectional crisis. As 1860 approached, many Democrats spoke of Breckinridge as a presidential contender, but he seems to have realized that his party was so fragmented that only a candidate who could unite all sections would have a chance, and he was too closely allied in the public mind with the more extreme Southern-rights wing of the party.

When the party did split in convention and the Southern-rights wing nominated him, he at first intended to decline, until persuaded that if he accepted, it would force the Northern Democrats' candidate, Douglas, to withdraw as well, and then a compromise candidate could be found. But Douglas would not agree to the bargain, and Breckinridge remained in the race. Though never an extremist himself, and entirely out of sympathy with the Fire-Eaters, who were destroying the party and the Union, he felt that he had to try to represent the views of conservatives who opposed federal interference with slavery in the territories, though still personally opposed to slavery himself. On election day, as predicted, the Democrats split their votes and gave Abraham Lincoln the election, though Breckinridge came in second to Lincoln in the electoral college. As vice president, he presided over the official count of electoral votes and declared Lincoln the winner, firmly condemning any efforts to disrupt the proceeding.

In the fall of 1859 the Kentucky legislature had elected Breckinridge to the Senate for the term beginning in 1861, so when he left his chair as vice president, he was immediately sworn in as a member of the U.S. Senate. There for the next several months he spoke out against extremism, sometimes supporting his friend Lincoln's administration, but opposing all attempts to coerce South Carolina and other seceding states into remaining in the Union. Not a friend of secession, Breckinridge still believed that Washington did not constitutionally have the power to force a state to stay. At the same time he believed that coercion, and military conflict, would only exacerbate Southern feelings and make it more difficult for a reconciliation, which is the end he always sought.

By the summer of 1861 Breckinridge's position was becoming increasingly untenable. In the public eye his speeches against the administration and his expressions of sympathy for Confederate soldiers wounded in the battle of Bull Run convinced more and more that he was a traitor in spite of his protestations of loyalty to the Union. Back in Kentucky a struggle raged between Union and Confederate sympathizers for control of the state, and on September 18 the state legislature finally sided with the North. At once the political arrests began, and the next day Breckinridge's political foes persuaded Union military authorities that he was too dangerous to run free in the state. Advised of the order for his arrest, Breckinridge made the choice he had been avoiding. Rather than languish in prison as a political prisoner for doing nothing more than speaking out as was his right as a senator and an American, he would cross the line into the Confederacy. It was a decision he ever after regretted being forced to make.

The Confederacy welcomed Breckinridge warmly, not for his military experience—which was very limited—but for his personal prestige. Jefferson Davis immediately commissioned him a brigadier general November 2, 1861, and assigned him to the small army being raised in Bowling Green, Kentucky, under Gen. Albert Sidney Johnston. After Johnston had to abandon his line in Kentucky in February 1862, he reorganized his army into four corps, eventually giving Breckinridge command of the smallest, the Reserve Corps, just six days before the army went into action. On April 6, at Shiloh, Johnston at first did not intend to put Breckinridge into action, but the battle quickly got out of hand and sucked the reserve into its maw along with the rest of the Confederate army. In his first action, Breckinridge performed very well, showed that he was cool under fire, could think and act and command the obedience of his men. Like other generals that day, he did not control his command very well, as it was a learning experience for all of them, but still he did well, being in on the capture of the Hornet's Nest late in the day.

When the Confederates were driven from the field the next day, Breckinridge covered the retreat to Corinth, Mississippi, winning promotion to major general on April 14. Soon he was ordered to take his small corps to Vicksburg to aid in defending that bastion on the Mississippi River. After several weeks there, he was ordered south to take Baton Rouge, and in a combined land and naval operation largely planned by Breckinridge, the Confederates attacked and all but took the town on August 5, until the failure of the naval component forced Breckinridge to retire. Instead he identified the bluffs at nearby Port Hudson as a prime location for defending the river against naval approach from below and began fortifying the heights that would stand as a major defense for the next year.

That summer Gen. Braxton Bragg, commanding now after the death of Johnston, planned a major invasion of Kentucky to wrest it back from the Yankees, and he wanted Kentuckians like Breckinridge with him for the moral force they might exert in the Bluegrass. One delay after another kept Breckinridge from reaching Bragg in time for the abortive invasion, but he did link with him late that fall. At the battle of Murfreesboro at the end of December 1862 and early January 1863, Breckinridge commanded a division in the action and conducted what was for its time one of the greatest infantry assaults yet. He did it against his wishes, and the severe pummeling his division received, in addition to other provocations, cemented his place among the dissidents opposed to Bragg's command of the army. For the next year Breckinridge would be the object of Bragg's animosity, and occasional plotting, while he himself stayed out of the active scheming and politicking done by other Bragg opponents, though there was no doubt where his sympathies lay.

In the summer of 1863 Breckinridge returned to Vicksburg in the abortive attempt to relieve the beleaguered garrison there. He got only as far as Jackson, Mississippi, where he commanded part of Joseph E. Johnston's army in the effort that was too little and too late. Breckinridge was soon ordered back to Bragg and commanded his division at the battle of Chickamauga, where his hard-hitting attacks helped to open the gap in the Union line that led to the rout of its army. Shortly afterward he took command of a corps in Bragg's army as it besieged the Yankees in Chattanooga. On November 23 Breckinridge was in command of the line on Lookout Mountain when it fell to the Yankees, and two days later his corps, spread too thin on a line far too long, fell back in a rout from Missionary Ridge. Bragg would try hard to blame the defeat on Breckinridge, accusing him of being drunk and absent from his command, while ample evidence showed that Bragg was lying, just as he had when he had ordered subordinates to furnish him with perjured testimony a year before to try to lay blame for the defeat at Murfreesboro on Breckinridge. In the end it was Bragg who suffered, resigning his command in disgrace.

In February 1864 Richmond assigned Breckinridge to command of the Trans-Allegheny or Western Department of Virginia, comprising the southwestern counties of the state that controlled a vital east-west rail link of the Confederacy, and a back door to invasion from Kentucky and East Tennessee. Breckinridge would intermittently hold this command for the next eleven months, his most notable achievement being his victory in the battle of New Market on May 15, 1864, when he turned back a Yankee invasion of the Shenandoah Valley. Immediately afterward he was called east to join Robert E. Lee's army as it faced advancing Federals pressing toward Richmond. Breckinridge held the center of Lee's line at Cold Harbor, suffering a serious injury when his horse was killed under him, yet went back into action and later commanded in the defense of Lynchburg from a sick litter.

That summer Breckinridge commanded a corps in the army of Gen. Jubal Early as it marched into Maryland and tried to threaten Washington. Breckinridge himself chiefly directed the battle of Monocacy and later served with Early in the battles at Kernstown and Winchester in the unsuccessful defense of the Shenandoah against Sheridan. That fall there were calls in the army for Breckinridge to replace Early in command, but Richmond instead sent him back to southwest Virginia. Then in February 1865 Jefferson Davis, under criticism for his management of the war, made Breckinridge secretary of war. By that time, Breckinridge recognized that the war was lost and directed all his efforts toward bringing about an honorable surrender on terms that would get the best conditions possible for the South in a reunited Union. Consequently, he engaged in a steady, yet respectful, tug-of-war with President Davis that lasted through the evacuation of Richmond and on through the flight of the government. Present at the surrender negotiations of the Army of Tennessee in mid-April, Breckinridge commanded the fleeing government party and escort until it broke up on May 4 in Georgia.

After the capture of Davis, Breckinridge himself made a hair-raising escape through Georgia and Florida and across the Straits of Florida to Cuba, where he issued orders calling on all remaining Confederate soldiers to disband and give their paroles. Thereafter he spent more than three years in Europe and Canada in exile, as multiple treason indictments were in effect against him in Kentucky and Washington. He spoke up repeatedly for reconciliation and amity between the sections and finally returned to

Lexington early in 1869 after a general amnesty. He lived only another six years, his health ravaged by the war. He resumed his law practice but also championed rebuilding, becoming president of a life insurance company, helping construct a railroad in eastern Kentucky, and fostering education and some degree of equal rights for former slaves. He died at his home in Lexington on May 17, 1875, of pneumonia resulting from complications of his war injury and is buried in Lexington Cemetery.

BIBLIOGRAPHY

Davis, William C. *Breckinridge: Statesman, Soldier, Symbol.* Baton Rouge: Louisiana State University Press, 1974.

————, ed. *The Confederate General.* 6 vols. Harrisburg, PA: National Historical Society, 1991.

————. *An Honorable Defeat: The Last Days of the Confederate Government.* New York: Harcourt, 2001.

U.S. War Department. *The War of the Rebellion: A Compilation of the Official Records of the Union and Confederate Armies.* 70 vols. in 128 pts. Washington, DC: Government Printing Office, 1880–1901.

—WILLIAM C. DAVIS

Lt. Gen. Simon Bolivar Buckner

SIMON BOLIVAR BUCKNER was born April 1, 1823, on a large farm some nine miles from the village of Munfordville, Kentucky. His father, Aylett Hartwell Buckner, was a Virginian who moved to Kentucky about 1803. Mother Elizabeth Ann Morehead Buckner was also a Virginian. They married in Bowling Green on December 8, 1819.

Young Buckner did not attend school until he was nine years old. His most important early formal schooling was at the Christian County Seminary in 1838–1839. When Buckner learned that a cadet at West Point from the local district had withdrawn from the school, he applied to Congressman Philip Triplett, who appointed him to the vacancy. During his four years there Buckner became acquainted with many of the future Union and Confederate officers of the Civil War. A sturdy six-footer with a powerful physique, Buckner was noted for his gymnastic skills. An omnivorous reader with a phenomenal memory, he excelled in mathematics, history, and draftsmanship. He ranked eleventh in the class of twenty-five that graduated in 1844.

Buckner was first assigned to Sackett's Harbor, New York, but he was recalled to teach ethics at West Point in 1845. He resigned from the faculty in May 1846 to join the Sixth Infantry, which was going to Mexico. Most of Buckner's service during the Mexican War was with Gen. Winfield Scott, whom he greatly admired. Buckner received one minor wound, performed well, and got two brevet promotions. When he returned to duty at West Point, he refused as a matter of principle to accept compulsory chapel attendance on Sundays. He and some other protesters were dismissed from the faculty. Buckner was assigned to duty in New York City. During his stay there he married Mary Jane Kingsbury, whom he had met during his tour of duty at Sackett's Harbor. Her father was Maj.

Julius B. Kingsbury, who had the foresight to purchase considerable acreage in what became Chicago. His wife remained in the East while Buckner had several assignments on the western plains. His father died on December 11, 1851. Promotion was slow in the small army, but Buckner became a first lieutenant in the Sixth Infantry on December 31, 1851, and captain in the regiment's commissary department on November 3, 1852.

In poor health, Major Kingsbury retired from the army in 1853. He needed help in managing his investments in the growing Chicago area, and Buckner resigned from the army in March 1855 to help handle the investments. Kingsbury died in 1856, and Buckner assumed greater responsibility in managing the estate, but he retained an active interest in the Illinois State Militia.

The Buckners were living in Louisville in 1858 when daughter Lily was born on March 7. Buckner became interested in reorganizing the moribund Kentucky State Guard, for which he was appointed inspector general. As the sectional controversy worsened, Gov. Beriah Magoffin, pro-Southern in sentiment, used Buckner as his representative in missions to Tennessee, Missouri, and Washington, D.C., in efforts to maintain Kentucky's unusual neutrality. In May 1861, with admirable foresight, Buckner transferred all of his and his wife's extensive property holdings in Chicago to her eighteen-year-old brother. His own holdings in Kentucky amounted to some $64,000.

Elections in the summer of 1861 showed that a majority of Kentuckians were pro-Union. After a visit from Buckner in an effort to preserve Kentucky's neutrality, President Abraham Lincoln ordered a brigadier general's commission for Buckner if he remained loyal to the Union. Despite his sincere attachment to the Union, Buckner believed that the North had violated so many terms of the union that the Southern states were justified in leaving it. Long after the war, Buckner said that the general government had frequently violated the principles of the Constitution. "I therefore cast my lot with those who opposed those arbitrary assaults upon individual rights."

Almost as soon as he made his decision, Buckner became a brigadier general in the Confederate army, to rank from September 14, 1861. Gen. Albert Sidney Johnston, who commanded the vast western theater for the Confederacy, ordered Buckner to seize Bowling Green, Kentucky, a town of some 2,500 people, which was located astride important transportation routes in south-central Kentucky. Buckner occupied Bowling Green on September 18, 1861, then sent troops northward to protect against possible Union advances from Louisville. A young son, Henry, died in Bowling Green in early December. When Brig. Gen. Ulysses S. Grant captured Fort Henry, Buckner was ordered to take his division to Fort Donelson. Grant's army was to be checked there until most of the Confederates in Kentucky had time to withdraw to Nashville. Brig. Gens. John B. Floyd and Gideon J. Pillow outranked Buckner. Buckner was placed in command of the right wing of the Confederate defenders. On the morning of February 15, Buckner was late in attacking when some of his troops were not on line in time, but then they pushed the Federal troops back some two miles. The way out had been opened, but after nearly a day of severe fighting, General Pillow ordered the troops to return to their original positions in the entrenchments. But Union forces held part of Buckner's line, and he was not able to dislodge them. During the night of February 15–16, the three generals met to decide what should be done. Buckner said that he could not hold his position for over half an hour when attacked. When Floyd and Pillow both decided to avoid being captives, the command fell to Buckner, who was determined to share the fate of his men. When he asked Grant for the appointment of commissioners to determine terms of surrender, Grant replied that "no terms except unconditional and immediate surrender [could] be accepted." Afterward, Grant quietly offered Buckner what personal funds he might need. Regardless of the circumstances of the surrender, Buckner received considerable criticism for his role, but he did not lose the confidence of President Jefferson Davis.

Buckner was imprisoned at Fort Warren, near Boston, where he indulged his interest in writing poetry. An exchange was made in the summer of 1862, and Buckner returned to Richmond. Despite some criticism of his Donelson surrender, he was promoted to major general on August 16, 1862. Although Gen. Robert E. Lee had asked for him, he was sent to Braxton Bragg in Chattanooga. Assigned to command a division in Maj. Gen. William J. Hardee's corps, he was soon involved in the 1862 invasion of Kentucky. At Munfordville he was asked by inexperienced Union colonel John R. Wilder what he should do when surrounded by a much larger Confederate force. Buckner provided an honest range of options and accepted the surrender of the Union force. After some early successes, including the only Confederate capture of a Union state capital during the war, the campaign's decisive battle was fought at Perryville on October 8. Neither army used its full strength, but during the heavy afternoon fighting, Buckner's division succeeded in forcing back the Union left wing despite enduring heavy casualties. But Bragg had been discouraged by the small number of Kentuckians who had volunteered for Confederate service, and Buckner's division was soon in the retreat through Cumberland Gap.

Buckner was next assigned to command the District of the Gulf at Mobile, where he worked to strengthen the defenses of that port. Then in April 1863 he was assigned to command the Department of East Tennessee, an area with vital supplies of salt and lead but with a population that contained a high percentage of Unionists. Buckner's force consisted of some four thousand infantry and some two thousand cavalry, and equipment was lacking. The district was placed in Bragg's jurisdiction, but Buckner was told to continue to report directly to the War Department. He was able to send a few small raids into eastern Kentucky, but his primary duty was to defend the region.

As Union forces advanced southward, Buckner was ordered to leave Knoxville and join Bragg. At Chickamauga on September 19–20, Buckner had a corps of two divisions, those of A. P. Stewart and William Preston. They were assigned to the command of Lt. Gen. James Longstreet, who had come west from the Army of Northern Virginia. Bragg's plans were altered frequently and poorly executed. Buckner's two divisions fought on different sectors of the battlefield, but they contributed to the victory that cost heavy casualties but sent the Union army retreating toward Chattanooga. During the two days, there were numerous errors and misdirections that increased discontent among many members of the army's high command. A secret meeting of corps commanders on October 4 called for Bragg's removal on the grounds of poor health. The precise authorship of the request is unknown, but Buckner, with his skill in writing and his dislike of Bragg, may have been the primary author. President Davis hurried westward in an effort to resolve the festering problem. Buckner was reduced to the command of a single division, and his department was abolished. On November 23, 1863, Buckner was ordered to join Longstreet, who was attempting to capture Knoxville.

Illness prevented Buckner from participating in that campaign. He went to Richmond before Christmas, commanded Hood's Division for a few weeks, then was reassigned to his old command of the Department of East Tennessee, where the problems of too few troops and inadequate equipment remained. His stay was brief, for Gen. Edmund Kirby Smith, commander of the vast area west of the Mississippi, requested his services. Promoted to lieutenant general on September 2, 1864, Buckner crossed the Mississippi and assumed the command that had been held by Maj. Gen. Richard Taylor in western Louisiana. In April 1865 his command was extended to include the District of Arkansas. Many of his problems concerned the growing desertion of troops and the extensive speculation in cotton. On May 9 Kirby Smith appointed Buckner as his chief of staff.

News of Lee's surrender led Kirby Smith and others to consider going to Mexico rather than accept surrender. If Buckner considered going into such exile, he abandoned the idea. Instead, he went to New Orleans to consult with Maj. Gen. E. R. Canby about terms of surrender. The terms agreed upon on May 26 were almost the same as those Lee and Joseph E. Johnston had accepted. General Kirby Smith accepted the terms on June 2 with one slight change.

Buckner was a competent military commander who believed strongly in well-trained and disciplined troops. Despite his surrender at Donelson and his protracted quarrel with Bragg, he had a generally favorable reputation in the Confederate army. His troops performed well at Donelson, Perryville, and Chickamauga; his resources were inadequate for much success in East Tennessee. He was trusted with some important semi-independent assignments, in which he performed well, despite limited resources.

Buckner said farewell to his staff and his troops on June 8–9, 1865. Ordered to remain in Louisiana, he sought ways to earn a living. He wrote editorials for the *Daily Crescent* and worked with various insurance companies, cotton factors, and commission houses. On February 5, 1866, General Grant gave him permission to travel within the United States to conduct business. In 1867 the Kentucky legislature passed the Amnesty Act, which protected individuals from legal actions resulting from actions taken under military authority or under military compulsion. Buckner secured the return of his Kentucky property. The death of Col. Henry W. Kingsbury, Buckner's brother-in-law to whom he had entrusted his wife's share of his father's estate, resulted in a protracted legal battle. Buckner and his wife regained the sizable property, which ensured a comfortable life. In 1868 Buckner edited the *Louisville Daily Courier* until it became part of the *Courier-Journal*. On January 5, 1874, Mary Buckner died of tuberculosis in Elizabethtown, where they were living at the time. Buckner made his home in Louisville until 1877, when he returned to Glen Lily, his plantation outside Munfordville.

One of the founders of the Southern Historical Society in 1869, Buckner wrote and spoke frequently about the Confederate experience. Often mentioned as a candidate for the governorship, he had a keen interest in state and national politics. On June 10, 1885, Buckner married twenty-eight-year-old Delia Claiborne of Virginia. During a bridal tour they visited Ulysses S. Grant shortly before his death; Buckner was one of the pallbearers at Grant's funeral. Son Simon Bolivar Buckner Jr. was born at Glen Lily on July 18, 1886. (A career army officer, Lieutenant General Buckner was killed on Okinawa on July 18, 1945.)

Elected governor in 1887, Buckner gave Kentucky four years of honest, efficient administration. He vetoed more private bills than had all of his predecessors combined. After the state treasurer decamped with most of the state's funds and the legislature voted appropriations that exceeded revenue, Buckner quietly loaned the commonwealth enough money to keep it solvent until tax revenues came in. Few of his progressive ideas were accepted by the legislature. He left his party in 1896 to run for vice president on a Gold Democrat ticket in opposition to William Jennings Bryan. He attended Confederate encampments whenever possible. When cataracts threatened to blind him, at age eighty he memorized five more of Shakespeare's plays so that if necessary he "could read Shakespeare in the dark." The operations for the cataracts were successful. After 1908 he was the only surviving Confederate of lieutenant general rank. In 1909 he visited his Mexican War battlefields. His health gradually broke down, and he died of uremic poisoning on January 8, 1914, at Glen Lily. He was buried in State Cemetery, Frankfort.

Bibliography

Davis, William C., ed. *The Confederate General.* 6 vols. Harrisburg, PA: National Historical Society, 1991.

Harrison, Lowell H. "Simon Bolivar Buckner." In *Kentucky's Governors,* ed. Lowell H. Harrison, 119–22. Lexington: University Press of Kentucky, 2004.

———. "Simon Bolivar Buckner: A Profile." *Civil War Times Illustrated* 16 (February 1978): 36–45.

Stickles, Arndt M. *Simon Bolivar Buckner: Borderland Knight.* Chapel Hill: University of North Carolina Press, 1940.

—Lowell H. Harrison

Brig. Gen. Abraham H. Buford

IT SHOULD COME as no surprise that Abraham Buford's greatest service in the Civil War would be in the cavalry. The breeding, rais- ing, and training of horses would be his lifetime passion from his earliest years. In this pursuit he followed in the footsteps of his grandfather and father, who had, while living in Virginia and Ken- tucky respectively, both been not- ed for their blooded stock and celebrated racehorses. Buford was born January 18, 1820, in Wood- ford County, Kentucky, the son of William and Frances Walker Kirtley Buford. As a result of his father's financial standing, his early life was one of privilege. Much of his initial education was from the private tutoring of Verpyle Payne, a very much respected teacher. He then attended Centre College in his home state but left that institution in 1837 when he received an appointment to West Point. Graduating from the academy in 1841, Buford could not look back upon his four years as having produced an academic record of great distinction. His standing was fifty-first in a class of fifty-two. Among his classmates were future Union generals Don Carlos Buell, Albion P. Howe, and Horatio G. Wright. As this low ranking did not entitle Buford to an elite posting, he was commissioned a brevet second lieutenant and as- signed to the First Dragoons. This was probably much to his liking, as he could continue his association with horses. For the next thirteen years, the First Dragoons would be his home and its career would be his. From 1841 to 1846 he experienced life on the frontier, serving at various times at Forts Atkinson and Leavenworth in Kansas and at Forts Gibson and Washita in the Indian Territory. At Gibson on April 12, 1842, Buford was promoted to second lieutenant. While at Fort Gibson in the winter of 1844–1845, he courted and proposed to Amanda Harris, the sister of a former officer and a teenager from Canajoharie, New York. They were married in 1845.

Letters written during that same winter by another officer at Fort Gibson, 1st Lt. Robert H. Chilton, alleged that Buford was combative and unpopular and had made very disparaging remarks, even "grosser and filthier than those of any other person at the Post," about Miss Harris after they were engaged. The same officer, who would also become a Confederate brigadier, described Buford's fiancée as a "simpleton . . . with a whoring sister and a black leg brother." The veracity of Chilton's comments about Buford must be questioned, however, because of his obvious bias against Buford as contained in the entire body of his correspondence.

From 1846 to 1848, Buford and the First Dragoons saw action in the Mexican War. Early in the war, on December 6, 1846, Abraham Buford was commissioned a first lieutenant. For gallant and meritorious conduct at the battle of Buena Vista on February 22, 1847, he was breveted captain.

When the Mexican War ended, Buford returned to Fort Gibson. Here on December 24, 1848, his only son, William A. Buford, was born. At that same time, Buford was sent to New Mexico. There he would spend the next three years, serving at such posts as Santa Fe, Socorro, Doña Ana, and Fort Fillmore. Finally, in 1852, Buford returned to the East, having been assigned as an instructor at the Cavalry School at Carlisle, Pennsylvania. On June 15, 1853, he was promoted to captain in the First Dragoons and appointed to serve as secretary of the Western Military Asylum, located in Harrodsburg, Kentucky.

In 1854, Abraham Buford was thirty-four years old. He was an extremely large man for the times, weighing well over three hundred pounds and standing over six feet tall. His character matched his size, as he was aggressive, domineering, and very much a martinet. The year 1854 would be pivotal in his life. Apparently his return to his native state, Kentucky, had kindled a desire to experience the life of a civilian family man and horseman. In that year he resigned from the army on October 22 and purchased the magnificent estate that would be his home for the next twenty-five years.

The family of Abraham Buford established their residence on 267 acres, three miles south of Versailles, Kentucky, in Woodford County. The purchase price was $21,396. Because of its scenic vistas, Buford named his new home Bosque Bonita, which means "beautiful woods." Here he began raising his beloved horses and also shorthorn cattle. Very quickly Buford established a national reputation for the quality of his stock, especially the racehorses. Evidencing an avid interest in politics and community affairs, he also served as president of the Richmond and Danville Railroad. As the sectional conflict, which would lead to the Civil War, continued to fester, Buford became an ardent advocate of states' rights, but counseled against secession. Therefore, when hostilities actually began, he adopted personally the neutral policy initially taken by Kentucky. He maintained this position until the summer of 1862. After the forces of John Hunt Morgan and Braxton Bragg entered the state, he decided to cast his lot with the Confederacy. He committed to the South despite the fact that his cousins John Buford and Napoleon Buford, both also native Kentuckians, had chosen the Union. He joined Morgan at Georgetown, and because of his prominence and prior military service, he was authorized to raise a command. After setting up a recruiting camp near Lexington, he was able to enlist several thousand men, who were formed into a cavalry brigade consisting of three regiments of raw troops. These units were designated the Third, Fifth, and Sixth Kentucky Cavalry regiments.

Buford's command saw its first action after the battle of Perryville as it covered Bragg's retreat. Their route took them through Cumberland Gap into East Tennessee. A family history, first written in 1903, claims that when the army reached Knoxville, Buford became embroiled in a dispute with Edmund Kirby Smith. As the story goes, the latter ordered Buford's Brigade dismounted so that the horses could be used in the artillery service. Supposedly Buford, after protesting to no avail, withdrew from his command and traveled to Richmond to see Jefferson Davis. This family history states that this alleged dispute with Kirby Smith and the meeting with Davis were the reasons for Buford's promotion to brigadier general and transfer to an infantry brigade. However, no documentary evidence exists to verify this version; further, the known facts clearly establish that it is not accurate. No record exists of any interview by Buford with Davis regarding a conflict with Kirby Smith. More importantly, Buford's Brigade did serve as cavalry during the Murfreesboro campaign, only two months after the battle of Perryville. It is true that Buford was promoted to brigadier general on November 29, 1862, to rank from September 2, 1862. A similar dispute was much more likely the cause of the transfer to an infantry command, but it was with a subordinate not a superior. In January 1863 Buford filed charges against Col. John R. Butler of the Third Kentucky Cavalry for misbehavior before the enemy. Butler was acquitted of all but one complaint and filed retaliatory charges against Buford. The army commander, Braxton Bragg, ended this situation by refusing to prosecute Butler's accusations, separating the Third Kentucky from the rest of the brigade, and having Abraham Buford transferred to John Pemberton's forces in Mississippi. Whether Buford's contentious personality played a role in this affair is not known for sure but certainly is problematic. He also outranked Joe Wheeler, whom Bragg wanted to command all his cavalry.

Pemberton, desperate for reinforcements in the face of Ulysses S. Grant's continuing pressure on Vicksburg, could not have been overjoyed at the arrival of a supernumerary brigadier who came without troops or an assigned command. Already short on soldiers but long on generals, Pemberton had no units to give to Buford, but he did have an idea. He conceived a plan whereby Franklin Gardner, Confederate commander at Port Hudson, downriver from Vicksburg, would form a brigade of infantry and cavalry to be commanded by Buford. As was true with many of Pemberton's ideas during the Vicksburg campaign, this one too had no merit. Gardner so informed Pemberton, stating that there was no available cavalry to make the plan feasible. Instead Gardner took units from various states from other brigades and assigned Buford to command the newly formed brigade. Separated from the cavalry for the first time in his military career, Buford quickly adapted to his new role as the leader of foot soldiers. His brigade initially occupied the left end of Gardner's line at Port Hudson. However, it did not stay there long, as Pemberton continued to shift troops in an attempt to counter Federal movements. From April 6 to April 16, 1863, Buford's brigade traveled through parts of Louisiana, Mississippi, Alabama, Georgia, and Tennessee en route to and from ever-changing assignments. Finally, while moving to Jackson, Mississippi, to join William Wing Loring's division of Pemberton's main army, Buford was ordered to stop temporarily at Enterprise, Mississippi, in response to Union colonel Benjamin Grierson's diversionary cavalry raid.

Never reaching Jackson, Buford was en route to Vicksburg but was halted at Edwards' Station. Participating in the subsequent battle of Champion Hill proved, despite the Confederate defeat, to be a stroke of good fortune for Buford's brigade. As a result of the battle, almost all of Loring's division became separated from the rest of the army. It could not retreat toward Vicksburg, as Union troops were interposed between the division and Pemberton. Instead, Loring headed east to Jackson, Mississippi, where his division joined the army then being organized by Joseph E. Johnston. Thus, in the summer of 1863 Buford's brigade twice avoided the fate of its former comrades, surrender, Pemberton at Vicksburg and Gardner at Port Hudson.

For the next eight months, Buford continued to serve as an infantry commander in Loring's Division. The brigade participated in the defense of Jackson, Sherman's Meridian campaign, and other engagements in Mississippi. During this time, Loring's Division operated as part of the forces led by Johnston, William Hardee, and Leonidas Polk.

Though 1864 saw the steady decline of the Confederacy, it marked the greatest period of Abraham Buford's military career. On March 2, he returned to his favorite branch of the service, the cavalry. That date saw him transferred to the command of the man with whom he would serve throughout the remainder of the war, Nathan Bedford Forrest. The success he would achieve under this renowned leader would result in Buford's being considered among the elite of Confederate cavalry subordinates in the western theater. The transfer of Buford to Forrest resulted from a decision by the department commander, Leonidas Polk, to reinforce Forrest's force with three additional regiments. The units selected were the three Kentucky infantry regiments of Buford's Brigade. Polk ordered Forrest to mount these regiments for cavalry service but left to Forrest's discretion just where the requisite horses were to be obtained. Forrest decided on Kentucky. Immediately upon Buford's arrival in Tupelo, Mississippi, Forrest organized a raiding party consisting of Buford's Brigade and a few other units. Left behind were the balance of his cavalry, the artillery, and the wagon trains. Their route would take them through western Tennessee and on into Kentucky by way of Paducah. By the time they were back in Jackson, Mississippi, they had captured more than enough horses to mount the entire brigade. In addition, supplies of all types had been taken, and Buford had been promoted to command one of Forrest's divisions. Soon afterward the raid was repeated with equal success. When Forrest moved next to attack Fort Pillow, Tennessee, he ordered Buford to make a diversion in the direction of Columbus and Paducah, Kentucky. This move resulted in unexpected but welcome benefits when Buford was able to intercept reinforcements bound for Fort Pillow and capture all the Federal artillery at Paducah.

Buford's finest hour on a major battlefield came at the battle of Brices Cross Roads on June 10, 1864. This battle, which is considered Forrest's greatest victory, resulted in the complete rout of the Union forces. Buford's Division played a major role in driving the Federals from the field, a fact that Forrest recognized in his after-battle comments. Apparently Abraham Buford found Bedford Forrest's style of fighting much to his liking. During the balance of the summer and early fall of 1864, Buford's Division participated in the battle of Tupelo and in one successful raid after another in Mississippi, Tennessee, Kentucky, and Alabama. These actions culminated in Forrest's famous gunboats' raid in October. During this foray, troops under Buford's command acquired enormous amounts of valuable supplies. Their greatest achievement, however, was the capture of four Federal ships on the Tennessee River on October 29. On November 4, they destroyed millions of dollars of Federal property at Johnsonville, Tennessee.

However, this freewheeling raiding ended on November 5, 1864, when Buford's Division was ordered to join John Bell Hood's Army of Tennessee as it moved north after the fall of Atlanta. Buford's Division was the first to see action at Spring Hill, Tennessee, on November 29. However, it missed the battle of Nashville, as just prior to the Federal attack, Hood had foolishly sent Forrest's cavalry off on a meaningless raid to Murfreesboro. Once the battle began, Forrest was recalled and Buford's Division returned in time to act as rear guard for Hood's routed army. While serving in this capacity, Buford was seriously wounded in a skirmish at Richland Creek on December 24. His injuries caused him to leave the field for seven weeks.

When he rejoined the army on February 18, 1865, Forrest dispatched him to Alabama to command all the cavalry operating in that state. As the war wound to its conclusion, Buford's forces were defeated at Selma, Alabama, on April 2, 1865, by a Federal column led by James Harrison Wilson. This was Buford's last major military action. In May, he surrendered at Gainesville, Alabama.

Upon the cessation of hostilities, Buford went back to Bosque Bonita, to his family, to his beloved horses, and to the lifestyle he had enjoyed before the war. Breeding, raising, and racing superior thoroughbreds quickly restored his reputation as one of the foremost turfmen in the nation. His stables were home to some of the greatest horses of the 1870s, including Crossland, Nellie Gray, Selena, Inquirer, and Versailles. Sportsmen from across the country traveled to Bosque Bonita to partake in its lavish hospitality and learn its breeding and training procedures.

Buford also maintained an avid interest in current events and postwar politics. Desirous of seeing the country reunited, he advocated reconciliatory policies. To advance these causes, he was elected to the Kentucky legislature in 1879. However, despite his fame, success, and prominence, the decade of the 1870s was also one of personal sorrow for Buford. On November 2, 1872, his only son, William, died at home at the age of twenty-three. This was followed by his brother's going insane and murdering a judge. On February 3, 1879, his wife, Amanda, died at Bosque Bonita. This trail of tragedy continued to haunt Abraham Buford. While he was still devastated by the loss of his wife and son, a series of severe financial reverses caused him to lose Bosque Bonita by foreclosure in April 1879. A month later, all of his horses were sold at a public sale to satisfy a judgment.

The weight of these events and the failure of his great physical prowess, resulting from his advancing age, caused Buford to fall into a deep depression. Unable to face his grief any longer, Buford committed suicide at his nephew's home in Danville, Indiana, on June 9, 1884. His final note contained the instruction that he was to be buried next to his wife and son in the Lexington City Cemetery, Lexington, Kentucky. Probably due to his poor financial situation, his grave was unmarked until 1977. In that year, a government headstone was placed on the grave. Its inscription identifies Buford as a "Brig Gen Cavalry Confederate States Army," a most fitting epitaph.

Bibliography

Bearss, Edwin C. *Forrest at Brice's Cross Roads and in North Mississippi in 1864.* Dayton, OH: Morningside Books, 1979.

Davis, William C., ed. *The Confederate General.* 6 vols. Harrisburg, PA: National Historical Society, 1991.

Hewitt, Lawrence Lee. *Port Hudson, Confederate Bastion on the Mississippi.* Baton Rouge: Louisiana State University Press, 1987.

U.S. War Department. *The War of the Rebellion: A Compilation of the Official Records of the Union and Confederate Armies.* 70 vols. in 128 pts. Washington, DC: Government Printing Office, 1880–1901.

—Marshall D. Krolick

Maj. Gen. Thomas James Churchill

THOMAS JAMES CHURCHILL was born March 10, 1824, to Samuel and Abby Oldham Churchill. He and his seven siblings grew up on the family farm near Louisville, Kentucky. Churchill graduated in 1844 from St. Mary's College in Bardstown and then completed law school at Transylvania University in Lexington. At the outbreak of the Mexican War, the twenty-two-year-old joined the First Kentucky Mounted Rifle Regiment as a first lieutenant. While camped in Little Rock, Arkansas, en route to Mexico, Churchill met his future wife, Ann Sevier, daughter of Sen. Ambrose Sevier.

Mexican cavalry captured Churchill while he was on a scouting mission in January 1847, and the war was nearly over before he was released. He returned to Little Rock and married Ann on July 31, 1849. They eventually had six children. Although Churchill dabbled in politics in the antebellum period, he devoted most of his attention to his large plantation in Big Rock, Arkansas, where, according to the 1860 census, he held twenty-eight slaves. In that year, Churchill's life, like the lives of most everyone in the United States, changed forever.

At the beginning of the Civil War, the Arkansas legislature sent Churchill north in an unsuccessful attempt to purchase armaments. He then struggled to raise a regiment of cavalry in the counties around Fort Smith. He had difficulty convincing volunteers to join for three years, but once the Confederate War Department allowed him to accept one-year enlistees, he was able to organize his regiment. The recruits elected Churchill colonel on June 9, 1861, and the unit was mustered into Confederate service as the First Arkansas Mounted Riflemen and joined Brig. Gen. Benjamin McCulloch's command at Fort Smith.

Churchill spent the better part of May 1861 training and equipping his men. Their first significant action occurred in July with the capture of the Federal garrison at Neosho, Missouri. By early August, the regiment and the rest of McCulloch's command had joined Maj. Gen. Sterling Price of the Missouri State Guard south of Springfield, Missouri. McCulloch assumed command of the combined force and moved to within ten miles of the city, determined to attack the Federal garrison under Brig. Gen. Nathaniel Lyon. The Federals, however, struck first. On the morning of August 10, Colonel Churchill's men were preparing for breakfast in an open field when they were surprised by a flanking force led by Col. Franz Sigel. Under fire, the regiment retreated to an adjacent wood, where Churchill and his officers calmed the men and organized them for battle. While McCulloch rallied his men, Churchill's unmounted regiment moved along a road in the direction of Springfield. They were met by General Price's aide, who was seeking support against Lyon's main assault. Churchill complied, and for the next three to four hours, his men engaged in repeated charges up "Bloody Hill" trying to dislodge the Federals. Under heavy musketry and artillery fire, Churchill had two horses shot from under him. Eventually, Confederate assaults and the death of Lyon broke the Federals' will, and they retreated toward Springfield. For Churchill's service at Wilson's Creek, Price awarded him a letter of commendation praising the actions of the colonel and his command. The tribute closed with the line, "Your own gallantry and skill were so conspicuous on that memorable day that every Missourian will always cherish the remembrance of you with pride and gratitude."

After the battle of Wilson's Creek, the Confederate forces separated. Churchill's regiment remained with McCulloch's Brigade and moved toward the Kansas border to attack Forts Scott and Lincoln in Kansas. Reports of a Union invasion from Missouri forced McCulloch to call off this campaign. Churchill's men and the rest of the brigade remained in northwestern Arkansas for the winter.

In January 1862, Jefferson Davis created the Military District of the Trans-Mississippi and placed Maj. Gen. Earl Van Dorn in command. McCulloch's force was made a division, with Churchill's regiment serving in Col. James McIntosh's brigade. In February, a Union force under Brig. Gen. Samuel R. Curtis forced Price's army out of Missouri, and it joined McCulloch's force in Arkansas. A month later, Van Dorn took command of the combined Confederate forces, which he christened the Army of the West. He made plans to pounce on Curtis's force at Pea Ridge along the Arkansas-Missouri border. During the battle on March 7, 1862, McCulloch and McIntosh were killed, and Col. Louis Hebert, commanding

McCulloch's other brigade, was captured. This created a command vacuum in the division. Churchill stepped into the vacuum and attempted to rally the broken Confederates. The next morning, Curtis's men swept the Confederates from the field in a complete rout. Van Dorn's forces scattered, and it took nearly two weeks to reassemble them.

Following the disaster, Churchill was commissioned a brigadier general to rank from March 4, and he assumed command of a brigade in Maj. Gen. John P. McCown's division. Churchill's brigade soon left for Mississippi as part of Van Dorn's fifteen-thousand-man Army of the West. The army arrived at Corinth, Mississippi, too late to participate in the battle of Shiloh and joined the Confederate retreat from Corinth later that spring. Churchill became a division commander under Braxton Bragg, but his division was soon sent to Chattanooga and then to Knoxville to support Maj. Gen. Edmund Kirby Smith's invasion of Kentucky. In August, Kirby Smith led Churchill's division and another under Brig. Gen. Patrick Cleburne through Roger's Gap and into the Bluegrass State. Kirby Smith wanted to cross the Kentucky River between Richmond and Lexington as quickly as possible to gain control of the state.

On August 30, Churchill's division engaged in a running battle with Union forces outside Richmond. In close cooperation with Cleburne's division, Churchill's men eventually routed the Federal forces and moved into Richmond, capturing thousands of prisoners and valuable ordnance. In a letter of gratitude given to Kirby Smith by the Confederate Congress for the victory at Richmond, Churchill was mentioned for his "promptness and intelligence."

Following the Confederate victory at Richmond, Kirby Smith moved on Lexington in September and maneuvered through northern Kentucky. His army occupied the Bluegrass for a month until the battle of Perryville in October. Then Bragg and Kirby Smith retreated back into Tennessee.

On December 10, Churchill was transferred west of the Mississippi and assumed command of the second division of Maj. Gen. Thomas Hindman's corps in the Army of the Trans-Mississippi. Lt. Gen. T. H. Holmes now commanded the department. In January 1863, Holmes placed Churchill in command of the five-thousand-man garrison at Fort Hindman, which guarded Arkansas Post on the Arkansas River. A force consisting of thirty-two thousand troops under Maj. Gen. John A. McClernand, and a small fleet of ironclads and gunboats under Rear Adm. David Porter assaulted this strategic point in early January. After a heavy bombardment on January 10, Union troops prepared for an attack on the afternoon of the eleventh. Much to Churchill's surprise, white flags appeared along the Confederate line prior to the infantry charge. The Confederate defenses collapsed. Although Holmes had ordered Churchill "to hold out until help arrives or all are dead," the unauthorized surrender of the Twenty-fourth Texas dismounted cavalry regiment forced Churchill to hand over to McClernand five thousand men and a huge quantity of stores. Churchill's men were paroled while he spent three months as a prisoner of war at Camp Chase in Ohio before he was exchanged.

In his official report written after his release, Churchill claimed that although heavily outnumbered, he planned to resist the Federal assault. He accused one of his brigade commanders, Col. Robert R. Garland, of dereliction of duty for not resisting the Union assault before he could arrive on the scene to remove the white flags from the Twenty-fourth Texas. Secretary of War James Seddon recommended a court of inquiry to Jefferson Davis, who left it to the discretion of the secretary pending more information. Holmes supported Churchill, but Garland took offense at the general's accusation. When Churchill's force was exchanged and sent to Richmond, Virginia, Churchill asked for a court martial to investigate the surrender.

Before the matter could be examined, however, the division reported to Bragg in Tullahoma, Tennessee, in August of 1863, and, because of its diminished size, the general ordered it reorganized as a brigade. The understrength regiments were then consolidated. When Garland was not chosen as a commander of a consolidated regiment, he felt slighted and protested to Churchill and the War Department, again demanding a board of inquiry into the surrender at Fort Hindman. The request wound its way through the levels of administrative red tape until the spring of 1864, when the War Department refused to see Churchill's censure in his report as cause for a court of inquiry. The matter was finally closed.

Churchill's next significant military action occurred in the Red River campaign of 1864. The new Trans-Mississippi commander, Gen. Edmund Kirby Smith, faced a combined Federal assault from Arkansas under Maj. Gen. Frederick Steele and from New Orleans under Maj. Gen. Nathaniel Banks. Kirby Smith sent most of his infantry to Shreveport to support either front as needed. These meager forces consisted of the two small divisions of Churchill and Brig. Gen. Mosby M. Parsons. When Confederate major general Richard Taylor requested Parsons and Churchill to join him south of Shreveport in DeSoto Parish, Kirby Smith delayed them, leading to a long-standing feud between the generals.

Taylor eventually convinced Kirby Smith to give him the two divisions but moved against Banks at Mansfield, Louisiana, before they arrived.

Taylor routed the Federal force on April 8, 1864, forcing Banks to retreat to Pleasant Hill. Taylor planned to use Churchill's and Parsons's divisions to finish off the Federals the next day. About 1:00 P.M. on April 9, Churchill's men arrived after having marched nearly fifty miles in only a day and a half. Taylor gave the exhausted men a short rest and then ordered Churchill to take command of his and Parsons's divisions and to get behind the Union left flank. Once Churchill's men were engaged with the enemy, the rest of the Confederates would assault the Union forces from the front. With Confederate cavalry riding behind the Federal lines cutting off retreat, the entire Union force would be destroyed or captured. At 3:00 P.M. Churchill's command commenced their march through the dense woods. The rebels soon became disoriented and failed to get beyond the Union flank. Instead, Churchill's men came out of the woods almost in front of the Federal left flank. Although the Yankee line cracked, reinforcements arrived to push back the exhausted and confused Confederates in savage hand-to-hand fighting. As darkness fell, the battle ended, and Taylor's plan to annihilate Banks had failed. Nonetheless, the Federals retreated toward Alexandria. This stage of the Red River campaign came to a close.

With Banks out of the way, Kirby Smith moved Churchill's and Parsons's commands toward Camden, Arkansas, to face Steele's invasion. With Steele's army in possession of Camden, Kirby Smith ordered Brig. Gen. James Fagan's cavalry to cut Steele's supply line. To divert Steele's attention, Churchill and Parsons made a feint against Camden. Fagan destroyed a Federal supply train at the battle of Marks' Mills and forced Steele to abandon Camden. Price immediately occupied the town with Churchill's and Parsons's men. Kirby Smith hoped to cut Steele's line of retreat at the Saline River. Unfortunately for the rebels, Fagan's cavalry failed to halt the Union army before it reached the river. Although Churchill's men marched rapidly without rest and little food for nearly thirty miles, they reached Jenkins' Ferry to see the Federal forces dug in and crossing the Saline. Kirby Smith ordered a hasty assault early on the morning of April 30, hoping to prevent the Federals from escaping. The narrow approach to the river landing and poor command decisions by Kirby Smith and Price, however, prevented the rebels from sending all of their men forward in a coherent attack. Instead, Churchill sent his brigades forward piecemeal, allowing the Union forces to repulse the attacks easily. As fresh Confederate troops arrived, they too were sent forward in uncoordinated attacks. At one point, Churchill leapt off a horse and seized a musket in an attempt to rally his disoriented and disheartened men.

Churchill spent the rest of the war in the Trans-Mississippi, eventually being promoted to major general on March 18, 1865. At the final surrender of Confederate forces, Churchill was in Texas preparing the defense of that state. Throughout his military career, he proved to be a competent yet hardly brilliant commander.

Following the war, Churchill returned to his plantation near Little Rock and again became active in politics. With the end of Reconstruction and the collapse of the Arkansas Republican Party, he joined the first wave of Redemption Democrats and became state treasurer in 1874. He served a total of three terms before becoming governor in 1880.

As governor, Churchill supported the establishment of a state mental hospital, educational funding for a new normal and medical school, creation of a state board of health, provisions for the collection of overdue taxes, and a strange resolution stating how Arkansas should be pronounced.

Allegations of discrepancies in the treasurer's account for 1874–1880 emerged during the legislative session of 1881 and haunted his tenure as governor. Churchill and his supporters faced a coalition of antiadministration Democrats, Republicans, and Greenbackers who took advantage of the missing funds to discredit him. An investigating committee found $233,616 missing from the state coffers. As soon as Churchill left office, he faced a suit filed in Pulaski County Chancery Court. In a case that eventually wound its way to the state supreme court, Churchill's attorneys argued that the alleged shortages were due to bookkeeping errors and unintentionally burned state scrip that had failed to be accounted for. Churchill eventually paid $23,973 to the state yet refused to admit embezzlement.

A second major scandal of Churchill's term as governor occurred in 1881 and involved factional differences in Perry County. The county judge reported to Churchill that extensive lawlessness in the county prevented him from performing his duties. Churchill sent in the state militia to maintain order. Such a display of force, however, reminded white Arkansans too much of Reconstruction, and the presence of the militia in Perry County weakened Churchill's stature in the state.

Charges of corruption, the use of militia, and a series of natural disasters in 1881–1882 fueled mounting discontent with Churchill's administration and ended his political career. After retiring as governor in 1883, he never again sought public office but instead devoted his attention primarily to his plantation. Active in the affairs of the United Confederate Veterans, he eventually served as the commanding major general of the Confederate Veterans of Arkansas. Following a prolonged illness, he died in Little Rock on May 14, 1905, shortly after his eighty-first birthday. He was buried with full honors in his Confederate uniform at Mount Holly Cemetery.

Indeed, Churchill would be remembered most for his military career. At the 1928 National Convention of the United Confederate Veterans in Little Rock, a memorial boulder honoring Churchill was unveiled. The commander of Robert C. Newton, Camp 197, Sons of Confederate Veterans, Joseph S. Utley, closed his address with a stirring hagiographical tribute honoring Churchill's patriotism and personal bravery, two attributes that cannot be questioned.

BIBLIOGRAPHY

Bearss, Edwin C. *Steele's Retreat from Camden and the Battle of Jenkins' Ferry.* Little Rock: Pioneer Press, 1967.

Davis, William C., ed. *The Confederate General.* 6 vols. Harrisburg, PA: National Historical Society, 1991.

Donovan, Timothy Paul, Willard B. Gatewood, and Jeannie M. Whayne. *The Governors of Arkansas: Essays in Political Biography.* 2nd ed. Fayetteville: University of Arkansas Press, 1995.

Joiner, Gary D. *Through the Howling Wilderness: The 1864 Red River Campaign and Union Failure in the West.* Knoxville: University of Tennessee Press, 2006.

—JOHN D. FOWLER

Brig. Gen. George Blake Cosby

A NATIVE OF Louisville, Kentucky, born on January 19, 1830, George Blake Cosby was the son of Fortunatus Cosby Jr. and Ellen Mary Jane Blake. His father had served as U.S. consul at Geneva, Switzerland, as editor of the *Louisville Examiner* (which espoused gradual emancipation), and later as superintendent of public schools in Louisville. The future Confederate general was also the brother of Frank Carvill Cosby, who served in the U.S. Navy throughout the Civil War and retired from Federal service as a rear admiral. George Cosby received his early education in private schools and, in 1848, received an appointment to the U.S Military Academy at West Point. Graduating in 1852, Cosby stood seventeenth out of forty-three cadets who were commissioned that year. Among the future Union and Confederate generals who graduated with Cosby were Henry W. Slocum, David Stanley, John Forney, Alexander McD. McCook, August Kautz, and George Crook.

Following commissioning, he was assigned to the Cavalry School for Practice at Carlisle Barracks, Pennsylvania, where he served until May 1853. From there he proceeded to Texas for duty with a unit of mounted rifles stationed on the frontier at Fort Ewell but was soon transferred to Fort Merrill. Located on the right bank of the Nueces River where the Corpus Christi–San Antonio road crossed the river, Fort Merrill was near the present-day town of Dinero in Live Oak County, Texas. In May 1854, Cosby rode out of Fort Merrill with his command in the direction of Laredo. On May 9, the soldiers found and attacked a band of about forty Lipan (Apache) Indians near Lake Trinidad, approximately forty miles northwest of Corpus Christi. Although his men killed three Indians, Cosby was severely wounded in the saber arm but retained the command throughout the engagement. The injury pained him for the remainder of his life.

In 1855, while stationed at Fort Clark, Texas, he was transferred to the celebrated Second Cavalry, in which unit also served such future Civil War notables as Albert Sidney Johnston, Robert E. Lee, George H. Thomas, William J. Hardee, John Bell Hood, Earl Van Dorn, and George Stoneman. From September 1855 through January 1857, Cosby was an assistant instructor of cavalry tactics at West Point. Rejoining his command at Camp Colorado, near Coleman, Texas, in April, he accompanied Capt. John Pope (future commander of the Union Army of Virginia) on a survey of the thirty-second parallel for a proposed railroad route to the Pacific Ocean. During this march from Santa Fe to the Wachita Mountains, Cosby engaged in raids against hostile Comanche Indians. In April 1859, he rejoined his company at Camp Radziminski, Indian Territory, and the following month participated in the action at Small Creek, in the Nescutunga Valley, and was commended in the official reports for conspicuous gallantry.

Cosby was stationed at Fort Mason, situated north of the Llano River between San Antonio and Abilene, when John Brown launched his raid against the U.S. arsenal at Harpers Ferry in October 1859. Although deeply troubled by the sectional crisis that threatened to tear the nation asunder, the young officer was more concerned with passions of the heart and, in 1860, married Antonia Johnson, niece of future Union general Richard W. Johnson. The couple had five children, four of whom were born following the Civil War.

As the nation drifted to the brink of civil war, Cosby took a leave of absence from his post and returned home to Louisville to determine what course he would take in the pending conflict. On May 9, 1861, he was commissioned captain in the U.S. Army but resigned the following day and offered his sword to the Confederacy. Appointed captain in the Confederate service to rank from March 16, 1861, Cosby first served with John Bell Hood and Thomas Hart Taylor recruiting in Kentucky before becoming an instructor of cavalry troops. He later served at Yorktown as chief of staff to John Bankhead Magruder. Promoted to major in September to rank from June 20, 1861, he served under Simon Bolivar Buckner in south and central Kentucky and was Buckner's chief of staff at Fort Donelson. Following the shameful abandonment of their post by John B. Floyd and Gideon Pillow, command of the garrison fell upon Buckner, who made the decision to surrender the fort. On February 16, 1862, he dispatched Cosby to deliver to Brig. Gen. Ulysses S. Grant a note proposing an armistice and the appointment of commissioners to work out terms of capitulation. The Federal commander replied, "No terms except unconditional and immediate surrender can be accepted. I propose to move immediately against your works." Buckner was visibly shaken by Grant's reply but was compelled to accept what he considered "ungenerous and unchivalrous terms."

Imprisoned at Fort Warren, on Georges Island at the entrance to Boston Harbor, Cosby was one of several Confederate officers granted a parole by order of Maj. Gen. Henry W. Halleck, commander of the Federal Department of the Mississippi. Returning to Louisville, Cosby enjoyed a brief period of freedom in the company of family and friends. On April 2, Halleck wrote to Brig. Gen. Richard W. Johnson (Mrs. Cosby's uncle) in Louisville, "I released Major Cosby on parole on the representation of prominent citizens of Kentucky. On his arrival at Louisville he permitted himself to be feted and lionized by his secession friends. His general conduct so little comported with his position of a prisoner on parole that I have been obliged to direct his return to [the depot of prisoners at] Columbus." Returned to Fort Warren, Cosby remained there until late May, when he was sent to Fort Monroe to await exchange.

Upon his arrival at Fort Monroe, Cosby was disappointed to learn that by the direction of Secretary of War George W. Randolph, the Confederate War Department declined to make any special exchanges, believing them to be "unjust and arbitrary." (Cosby had been working to secure an exchange for Maj. Israel Vogdes of the First U.S. Artillery, who had been captured on Santa Rosa Island, Florida, on October 9, 1861.) Securing a parole for ten days, he visited the Confederate capital in Richmond in hope of effecting his exchange but failed in the endeavor. However, he was provided with a note from Secretary Randolph to Union major general John E. Wool offering to send an officer authorized to execute a cartel of exchange. Discussions eventually followed and in July resulted in the Dix-Hill Cartel, which governed prisoner exchange for much of the war.

Upon his return to Fort Monroe from Richmond, Cosby was sent to Fort Delaware, on Pea Patch Island in the Delaware River, where he remained until exchanged in August 1862. Rejoining the staff of General Buckner, Cosby was elevated to colonel and participated in the battles of Munfordville (September 14–17) and Perryville (October 8) in Kentucky. He continued to serve as Buckner's chief of staff when that general was given command of the District of the Gulf, headquartered in Mobile, in December 1862.

In January 1863, Cosby was given command of a brigade of cavalry under Maj. Gen. Earl Van Dorn. The Confederate horsemen moved from Mississippi through northern Alabama and into Tennessee to cooperate with Gen. Braxton Bragg's Army of Tennessee. On March 4–5, Van Dorn's command clashed with a combined force of Union infantry and cavalry at Thompson's Station, located on the Nashville and Decatur Railroad nine miles south of Franklin. In this sharp engagement, Cosby's first as a brigade commander, the Southern horsemen overwhelmed a smaller enemy force and compelled the surrender of more than 1,200 Federals, including their brigade commander Col. John Coburn.

On April 23, 1863, upon the recommendation of Buckner and Van Dorn, Cosby was elevated to brigadier general at the request of Joseph E. Johnston. His commission dated from January 20. In mid-May, Cosby's Brigade and the division to which it was attached, that commanded by Brig. Gen. William H. Jackson, was directed to march from Tennessee to Canton, Mississippi, for incorporation into the Army of Relief. This force was assembled in the Jackson-Canton area by Joe Johnston for the purpose of relieving the garrison of Vicksburg, then besieged by Grant's Union army. On June 9, shortly after his arrival in Canton, Cosby was ordered to place his brigade to guard the "Mechanicsburg Corridor," the country between the Yazoo and Big Black rivers, northeast of Vicksburg. He established his headquarters near Mechanicsburg and spent the balance of the month occasionally reconnoitering the Federal positions north of Vicksburg. Although Johnston's force finally took up the line of march toward Vicksburg, it was too late to be of any assistance, as the fortress city surrendered on July 4, 1863. In the aftermath of the city's surrender, Cosby's Brigade helped cover the retreat of Johnston's army to Jackson, where the Confederate forces were also besieged. When Johnston evacuated the capital city on the night of July 16, Cosby's troopers covered the retreat eastward across the Pearl River, through Brandon, to Morton, Mississippi. For the balance of the year, Cosby's men occasionally skirmished with Federal units operating out of Vicksburg.

On December 23, 1863, Cosby was relieved of command with Jackson's Division and instructed to report to departmental headquarters for orders. Sent to the Department of Western Virginia and East Tennessee, he served for a short period with the celebrated raider, John Hunt Morgan. On August 10, 1864, Secretary of War James A. Seddon ordered that Cosby be given command of the brigade formerly led by Brig. Gen. George B. Hodge, who had been sent to the Department of Alabama, Mississippi, and East Louisiana. Cosby, however, did not assume command until September 5, at which time his new brigade numbered fewer than three hundred men, many of whom were dismounted due to lack of horses. His brigade moved throughout southwestern Virginia and eastern Tennessee as the situation demanded but saw little action. In October, Cosby's horsemen were ordered to the Shenandoah Valley, where they joined the command of Jubal Early but arrived too late to participate in any action. The brigade later joined Maj. Gen. John C. Breckinridge at New Market, and in December Cosby's men returned to southwestern Virginia, where they remained for the balance of the war.

Following the surrender of Gen. Robert E. Lee, Cosby attempted to evade the Federals and join Joe Johnston in North Carolina. But his efforts were futile. Disbanding his unit, Cosby returned to Kentucky, where he was paroled in May 1865. As with many other former Confederates, Cosby made his way to Canada, where he lived for a year before returning to the United States. In 1868, he moved to California and settled in Butte County, where he first worked as a manager of a mountain stage route and later as a contractor to supply U.S. Army posts. For a brief period he was a sutler at Fort Warner in Oregon and even tried his hand at farming.

Returning to California, Cosby held a number of state and federal positions. From 1878 to 1883 he was the secretary of the board of state engineers. In January 1883, Gov. George Stoneman, a former Union general, appointed him adjutant general of California, a position he continued to hold in the administration of Gov. Washington Bartlett. In 1886, while serving as adjutant general, he was appointed by President Grover Cleveland a member of the board of visitors to the U.S. Military Academy. (Cosby and Francis T. Nicholls of Louisiana, who was also appointed that year, thus became the first former Confederates to serve in that capacity.) Working with the committee on buildings and grounds, Cosby and his fellow board members recommended the construction of a new gymnasium in which to conduct drill during inclement weather, a separate building for the Department of Chemistry and Philosophy, sixteen sets of quarters for enlisted men, and workshops for the quartermaster. Overall, the board of visitors reported to Congress that there was "much to approve and little to criticize" about the academy, whose superintendent at that time was former Union general Wesley Merritt.

Resigning as adjutant general in 1887, Cosby was appointed U.S. commissioner with certain Indians in California. The following year he superintended the construction of the post office building in Sacramento. In 1897 he was appointed receiver of public moneys of the Sacramento land office, a position he held until debilitated by a paralytic stroke in the early years of the twentieth century. An invalid for the final years of his life,

Cosby suffered intense pain that doctors attempted to alleviate by administering opiates. In time, even these powerful drugs lost their efficacy, and he sank further into depression. On June 29, 1909, he took his own life; the local papers reported that "the open valve of a gas pipe told its mute story." His remains were cremated and placed in an urn and interred in City Cemetery in Sacramento, California. Cosby was survived by his wife.

In June 1915, the federal government placed a bronze bust of Cosby on the grounds of Vicksburg National Military Park. Sculpted by Anton Schaaf, the monument is located on Kentucky Avenue across from the Kentucky Memorial.

BIBLIOGRAPHY

Davis, William C., ed. *The Confederate General.* 6 vols. Harrisburg, PA: National Historical Society, 1991.

Johnston, J. Stoddard. *Kentucky.* Vol. 11 in *Confederate Military History,* ed. Clement A. Evans. Atlanta: Confederate Publishing, 1899. Rev. ed. Wilmington, NC: Broadfoot Publishing, 1988.

U.S. War Department. *The War of the Rebellion: A Compilation of the Official Records of the Union and Confederate Armies.* 70 vols. in 128 pts. Washington, DC: Government Printing Office, 1880–1901.

—TERRENCE J. WINSCHEL

Maj. Gen. George Bibb Crittenden

BORN ON MARCH 20, 1812 in Russellville, Kentucky, George B. Crittenden was the oldest son of John Jordan Crittenden and Sarah Lee. The able lieutenant of Henry Clay, John J. Crittenden was one of the most powerful political figures in antebellum Kentucky. The elder Crittenden served as Kentucky governor (1848–1851), held the office of attorney general in the cabinets of both William Henry Harrison and Zachary Taylor, and served four terms in the U.S. Senate. He inherited Clay's mantle as an eloquent advocate of Union and compromise as the nation drifted toward war in the 1850s.

Raised in Frankfort, George was initially sent to a Lexington, Kentucky, boarding school in 1824. He was subsequently admitted to West Point on July 1, 1828, and graduated in 1832. He was appointed brevet second lieutenant in the Fourth U.S. Infantry and saw active service in the Black Hawk War. After a brief tour of duty in the Arkansas Territory, he resigned his commission on April 30, 1833, and returned to Kentucky. Receiving his LL.B. degree at Transylvania University later that same year, he began the practice of law. Despite his youth, Crittenden's heavy drinking had become a source of serious concern to his father by the late 1830s.

Without telling his father, young Crittenden abruptly left Kentucky and settled in the Republic of Texas. Incursions by Mexican forces led to the formation of the Southwestern Army of Operations in the fall of 1842. Crittenden volunteered for active duty and was among a detachment led by Col. William Fisher that refused orders to suspend active operations and advanced into Mexico. Fisher was defeated at the battle of Mier on December 26, 1842, and his entire command was forced to surrender. The prisoners were confined in the grim castle of San Carlos de Perote.

Upon their arrival in March of 1843, the Texans were informed that they would be forced to draw lots and one of every ten would be executed by firing squad. According to one tradition young Crittenden drew a white bean but gave it to a comrade who had a wife and children. He then made a second draw but the fatal black bean was not grasped and he was spared. Senator Crittenden used all the powers at his disposal to arrange the release of his wayward son. Ironically, his political foe, former president Andrew Jackson, was instrumental in securing young Crittenden's release. Sailing from Vera Cruz, the young Kentuckian reached New Orleans by way of Havana on May 7, 1843.

Crittenden returned to Kentucky and apparently resumed the legal profession until the outbreak of the Mexican War. On May 27, 1846, he was appointed captain in the U.S. Regulars and served in Maj. W. W. Loring's Mounted Rifles Regiment in Winfield Scott's advance on Mexico City. Crittenden nearly missed the campaign however when he was arrested for being drunk on duty. The young officer tendered his resignation but immediately left for Washington, where he persuaded the secretary of war to restore him to duty. In the fighting near Mexico City, he was brevetted major on August 20, 1847, for bravery at the battles of Contreras and Churubusco. Crittenden's demons continued to haunt him, and during the winter of 1848 he was arrested a second time for drunkenness. He resigned again but was restored to command a second time due to his father's political influence. Promoted to major on March 15, 1848, Crittenden was subsequently arrested for drunkenness a third time, court-martialed, and dismissed from the service on August 19, 1848. Once again the elder Crittenden used his powerful political connections to have his troubled son restored to duty on March 15, 1849.

Crittenden rejoined his command at Jefferson Barracks in St. Louis and subsequently participated in the regiment's two-thousand-mile, six-month march to the Oregon Territory. After establishing posts along the Oregon Trail, the Rifles reached Oregon City in November 1849. The regiment moved northward to present-day Washington and occupied Columbia Barracks. In 1851 the command was ordered back to Jefferson Barracks in Missouri. Fresh reports of Crittenden's heavy drinking concerned his father so much that he urged his son to resign rather than risk further disgrace. However, the young officer promised to reform and served ably when his command was subsequently ordered to the Texas frontier in 1852. Crittenden was promoted to lieutenant colonel on December 30, 1856, and briefly commanded Fort Union on the Sante Fe Trail in the New Mexico Territory in late 1860 and early 1861. Crittenden frequently led his command in operations against hostile Indians and his victory over a band of fierce Comanches on January 2, 1861, was duly noted in the nation's major newspapers. He was preparing for an expedition against the Apaches when the guns roared at Fort Sumter in 1861.

As Kentucky's foremost champion of the Union, the elder Crittenden urged his son to "be true to the government that has trusted in you. And stand fast by your national Flag, the Stars & Stripes." However Lieutenant Colonel Crittenden was determined to cast his lot with the Confederacy and resigned his commission on June 10, 1861. His decision reflected the divisions that split many Kentucky families, as his brothers Thomas L. and Eugene subsequently achieved high rank in the Union army. While he regretted George's decision, John J. Crittenden never renounced him and in 1862 chastised his old Whig ally, the noted Kentucky journalist George D. Prentice, for denouncing his eldest son in the pages of the highly influential *Louisville Journal.*

Making his way to Richmond, Crittenden was appointed brigadier general on August 15, 1861. On August 21 he was ordered to report to Manassas, Virginia, where he assumed command of a brigade in Gen. Joseph E. Johnston's Army of the Potomac. On October 25, President Jefferson Davis sent an informal letter advising Crittenden that he was his "first choice" to lead a column to redeem Kentucky and inquired whether the Kentuckian would be willing to undertake the task. Davis's friendship with the Crittendens dated back to his Mexican War service, when he became close friends with Thomas, George's younger brother. Indeed, a newly elected Senator Davis worked hard to have George restored to rank in 1849. Crittenden must have agreed, for on November 9 he was promoted to major general and ordered to assume command of the Eastern District of Kentucky. On November 24 while en route to Cumberland Gap, he sent a formal request to Gen. Albert S. Johnston, the Confederate commander in the western theater, seeking to determine both the limits of his district and the troops at his disposal. Holding the extreme right of Johnston's line of defense, which stretched from Columbus on the Mississippi through Bowling Green to Cumberland Gap, Crittenden was apparently ordered to assume command of all Confederate forces in East Tennessee and southeastern Kentucky.

Crittenden established his headquarters at Knoxville on December 1. Summoned to Richmond, he was subsequently advised by Davis that his district was reduced to the extreme corner of southeastern Kentucky. The secretary of war confirmed in written orders dated December 13 that Crittenden would have no authority in East Tennessee or northeastern Kentucky, where Brig. Gen. Humphrey Marshall sought to establish his own field of operations. The force Crittenden was ordered to lead into Kentucky was therefore limited to Brig. Gen. William Carroll's brigade in Knoxville and Brig. Gen. Felix Zollicoffer's brigade, which held an advance position just over the Cumberland River at Beech Grove, Kentucky. Crittenden had just returned to Knoxville on December 15 when he learned that Zollicoffer's position was threatened by the advancing enemy. He advised Johnston that he considered Zollicoffer's situation so "critical" that he ordered his subordinate to withdraw to the south side of the Cumberland.

High water prevented a withdrawal, and on January 2, 1862, Crittenden joined Zollicoffer on the Cumberland. Four days later the new commander issued a "Proclamation to the People of Kentucky," which concluded, "Will you join in the moving columns of the South or is the spirit of Kentucky dead?" The arrival of Carroll's brigade prompted Crittenden to summon a council of war on the night of January 18. Brig. Gen. George H. Thomas and two Union brigades had advanced as far as Logan's Cross Roads only ten miles away. The Federal commander expected to form a juncture with Brig. Gen. Albin Schoepf's brigade before attacking the Confederate position. However, Crittenden had learned that the two enemy columns were separated by high water and determined to launch an immediate attack before the two forces could unite.

Crittenden moved forward at midnight and struck Thomas's force on the morning of Sunday, January 19. The battle of Mill Springs was fought in heavy rain and fog. Zollicoffer was killed early in the fighting, and Crittenden's poorly armed, poorly trained force fell apart and fled in panic to the banks of the Cumberland. Crittenden abandoned his artillery and stores to the pursuing enemy and ferried his shattered command across the river during the night. By the time he reached Gainsboro, Tennessee, his command was nothing more than an armed mob. Crittenden had made a desperate gamble and lost not only his command but also his reputation. In the weeks that followed, rumors were rife that he was drunk during the fighting and that his men, embittered by Zollicoffer's death, no longer wished to serve under him. Despite published statements from officers who claimed that Crittenden "deported himself as a brave and gallant soldier," the Kentuckian requested an official court of inquiry in February.

Crittenden's reorganized division was subsequently ordered to Murfreesboro, where the command was attached to Hardee's corps of Johnston's army. During the Confederate concentration at Corinth, Mississippi, on the eve of Shiloh, Crittenden's reserve division was based at nearby Iuka. On April 1, 1862, the ill-fated Kentuckian was arrested for being drunk on duty and relieved of command. Crittenden tendered his resignation and requested a leave of absence on April 11. However, his resignation was not accepted, and on July 24 a court of inquiry was convened to investigate the Kentuckian's conduct. The court found enough evidence to recommend a court martial. However on September 23, he was released from arrest and, perhaps due to the intervention of President Davis, permitted to resign on October 23, 1862.

Most sketches of Crittenden end with his final disgrace and only brief mention is made of his subsequent service. However, almost as an act of penance, Crittenden continued to serve ably until the end of the conflict. On April 7, 1863, he resumed active duty as colonel in the regular Confederate army and was ordered to report for duty under Brig. Gen. John S. Williams, who commanded a small cavalry brigade at Saltville in the Department of Western Virginia. Although a minor theater during the conflict, the mountainous region contained vital strategic targets including the Virginia and Tennessee Railroad, which connected the major eastern and western theaters. When a large Union cavalry force struck the depot at Wytheville on July 18, Crittenden, as a member of Williams's staff, played an active role in operations against the raiders.

In a strange twist of fate, the abandonment of East Tennessee in August of 1863 found Colonel Crittenden placed temporarily in command of the scattered forces in his old district. The transfer of virtually all Confederate forces in the region to Bragg's Army of Tennessee led to the occupation of Cumberland Gap and Knoxville by the advancing Union forces of Gen. Ambrose Burnside. As Burnside's cavalry advanced along the railroad toward the Virginia border, Crittenden was ordered to organize a skeleton force to fight a series of delaying actions between September 10 and 23. The Kentuckian did his work well, buying General Williams enough time to organize a defensive force that checked the enemy advance at the Virginia line. He was subsequently praised by Maj. Gen. Sam Jones, commander of the Department of Western Virginia, for leading his little force with "judgment, boldness and skill."

Crittenden resumed the duties of a staff officer and apparently remained in southwestern Virginia during the long struggle for East Tennessee during the winter of 1863–1864. However, when the colorful raider John Hunt Morgan took temporary command of the Department of Western Virginia in the spring of 1864, Crittenden saw action again at Crockett's Cove near Wytheville on May 10. Posted in a key pass with a small detachment, Crittenden delayed the Federal raiders until Morgan brought up his main force and routed the enemy. Morgan's subsequent ill-fated raid into Kentucky and the temporary transfer of Brig. Gen. William E. Jones to the Shenandoah Valley led Confederate authorities to place Crittenden in command of the recently organized Department of Western Virginia and East Tennessee on May 31. Crittenden, who suddenly found himself in command of a department defended largely by reserves, petitioned Richmond on June 4 to be relieved of the responsibility.

Morgan's return to Virginia in late June only brought Crittenden a temporary respite from command. On July 30, 1864, he was ordered to assume command of all mounted forces operating in East Tennessee. Crittenden's small force, soon reinforced by Col. Henry L. Giltner's Kentucky cavalry brigade, frequently clashed with Union troops in the vicinity of Bulls Gap. Crittenden requested to be relieved of command when General Morgan advanced into East Tennessee with his entire force in early September. However, the movement abruptly ended when Morgan was killed in a surprise raid on his headquarters at Greeneville, Tennessee, on September 4. Crittenden led the solemn funeral procession for his fallen commander at Abingdon, Virginia, on September 6.

On September 5, Crittenden was ordered to turn over the command of his small mounted force to Brig. Gen. John C. Vaughn and was subsequently assigned to duty as inspector general of all troops in East Tennessee. Although placed in command of the department in March, Maj. Gen. John C. Breckinridge was ordered on active duty in eastern Virginia until the fall of 1864. Shortly after Breckinridge's return to southwestern Virginia, Crittenden was appointed to his staff on October 12, 1864. On November 9, Breckinridge advanced against a sizable Union force in East Tennessee. He drove the Federals from an advance post at Lick Creek on November 10 and on the following day attacked the main enemy position at Bulls Gap.

Crittenden was ordered to support Breckinridge's artillery and make a demonstration with three hundred men along the enemy's front while the main assault was launched against the Union right flank. The Confederates failed to break the enemy lines on November 12. However, the arrival of reinforcements in Breckinridge's camp led the Union commander to attempt a retreat under the cover of darkness on the night of November 13–14. A vigilant Breckinridge overtook and routed the retreating foe in a running fight that finally drove the Federals across the Holston River.

Southwestern Virginia continued to be the target of large Union cavalry raids from Kentucky and East Tennessee until the spring of 1865, and

Crittenden served ably at Breckinridge's side at the battle of Marion, Virginia, on December 17–18, 1864. Often stationed at Wytheville, he apparently spent the closing months of the war performing routine administrative duties. Upon learning of the fall of Richmond, Brig. Gen. John Echols, Breckinridge's successor, abandoned the department and led his small command eastward to join Lee's retreating forces. Echols learned of Lee's surrender when he reached Christiansburg, Virginia, on April 12 and determined to join Gen. Joseph E. Johnston's beleaguered Army of Tennessee in North Carolina. Crittenden was among those present at the final surrender in Greensboro and was paroled on May 5, 1865.

Crittenden returned to Kentucky, where he had been indicted for treason in the Federal courts, and on November 9, 1867, was formally pardoned by President Andrew Johnson. Although he served as the state librarian from 1867 to 1874, Crittenden spent his final years in relative obscurity. A lifelong bachelor, he lived with his sister Sarah Watson in Frankfort and died on November 27, 1880, at the residence of another sister, Mrs. John C. Young, in Danville, Kentucky. Although his funeral was well attended, no eulogy was delivered and Crittenden was laid to rest in the family plot beside his illustrious father in the State Cemetery in Frankfort.

A tragic figure, Crittenden still bore himself with dignity during the closing days of the war. Years after the conflict a Kentuckian who served with Crittenden in southwestern Virginia recalled that he "was a small man, genial and courteous, a trained soldier, plain in dress and unostentatious in manner, often thoughtful and abstracted as if pondering deeply some military problem. I remember I felt profoundly respectful when in the presence of General George B. Crittenden."

BIBLIOGRAPHY

Davis, William C., ed. *The Confederate General.* 6 vols. Harrisburg, PA: National Historical Society, 1991.

Hafendorfer, Kenneth A. *Mill Springs: Campaign and Battle of Mill Springs, Kentucky.* Louisville, KY: KH Press, 2001.

U.S. War Department. *The War of the Rebellion: A Compilation of the Official Records of the Union and Confederate Armies.* 70 vols. in 128 pts. Washington, DC: Government Printing Office, 1880–1901.

—JAMES M. PRICHARD

Brig. Gen. Basil Wilson Duke

BASIL WILSON DUKE was born on May 28, 1837, on his uncle's estate just north of Lexington, Kentucky, the only child of Nathaniel Nelson Duke and the former Mary Currie. Because Duke's father, a career naval officer, was frequently away, and because his mother died when he was only eight years old, Duke was raised with his ten cousins on his uncle's thousand-acre homestead, Richland. As the result of hard work, good fortune, and ample inheritance, the Dukes were a prominent family in antebellum Kentucky.

The sight of blood and the smell of gunpowder were common components of a rural farm like Richland. Duke's early contact with Kentucky-bred horses, the duties of farm life, and his natural development as a young hunter brought him into contact with the violence and energy of nineteenth-century Kentucky. Another long-standing aspect of wealthy Kentucky farm life was the unquestioned existence of slavery. To Duke, nothing in his environment hinted that slavery was in any way improper or unjustified. In great part, the defense of the traditions that made up this way of life created the sense of honor and pride that were so much a part of the Bluegrass region.

In contrast to the aggressive self-confidence engendered by the horse and the gun was the obligation for the teenage Duke to cultivate the skills necessary to acquire a respectable occupation. The Duke family believed that a young man must receive a proper education, and Duke attended both precollege and college classes. His older cousin and his uncle were both lawyers, and Duke's exposure to their lifestyles may have influenced him to attend Transylvania Law School in Lexington. Living a block away from the main Transylvania Law School building was the family of John

Hunt Morgan, a successful, well-known Mexican War veteran who would play a pivotal role in Duke's future.

Duke graduated from law school in 1858, moved to St. Louis, and opened his law practice. He quickly became embroiled in the political maneuvering upon which the future of Missouri rested. In the months between the 1860 election and the secession of several Southern states, Duke was one of the most active voices in support of St. Louis's Southern aspirations. During the spring of 1861, Duke successfully executed a clandestine mission to Baton Rouge, Louisiana, in order to transport weapons back to St. Louis to arm Southern sympathizers. It was this exploit that, once St. Louis was secured by federal troops, put Duke on the wrong side of a treason charge. Now a wanted man for treason, Duke headed for Kentucky.

On June 19, 1861, Basil Duke married Henrietta Morgan, John Hunt Morgan's sister. This act set in place the two personal relationships that would define Duke's life. After his marriage, Duke returned to southern Missouri and served the Confederate cause in both a regimental staff aide position and as a scout. This service taught Duke the value of military organization, discipline, and the hit-and-run tactics that would become Brig. Gen. John Morgan's calling card.

Once Kentucky's neutrality was clearly violated in the fall of 1861, men were forced to take sides in the looming conflict. John Hunt Morgan had command of a company called the Lexington Rifles, and Duke joined his brother-in-law's unit. The military experience Duke had obtained in Missouri was enough to distinguish him to Morgan, and the two enjoyed a rapport that would catalyze historic success for the next twenty-one months. They found they complemented each other; Morgan had charisma and audacity, while Duke attended to discipline, training, and the development of tactics.

In April 1862, Morgan's men became part of the Confederate strike force headed for Pittsburg Landing, Tennessee. As part of Brig. Gen. John C. Breckinridge's Reserve Corps, Duke sat with Morgan's cavalry through the anxious morning hours of April 6, listening to the maelstrom of the Shiloh battle while awaiting orders. At midday, Morgan and Duke led their men onto the battlefield and witnessed the shocking results of combat for the first time, picking their way past the grisly visages of the dead and dying. During a cavalry charge that afternoon, Duke was wounded in both shoulders; he would not recover from his wounds for two months.

During Duke's convalescence, Morgan suffered one of his most humiliating defeats. His command was completely surprised and nearly destroyed by Union cavalry at Lebanon, Tennessee, in May. One of Duke's first tasks upon his return to duty was to reconstitute Morgan's cavalry.

Refitted and reinforced, Morgan was given permission to execute a freewheeling raid through the heart of Kentucky in July 1862. In preparation for the raid, Duke, now a lieutenant colonel, having been promoted in June, was given command of Morgan's best men, the newly formed Second Kentucky Cavalry. Rampaging through central Kentucky, Morgan's cavalry rolled through town after town picking up recruits, capturing home guard garrisons, and creating havoc for the Union command. After the success of his "First Kentucky Raid," Morgan reported to his superiors that Kentucky sentiment ran strongly with the South and that tens of thousands of recruits would be forthcoming if the Confederate army entered Kentucky. Thus Morgan and Duke were responsible, in part, for the miscalculation that launched the Confederate invasion of Kentucky in August of 1862.

For six weeks from mid-August through September of 1862, the Confederate occupation of Kentucky met with civic approval and battlefield success. Morgan's cavalry, having hastily quit Lexington as "rebels" a year previously, returned home to the pomp of conquering heroes. To many, the high-water mark of their Civil War service was to parade in front of euphoric family members as triumphant soldiers of victory and honor. Two weeks after his homecoming, Duke received orders to conduct a diversionary attack threatening Cincinnati, Ohio, and his detachment rode to Augusta, Kentucky, near a good ford a few miles downriver from the town. Unexpectedly, Duke was checked by the spirited defense of the local home guard, and the losses suffered in street fighting at Augusta prompted him to cancel his plans to feign an attack on Cincinnati. To compound Duke's disappointment, Confederate general Braxton Bragg decided to end the Kentucky campaign after the battle of Perryville, due primarily to a dearth of fresh Confederate recruits—a repudiation of the claims made by Duke and Morgan after their First Kentucky Raid in July.

His successful December raid on Hartsville, Tennessee, garnered a promotion to brigadier general for Morgan, and Duke moved up to colonel of the Second to rank from December 7, 1862. Morgan then planned to attack railroads in Kentucky. The objective of Morgan's 1862 "Christmas Raid" was to destroy the massive Muldraugh's Hill train trestles. Morgan's raiders reduced the blockhouses guarding the trestles and burned the bridges as planned. During Morgan's retreat from the area on December 29, his men were surprised by a Union detachment as the rebels crossed the Rolling Fork River. It was here that a fragment from an artillery shell struck Duke in the head. He fell to the river's edge, motionless, and initially was thought to be dead. After Duke was treated by a physician in Bardstown, his men brought him back to Confederate lines, where he slowly recovered from his wound before rejoining his brigade in March 1863.

In the summer of 1863, Morgan wangled authorization for yet another summer raid into Kentucky; however, he was specifically prohibited from crossing north of the Ohio River. Morgan purposefully flouted his orders and began what is known as the "Great Raid." Morgan's advance squadron captured two steamers at Brandenburg, Kentucky, and used the boats to ferry his entire command north of the Ohio River on July 8, 1863. The next day, Col. "Stovepipe" Johnson executed a coordinated attack on home guard forces in Corydon, Indiana, eventually subduing the garrison. This was the last significant offensive action for Morgan's raiders north of the Ohio River. After Corydon, the Great Raid turned into an unrelenting chase through the farm fields of southern Indiana and Ohio. Riding ahead of pursuing Union cavalry, Duke became impressed with the undisturbed abundance of the North and understood, perhaps for the first time, the true scale of the barriers that had to be surmounted to defeat the Union.

After eleven relentless days, it became obvious to both Union and Confederate forces that the most likely location for Morgan to return southward was at a ford on the Ohio River at Buffington Island, Ohio. Just as the Confederates were about to cross the river to safety, they were hit by Union gunfire coming from three directions. On July 19, Duke's men courageously grappled with Union troops at Buffington long enough for Morgan and Stovepipe Johnson to escape with more than half the Confederate command. Duke, however, was among the hundreds captured. Within a week, the remainder of Morgan's raiders were captured and Morgan with his staff was incarcerated with Duke behind the fourteen-foot-high walls of the Ohio State Penitentiary at Columbus.

The restrictions of detention, and the knowledge that he was no longer of help to his chosen cause, unsettled Duke during his captivity. With his wife and two young children on the run from Federal troops, Duke became despondent. For the next eleven months, he was shuttled from the Ohio Penitentiary in Columbus to Camp Chase, back to the Ohio Penitentiary, and then on to Fort Delaware with no apparent relief to his frustrating status.

In June 1864, rumor had it that Confederate commanders were planning to station Union prisoners of war in the streets of Charleston, South Carolina, in order to restrain the wanton shelling of the town by federal artillery. In retaliation, the Union command decided to station Confederate prisoners at Morris Island, South Carolina, for the same purpose. Duke was chosen as one of the rebel inmates to be used as a human shield on Morris Island and was shipped off to South Carolina.

The Confederate intention to use human shields proved false, and Duke lingered in limbo for weeks in South Carolina. While there, the prisoner-exchange impasse that had stymied his release was suddenly resolved. Duke was taken aboard the Confederate steamer *Chesterfield* and discharged onto the Charleston wharf on August 3, 1864. After almost thirteen months of captivity, Duke was reunited with his wife and children. Toward the end of August, Duke and Morgan also reunited, but the meeting was short and bittersweet. When the two warriors met, Morgan had just completed his 1864 raid into Kentucky, this time with disastrous results, as his cavalry had nearly disintegrated in defeat and desertion. Relieved of command and placed under investigation, Morgan, in defiance of orders to stay put, rounded up 1,500 men and left Virginia to strike Union forces in Tennessee. This time, ominously, Duke did not follow his friend and mentor. Gen. John Hunt Morgan was killed on September 4, 1864, at Greeneville, Tennessee. The man that Duke considered his best friend was now gone forever.

Duke was promoted to brigadier general on September 15, 1864, and given command of the meager remnants of Morgan's cavalry, at the time fewer than three hundred battle-ready soldiers. Once again, Duke took on the task of rebuilding Morgan's men. Through effective recruitment, discipline, training, and leadership, Duke had doubled the size of his unit when he was called to report to the District of Southwestern Virginia.

In the spring of 1865, the tattered remains of Duke's cavalry evacuated southwestern Virginia in a bid to join with Lee's Army of Northern Virginia. On April 10, news came that Gen. Robert E. Lee had surrendered. Duke saw only two realistic choices: surrender, or fight on with Gen. Joseph E. Johnston's army in North Carolina. Dutiful to the end, Duke chose to fight on. As the depleted veterans fell away from the last vestiges of Morgan's old command, those willing to continue to the bitter end joined with Duke for the final hours.

Even though President Jefferson Davis agreed to the initial terms of surrender secured by Johnston, Davis himself continued to flee. Duke was with Davis and the fugitive Confederate cabinet in Charlotte, North Carolina, and from there escorted the group to Abbeville, South Carolina. At

Abbeville, the Confederate government was dissolved and the curtain came down on a play that had cost so much for all involved. Duke surrendered soon thereafter in Georgia.

Duke learned and sacrificed much during the four years of the conflict, and when the war ended, he was just twenty-eight years old. Back in Lexington, Duke anxiously considered his options. Not wishing to return to St. Louis, and possessing no client base in Lexington, Duke decided instead to capitalize on the depressed value of cotton in the South and opened a commission trading business with his cousin.

With Duke's business prospects improving, he quickly turned his attention to his grand war memoir, *A History of Morgan's Cavalry*. Glossing over his own wartime contributions, Duke spared no effort to lionize his former superior and brother-in-law. The work is considered the most valuable firsthand source in the documentation of Morgan's actions during the war. *Morgan's Cavalry* also pioneered the genre of the Lost Cause, the belief that overwhelming opposing numbers doomed the struggle for Southern independence, leaving only patriotic honor and dignity as the reasons to fight.

The movement of the Kentucky electorate from Unionist Whig to Southern Democrat had been under way since 1862, and the twin forces of Reconstruction and emancipation hastened the breathtaking realignment in postwar Bluegrass politics. Soon, Duke concluded that his career as a Confederate general was an asset, and he renewed his interest in governmental affairs. By 1868 he was ready to assume a higher public profile, so he moved his family to Louisville and returned to the practice of law. After a short stint as a member of the Kentucky House of Representatives, Duke sought and won the office of commonwealth attorney for Jefferson County (which included the city of Louisville). More than once, Duke's experience as a hardened combatant proved useful in quelling the criminal unrest that swept Louisville after each economic downturn.

In the 1880s Duke became an advocate, attorney, and lobbyist for one of the most monolithic businesses in Kentucky, the Louisville and Nashville Railroad—a business he had zealously tried to destroy during the war. Despite the fact that the L & N became a populist target for the economic ills of Kentucky, Duke successfully fought many legal and legislative battles for his wealthy client and benefited from his effective service. In the last thirty years of his life, Duke's public persona became closely associated with the ordeals of the L & N Railroad.

Between 1885 and 1894, Duke's political views and Civil War remembrances found a vehicle when he became involved in editing two magazines focused on Civil War history and Southern literature, the *Southern Bivouac* and *Southern Magazine*. Although Duke's literary contributions were considerable, neither magazine was financially stable. Duke reluctantly left the magazine business in 1894.

A man of reconciliation, Duke was involved in veterans' affairs until the very end of his life and was appointed commissioner of the Shiloh Battlefield in 1904 by his good friend President Theodore Roosevelt. Basil Wilson Duke died in New York City on September 16, 1916, as a result of an infection after surgery. He was brought home to Kentucky and is buried in the Lexington Cemetery.

After Duke's death, his legacy slipped behind the shadow of that of his old cavalry commander. Recently, however, Duke has taken his own turn on the stage, and his performance has been a revelation to those interested in nineteenth-century American history.

BIBLIOGRAPHY

Davis, William C., ed. *The Confederate General.* 6 vols. Harrisburg, PA: National Historical Society, 1991.

Duke, Basil W. *A History of Morgan's Cavalry.* Cincinnati: Miami Printing and Publishing, 1867. Reprint, West Jefferson, OH: Genesis, 1997.

———. *Reminiscences of General Basil Wilson Duke, C.S.A.* New York: Doubleday, 1911. Reprint, West Jefferson, OH: Genesis, 1997.

Matthews, Gary Robert. *Basil Wilson Duke, CSA: The Right Man in the Right Place.* Lexington: University Press of Kentucky, 2005.

—Raymond Mulesky

Maj. Gen. James Fleming Fagan

JAMES FLEMING FAGAN was born on March 1, 1828, in Clark County, Kentucky, to Steven and Catherine Stevens Fagan. When Fagan was ten, his family moved to the new state of Arkansas, where his father had taken a position as a contractor for the statehouse at Little Rock. Not long after, Fagan's father died, and in December 1842 his widowed mother married Samuel Adams, a prominent planter and future governor (1844) and state treasurer (1845–1849) of Arkansas. After his stepfather died in 1850, Fagan took charge of the family farm on the Saline River and also served for one term in the Arkansas state legislature. He fought as a second lieutenant in the Mexican War in the First Arkansas Volunteer Cavalry. After the war, Fagan returned to his farm and in 1851 married Myra Ellisiff Beall, the sister of future Confederate general William Nelson Rector Beall.

At the start of the Civil War, Fagan raised a company for Confederate service and was elected its captain. His company joined with others to form the First Arkansas Volunteer Regiment. Although the regiment was created at Little Rock in May 1861, it was actually organized at Lynchburg, Virginia, later that month, when ten companies, including Fagan's, enlisted for one year. There, the men elected Fagan colonel of the regiment on May 8. Although present at the battle of First Manassas in July, the First Arkansas was not actively engaged. Indeed, the regiment was assigned primarily to garrison duty for the first year of the war.

The regiment was transferred to the Army of the Mississippi in February 1862 and assigned to Col. Randall L. Gibson's brigade of Brig. Gen. Daniel Ruggles's division in Maj. Gen. Braxton Bragg's corps. Fagan's men saw their first real action at the battle of Shiloh, April 6–7, 1862. There, in the thickets along the Tennessee River, Fagan's untried regiment became part of the first wave of Confederate attacks and suffered 364 casualties out of 800 engaged—a horrific 45 percent casualty rate. Despite the regiment's losses, Bragg questioned the initiative and bravery of Fagan and the rest of the officers in Gibson's brigade. This challenge launched a long dispute of honor.

On the morning of April 6, Bragg claimed that he discovered Gibson's fresh brigade standing idle in Barnes's Field. He apparently assumed that Gibson was avoiding the action occurring all along the line. Bragg dismissed Gibson's assertion that one of Bragg's own staff officers had instructed him to advance slowly toward the front. The general promptly ordered Gibson forward. As the brigade entered the thickets, the men became disoriented, and a company of the Fourth Louisiana Infantry fired on Fagan's regiment. Fagan moved quickly to stop the slaughter. Once order was restored, heavy Union fire drove Gibson's brigade back. An angry Bragg repeatedly ordered the brigade to attack. With his ego bruised, Gibson thrust his brigade forward in four piecemeal assaults from noon to 2:00 P.M. that left his regiments shattered. The brigade retired in the afternoon, mauled and defeated. The feud between Bragg and the brigade officers, including Fagan, did not end at Shiloh but continued until Bragg's death in 1876. The officers believed that Bragg had sacrificed the men in fruitless attacks. Bragg countered that the regiments needed repeated rallying by his staff officers and that the high casualties were the result of poor management by the officers.

At the reorganization of Confederate forces in April, the men of the First Arkansas reelected Fagan as their colonel. He led his regiment at the battle of Farmington, Mississippi, on May 9, 1862, but he continued to feud with Bragg. Although he was commanding the fourth brigade of Ruggles's division, he again fell into disfavor with Bragg after he reported sighting an enemy force at Farmington that Bragg did not believe existed. Bragg complained to Gen. P. G. T. Beauregard that he would have to suspend the colonel. Fagan took exception to what he considered to be Bragg's continued harassment, and, according to one source, he apparently tendered his resignation and left, along with other Confederate officers, for Arkansas. Other sources, however, state that Colonel Fagan was reassigned to the newly created Trans-Mississippi Department, where Maj. Gen. Thomas Hindman placed him in command of a regiment of mounted riflemen, the First Arkansas. He was appointed a brigadier general on October 2, to rank from September 12, 1862, and Lt. Gen. Theophilus Holmes, the department commander, soon gave Fagan a brigade composed of four Arkansas infantry regiments. Fagan led his brigade in the battle of Prairie Grove on December 7, his 1,500 men holding a ridge line on the Confederate right until ordered to retreat that night.

On July 4, 1863, Fagan took part in the attack on Union-held Helena, Arkansas, on the Mississippi River. General Holmes, who had been demoted to district commander of Arkansas after Prairie Grove, was eager to rebuild his military reputation by capturing the Federal supply base at Helena. He planned to secure the heavily fortified hills overlooking Helena and from that position attack the main Federal garrison in the town. Fagan's men displayed incredible tenacity as they charged the Federal defenses of Battery D on Hindman Hill. Fighting from 4:30 A.M. until 7:00 A.M., the brigade stormed four lines of rifle pits but lacked the strength to assail the fifth line. Moreover, because of Maj. Gen. Sterling Price's late attack, Fagan's men received artillery fire from Union batteries on Graveyard Hill. Even with these setbacks, by 8:00 A.M. Fagan had rallied and organized his men for another assault, which captured the last line of rifle pits but could not capture the battery itself. Holmes's piecemeal attacks and lack of coordination prevented him from reinforcing Fagan or his other units, and by 10:30 A.M. Fagan was forced to call a retreat. Even without support, Fagan's men had fought well, but they ultimately failed to achieve their objective. Still, Holmes commended Fagan and blamed Price for the Confederate failure at Helena.

Following the struggle for Helena, the aged Holmes succumbed to exhaustion and transferred command of the District of Arkansas to Price. Fagan temporarily replaced Price as division commander. In July 1863, Fagan assumed command of Price's Division (with Fagan's, Brig. Gen. Mosby Parsons's, and Brig. Gen. Dandridge McRae's brigades) headquartered at Searcy. As Federal troops advanced on Little Rock, Fagan withdraw his forces from Searcy and Des Arc and assumed a position on Bayou Meto. General Frost replaced Fagan as division commander in August, and he returned to his brigade. The brigade took part in the unsuccessful defense of Little Rock, which fell to Union forces in September 1863.

Fagan's command was operating in southern Arkansas during the Federal campaign against Shreveport in 1864. After Union major general Nathaniel Banks's defeat at Mansfield and Pleasant Hill, Gen. Edmund Kirby Smith ordered Fagan (now in command of a cavalry division comprising the Arkansas brigades of Brig. Gen. William L. Cabell, Brig. Gen. Thomas P. Dockery, and Col. William A. Crawford) to operate against the Federal expedition of Union major general Frederick Steele at Camden. After watching the Federal forces under Steele move into Camden on

April 16, Fagan's Arkansans camped nearby. The next day, two brigades of Fagan's Division (Cabell's and Crawford's) joined in the successful attack on a Federal supply train at Poison Spring. While Banks's army retreated in Louisiana, Kirby Smith moved into Arkansas and took personal command of the campaign against Steele at Camden. Kirby Smith ordered General Price to dispatch a cavalry force across the Ouachita River to curtail Federal foraging and sever Steele's communications with Little Rock and Pine Bluff. Fagan commanded this force of 4,000 hand-picked troopers. He organized his task force into two divisions under Cabell and Brig. Gen. Joseph O. Shelby. Fagan learned on April 24 that a large supply train with an escort of 1,500 men had left Camden for Pine Bluff. Fagan planned to envelop the Federals at Marks' Mills. His wing hit the train first, and Shelby's wing assaulted the rear of the Yankee force a little later. The attack lasted less than two hours, and the Confederates inflicted at least 1,300 casualties (mostly prisoners), captured four cannon and hundreds of small arms, and secured or destroyed more than three hundred wagons. Fagan lost about 500 men. The smashing Confederate victory at Marks' Mills convinced Steele to abandon Camden and retreat toward Little Rock.

For his performance in the campaign, Fagan was promoted to major general on June 13, 1864, to rank from April 2. Although Marks' Mills ranks as Fagan's greatest success as a general, it was a hollow triumph. His tactics were poor; he committed his command piecemeal. Moreover, following the victory, he apparently misinterpreted the strategic situation and foolishly led his cavalry toward Arkadelphia in a futile attempt to find forage for his horses. In doing so, he disobeyed his orders to maneuver between Camden and Little Rock to cut Steele's line of communications and retreat. In fact, only after being prodded by subordinates did Fagan attempt to contact Kirby Smith to discover any changes in the general's orders. As a result of Fagan's blunder, Steele's army passed Fagan's force before they could block it and crossed the Saline River at Jenkins' Ferry. Kirby Smith did not censure Fagan for his lack of initiative. In fact, he praised him, stating correctly that "Fagan's destruction of Steele's entire supply train and the capture of its escort at Marks' Mills precipitated Steele's retreat from Camden." Kirby Smith goes on to say that "had General Fagan, with his command, thrown himself on the enemy's front on his march from Camden, Steele would have been brought to battle and his command utterly destroyed long before he reached the Saline. I do not mean to censure General Fagan. That gallant officer taking the road to Arkadelphia after the battle of Marks' Mills was one of those accidents which are liable to befall the best of officers." Despite Kirby Smith's support, it is clear that had Fagan covered the roads north of Camden, he would have delayed Steele's retreat. Yet, Fagan's subsequent actions were what allowed Steele to escape with his army.

In the fall of 1864, Kirby Smith sent Sterling Price into Missouri in the hopes of capturing St. Louis and spoiling Lincoln's chances for reelection. Price's twelve-thousand-man force, dubbed the Army of Missouri, comprised three divisions led by Fagan, Brig. Gen. John S. Marmaduke, and Shelby. After eluding Steele's forces in northeast Arkansas, Price set forth from Pocahontas, Arkansas, on September 19. The army entered the state from three different points; Fagan took the center route through Martinsburg, Reeves Station, and Greenville, with Marmaduke on his right and Shelby on his left. They planned to rendezvous at Fredericktown. On September 26, Fagan's men captured Arcadia and drove the Federals out of Ironton. The next day, the Confederates reached Pilot Knob, and Marmaduke's and Fagan's troops surrounded the stronghold of Fort Davidson. After a sharp fight in which Fagan's men were bloodily repulsed, the Federals abandoned the fort. The rebels wangled their way deeper into the state. Fagan's men took the heights around Jefferson City on October 7, but Price lacked the manpower to defeat the garrison. Price then resolved to move toward the Kansas border, routing small garrisons and obtaining arms for his men. Fagan brushed aside an attack from the Jefferson City garrison, and his men continued to forage and destroy railroads in their path.

The Confederates arrived in Boonville on October 10. Fagan's Division, along with Marmaduke's, again drove off a Union cavalry force from Jefferson City. Price's men won the engagements of Glasgow on October 15 and Lexington on October 19, where they encountered part of Maj. Gen. Samuel Curtis's Army of the Border southeast of the city. On October 21 and 22, the Union cavalry under Maj. Gen. Alfred Pleasonton routed Price's rear guard under Fagan on the Little Blue, and on October 23 at Westport, Fagan and Shelby counterattacked the Federal force but failed to drive them from the field.

Westport was the decisive battle of Price's campaign. His force continued to fight rearguard actions as it headed back toward Arkansas. They fought engagements at the Marais des Cygnes and Marmiton rivers on October 25 and Newtonia on October 28. By November 1, Price's force had returned to Arkansas battered and beaten. They would take part in no future raids. Missouri was permanently in Union control. From February 1 until the spring of 1865, Fagan commanded the cavalry in the District of Arkansas. In April he was the only major general on active duty in Arkansas and was placed in charge of the district until the end of hostilities in May 1865.

Fagan's military career was unremarkable. The general exhibited no tactical or strategic brilliance. He was merely a solid commander who, through his personal bravery and dedication, earned the respect of his men and the people of Arkansas.

Following the surrender of Confederate forces, Fagan returned to his farm and family. After the death of his first wife, he married Lizzie Rapley of Little Rock, a niece of Maj. Benjamin J. Field, brother of the first wife of former governor Henry M. Rector. President Ulysses S. Grant appointed Fagan U.S. marshal in 1875. He also served as a receiver for the U.S. Land Office in 1877. In 1890, he ran for Arkansas railroad commissioner but was defeated, perhaps because he had accepted federal patronage positions under the Grant administration. Fagan died in Little Rock on September 1, 1893, at the age of sixty-five and was buried at Mount Holly Cemetery. General James Fleming Fagan, Chapter 280, Military Order of the Stars and Bars was christened in his honor.

BIBLIOGRAPHY

Bearss, Edwin C. *Steele's Retreat from Camden and the Battle of Jenkins' Ferry.* Little Rock: Pioneer Press, 1967.
———. "The Battle of Helena, July 4, 1863." *Arkansas Historical Quarterly* 20 (Autumn 1961): 256–97.
Davis, William C., ed. *The Confederate General.* 6 vols. Harrisburg, PA: National Historical Society, 1991.
DeBlack, Thomas A. *With Fire and Sword: Arkansas, 1861–1874.* Fayetteville: University of Arkansas Press, 2003.

—JOHN D. FOWLER

Maj. Gen. Charles William Field

CHARLES WILLIAM FIELD was
the son of Willis Field and Isabella Miriam Buck Field. He was
born at his parents' home, Airy
Mount, in Woodford County,
Kentucky, on April 6, 1828. Field
received an at-large appointment
to the U.S. Military Academy at
West Point in 1845 and graduated twenty-seventh in his class on
July 1, 1849. Appointed a brevet
second lieutenant, Field joined
the Second U.S. Dragoons. His
first assignment placed him at the
Cavalry School for Practice at
Carlisle Barracks, Pennsylvania,
where he reported for duty on

October 1. Field did not remain long at Carlisle Barracks. The following
month he received orders to take seventy-four recruits to Fort Leavenworth, Kansas.

From Fort Leavenworth, Field went on to serve with the Second Dragoons at various frontier posts in New Mexico and Texas. He received
promotion to second lieutenant on June 30, 1851, and became regimental
quartermaster on September 30, 1853. While on duty at Jefferson Barracks, Missouri, he received promotion to first lieutenant of Company I on
March 3, 1855. Field accompanied his regiment on the long march from
that post to Fort Mason, Texas, from October 1855 to January 1856. During this trip, Field became the subject of camp gossip among some of the
officers' wives, including Eliza Johnston, wife of Col. Albert Sidney Johnston. One rumor said that Field had seduced the wife of an officer of another regiment at Jefferson Barracks and even hid her among the camp
followers who accompanied the column to Texas. Mrs. Johnston's cook
supposedly claimed that the young lieutenant had an affair with one of the
laundresses, who had a child, and then lived openly with her.

Perhaps because of these scandals, Field soon received orders to return
to the Cavalry School at Carlisle Barracks. He arrived there on July 31,

1856, and became acting assistant quartermaster and acting assistant commissary of subsistence for the post. On August 26, the War Department ordered Field to go to West Point. There he became assistant instructor of cavalry tactics. On January 31, 1861, he received promotion to captain of the Second U.S. Cavalry. Field remained at the academy until March 16 of that year. With the secession of Virginia, he resigned his commission on May 30. Field offered his services to the new Confederate States of America and received a commission as captain of cavalry effective March 11.

Field's first duty in the Confederate army undoubtedly came as a result of his recent posting at West Point. He commanded the Cavalry Camp of Instruction at Ashland, Virginia, about seventeen miles northwest of Richmond. A number of cavalry companies received training there during the spring and summer of 1861. When the Sixth Virginia Cavalry Regiment was organized on September 16, Field received a commission as its colonel. He and his men moved to Manassas Junction to join Gen. Joseph E. Johnston's Army of the Potomac and became a part of Brig. Gen. James E. B. Stuart's cavalry brigade. Field first led his men in combat on December 2. He took a detachment of ninety men from four of his companies on a scouting mission toward the village of Annandale, about fourteen miles from his camp. When this force came upon Union pickets, Field led an attack on them. The Confederates killed four or five enemy soldiers and captured fifteen prisoners. Two of Field's troopers fell into Federal hands.

On March 14, 1862, Field was promoted to brigadier general to rank from March 9. On the twenty-seventh he left his regiment to report to Maj. Gen. Gustavus W. Smith, commander of the Aquia District. The district covered the land between Powell's River and the mouth of the Potomac River, which included the Northern Neck and the counties on both sides of the Rappahannock River from its mouth up to Fredericksburg. Field assumed command of a small infantry brigade consisting of two Virginia regiments (Fortieth and Fifty-fifth) and an Alabama battalion. Smith's departure for Richmond early in April left Field in nominal charge of the district, with headquarters at Fredericksburg. Troops of Union major general Irwin McDowell's Department of the Rappahannock began advancing toward Fredericksburg on April 17. Some of Field's men skirmished with the Federals the following morning. When he saw that the enemy outnumbered him about two-to-one, Field ordered an evacuation of Fredericksburg after burning the bridges over the Rappahannock River and supplies that he could not take with him. He took up a position about seven miles south of the town and soon began receiving reinforcements from Richmond. Gen. Robert E. Lee sent Brig. Gen. Joseph R. Anderson with his brigade to Field's camp with orders to assume command and oppose any effort by the Union forces to advance toward the Confederate capital. A stalemate ensued, with McDowell's men tied down in the area so they could not go to the Shenandoah Valley to fight Maj. Gen. Thomas J. "Stonewall" Jackson's army if needed.

About April 30, 1862, the Sixtieth Virginia Infantry Regiment joined Field's brigade. Field took his brigade to Guiney Station about May 18 in response to the Union Army of the Potomac's movement up the Peninsula. He received orders to go to Richmond and left on May 24. By May 27, the brigade had reached Stony Run. There the brigade became a part of Maj. Gen. Ambrose P. Hill's division, which would soon become one of the finest fighting units of the Army of Northern Virginia. The brigade was at Ashland on May 28 and at Brook's Run by the thirty-first. Sometime during this month, the Twenty-second Virginia Infantry Battalion received assignment to Field's brigade, and the Forty-seventh Virginia joined it on June 11.

Field and his men fought with Hill's "Light Division" during the Seven Days' Battles. At Mechanicsville on June 26, the brigade charged the Federal position on the heights overlooking Beaver Dam Creek. Union artillery and musketry fire thinned Field's ranks as they advanced. The Virginians eventually took shelter in a thicket of woods along the creek and exchanged musketry fire with the enemy until after dark. During the night, the Federals withdrew to Gaines' Mill. Field's men again assaulted the enemy at the latter point the following day, going up against the enemy center. Forced to fall back after the first attack, Field's men went forward again. Unable to breach the Union line, his men dropped to the ground and continued to fire at their foes. The brigade saw its last action of the campaign on June 30 at Frayser's Farm, or White Oak Swamp. Hill reported that, during the assault that afternoon, "Field pressed forward with such ardor that he passed far in front of my whole line." Two of Field's regiments engaged in hand-to-hand combat with the Federals and captured two Union artillery batteries. The brigade held that part of the battlefield until relieved that night. Field reported casualties of 603 men killed and wounded during the Seven Days' Battles, about half of his force.

In early August, Field and his men accompanied the division on the march northward to engage Maj. Gen. John Pope's Army of Virginia. His was the last brigade of Hill's division to arrive on the battlefield at Cedar Mountain on August 9. The sun was beginning to set, and the fighting had all but ended. His men supported Capt. Willie Pegram's Virginia Battery as it dueled with three Union batteries. Brigade losses that evening totaled nine men killed and eighteen wounded. Following this battle, the Sixtieth Virginia was detached from the brigade and sent to southwestern Virginia. The men found themselves in the famous railroad cut at the battle of Second Manassas on August 29. One of the Union assaults that afternoon temporarily drove back portions of Field's Brigade. It may have been at this time that Field received a severe wound in the hip. At first the surgeons apparently thought he would not survive and did not do much other than to examine the wound. The following morning the surgeons looked at Field again and tended to the injury. He was taken to the home of Dr. and Mrs. Marsteller to recover. That process would be a long one. Field's friend, E. Porter Alexander, recalled after the war that Field "carried the bullet for twenty years, & it was then cut out nearly below the knee on the opposite side of its entrance, having gradually worked down as bullets often have a way of doing."

Field seemed to have recovered sufficiently from his wound to attempt to do active duty again in the spring of 1863. On May 25, he received assignment as superintendent of the Bureau of Conscription in Richmond. There are indications that his assistant had to fill in for him from time to time. The War Department removed him from this position on July 30 citing "the state of [his] health." By the following spring, Field was finally ready again for a field command. President Jefferson Davis nominated him on February 12 for promotion to the rank of major general, and the Confederate Senate confirmed that promotion the same day. He received orders to report to Lt. Gen. James Longstreet and the First Corps of the Army of Northern Virginia, which was then located in eastern Tennessee. The assignment was for Field to take command of the division formerly commanded by John Bell Hood. Field was also named as a member of the court-martial panel looking into charges against Gens. Lafayette McLaws and Jerome Robertson. It is unclear if he actually performed this duty.

Longstreet at first ignored the instructions of the War Department and assigned Field to command a small division formerly headed by Maj. Gen. Simon B. Buckner and placed the latter over Hood's Division. His motivation seems to have been his hope to see Brig. Gen. Micah Jenkins promoted and given command of Hood's Division. If Buckner received orders transferring him somewhere else, which was likely to happen, then Jenkins would have taken over the division as its senior brigadier. Following an exchange of letters and telegrams back and forth between Longstreet and Gen. Samuel Cooper, the latter finally responded that

Longstreet's tone was "considered highly insubordinate and demands rebuke." Field took command in time to move his division with the rest of Longstreet's corps to rejoin the army in northern Virginia in mid-April 1864.

On the morning of May 6, during the second day of fighting in the Wilderness, Field led his division into combat for the first time. His and Brig. Gen. John B. Kershaw's divisions rushed onto the field in time to stop a Union assault that had routed two divisions of A. P. Hill's Third Corps. By midmorning Longstreet's corps had begun pushing the Federals back. Longstreet then organized a flank attack against them, which included Field's and Kershaw's divisions hitting them in front. The plan worked well, and the Union line was almost ready to crumble. Longstreet stopped briefly to congratulate Field on the fighting his men had done. Longstreet rode forward with Kershaw, Brig. Gen. Micah Jenkins (one of Field's brigade commanders), and some staff and couriers. Confederate troops accidentally fired into this group of men, killing Jenkins and badly wounding Longstreet. Learning of this incident, Field rode forward, and Longstreet told him to assume command of the corps and to press the enemy. Field did so, receiving two wounds before Lee called off the attack so that the troops could realign themselves. Field and his division saw no more heavy combat that day.

Maj. Gen. Richard H. Anderson assumed command of Longstreet's corps on May 7, and Field returned to his division. The armies had moved to Spotsylvania Court House and begun entrenching by that time, and Field's men soon found themselves under attack by portions of Lt. Gen. Ulysses S. Grant's army. On May 10, some Federal troops got into the ditch in front of one of Field's brigades but were killed or captured as they attempted to clamber over the parapets. Violent assaults hit Field's trenches again on May 12, but his men again repelled them, causing heavy casualties in the blue ranks. When the two armies shifted southward again to the North Anna River, Field and his men did not become engaged in any of the fighting there. The division supported Kershaw's Division in repelling a Union attack at Cold Harbor on June 1. Field appears to have been absent from his division for several days following the fighting at the latter point, perhaps suffering from his Second Manassas wound.

As the armies moved toward Petersburg, Field's Division supported that of Maj. Gen. George E. Pickett in driving Union forces out of some Confederate entrenchments they had overrun near Bermuda Hundred. The men then occupied trenches east of Petersburg for several weeks before receiving assignment to the forces protecting the approaches to Richmond on the north side of the James River. Field became nominal commander of Confederate forces there and was responsible for repelling Union attacks on August 14 and 16, 1864, in the second battle of Deep Bottom. His actions there, particularly on the sixteenth, probably saved Richmond from being captured. Union troops attacked and captured Fort Harrison on September 29 and pushed toward Fort Gilmer. Field brought his men up in time to repulse the assault on that place. The following day, the division made an unsuccessful attempt to retake Fort Harrison. Again on October 27, Field and his men played an important role in defeating a Union offensive along the Darbytown Road. This closed the major fighting north of the James River for the year.

The Union victory at Five Forks west of Petersburg on April 1, 1865, resulted in orders for Field to take his division to Petersburg in anticipation of an assault on the fortifications around that town. One of his brigades reached the trenches on the morning of April 2 in time to bolster the defenses and stall Federal forces that had overrun Lee's lines southwest of the town. That night, Field and his men joined the army in evacuating Petersburg and beginning the long march westward. His was the largest division in the army at the time and engaged the Federals several times during the retreat that ended at Appomattox Court House on April 9. At the surrender there, his division had 462 officers and 4,491 enlisted men paroled. Field himself then went to his father-in-law's home in King George County. In the final year of the war, he had proven himself one of the most reliable of Lee's lieutenants.

After the war, Field worked for a time for the Piedmont and Arlington Life Insurance Company of Virginia. The company failed in 1873, so two years later he joined other former Civil War generals in Egypt to serve in the army of Ismail Pasha, the khedive of that country. Field remained there until 1877, having acted as inspector general of the army during an expedition into Abyssinia. Returning to the United States, he became a civil engineer in Washington, D.C. Field was elected doorkeeper of the U.S. House of Representatives and served in that capacity from April 18, 1878, until March 4, 1881. From 1881 to 1885, he was a civil engineer in the service of the United States. President Grover Cleveland appointed him as superintendent of the Hot Springs Reservation in Arkansas in 1885, and he held that post until 1889. He then returned to his residence in Washington and helped compile the official records of the Civil War.

Field married Monimia Fairfax Mason in 1857. She was the daughter of Wiley Roy Mason and Susan Taylor Smith Mason of Cleveland Plantation in King George County, Virginia. They had two sons, Charles A. Field and Wiley Roy Mason Field.

On April 9, 1892, Field died at his home in Washington of what was called Bright's disease. His body was buried in Loudon Park Cemetery in Baltimore.

BIBLIOGRAPHY

Davis, William C., ed. *The Confederate General.* 6 vols. Harrisburg, PA: National Historical Society, 1991.

Field, Charles W. "Campaign of 1864 and 1865. Narrative of Major-General C. W. Field." *Southern Historical Society Papers* 14 (1886): 542–63.

Hesseltine, William B., and Hazel C. Wolf. *The Blue and Gray on the Nile.* Chicago: University of Chicago Press, 1961.

—ARTHUR W. BERGERON JR.

Brig. Gen. Richard Montgomery Gano

RICHARD MONTGOMERY GANO was born on June 17, 1830, in Bourbon County, Kentucky, to one of that state's pioneer families. Of Huguenot extraction, the members of the Gano family contributed significantly to the military and religious development of the Kentucky frontier. Richard Montgomery Gano continued the history of contribution in both those areas. The Ganos settled in the area of Bourbon, Franklin, and Scott counties when its possession was still contested by American Indians. They fought as members of the state militia to make the area safer for white settlement. Gano's grandfather for whom he was named, Gen. Richard M. Gano, distinguished himself in the War of 1812. At least four additional relatives were addressed with military rank up to major general because of their service in the nation's wars. Other members of the family were physicians and preachers. His father, John Allen Gano, helped Alexander Campbell and Barton Stone create the Disciples of Christ denomination after a split with the Baptists. The Ganos were prominent in the early history of Georgetown College and in the creation of Bacon College, which would evolve into Kentucky University. Gano's mother, Catherine Conn, was also a member of a prominent Kentucky family.

Gano entered Bacon College at the age of twelve. He studied at Bethany College in Bethany, Virginia (now West Virginia), then trained to be a physician at the medical college in Louisville, Kentucky.

Graduating in 1849, Gano established his practice in Kentucky, but medicine was not a lucrative profession for a young man even if he did have strong connections through relatives. On March 15, 1853, Richard Gano married Martha "Mattie" Jones Welch of Crab Orchard, Kentucky, and the couple sought a place where he could provide for a family. In the 1850s the Ganos were back and forth between Kentucky, Louisiana, and Texas. In addition to an independent medical practice, Gano served as the physician for the Louisiana State Prison from 1856 to 1858.

In 1856 Gano began to buy land in Grapevine Prairie, Texas (near the present site of the Dallas/Fort Worth International Airport). Three years later his growing family settled in a small dogtrot cabin now preserved in Dallas's Old City Park. Gano quickly became a leader in the community. Like most of his relatives and friends among Kentucky's pioneer families, he wanted to make money. While practicing medicine he also became a farmer and stockman. Gano raised cattle and introduced the Kentucky racehorse to Texas.

He gained military experience suitable to a future cavalry officer fighting the Comanche Indians. When a war party raided Parker and Wise counties in 1858, Gano helped organize a company to pursue them. Impressed by his efforts, the citizens of Tarrant County awarded him a sword in gratitude and elected him to represent the county in the Texas legislature.

As a legislator Gano championed the cause of his fellow citizens living on the frontier. He argued that the government had a responsibility to protect its citizens against the Indians. Additionally, he lobbied for the growing livestock interests in the state.

With the outbreak of the Civil War, Gano faced a serious quandary. Like many Kentucky families, the Ganos suffered divided political loyalties. Kentucky was a border state. Its elite citizens owned slaves, but Kentuckians also held deep loyalties to the concept of union. Rev. John A. Gano, Richard's father, like many Kentuckians, prayed that war would be avoided by another compromise in the tradition of Henry Clay. However, his great-uncle, Dr. Stephen F. Gano, remained fiercely loyal to the Union. When secessionist students raised the Confederate flag over Recitation Hall at Georgetown College, Dr. Gano, a trustee of the college, climbed to the top of the building along with an elderly black man to remove it. He later helped organize a Union home guard unit. His name was also carried by the Union general Kentuckians hated most, Stephen Gano Burbridge, better known as "Butcher" Burbridge. Ironically, Richard M. Gano and Stephen Burbridge most likely played together as boys. But Richard offered his services to the Confederacy. He resigned his seat in the legislature and in June 1861, encouraged by his friend Gen. Albert Sidney Johnston, raised two companies of cavalry, ten officers, and 181 men. After being mustered into the Confederate army, the Grapevine Volunteers reported to Gen. P. G. T. Beauregard, Army of the Mississippi, on May 15, 1862. Beauregard assigned Gano's troop to Col. John Hunt Morgan's command, the Second Kentucky Cavalry, at Chattanooga, Tennessee.

Gano entered the war with the sense that he was on a noble and religious mission. Devoutly religious, he firmly believed God would bless the efforts of the Confederacy. His reports are written in a highly moralistic and religious tone and often quote scripture in support of the cause. Most end with the words "God has blessed us." He expressed dismay that Kentuckians could believe some of the things attributed to Confederate soldiers. Repeatedly he argued that his men treated captured soldiers with kindness and respect. Disappointed that Kentuckians did not flock to the Confederate banner, he nevertheless praised Kentucky women for their demonstrations of loyalty. The Confederacy found a champion of the Lost Cause interpretation in Richard M. Gano long before the end of the Civil War.

Gano's Texans were perfectly suited to serve with John Hunt Morgan. Morgan preferred the slashing attacks that took the enemy by surprise, disrupted communications, and destroyed supply lines. Gano's unit participated in Morgan's first two raids into Kentucky. In the First Kentucky Raid, in July 1862, Gano distinguished himself as a dependable commander. He played a major role in the capture of Tompkinsville, Harrodsburg, and many other central Kentucky towns, creating panic in local citizens and Union soldiers alike. His Texans were dashing men who gained a reputation for bravery. Having grown up in Kentucky, Gano knew the region well, and Morgan used him to disrupt supply lines, attack trains, and burn bridges. Morgan frequently sent Gano to circle the enemy, or a town as in the case of Cynthiana, to block the enemy's escape.

Family loyalties affected military action on that first venture into Kentucky. On July 18, Gano stopped in Scott County to have tea with his father, Rev. John A. Gano, and an old friend, the evangelist W. H. Hopson, who was holding a revival at the Old Union Church. Also on the First Kentucky Raid, having stopped at the farm of John F. Payne, Gano learned that Stephen Gano and the Union state militia were coming after him. Gano sent a message to his uncle: "Tell him that I am his nephew, Richard M. Gano, commanding some Texas cavalry: that I am not hunting a fight with him and that he . . . had better turn back . . . and remain quiet; but if they follow me one hundred yards from Donerail, that I shall attack them." No battle occurred, so Uncle Stephen Gano must have turned back. In a report filed from Hartsville, Tennessee, in August, John

Hunt Morgan praised Gano and his Texans for their bravery and their "good soldier-like conduct."

Gano also participated in Morgan's raid on the Louisville and Nashville Railroad in August. During that expedition, he earned promotion to major and commanded a full battalion at the engagement at Gallatin, Tennessee.

In September 1862, a new cavalry unit, the Seventh Kentucky Cavalry, was created for John Hunt Morgan. Gano became the commanding officer of the new Seventh Kentucky Cavalry Regiment, earning a promotion to colonel on September 2. Morgan, Basil Duke, and Gano greatly overestimated the loyalty of Kentuckians to the Confederate cause. After their raid they believed thousands of men would join the Confederacy if a military presence was shown in the state. It was largely upon their recommendation that Gens. Edmund Kirby Smith and Braxton Bragg invaded Kentucky in September 1862. Gano led his forces as far north as the Ohio River, capturing Maysville, Kentucky, on September 11, 1862, without firing a shot. On October 18, Gano participated in the skirmish at Ashland, the estate of Henry Clay. However, early success quickly waned. Kentuckians did not rally to the Southern cause as its Confederate leaders had hoped, and promised. Union and Confederate forces stumbled into one another at Perryville in early October, fighting the bloodiest battle Kentucky would experience in the war. Gano's cavalry covered the retreat of Braxton Bragg's army back to Tennessee.

Gano's Seventh Kentucky Cavalry subsequently took part in Morgan's Christmas Raid into Kentucky in December 1862. Then, back in Tennessee he fought with Morgan in the engagement at Milton, or Vaught's Hill, in late March 1863. More accustomed to fighting offensively, he made bad decisions when ordered to establish a line of defense at Snow Hill. His troops were easily flanked and forced to withdraw by Union forces.

Temporarily attached to another unit, Gano's Seventh Kentucky Cavalry missed Morgan's disastrous Great Raid. After Morgan's capture in Ohio, the remnants of Morgan's men joined Gano and fought under Brig. Gen. Nathan Bedford Forrest in the battle of Chickamauga. His health broken, Gano received a furlough after the fighting at Chickamauga. Accompanied by approximately eighty survivors of the original Grapevine Volunteers, now called the Gano Guards, Gano returned to Bonham, Texas.

The circumstances of Gano's promotion to brigadier general are unclear. The *Official Records* contains Lt. Gen. Edmund Kirby Smith's Special Order No. 172, dated October 24, 1863, ordering Brig. Gen. Richard M. Gano to the District of the Indian Territory. It is known that Kirby Smith later recommended the promotion of Gano, but President Jefferson Davis did not make it official until March 17, 1865. From October 24, 1863, however, Gano commanded with the rank of brigadier general.

Accompanied by the Gano Guards, Gano reported to Brig. Gen. William Steele, commander of the Indian Territory, on November 1, 1863, and was assigned to command acting brigadier general Smith P. Bankhead's brigade of Texas cavalry. On December 31, the brigade amounted to only 946 officers and men present for duty. Much of Gano's time was spent arresting stragglers and deserters from both armies, and he was encouraged to establish communications with partisans fighting in the area. In April 1864, Gano suffered an arm wound at the battle of Poison Spring in Arkansas. In the same year he commanded operations against Fort Smith and Massard Prairie in Arkansas.

In August Gano was ordered to organize Texas militia units. In that task he sought to allay the fears that all the men would be ordered away from their homes, leaving their families in danger. Much of the Trans-Mississippi Department had deteriorated into a very harsh guerrilla war, and Gano understood the concerns. He urged his commanding officer to keep the men on the frontier. Again, official records speak to the respect other officers had for his opinions as well as his courage.

Returning to the Indian Territory, Gano combined forces with Brig. Gen. Stand Watie, a Native American who commanded an Indian brigade that included Cherokee, Creek, and Seminole Indians. Any combination of Texans and Indians was problematic. By right of seniority Gano was in charge, but each general commanded his own troops in action. On September 19, 1864, Gano successfully attacked a large Union wagon train near Cabin Creek. Union forces reported losses of 202 wagons, forty horses, and over a thousand mules valued at $1.5 million. Gano was wounded again at Cabin Creek, and his war was essentially over. On May 26, 1865, the Army of the Trans-Mississippi surrendered.

Gano's record as a soldier rests mostly on his courage, his aggressiveness, and his loyalty to the Southern cause. Gen. Basil Duke claimed he saw Gano frightened on only one, very brief, occasion throughout the entire war, and his Texas troops repeatedly demonstrated their loyalty to him. His knowledge of warfare and his judgment, however, were sometimes suspect. On more than one occasion his enthusiasm and the tactics employed by Morgan led to near disaster. At the skirmish of Ashland and several other encounters, Gano's men, positioned to block the retreat of the enemy, fired recklessly, endangering other Confederate units. At Snow Hill his deployment of troops in a defensive position showed his ineptitude in battlefield tactics. But the greatest blemish on his record occurred in the Indian Territory. According to historian Jay Monaghan in *Civil War on the Western Border, 1854–1865*, Gano and Stand Watie attacked an encampment of Union hay cutters in September 1864 near the modern city of Wagoner, Oklahoma. The hay cutters were Negroes, and the Confederates massacred them, refusing to accept surrender, and later killing those wounded in the initial attack. Officers' reports in the *Official Records* substantiate the claim in part. Reports of Confederate officers merely hint at the killing, but Union officers stated that the Confederates killed "all the Negroes they could find." Another Union officer said the Cherokee soldiers, "having procured liquor, became intoxicated and slaughtered indiscriminately." Such an atrocity may have resulted from an inability to control Indian troops. Gano, however, was officially in charge of the entire military force and therefore bears responsibility.

After the war Gano turned his attention to religion. He returned to Kentucky where his father and the Reverend Hopson officiated as he was ordained to the Disciples of Christ ministry. In the years after the war he preached in Dallas and San Antonio. He was responsible for establishing many churches in Texas and Kentucky. He also played an active role in the Prohibition movement of the 1880s.

In Texas, Gano resumed his role as a farmer and stockman, raising purebred cattle, horses, sheep, and hogs. He established a real estate company, served as vice president of the Estado Land and Cattle Company, and was a director of the Bankers and Merchants National Bank in Dallas.

In the postbellum era Gano played an active role in the United Confederate Veterans. A frequent speaker, he contributed to the glorification of the Confederate cause that became known as the Lost Cause mentality. He served as chaplain of his camp and attended most regional and national meetings.

Gano and his wife, Mattie, had twelve children, nine of whom lived to maturity. Gano died on March 27, 1913, at his daughter's home in Dallas and is buried in the Oakland Cemetery, Dallas, Texas.

Bibliography

Apple, Lindsey, Frederick A. Johnston, and Ann Bolton Bevins, eds. *Scott County, Kentucky: A History*. With an introduction by Thomas D. Clark. Georgetown: Scott County Historical Society, 1993.

Davis, William C., ed. *The Confederate General*. 6 vols. Harrisburg, PA: National Historical Society, 1991.

Matthews, Gary Robert. *Basil Wilson Duke, CSA: The Right Man in the Right Place*. Lexington: University Press of Kentucky, 2005.

Monaghan, Jay. *Civil War on the Western Border: 1854–1865*. Lincoln: University of Nebraska Press, 1955.

U.S. War Department. *The War of the Rebellion: A Compilation of the Official Records of the Union and Confederate Armies*. 70 vols. in 128 pts. Washington, DC: Government Printing Office, 1880–1901.

—LINDSEY APPLE

Brig. Gen. Samuel Jameson Gholson

ESTEEMED FOR HIS COURAGE
and his character, Samuel J. Gholson gave total commitment to the
Confederacy. Due to circumstances beyond his control, he
never had the opportunity to lead
a brigade in a major battle. With
his age, his wounds, and his lack
of cavalry experience, he probably
wouldn't have distinguished himself had he done so. However, his
labors in recruiting and organizing the Mississippi state troops
proved valuable. Gholson's greatest contribution to the Confederate cause was the unglamorous
day-to-day struggle reconciling
the state army forces with their Confederate army counterparts.

Samuel Gholson was born near Richmond, Madison County, Kentucky, May 19, 1808, the son of Francis and Susanna Brown Gholson. The
parents moved to northern Alabama in 1817, settling in Franklin County.
The future general was educated in the common schools of Franklin
County, where he read law under the tutelage of Judge Peter Martin of
Russellville. Admitted to the Alabama bar in 1829, the young Gholson
moved to Athens, Monroe County, Mississippi, and started practicing
there. He soon became a leader of the local bar. According to his sometime political rival, Reuben Davis (who defeated him in a race for district
attorney), Gholson was a famed orator and a feared opponent in the court-
room. An active Democrat and supporter of President Andrew Jackson,
he was elected to the Mississippi House of Representatives in 1835. By
1840 he and his new wife bought a large home in Aberdeen, Monroe
County, where they lived the remainder of their lives.

In the summer of 1837 President Martin Van Buren unexpectedly re-
convened Congress. Mississippi's two representatives had been elected in
1835 to the Twenty-fourth Congress for a two-year term to end March 4,
1837, the traditional end date for Congress. Mississippi's governor called

a special election that summer to elect representatives for the special fall session. Gholson, a Democrat activist, was chosen to fill one of the seats, and the two Democrats cruised to victory. Once in, however, the Democratic majority of the House, ignoring strenuous Whig objections, declared that the election was not only for the unexpired portion of the Twenty-fourth Congress but for the forthcoming Twenty-fifth Congress as well. At the regular November election Gholson and his colleague refused to campaign, asserting that the House decision rendered the election null and void. The two Whig candidates, benefiting from a nationwide Whig trend and the Democratic boycott of the election, won handily, and presented their credentials as members-elect. The ensuing nasty, partisan debate almost resulted in Gholson's death. Congressman Henry Wise noted that while the Whig challengers were paying for their own presentation, Gholson and his colleague were charging their printing fees to the government. Gholson found this insinuation that he was milking the Treasury "unworthy of [Wise] and his station." The hot-tempered Wise turned to Gholson and proclaimed that "if ignorance and impudence constitutes a blackguard, there he stands," to which Gholson shot back that Wise was "a scoundrel and coward." In consequence of what one newspaper called "this disgraceful affair," only the intervention of John C. Calhoun and others prevented the two from fighting a duel. The upshot was that the House unseated both sets of claimants and ordered a new election. Perhaps wisely, Gholson declined to run, and the Whigs won both seats.

As consolation for his unseating, President Van Buren rewarded Gholson with an appointment as judge of the U.S. District Court of Mississippi. He served on the bench, with honor and distinction, until 1861, all the while remaining an active Democrat, backing Jefferson Davis's 1851 campaign for governor, and presiding over the 1860 state Democratic Party convention. Monroe County elected its distinguished judge to the 1861 Mississippi Secession Convention, where he urged immediate secession. Gholson was a member of the committee that drafted the secession ordinance.

Although way overage for combat duty, Judge Gholson resigned his post and enlisted as a private in the Monroe Volunteers. When on May 30, 1861, the company entered Confederate service as Company I, Fourteenth Mississippi Infantry, Gholson was elected captain. At Fort Donelson the Fourteenth participated in the defense against Ulysses S. Grant's investing Union army. Gholson took a bullet in the right lung during the fighting but was evacuated before the fort surrendered. Upon his recovery,

Gholson returned to northeast Mississippi to recruit a battalion but only succeeded in raising another company, Gholson's Rebels. Gholson took this company into the camp of the newly formed Forty-third Mississippi and joined the regiment—on the condition that Col. William Moore of the Forty-third hold a new election for colonel of the regiment! Gholson ran for colonel but lost to Moore, at which point Gholson pulled his company out of camp. As an independent company (which eventually became Company L of the Forty-third) Gholson's Rebels served in northern Mississippi during late 1862. Gholson was wounded yet again (in the left leg) in the fighting near Corinth. According to one newspaper account, "in the fierce battle of Corinth he drew his sword and was flourishing it. While thus engaged an enemy bullet hit the sharp edge of his sword and was literally split in two. Both parts were, of course deflected from the original course, one of the halves embedding itself in the Captain's leg just above the knee." This wound finally convinced the old judge that his days as a junior field officer had to end. On January 29, 1863, he submitted his resignation as captain of Gholson's Rebels, Accompanying the resignation was a surgeon's report stating that his thigh wound had developed "several abscesses" and inflammations that further field duty would aggravate more.

On October 22, 1862, Gholson had written his old friend and political associate Jefferson Davis asking for another assignment: "If there is anything that I can do in Mobile or some place south until Spring, I would be glad to do it." President Davis endorsed the application, noting that he knew Gholson as "a gallant man," and in April of 1863 nominated Gholson to the rank of colonel of cavalry (to rank from December 16, 1862) and judge of the military court of Hardee's Corps, Army of Tennessee. However, Gholson declined the appointment, apparently on June 16, 1863, as his successor judge was nominated to take rank from that date. Gholson's state had asked for his services.

Maj. Gen. T. C. Tupper of the Mississippi militia had become convinced that independent (i.e., non-Confederate) state forces were of little use, taking men away from the farms and draining the state treasury. He recommended to Gov. John J. Pettus that the state militia be disbanded and the active elements transferred to the Confederate army. Pettus, wishing to preserve the militia to protect the state's grain harvest, appointed Gholson to Tupper's position on April 18, though the commission was not issued until October 15, 1863.

Gholson's state troops consisted of several scattered cavalry regiments, battalions, and independent companies, understrength, underpaid, "poorly and only partly armed," and plagued by desertion. Gholson's task was to recruit and organize these forces, then use them, in cooperation with regular Confederate army troops, to protect northern Mississippi from Federal raids. Gholson sparred with local Confederate commanders as to who had the right to issue orders to his troops. Brig. Gen. James Chalmers, for one, protested to his superiors that Gholson was ordering state troop movements inside Chalmers' district without even notifying him. Along with other Confederate generals, Chalmers thought the whole "state troops" organization a haven for men trying to evade conscription by volunteering for local duty and proposed that Gholson's units be transferred to Confederate service. Confederate department commander Joseph E. Johnston agreed and on June 2, 1863, ordered Gholson's newly raised state cavalry transferred into Confederate service when organized.

This order helped clarify the future status of Gholson's men. But current problems remained. Gholson led a detachment opposing a May 1863 Union raid toward Okolona, and his troopers helped out that November when Confederate cavalry thrust north in harassing raids against the Memphis and Charleston Railroad. In December he impressed slave labor to help repair the Mobile and Ohio Railroad. He also quarreled with Confederate area commander Samuel W. Ferguson. Ferguson complained that Gholson seized equipment that belonged to Ferguson's men. Gholson counterclaimed that Ferguson seized the corn that was being stored for the state troops. Gholson piously assured Confederate authorities that he desired "perfect harmony between the two commands" but would not submit to Ferguson's "aggressions."

During Union brigadier general William Sooy Smith's raid into northern Mississippi in February 1864, Gholson's men provided initial opposition, without much success. They were routed and pushed aside in a February 19, 1864, skirmish near Houston, Mississippi. However, after Bedford Forrest and his men repulsed Smith's raiders at Okolona (February 22), Forrest turned over the pursuit to Gholson's fresher men. The state troops (only seven hundred strong) harried the retreating Union invaders and captured "a good many prisoners." Usually a hard man to please, Forrest was impressed by Gholson's energy and his willingness to cooperate. During Forrest's raid into West Tennessee (April 1864) Gholson's men, stationed at Tupelo, guarded Forrest's rear and after the raid took charge of 550 Union prisoners captured in the raid.

By this time the brigade was completing its organization and was ready for transfer to the Confederate army. It consisted of two regiments (with a third forming) and two battalions of cavalry, 1,172 effectives and 1,968 aggregate. Recommendations poured in for Gholson to be appointed a Confederate brigadier general, to command the brigade upon transfer. Gov. Charles Clark of Mississippi noted that the transfer "could not have been made except with assurance that I will do all in my power to retain Genl. Gholson." General Forrest added his support, as did other influential Mississippians. President Davis wrote back to Clark that "I have long recognized the patriotic service of Genl. Gholson. It will give me pleasure to nominate him for the brigade transferred by you to the Confederate Service." The transfer occurred on May 1, 1864, and Gholson received his commission as brigadier general June 1, 1864, to rank from May 6.

As could be predicted, the transfer caused turmoil within the brigade. One problem was caused by the state government's retaining most of the arms and equipment of the brigade. It entered Confederate service, in the words of General Ferguson, "green and imperfectly armed." Gholson pleaded for supplies, noting that "one-half of my men are without saddles, and at least one-half of those in use are worse than nothing." Another problem arose from the ambitions of younger officers in the brigade. The politically connected Col. William L. Lowry, one of Gholson's regimental commanders, wrote to President Davis asking for a transfer. Lowry admitted Gholson's courage and good character but complained that "'Old Slow' . . . is egregiously ignorant of military discipline, knows nothing whatever of drill and in consequence of age is entirely too slow for a cavalry commander. . . . He is, in military circles, an object of derision."

In late May 1864, Maj. Gen. Stephen D. Lee, commander of Confederate forces in Mississippi, ordered Gholson's men south to Canton, Mississippi, to assist in containing the Union garrison at Vicksburg. Gholson's Brigade was assigned to Brig. Gen. Wirt Adams, who thought the brigade "not a reliable command" and recommended that they all be dismounted and the units broken up. The brigade opposed a Union expedition from Vicksburg to the Pearl River that July, and on July 7, in a skirmish near Jackson, Mississippi, Gholson was once again wounded, this time struck twice by minié balls in the left shoulder and arm. The wound was serious enough to keep him out for months. In the meantime the brigade, commanded by its senior colonel, fought at the battle of Tupelo, then was ordered to Atlanta, where it participated actively in the latter stages of the Atlanta campaign. The troopers lost one-third of their number at the battle of Ezra Church and lost further in Hood's fall campaign against Sherman's supply line.

By December 1864 Gholson had recovered enough from his summer wounds to resume active duty. On December 2 he was posted to northeast

Mississippi, charged with rounding up the numerous absentees from his brigade. Gholson was laboring to collect what one superior officer labeled "the debris" of his command when Union forces under Brig. Gen. Benjamin Grierson launched a raid designed to cut the Mobile and Ohio Railroad. Gholson collected his remnant, some two hundred men, and skirmished with the raiders while falling back onto Egypt Station, Mississippi. There Gholson joined what was perhaps the least likely combat unit in the Confederate army: a regiment of former Union soldiers, let go from Andersonville and other prisons on the promise that they'd fight for the South. Gholson's "debris," short on ammunition, and the "Galvanized Confederates" proved no match for the Union cavalry assault that December 28. A charge by the Fourth Illinois Cavalry dislodged Gholson's men, positioned behind a railroad embankment. Gholson himself received a left-arm wound reported as mortal in several Union (and at least one Confederate) accounts of the engagement. The Galvanized Confederates withdrew to a blockhouse where, after a short stand, they surrendered. Gholson was captured on the field, and when the Union raiders withdrew, they left him in the care of a Union army physician. Gholson survived but only at the cost of amputating his wounded arm at the shoulder joint.

In March 1865 the regiments of the brigade, still under Colonel Lowry, were consolidated into one regiment by General Forrest's order and placed permanently in Forrest's Cavalry Corps. In a letter to Gholson, Forrest expressed a "high appreciation of [his] gallantry and capacity as a soldier and officer" and hoped that Gholson would be fit for field duty soon. But the letter also threw into doubt the status of Gholson and his brigade, noting that the secretary of war had no authentication of the brigade's transfer to Confederate service (a telling commentary on the paperwork at the War Department). The fifty-seven-year-old Gholson's combat career had reached an end.

Gholson returned to his Aberdeen, Mississippi, home, and was paroled there. The voters of Monroe County honored their "able, brave, and generous gentleman" by electing him to the state house of representatives, where his colleagues made him speaker. He served as such from 1865 to 1867 and was elected again to the house in 1878. In office this loyal Southerner, while accepting the results of the war, labored to overthrow the Reconstruction government of the state. When not in government the "old warhorse" (as he was called by his friends) practiced law, in one case successfully defending alleged Ku Klux Klan members.

Age and wounds finally took their toll on the crippled warrior. In the flowery language of his obituary, "for many months he has stood at the

margin of the grave confronting disease and debility with a will power
that was almost proof against their cruel attacks; but the nerve that was
iron a few years ago had succumbed to the combined assaults of time and
disease, and the ripe sheaf yielded to the scythe."

General Gholson died at his Aberdeen home on October 16, 1883. As
a mark of respect, all the businesses in Aberdeen were closed the day of his
funeral, the townspeople attending the services at the local Presbyterian
church. He was buried in Odd Fellows Cemetery, Aberdeen.

Gholson married local heiress Margaret Ragsdale in 1838. The couple
had no children.

BIBLIOGRAPHY

Davis, William C., ed. *The Confederate General.* 6 vols. Harrisburg, PA: National
    Historical Society, 1991.

Hooker, Charles E. *Mississippi.* Vol. 9 in *Confederate Military History,* ed. Clem-
    ent A. Evans. Atlanta: Confederate Publishing, 1899. Rev. ed. Wilmington,
    NC: Broadfoot Publishing, 1988.

U.S. War Department. *The War of the Rebellion: A Compilation of the Official Re-
    cords of the Union and Confederate Armies.* 70 vols. in 128 pts. Washington,
    DC: Government Printing Office, 1880–1901.

—BRUCE S. ALLARDICE

Brig. Gen. Randall Lee Gibson

RANDALL LEE GIBSON was born on September 10, 1832, at Spring Hill, the home of his maternal grandparents, near Versailles, Woodford County, Kentucky, the son of Tobias Gibson and Louisiana Breckinridge Hart. His father was a native of Mississippi and a member of a well-known pioneer family, while his mother was descended from distinguished Kentucky forebears. By the 1840s Tobias was one of the largest sugar planters in Louisiana and had amassed several plantations along Bayou Black near the town of Houma, which Louisiana Gibson named. Randall was educated by his parents' instruction, by private tutors, and in the schools of Lexington, Kentucky, and Terrebonne Parish, when his family traveled south for the cane-growing season. At the age of sixteen, Randall went to Yale University, where he enjoyed academic success and popularity, being elected by his fellow students to deliver the valedictory address at their 1853 commencement. After graduation from the law school of the University of Louisiana in New Orleans in 1855 and extensive travel in Europe, Gibson bought seven hundred acres of land on Bayou Lafourche near Thibodaux, Louisiana, in 1858, where he planted sugar cane and practiced law. A supporter of the Sen. John Slidell faction of the Louisiana Democratic Party, Gibson wrote about the growing alienation between the North and South in pro-slavery essays in *DeBow's Review*. An ardent secessionist, he was an unsuccessful candidate for the state secession convention in 1860.

Gibson served on Gov. Thomas O. Moore's militia staff until it was disbanded in 1861, when he enlisted in the Louisiana state military forces and became a captain of artillery in the First Louisiana Regular Artillery Regiment prior to his election on September 16, 1861, as colonel of the

Thirteenth Louisiana Volunteer Infantry Regiment. With no prior military training, Gibson worked hard to learn military tactics and regimental leadership before joining Gen. Albert Sidney Johnston's Army of the Mississippi in Corinth, Mississippi, where his regiment was assigned to the First Brigade of Brig. Gen. Daniel Ruggles's First Division in the Second Army Corps under Maj. Gen. Braxton Bragg. Because the leader of the First Brigade, Brig. Gen. Lucius Marshall Walker, was on sick leave, Gibson, as senior colonel, commanded the brigade and led his green troops in one of the most notorious actions of the battle of Shiloh. On the orders of Bragg and despite Gibson's objections, the First Brigade made four unsuccessful frontal assaults on the Hornet's Nest, and Bragg, refusing to acknowledge his own failure to provide artillery support or the difficulties created by the impenetrable thicket that protected the Union forces, blamed the failure on Gibson's faulty leadership. This sparked bitter enmity that marred much of Gibson's military career, especially after President Jefferson Davis tapped Bragg to succeed Gen. Pierre Gustave Toutant Beauregard as commander of the western army.

Gibson returned to the leadership of the Thirteenth Louisiana, which was now part of Brig. Gen. Daniel Adams's brigade, and performed so well at the battle of Perryville, Kentucky, that Adams reported his intention to recommend Gibson's promotion to brigadier general. His regiment suffering from a severe shortage of manpower, Gibson commanded the merged Thirteenth and Twentieth Louisiana Regiment (Consolidated) in the reorganized army that Bragg named the Army of Tennessee in November 1862. Adams was wounded during the battle of Murfreesboro, and Gibson again took command of the brigade and was commended by the division commander, Maj. Gen. John C. Breckinridge, for his courage and skill. In the contentious atmosphere of the Army of Tennessee after Murfreesboro, Bragg relieved Gibson of his command on March 1, 1863, and ordered him to conscript duty. These were the darkest days of Gibson's military career.

Convinced that Bragg would never promote him, Gibson now believed that the irascible army commander intended to drive him from the army. Gen. Joseph E. Johnston, however, returned Gibson to the command of the Thirteenth and Twentieth Louisiana (Consolidated) when Breckinridge's troops joined Johnston in the campaign against the Union army during the siege of Vicksburg. In Adams's absence, Gibson remained in command of the brigade at the battles of Chickamauga and Missionary Ridge. But it was only after President Davis reluctantly removed Bragg and appointed General Johnston to command the Army of Tennessee that Gibson finally received promotion to brigadier general on January 11, 1864.

General Johnston was popular with the army's rank and file during the opening months of 1864 as Union major general William Tecumseh Sherman began his invasion of Georgia. Gibson, however, disapproved of Johnston's defensive strategy as Sherman moved relentlessly toward Atlanta and was not sorry to see him replaced by Gen. John Bell Hood in July. Gibson's Brigade, now under corps commander Lt. Gen. Stephen D. Lee and division commander Maj. Gen. Henry D. Clayton, fought valiantly in the fruitless battle of Atlanta and in the final doomed Tennessee campaign. Through the horrific suffering of the engagements at Spring Hill and Franklin (where Clayton's Division was luckily held in reserve), Gibson never lost faith in Hood's aggressive tactics, not even following the terrible rout at Nashville. After the remnants of the Army of Tennessee arrived in Mississippi in January 1865, Lt. Gen. Richard Taylor, head of the Department of Alabama, Mississippi, and East Louisiana, arranged for Gibson and his remaining men to go to Mobile, where the Confederates were concentrating troops to foil Union plans to invade the state through southern Alabama and destroy industrial and agricultural resources. Gibson commanded about three thousand men at Spanish Fort in April 1865 and withstood a two-week siege by three times as many Union troops in one of the final actions of the war. He always believed that the failure to remove Bragg more promptly from the command of the Army of Tennessee cost the Confederacy its independence.

Gibson returned to Terrebonne Parish, where his father had struggled to keep the plantations afloat during the Federal occupation. The Gibson family had been fortunate: all six of the Gibson sons (Randall, Hart, William Preston, Tobias, Claude, and McKinley) had served in the Confederate army; all survived except one (Claude), who died of natural causes in New Orleans. Gibson suffered the lethargy and depression endured by many of the Confederacy's veterans, but he soon adjusted to civilian life and was back on his feet, planting sugar cane and practicing law in New Orleans in partnership with Maj. John Austin, a former member of his brigade. Gibson received a letter of amnesty in 1866 and the next year accepted the terms of his pardon by President Andrew Johnson. His Northern friends were anxious to reconcile with him, but it was difficult for them to understand the fears that former Confederates had of Radical Republican government and of a landless black majority empowered to vote. Tempered by the suffering of the war, Gibson welcomed the end of slavery and set about rebuilding his world with stoic resolve.

In 1868 Gibson married Mary Montgomery of New York City, daughter of a wealthy former New Orleans merchant, Romanzo Warwick Montgomery, and Virginia Carolina High Montgomery, who was born in New Orleans. Gibson and Mary enjoyed the social whirl of New Orleans, where Dr. Tobias Gibson Richardson, his father's namesake, and Edward Douglass White, a prominent young attorney, were close friends and frequent guests. Gibson and his brothers continued to assist their father on the family's plantations but struggled with the shortage of labor and the frequent disastrous flooding of the Mississippi River. Realizing that the Civil War had permanently and radically changed patterns of civilization in the South, Gibson joined with former Confederate general Beauregard, prominent Conservative Democrats, and a number of blacks in the Grand Unification Movement, which endorsed the civil and political rights of all people. Although the movement was ultimately unsuccessful in unifying the racial groups, Gibson's participation indicates the sea change that the Civil War effected in his prewar racial attitudes.

Gibson ran for Congress in 1872, but the seat was awarded to his Republican rival. In 1874 his congressional campaign was successful, and he took his seat in the Forty-fourth Congress. Reelected in 1876, Gibson was instrumental in the effort to forge a peaceful settlement of the presidential election that resulted in the Compromise of 1877 and ended Reconstruction in the South. A Conservative Democrat, Gibson was increasingly disillusioned with Louisiana's politics, where Bourbon Democrats, a powerful New Orleans Ring, and the Republican Party battled the Conservatives for primacy. As one of the "rebel brigadiers" in the House of Representatives, Gibson grappled with policies affecting tariffs, money, banks, railroads, and, most important for his constituents, the construction of levees on the Mississippi River. Gibson crafted the bill for the Mississippi River Commission, to be composed of engineers and other civilian river experts, which would give scientific credibility to the South's attempt to secure federal funding for levee construction. He also supported the creation of the Monetary Commission, the only congressman to endorse the group's minority report, which endorsed the gold standard. A member of the Ways and Means Committee, Gibson favored the establishment of the Tariff Commission and became a leading spokesman for the protective tariff. In 1880 when the Louisiana legislature met to elect a U.S. senator to the seat to be vacated in 1883, Gibson was selected for the position. He had to seek reelection to the House one more time in 1880, when he easily defeated his Republican challenger.

In 1881, Paul Tulane, a wealthy former New Orleans merchant who had built a large fortune before retiring to his boyhood home of Princeton, New Jersey, chose Representative and Senator-elect Gibson to serve as trustee of a group of properties in New Orleans to be used for the educational benefit of the young people of Louisiana. Gibson reluctantly agreed to accept Tulane's commission and, following the model of the Peabody Fund, created a seventeen-member board of Louisiana leaders, including Tobias Richardson and Edward Douglass White, to administer Tulane's bequest. Gibson also sought the advice of one of his best Yale friends, Andrew Dickson White, the founding president of Cornell University. Gibson influenced the board to name his cousin and close friend, William Preston Johnston, to be the first president of the university. Gibson struggled with Bourbon Democrats to secure from the Louisiana legislature tax-exempt status for the New Orleans university, which absorbed the former University of Louisiana. He also quietly but forcefully persuaded Paul Tulane to allow the potential enrollment of women, overcoming the influence of James McCosh, president of Princeton University, who was urging Tulane not to allow women in his new university. Above all, Gibson was a strong voice for high standards of scholarship despite the pressure from some community leaders to increase enrollment and to adopt a more pedestrian mission.

Gibson began his Senate career at age fifty-one, a vigorous and energetic man despite frequent bouts of debilitating gout. He and Mary, now thirty-eight years old, and their three sons took up residence in a larger Washington, D.C., home as they assumed the enhanced social obligations of a U.S. senator. The basic political issues were familiar ones, and Gibson said that he often felt as if he were standing atop a levee, keeping watch on the river, rice and cane fields, and the protective tariff. He was an ardent supporter of the Blair education bill, which would provide federal funds for public education, funds that would have enormously benefited the South, and which, ironically enough, the Bourbons vehemently opposed. With the election of Grover Cleveland in 1884, the first Democrat to occupy the White House in twenty-five years, patronage issues soon swamped Gibson. Doling out federal largesse was complicated by the fractured state Democratic Party and the fact that the presence of the New Orleans Custom House meant more lucrative and abundant federal patronage was available in Louisiana than in most states. Gibson's Senate career was also impacted by the fact that the other Louisiana Senate seat was occupied by a Bourbon Democrat who opposed many of the measures, such as federal aid to education and the gold standard, that Gibson supported.

After Mary's death in 1887, Gibson assuaged his grief by plunging into the politics of the 1888 gubernatorial election and his own reelection to the Senate by the Louisiana legislature. The legislature unanimously elected Gibson to the Senate, but Republicans tabled his credentials for the term beginning March 4, 1889, and Sen. William Chandler of New Hampshire announced a resolution calling for an investigation of the 1888 Louisiana election. In the greatest battle of his political life, Gibson managed to defeat Chandler's resolution and to take the seat to which he had been elected, but he implored members of the Louisiana legislature to reform the election process, which he considered a greater threat to the state than the presence of a corrupt and powerful lottery company that had insinuated itself into every aspect of state government.

Gibson's advocacy of the gradual abolition of the lottery, as opposed to its immediate dissolution, and his conviction that election reform was the most important issue facing the state were out of step with the beliefs of most of his supporters. Gibson finally realized that election reform would have to go on a back burner, and he joined the antilottery forces in supporting its immediate abolition and worked for the election of a Conservative Democrat to the governorship in 1892. Although he was victorious on both counts, he created enemies for himself in the legislature where the reelection to his Senate seat for the term beginning in 1895 would be held. The Senate election was deadlocked and finally delayed until 1893, but it was obvious that Gibson's leadership of state politics had been dealt a severe blow. The Conservative Democrats now aligned themselves with the Bourbons, and when Gibson died on December 15, 1892, at Hot Springs, AR, he was one of the last of the patrician Conservative Democrats who espoused noblesse-oblige politics and sought middle-of-the-road positions apart from the extreme racial, economic, and social politics of the age. Gibson was buried in the family plot in Lexington Cemetery, Lexington, Kentucky, with great praise and accolades for his life's work serving as, in the words of Edward Douglass White, a minister between the people of the North and the people of the South.

Bibliography

Davis, William C., ed. *The Confederate General.* 6 vols. Harrisburg, PA: National Historical Society, 1991.

Gibson and Humphreys Family Papers, 1846–1919. Southern Historical Collec-
    tion. Wilson Library, University of North Carolina at Chapel Hill.
Johnston, Albert Sidney, and William Preston Papers. Mrs. Mason Barret Col-
    lection. Manuscripts Division, Howard-Tilton Memorial Library, Tulane
    University, New Orleans.
McBride, Mary Gorton, and Ann Mathison McLaurin. *Randall Lee Gibson of
    Louisiana: Confederate General and New South Reformer.* Baton Rouge: Loui-
    siana State University Press, 2007.

—MARY GORTON MCBRIDE

Brig. Gen. John Breckinridge Grayson

JOHN BRECKINRIDGE GRAYSON was born into a politically well-connected family on October 18, 1806, at Cabell's Dale, his maternal grandfather's plantation near Lexington, Kentucky. His parents, Alfred William Grayson and Letitia Preston Breckinridge, married there on October 28, 1804, and named their middle child, the only one to survive to adulthood, after her father. John Breckinridge had served as U.S. senator from Kentucky (1801–1805) and attorney general (1805–1806) under President Thomas Jefferson before his death at Cabell's Dale in December 1806. The boy's other grandfather, William Grayson, former aide-de-camp to George Washington and U.S. senator from Virginia (1789–1790), died before John was born. Alfred Grayson also held public office, serving as Kentucky's secretary of state from March 1, 1807, to February 22, 1808.

Following Alfred's death on October 10, 1810, John, baby brother William Lewis, and his mother returned to Cabell's Dale. John's early education appears to have come entirely from private tutors on the plantation. On October 16, 1818, his mother remarried. John's new stepfather, Maj. Gen. Peter Buel Porter, a future secretary of war (1828–1829), was a native of Connecticut, former U.S. congressman from New York, and a hero of the War of 1812. The family immediately relocated to Black Rock, Niagara (later Erie) County, New York.

Appointed from Kentucky, fourteen-year-old John entered the U.S. Military Academy at West Point about June 26, 1821. In June 1824, he "was turned back to repeat the studies of his Second Class [junior] year" because of a deficiency in philosophy. He graduated (along with fellow Kentuckian Albert Sidney Johnston) on July 1, 1826, twenty-second out of a class of forty-one cadets. Brevetted second lieutenant, Third Artillery, upon graduation, he was promoted that same day to second lieutenant, Second Artillery and ordered to Fort Monroe, Virginia, for duty at the Artillery School for Practice. Because geographical dispersal of the companies of artillery regiments undermined discipline and efficiency, the school had been established so that the various companies could rotate through it.

Despite being assigned to topographical duty on June 4, 1828, Grayson found time to court Caroline Searle, daughter of the deceased Sir Francis Searle and "celebrated for her beauty and finely cultivated voice." The couple married in Washington on November 10, 1828. Maj. Gen. Alexander Macomb Jr., commander of the U.S. Army, walked Caroline down the aisle, and President John Quincy Adams hosted a subsequent dinner and reception in the White House. Grayson's parents attended, his stepfather then serving in Adams's cabinet as secretary of war.

Grayson's topographical duty ended on March 29, 1832. He was briefly stationed at the Augusta (Georgia) Arsenal before joining the garrison at Fort Mitchell, Alabama, in 1833. Promoted first lieutenant on April 30, 1834, he was transferred to Fort Wood (now Macomb), near New Orleans. There Grayson remained except for a brief assignment to Bay of St. Louis, Mississippi, before taking part in the Second Seminole War. The Graysons' only child, John Breckinridge Grayson Jr., was born in New Orleans on September 9, 1835.

Grayson saw action in Florida against the Seminoles at Camp Izard (February 27–29, March 5) and Oloklikaha (March 31) in 1836 before being ordered back to New Orleans. He performed commissary duty there until 1847, being promoted to captain, staff, Commissary of Subsistence, July 7, 1838, and captain, Second Artillery, December 11, 1838 (though he only held the second rank through June 18, 1846). In July 1845, Grayson became responsible for securing and transporting the foodstuffs for Bvt. Brig. Gen. Zachary Taylor's 1,500-man Army of Occupation, which had been dispatched to secure the newly annexed Republic of Texas. Already-strained relations with Mexico rapidly deteriorated when President James K. Polk reinforced Taylor and ordered him to advance to the Rio Grande in January 1846. Hostilities broke out on April 25, and the U.S. Congress responded by declaring war on May 13. Grayson's commissary duties expanded exponentially: by August, Taylor commanded nearly 20,000 troops, mostly volunteers.

Grayson's performance impressed Maj. Gen. Winfield Scott. When he began assembling a second army to capture Mexico City in February 1847, he appointed Grayson to his staff as chief of commissariat. Present at the siege of Vera Cruz and the battles of Cerro Gordo, Molino del Rey, and Mexico City, Grayson was brevetted major (August 20, 1847) for "gallant and meritorious conduct" in the battles of Contreras and Churubusco, and lieutenant colonel (September 13, 1847) for similar behavior at the battle of Chapultepec.

On October 13, 1847, during the occupation of Mexico City, several officers, including Grayson and future president Franklin Pierce, initiated the Aztec Club, a social club and resort for officers, whose members "could drink, dine and entertain themselves, and their invited guests, while stationed on duty far from home." Later that day, Maj. Gen. John A. Quitman was elected president, and Grayson and Col. Charles F. Smith were elected first vice presidents. Founding members included Robert E. Lee, Ulysses S. Grant, Joseph E. Johnston, P. G. T. Beauregard, George B. McClellan, Joseph Hooker, and Kentuckians Gustavus W. Smith and John Stuart Williams. Headquartered in the eighteenth-century palace that had been built for the viceroy of Spain, the Aztec Club quickly became *the* place in the city. Winfield Scott, whose headquarters was nearby, was made an honorary member. The ranks of the organization swelled quickly, including William T. Sherman, George G. Meade, and Kentuckian Simon Bolivar Buckner. With evacuation of Mexico City looming, a meeting was held on May 26, 1848, in which Grayson was elected "Substitute President and Acting Treasurer" for a four-year term; in fact, he would serve as both.

When Scott departed Mexico in February of 1848, his successor, Maj. Gen. William O. Butler, retained Grayson. But later that year Grayson received orders to report to Detroit. He passed through New Orleans so his family could travel with him to Michigan. While in the Crescent City, local officials presented him with a sword for "his distinguished service" and to express "their admiration and esteem for him as an officer and gentleman." Grayson served as commissary officer at Detroit for seven years, being promoted major, staff, Commissary of Subsistence, October 21, 1852.

While stationed in Detroit, Grayson met Charles E. Whilden, and in 1855, when Grayson was ordered to report to Santa Fe as chief of commissariat of the Department of New Mexico, he invited Whilden to accompany him to his new post and serve as his personal secretary. If Whilden is any indication, Grayson was an excellent judge of men. Whilden went on to be "the unsung hero of the Bloody Angle at Spotsylvania Court House" until rescued from obscurity by author Gordon C. Rhea.

Operating out of St. Louis, Grayson spent most of that spring assembling a wagon train at Fort Leavenworth that would eventually consist of some five hundred soldiers, seven hundred mules and horses, nearly one hundred wagons, and $200,000 in specie. Low water in the Missouri River hampered the forwarding of supplies, but the column finally moved out June 28. The arduous journey was made even more so when a slave dropped hot coals that ignited the prairie grass. The blaze consumed numerous tents and muskets, and stray bullets wounded several, one fatally. Two more soldiers drowned while swimming horses and wagons across a rain-swollen river.

Grayson reached Santa Fe on August 27. A few weeks passed before he got settled into a five-room building that contained both office and residence. The one-story structure also housed Whilden, two servants, and an Italian cook. Other than the scenery, there was little to recommend Santa Fe. And though most found it a healthy climate, Grayson was bedridden with pneumonia at least once while stationed there.

By the time Grayson, "at home on every subject whether civil or military," was selected as keynote speaker for the Independence Day celebration in 1856, he had acquired a staff of four servants. One was devoted entirely to caring for Whilden, who described Grayson as sharing everything with him and as being "more like a Father and a bosom friend than a Superior." As with so many officers separated from their families, Grayson had plenty of time to kill. Unlike so many of them in similar surroundings, he did not turn to alcohol to relieve the loneliness.

He sought diversion instead. One such diversion was the Historical Society of New Mexico, founded in late 1859, at a meeting in Grayson's quarters. Appropriately, Grayson served as its first president—and its second also. The society was a purposeful aggregation dedicated to the study of a host of subjects, such as history, geography, geology, climatology, and Indian races and presentation of their findings in learned addresses.

When the Civil War broke out, Grayson sided with the South. His resignation from the U.S. Army had been accepted on July 1, 1861, and he headed east not knowing how the Confederate government would receive him, since his native Kentucky had declared itself neutral. He stopped briefly in New Orleans to visit his family before pressing on to Richmond, where President Jefferson Davis warmly welcomed him. Two years behind Grayson at West Point, Davis nominated his former schoolmate to be brigadier general from Louisiana on August 13, 1861. Confirmed by the Senate on the sixteenth, Grayson accepted his commission four days later.

On August 21, the War Department assigned him to command the Department of Middle and East Florida.

Grayson reached Florida on September 4 and established his headquarters at Fernandina on the eighth. Located on Amelia Island south of Fort Clinch, the town constituted the eastern terminus of the Florida Railroad, which traversed the state to Cedar Key on the Gulf of Mexico. Because of the rail connection, many thought Fernandina would become a haven for blockade runners. Instead, disruption of the coastal trade brought near starvation to the residents. Before Grayson's arrival, foodstuffs had dwindled to a three-day supply, and Yankee blockaders were visible from the rooftops.

Obviously harbor defense was essential. Grayson's primary concerns were St. Augustine, Amelia Island, and the mouth of the St. John's River on the Atlantic coast and Cedar Key, St. Marks, and Apalachicola on the Gulf. Though fortifications had already been built and cannon mounted at all of these locations, Grayson found that some of the earthworks had to be completely redone and all of the sites needed augmenting with heavier, rifled cannon. On September 13 Grayson wrote Secretary of War Leroy P. Walker outlining the deplorable conditions: "As sure as the sun rises, unless cannon, powder, &c., be sent to Florida in the next thirty days, she will fall into the hands of the North. Nothing human can prevent it." He enclosed a requisition for eighteen siege cannon, twelve fieldpieces, and twenty-three thousand pounds of cannon powder. Though Grayson did not exaggerate, Florida's coastal ports held, but only because the Union was not ready to occupy them.

On September 14, Grayson began a tour of his department. Although his delicate health threatened to collapse entirely in the weather, he journeyed on to Tallahassee, to meet with Florida governor-elect John Milton. Even before his election, Milton was proffering unsolicited advice to Secretary of War Walker. Apparently, Milton pressed his ideas on military matters to Grayson on September 25, but the general decidedly disagreed. Milton wrote Secretary of the Navy Stephen R. Mallory on October 2 telling him of the meeting with Grayson and commenting on his poor health: "He is nearly spent with consumption. I thought he would die last Wednesday night, and I fear will not have physical strength to discharge necessary duties in Florida." When the War Department failed to relieve Grayson immediately, Milton did his best to prevent the general from issuing orders from his sickbed.

On October 10, the War Department changed course by assigning another brigadier general to relieve Grayson, because his health prevented his performance of duty. Members of his command immediately protested. Col. William S. Dilworth wrote Secretary of War Walker on October 14 that Grayson, despite his illness, "has done everything that man could," and his men had "perfect confidence in him." Dilworth scoffed at the "officious meddling of scared politicians" and hoped headquarters would deliver them a "merited rebuke." Others concurred with the new governor, however, believing disease had rendered Grayson "non compos mentis" and not responsible for his actions.

The struggle between governor and general came to an abrupt end in Tallahassee on October 21, when Grayson died before being relieved of his command. His son had been with him at the end. He and a member of the general's staff brought the body to New Orleans via Mobile for burial. Maj. Gen. Mansfield Lovell received the remains on October 27, and the body lay in state in the mayor's parlor in city hall. Brig. Gen. James Trudeau organized the funeral procession. The funeral began at four o'clock the following day; the procession, which included more than two thousand soldiers, proceeded to St. Louis Cemetery No. 2, where Grayson's remains were placed in one of the tombs belonging to the Thomas Layton family. The general had died a Roman Catholic, held the highest post in the Masonic order, and was a prominent member of the Odd Fellows. His wife, Caroline, was then residing in Madisonville, Louisiana, where she operated a hotel. She did not need the revenue: the general left an estate worth $56,000 in real property and $58,000 in personal.

Three of the general's close relatives would serve with distinction during the Civil War. His son, John Breckinridge Grayson Jr., entered Confederate service as a first lieutenant in the First Louisiana Heavy Artillery. Later promoted to captain, he successfully defended Fort Coburn, near Grand Gulf, Mississippi, on April 29, 1863, forcing Ulysses S. Grant to cross the Mississippi farther downstream. Captured at Vicksburg and exchanged, he was serving as chief of artillery for Brig. Gen. St. John R. Liddell when he was captured at Fort Blakely, Alabama, April 9, 1865.

General Grayson's half brother, Peter Augustus Porter, entered the Union army in the summer of 1862 as colonel of the Eighth New York Heavy Artillery Regiment. His first and last major engagement came at Cold Harbor, Virginia, on June 3, 1864, when he was killed, shot six times while leading an assault on Confederate fortifications.

Grayson's most illustrious relative was first cousin John C. Breckinridge, who also grew up at Cabell's Dale, was U.S. vice president (1857–

1861) and senator (1861), and Confederate major general and secretary of war (1865).

BIBLIOGRAPHY

Davis, William C., ed. *The Confederate General*. 6 vols. Harrisburg, PA: National Historical Society, 1991.

Ezra J. Warner Papers. Chicago History Museum.

U.S. War Department. *The War of the Rebellion: A Compilation of the Official Records of the Union and Confederate Armies*. 70 vols. in 128 pts. Washington, DC: Government Printing Office, 1880–1901.

—LAWRENCE LEE HEWITT

Brig. Gen. Roger Weightman Hanson

ROGER WEIGHTMAN HANSON
was born on August 27, 1827, in
Winchester, Kentucky. He was
the second son of Samuel Hanson, a Virginian of Swedish de-
scent, a prominent attorney and
judge in Clark County. His
mother, Matilda Calloway, was
the daughter of a general. The
Hansons had five sons. Roger W.
Hanson grew into a handsome,
solidly built, five-foot-nine-inch
man, with huge, round shoulders.
He was ambitious, good humored
yet with a fiery temper, a deep
guttural voice, and a rancorous
way with words. He had gray
eyes and a florid complexion.

In 1846, when he was eighteen years old, Hanson was elected first
lieutenant in Capt. John S. Williams's company of volunteers to serve in
the Mexican War. The company was attached to the Sixth U.S. Infantry
and was later part of the Fourth Kentucky Volunteers, with Williams as
colonel. Hanson served creditably and earned a reputation for reckless
bravery and camaraderie during the course of the conflict. His style, courage under fire, and lively sense of humor endeared him to his peers, who
were impressed with his aptitude for military principles despite his lack of
formal training. However, he was also noted for having a volatile temper.
It was this latter aspect of his character that ultimately led to his nickname
of "old Bench leg."

In January 1848, upon returning from the war, Hanson engaged in a
duel with William Duke over the affections of a young lady. Hanson denounced Duke as a coward. The wronged Duke demanded satisfaction.
The two combatants met on a cold January morning along the banks of the
Ohio River near Vevay, Indiana, and engaged in several rounds of personal combat in which they exchanged a series of shots. The aggrieved
Duke sustained a minor graze wound to the hand, but his return fire shat-

tered Hanson's right thighbone. The wound never fully healed, leaving Hanson with a perpetual limp and the unflattering nickname. Hanson lost both the duel and the lady, who married Duke.

During his convalescence, Hanson studied law and thereafter began a career in law and politics, following in the footsteps of his father. However, the California gold fever lured the young adventurer west on an ill-starred venture. Hanson set out on horseback but, losing the horse, was forced to walk two hundred miles to San Francisco. Hanson survived the odyssey, despite his game leg. Considering the endeavor a failure, he returned to Winchester, Kentucky, and was practicing law within the year. There he developed a successful law practice before moving to Lexington, Kentucky. It was said of Hanson, who lacked a formal education, that he "read less and comprehended more law than any member of his profession in Kentucky." Hanson was married to Virginia Peters of Woodford County in 1853. Hanson also became a Freemason and joined the Good Samaritan Lodge No. 174 in 1856.

Hanson lost little time involving himself in the politics of the day. As a staunch Whig and unionist, he ran for political office in 1851, losing a seat in the state house of representatives by the slender margin of six votes to his erstwhile Mexican War commander, John Williams. Hanson is credited with bestowing the sobriquet of "Cerro Gordo" upon his former commander. During the political campaign, Hanson derisively charged that Williams's boasts of capturing cannon during the battle of Cerro Gordo, on April 17–18, 1847, were false, that the guns had been spiked and abandoned by a retreating foe, not seized in combat. He further claimed that Williams's company, to which Hanson belonged, broke and ran from the field. Williams, according to Hanson, outpaced all of his men in the hasty retreat. Despite these claims, "Cerro Gordo" Williams, as he was thereafter known, won the seat and was reelected in 1853.

Hanson did get elected to the state legislature in 1853 and again in 1855, representing Fayette County. He ran for U.S. Congress in 1857 and was again defeated, this time by James B. Clay, son of the renowned compromiser, Henry Clay. At this time, Hanson formed a partnership with Richard Hickman Prewitt, a graduate of the University of Louisville's law school. Their firm, Hanson and Prewitt, was one of the foremost in Lexington, covering all aspects of criminal and civil law. They remained partners until Hanson's death.

Hanson was a stalwart Whig until the demise of that party, at which time he affiliated himself with the Know-Nothing Party. During the secession crisis, Hanson remained strongly pro-Union and actively campaigned for John Bell during the Kentucky gubernatorial election and the 1860 presidential campaign. Hanson served as one of the electors from Kentucky in the electoral college in both the 1856 and 1860 elections.

With the advent of the Civil War, Hanson was faced with the same dilemma that confounded many of his contemporaries. Torn between his love for the Union and his sense of obligation to the rights of the State of Kentucky, he determined to uphold the Constitution but desired to remain neutral. To George D. Prentice, editor of the *Louisville Journal,* Hanson publicly avowed to be a "Union man without ifs or buts." Soon, however, he did a political about-face and decided that his future and his ties lay with the Confederacy. Hanson was not alone in his decision. Two of his four brothers joined the Confederate ranks, and two others embraced the Union cause. Like Kentucky, the Hanson family was torn apart by the war.

Commissioned a colonel in the Kentucky State Guard on November 23, 1860, Hanson resigned the following year to accept a commission in the Confederate army. He was held in such esteem by his fellow officers that they presented him with a fine horse and saddle. One of the presenters was his old rival William Duke, who felt that since he had made it difficult for Hanson to walk, he could at least make it easy for him to ride.

On August 28, 1861, he was commissioned a lieutenant colonel to rank from August 18 and was assigned to the Second Kentucky Infantry, under Col. James M. Hawes. The Second Kentucky had been organized at Camp Boone, Tennessee, on July 16, 1861. When Hawes resigned in September, Hanson assumed the command as colonel to rank from September 2. Hanson's regiment was assigned to serve under Brig. Gen. Simon B. Buckner in central Kentucky, where his initial duties included preparing the defenses of Bowling Green. Hanson was the interim commander of the Kentucky brigade, known as the Orphan Brigade because it was exiled from its home state. Hanson held the command until he was superseded by Brig. Gen. John C. Breckinridge in November.

Military life and order came naturally to Hanson. He understood what needed to be done intuitively, having what he himself called "horse sense" about such matters. As a commander Hanson was no-nonsense, paying close heed to drill and discipline. "Old Roger," or "Old Flintlock," as he was called by the brigade, was the best disciplinarian they ever had. He took pains to see that camps were set up and maintained in an orderly manner, that guards were properly mounted and relieved, and that fatigue parties were organized. Hanson was often seen making the rounds through camp at all hours of the night. He knew the duties and responsibilities of each of his officers and saw to it that they were in strict compliance. His rigid discipline and watchful eye even extended to the medical roll. Concerned that some of his men were malingering, Hanson ordered that no more than two men from each company could be listed on the sick rolls at any one time. He visited the camp hospital on a regular basis to enforce his edict. The result of all of this activity and watchfulness on his part was a body of orderly and well-disciplined men, efficient soldiers with a sense of confidence and pride.

In late January 1862 Hanson was sent to reinforce Fort Donelson, on the Cumberland River. The Second Kentucky was posted on the extreme right of the Confederate line along Hickman Creek. There, atop high bluffs, his men began digging rifle pits with the few tools available. His men were clothed in butternut gray hooded parkas against the cold and equipped with a new battle flag. In February, Union forces commanded by Brig. Gen. Ulysses S. Grant, flush with a recent victory at Fort Henry, were investing the fort.

On the morning of February 15, 1862, the Confederates mounted an assault to break through the Union lines. Hanson, eager for the fight, attacked in conjunction with forces under Col. Nathan B. Forrest. The Confederates advanced through the steep ravines and attacked the forces under W. H. L. Wallace. During the fighting, Hanson chided his men for ducking as bullets whizzed by, as there was no danger if they heard the bullet, because it had already passed. When Hanson himself ducked, he replied in response to the laughs of his men, "Boys, you may dodge a little if they come too close." Hanson ordered his men to charge with bayonets and not to fire until at close quarters. Partially screened by the terrain, the Confederate attack was able to advance across open ground to the Union positions, losing fifty men in the process. When the furious charge struck, the Federals fled, abandoning their camp, tents, cannon, ambulances, and other material. Hundreds of bluecoats were taken prisoner. Hanson's men were described by Wallace as a "strange and snotty crowd," who shot "terribly smartly." After the successful attack, some of Hanson's men were sent to support other parts of the line.

Despite the successful attack, Grant was able to mount a successful counterattack and reestablish his lines around the fort. The Confederates were driven back to their original starting positions, securely sealing off the breach made by the Confederate attack. Hanson narrowly escaped serious injuries, despite losing his horse to a cannonball and having his clothing pierced with bullets. The next day, it fell to Brig. Gen. Simon B.

Buckner to surrender the Confederate forces, including Hanson and his command, to Grant. Thus, Hanson became a prisoner of war.

Hanson was imprisoned initially at Camp Chase, in Columbus, Ohio, and later at Fort Warren, Boston. During the period of his imprisonment, he corresponded regularly with his wife. His old nemesis, George Prentice, the Louisville editor, in response to a note from General Buckner, offered to send Hanson a demijohn of whiskey, which, he jokingly wrote, was "already jugged—like Roger himself." General Breckinridge and others actively lobbied to have Hanson exchanged. "I regard Colonel Hanson a most valuable officer," wrote Breckinridge. Eli M. Bruce, a Kentucky businessman, lobbied the Confederate government, stating that Hanson was "the best colonel in our service." Hanson was out of prison on parole in Baltimore for a brief period before being confined again in Fort Warren. Despite the behind-the-scenes machinations and an initial deal for his release in May, Hanson was not officially exchanged until August 5, 1862.

He rejoined the army at Knoxville, Tennessee, in October, after the battle of Perryville. Breckinridge gave him command of the Orphan Brigade, consisting of the Second, Fourth, Sixth, and Ninth Kentucky and the Forty-first Alabama regiments. The brigade was encamped at Murfreesboro, Tennessee, where Hanson resumed his regimen of discipline and order until his men were once again in top form. According to one soldier, Hanson "brought down upon the 'boys' the strictest kind of discipline." Nonetheless, accounts of excess drinking, gambling, and vandalism abounded in the Orphan Brigade.

Hanson's wife actively lobbied to have him promoted to brigadier general. In December 1862, with President Jefferson Davis reviewing the troops, Hanson's men marched so precisely that his men claimed Hanson was promoted to brigadier general on the spot. Whether this is in fact the case, his commission is dated December 13, 1862, the day of the review.

In late December, active campaigning resumed, culminating at month's end with the battle of Murfreesboro. On December 31, 1862, Gen. Braxton Bragg's Army of Tennessee attacked Union major general William S. Rosecrans's Army of the Cumberland with a furious early-morning assault. In what would prove to be one of the bloodiest battles in the western theater, the Federal army was driven back, but not broken, and never relinquished its grip on the Nashville Pike and the vital Nashville and Chattanooga Railroad.

At Murfreesboro, Hanson's brigade was posted on Breckinridge's extreme left on Whayne's Hill and saw but limited action in the first day's fighting. On January 2, 1863, the respite for the Orphan Brigade ended. Bragg massed his army against the division of Horatio Van Cleve, posted on a hill at McFadden's Ford. The Union position was supported by more than fifty pieces of artillery across the river. Bragg ordered Breckinridge's division to make the assault and take the Union position, despite vehement protestation from Breckinridge on the inadvisability of the order.

When Hanson learned of the order for the suicidal attack, he denounced it as murderous and went on a tirade, vowing to murder Braxton Bragg. No doubt believing the vitriolic Kentuckian meant what he said, Breckinridge and other officers restrained Hanson until he cooled off. Hanson prepared his men for the attack. "I believe this will be my last," he said.

At 4:00 P.M. the attack began. The Orphan Brigade advanced smartly enough to draw Breckinridge's admiration. Hanson ordered his men to load, advance with fixed bayonets, fire at one hundred yards, and then charge. His men crashed through the underbrush, fired, and then charged the Union line. The Federals fled from their position and retreated across the river. Hanson pursued. Union artillery on the hill across the river now began firing in earnest. Hanson was almost immediately struck in the left knee by a shell fragment and mortally wounded. The fragment tore through muscles and bone and severed his femoral artery. He was tended to on the field by Dr. John O. Scott and Dr. J. C. Legare.

Hanson was evacuated by ambulance to the house of I. J. C. Haynes, in Murfreesboro. There he was administered to by doctors and tended to by his wife, Virginia, and Mrs. Breckinridge until he died, on Sunday, January 4, 1863. His last words, reputedly said to General Breckinridge, were, "I shall die in a just cause, having done my duty."

Hanson's widow made arrangements to have his body borne to Kentucky, but Federal authorities would not let her proceed beyond Nashville. Thus the general was buried there. After the war, in November of 1866, Hanson's body was removed from his Nashville burial place and escorted by an honor guard of those who had served under him to Louisville. Again, Federal authorities intervened, not to prevent the ceremonies, but to forbid "wearing the uniform or side arms or carrying the flag of the late rebel army, or marching by military organization."

After memorial services were held, Hanson was escorted to Lexington and reinterred in City Cemetery (now Lexington Cemetery) on November 11, 1866. In 1895, the survivors of the Orphan Brigade erected a monument, funded by subscription, in memory of the general and his wife, who died in 1888. The monument was dedicated on July 9, 1895, before a large crowd. General Roger W. Hanson, Camp No. 1844, Sons of Confederate Veterans, in Winchester, Kentucky, was named in his honor. Kentucky Historical Highway Marker 951, in Clark County, honors the five Hanson brothers who served in the Civil War.

BIBLIOGRAPHY

Cozzens, Peter. *No Better Place to Die.* Urbana: University of Illinois Press, 1990.

Davis, William C. *The Orphan Brigade.* New York: Doubleday, 1980.

————, ed. *The Confederate General.* 6 vols. Harrisburg, PA: National Historical Society, 1991.

Thompson, Ed Porter. *History of the Orphan Brigade.* Louisville, KY: Lewis N. Thompson, 1898.

—ROBERT I. GIRARDI

Brig. Gen. James Morrison Hawes

WHEN THE CIVIL War broke out, few Kentuckians were as thoroughly prepared for the coming challenges as James Morrison Hawes. Reared in a prominent political family, he had graduated from West Point, fought in the Mexican War, taught at his alma mater, studied at the Cavalry School of Saumur in France, and helped quell the growing sectional unrest in Kansas Territory. His early successes, however, did not prepare him for the scale or severity of the Civil War. Like many commanders during that conflict, the well-trained and apparently able James Hawes had a wartime career that never lived up to expectations.

Born in Lexington, Kentucky, on January 7, 1824, to Richard and Hattie Nicholas Hawes, James grew up as the oldest child within a successful family. With his father's young law practice thriving by the time of his birth, James's youth progressed along with Richard's growing political career. As James entered his teenage years, Richard had already served several terms as a Whig in the Kentucky House of Representatives and took a seat in the U.S. House of Representatives in 1837. Having received a good preparatory education and possessing the necessary political connections, James gained admission to the U.S. Military Academy at West Point and began his education there on July 1, 1841.

Upon his graduation in the late spring of 1845, twenty-ninth in his class of forty-one, Hawes immediately departed for cavalry service in Texas. With that state recently joining the Union, an occupying force had been dispatched to prevent further conflicts with Mexico. He remained in Texas until war broke out in 1846. From 1846 until 1848, 2nd Lt. Hawes fought throughout Mexico including service during the siege of Vera Cruz. Brevetted to first lieutenant for his bravery in the battle of San Juan de los Llanos, he also saw action at Contreras, Churubusco, and Molino del Rey and finished his tour in Mexico in glory.

With the Mexican War ended and a strong start to his military career secured, Hawes returned to West Point in 1848 as assistant instructor of infantry tactics. While there, he also taught mathematics and took it upon himself to teach the school's first course in cavalry tactics in 1849. The next year, he left the academy and traveled to Saumur, France, where he studied at the French cavalry school until 1852. Upon his return to the United States, he was ordered to Texas.

In early 1857, he took leave from his western assignment and married Marie J. Southgate on February 3. Returning west later that year, he joined Philip St. George Cooke's Second Dragoons at Fort Leavenworth, Kansas Territory, where the regiment started west on an expedition against the Mormons. Under the command of Albert Sidney Johnston, the Utah Expedition got a late start crossing the mountains, and Cooke's command at the tail of the column suffered terribly. Moving into hostile Mormon territory in October and November, Johnston's expedition was bogged down in snowy mountain passes, and he pushed his men forward to Fort Bridger, Utah Territory, where they spent the hard winter. After having horses, mules, and oxen sent from Fort Union, New Mexico Territory, Johnston had the animals distributed into the nearby small meadows where they could graze under the guard of Hawes and others within Cooke's command. In addition to working under future Confederate general Johnston and Union general Cooke, Hawes's comrades in the march against the Mormons included future Confederate generals Henry Hopkins Sibley and John Pegram. In late 1858, Hawes returned to Kansas Territory, where a military presence was needed to deter the ongoing sectional violence in the region.

By 1860, James's father had become a pro-Southern Democrat offering his support to John C. Breckinridge, and James was considering his future if the crisis escalated further. On May 9, 1861, James Hawes resigned his commission in the U.S. Army and returned home to Kentucky. Ordered to Clarksville, Tennessee, the following day, he took command of the nascent Second Kentucky Infantry and spent the summer there organizing Kentucky volunteers. On September 18 he was ordered to advance with a portion of the Second Kentucky Infantry, a battery, and a company of cavalry to the Green River in Kentucky. There he remained watching for any advance of the enemy. On August 28, President Jefferson Davis had nominated him to be colonel of the First Kentucky Infantry, which had been organized in Virginia. Hawes declined the transfer and resigned as a

colonel in the Provisional Army on October 14. Gen. Albert Sidney Johnston somehow made Hawes a major and stationed him in Glasgow, Kentucky, to recruit and train volunteers. In an October 27 letter to Gen.
Samuel Cooper, Johnston remembered his former subordinate by recom-
mending him for brigadier general. He wrote, "There is no one available
who, in my opinion, has higher qualifications for that position than Major
Hawes." On November 29, Davis nominated Hawes to be a captain in the
Regular Army, to rank from March 16, 1861. Finally, Hawes's fortunes
rose when Davis nominated him brigadier general on March 14, 1862, to
rank from March 5. However, as would become legend, Braxton Bragg
later discounted Hawes's abilities when he included him in a long list of
general officers who were, "in [his] judgment, unsuited for their responsible positions."

Reunited with his former commander Albert Sidney Johnston, Brig.
Gen. James Hawes assumed command of his cavalry. He spent the following weeks protecting the army's flanks as the great showdown that would
become the battle of Shiloh began to appear on the horizon. During the
battle, however, Hawes played a rather disappointing part by being assigned to hold various cavalry and infantry units in reserve and apparently
saw little of the field. In the aftermath of Shiloh, Hawes's brigade was
dispatched south toward Tupelo, Mississippi, to secure a section of the
Mobile and Ohio Railroad near Rienzi. Within a week, Hawes resigned
his command and volunteered to command an infantry brigade under a
close friend of his father's, John C. Breckinridge. By the end of April,
James had been reassigned, and one month later, he was commanding
Breckinridge's First Brigade.

Richard Hawes's life had also been significantly altered at Shiloh. Although he had left Kentucky and joined the Confederate Army in late
1861, his abilities did not lie on the battlefield. While he was temporarily
serving as a brigade commissary, the Confederate government appointed
him governor of Kentucky after the first Confederate governor, George
Johnson, was killed during the battle. Richard Hawes was officially sworn
into office on May 31 at Corinth, Mississippi.

By the summer of 1862, few Confederate generals were as well con-
nected politically as James Hawes, but militarily Braxton Bragg's afore-
mentioned mistrust may have affected Hawes's professional situation.
After serving under Breckinridge for several months, he was reassigned to
Little Rock, Arkansas, in late September 1862 to serve as Maj. Gen.
Theophilus Holmes's cavalry commander. Upon reporting to Holmes,
Hawes was given command of a brigade of cavalry and immediately dis-

patched to the White River, where he was to watch for Union movements in and around Helena, Arkansas. The remainder of 1862 and the first months of 1863 saw similar duty.

With Ulysses Grant determined to take Vicksburg, Mississippi, the Confederacy sprang into action, hoping to save the river city. By early June 1863, Hawes, who had left the cavalry to take over a brigade in John G. Walker's Texas infantry division, had arrived at Milliken's Bend, just north of Vicksburg, on the Louisiana side of the river. On June 6, a column of Union soldiers, including a significant number of black men, started toward Richmond, Louisiana, when they met a Confederate force. After a brisk fight, the Federals retreated back to Milliken's Bend, where they were assured of help from Union gunboats. Very early the next morning, Confederates pressed forward into the Union lines and by late morning, the situation for the Federals was dire. Hand-to-hand fighting hallmarked the climax of the battle, which very nearly resulted in the complete destruction of the Union force. By noon on June 7, the beaten and battered Unionists withdrew to safety.

Hawes and his men were twenty miles from Milliken's Bend on June 6, but upon receiving orders, they marched toward the site of the initial skirmish. At 10:30 P.M., he found the only convenient bridge crossing Walnut Bayou out and sent scouts upstream six miles to report on the condition of the nearest available crossing. Receiving a positive report, Hawes hurriedly ordered his men forward, and twelve hours later, he and his men arrived on the field of battle. Approaching Milliken's Bend at Young's Point, the location of the Union camp, Hawes hoped to reach the camp undetected. However, Brig. Gen. Henry McCulloch's attacking force stalled and began to retreat to safety, and Union gunboats began shelling the area around Young's Point, forcing Hawes to withdraw. Hawes reported that his men were so exhausted from their night march and the day's heat during the battle that a full five hundred of his Confederates were "rendered unfit for duty" with two hundred requiring removal to the rear.

Not all of Hawes's superiors were satisfied with his conduct at Young's Point. Maj. Gen. Richard Taylor reported that Hawes had "consumed seventeen hours in marching 19 miles over a good road without impediments" and that Taylor had not received any report from Hawes until late in the evening, after the battle had ended. Similar to Hawes's own account, Taylor stated that when Hawes arrived at Young's Point, he found favorable circumstances for an attack, despite his tardiness. Taylor contended that the enemy gunboats only fired two shells, both of which were well placed and damaging, and that alone convinced Hawes to call off his attack, although "he was satisfied he could carry the position, but did not think it would pay." Taylor also noted with frustration that Hawes retreated all the way back to the main road "in less time than he had taken to advance." Despite Taylor's condemnation of Hawes's prosecution of the battle that day, Maj. Gen. John Walker gave him the benefit of the doubt when he wrote, "I am satisfied that the conviction must have been overpowering that the attack would fail after a useless sacrifice of life, or he would not have taken the responsibility he did."

Walker's conciliatory words had no influence on Taylor's opinion of Hawes's activities that day. When Jefferson Davis read the battlefield reports, he noted, "This report and the indorsement indicate such failure to execute orders as should not be overlooked." Secretary of War James Seddon concurred and asked, "Should there be a court of inquiry or a court-martial, or would it be better to simply relieve Brigadier-General Hawes?" General Samuel Cooper then stepped in and offered the opinion that the decision should be left with Lt. Gen. Edmund Kirby Smith. Seddon concurred with Cooper's opinion and left Hawes's fate in Kirby Smith's hands.

Kirby Smith needed men, particularly commanders, and he saw through some of the pettiness surrounding the Hawes question, so he chose not to act on the allegations. On February 11, 1864, however, Hawes requested his own removal from command. Five days later his former commander and professional nemesis, Richard Taylor, wrote to Kirby Smith trying to smooth over the difficulty. In his visit to Alexandria, Louisiana, Kirby Smith, knowing that Hawes's men loved their commander and wished to keep him, "made a minute inspection of Hawes' and Randal's brigades in this division, and [had] never seen any troops in finer condition." He added, "No troops ever exhibited greater improvement in all the qualities of soldiers, and their present condition reflects great credit on the division and brigade commanders." Finally, Taylor got to his point: "I respectfully ask that Special Orders, No. 34, be revoked. General Hawes' brigade is in splendid order and a change would be very unfortunate." Despite Taylor's attempt to draw Hawes back to his brigade, he changed his mind by early April and wrote Kirby Smith, "I respectfully recommend that the order assigning General Hawes to duty in this district be countermanded, as he was relieved from duty here at his own request, and I am satisfied it would be for the interest of the service to leave Colonel [Xavier B.] Debray in command of his brigade."

Hawes's final command of the Civil War was of the city of Galveston,

Texas, and its defenses. Taking charge on April 15, 1864, Hawes issued Special Orders, No. 4 declaring Galveston to be an entrenched city and all local civilians to be treated as camp followers. As part of this order, Hawes caused some controversy by forcing all of the city's inhabitants to register with the army and to obey a nighttime curfew. Local reaction was strong; the city's mayor and aldermen unanimously condemned the order. This response drew Hawes's ire to the point that he asked his commander, Maj. Gen. John Bankhead Magruder, for permission to arrest the officials and expel them from his lines. Magruder tried to temper the reaction by modifying the order to allow the citizens to register with local officials instead of military officers, but the damage to Hawes's popularity had been done. He was now an enemy of the people on the scale of Benjamin "Beast" Butler. However unfavorable their opinion of Hawes and his infamous order, the citizens of Galveston soon resided in one of the safest cities in the Confederacy.

The next month, Hawes's command was tested by what became known as the "bread riot." With the Union blockade working and Texas effectively cut off from the rest of the South, provisions began running low. In response, Hawes ordered that the commissary restrict its trade to the military alone and stop selling to soldiers' family members completely. Angry women converged on Hawes's residence and office in protest of his order, and Hawes responded by having them arrested. By the end of the day, all but a handful had been released from custody and sent home, but Hawes ordered those still jailed to be put on trains for Houston with orders to stay out of Galveston.

For the third straight month, June brought more difficulty for Hawes. A runaway slave had been captured and remanded to the city jail. As Hawes saw the case, the slave should be released to his master; however, the civil officials refused to give the man up until his owner paid a delinquent fee. Tired of having his orders questioned by civilians, Hawes sent soldiers to take the keys from the city officials and turn the slave over to his owner. The officials then petitioned for and received a court order declaring Hawes's actions unlawful. As part of the order, the slave had to be returned to jail, but Hawes issued his General Orders, No. 24, a scathing evaluation of the loyalty of Galvestonians. He saw himself as surrounded by subversive civilians and believed that "treason of the darkest dye" existed in the city. Hawes announced that he interpreted his position as commander to authorize him to determine military necessity and to place that above all other conditions.

Hawes's uneasy tenure in Galveston was complicated by a yellow fever epidemic during the fall of 1864. Even the commander was infected and forced to bed while Col. Ashbel Smith, a physician and Galveston resident, took temporary command of the city. On April 14, 1865, the locally popular Smith returned to command when Hawes was relieved of duty. It was then and there that his long military career came to an end.

Upon the end of the war, Hawes joined Edmund Kirby Smith and several others in San Antonio on their trek to the relative safety of Mexico. Along the way, they overtook a group including John Magruder, Sterling Price, Jo Shelby, and three Confederate governors, and the group of luminaries crossed the Rio Grande at Eagle Pass on June 26, 1865. Within months, the men began the process of repatriation to their homeland thanks to President Andrew Johnson's amnesty proclamation. Hawes returned to Kentucky and lived out the remainder of his life as a hardware merchant in Covington. He died on November 22, 1889, and is buried in Covington's Highland Cemetery.

If an epitaph must be written for James Hawes, the Civil War general, it has to focus on his extensive military background and the respect he garnered from his men. As a pioneer in the military training of cavalrymen, Hawes became an indispensable part of the U.S. Army's prewar activities. However tactically sound he was, or how many of his wartime failures can be credited to factors beyond his control, in the end his lack of political acumen strained the pivotal relationships with Richard Taylor and the citizens of Galveston, Texas. Always the soldiers' general, Hawes can be remembered as a great cavalry tactician, military innovator, and leader of men.

BIBLIOGRAPHY

Cotham, Edward T., Jr. *Battle on the Bay: The Civil War Struggle for Galveston.* Austin: University of Texas Press, 1998.

Davis, William C., ed. *The Confederate General.* 6 vols. Harrisburg, PA: National Historical Society, 1991.

U.S. War Department. *The War of the Rebellion: A Compilation of the Official Records of the Union and Confederate Armies.* 70 vols. in 128 pts. Washington, DC: Government Printing Office, 1880–1901.

—BRIAN D. McKNIGHT

Brig. Gen. Benjamin Hardin Helm

THE SECOND DAY on the heavily
wooded Chickamauga battlefield
found Benjamin Hardin Helm in
a cedar thicket and in the thick of
a short and furious mid-morning
engagement that seemed, at these
close quarters, all Kentucky. Although presently serving in the
Army of Tennessee, Helm commanded the First Kentucky Brigade, better known as the "Orphan
Brigade," the largest and perhaps
hardest-fighting Confederate unit
recruited from a state never officially seceding from the Union
and never successfully occupied by
Southern forces.

If these Bluegrass rebels couldn't easily go home again, their bitter exile
wasn't for lack of trying. In the fall of 1863, Helm and his brigade formed
part of Gen. Braxton Bragg's attempt to counter Union major general William Rosecrans's offensive against the vital gateway and railway city of
Chattanooga, Tennessee. If "Old Rosy" gazed farther down south and beyond to Atlanta, the Orphans looked back up north to their farms and families in Kentucky. On that particular twentieth day of September, while
encouraging and emboldening his men, Helm reportedly pointed his sword
toward the enemy positions and shouted, "This is the road to Kentucky."

Conspicuously mounted, the lean and lanky thirty-two-year-old Confederate brigadier general spurred his horse and his men forward across
the broken ground against efficient, if impromptu, Federal breastworks.
Manning those indifferently arranged but perilously sharp abatis were
bluecoated Kentucky Union soldiers commanded by Virginia-born but
Union-loyal Maj. Gen. George Thomas whose performance on the nearby
Horseshoe Ridge would soon earn him the soubriquet "Rock of Chickamauga" and save for the Federal forces some degree of pride in what finally turned into a spectacular Confederate victory.

At the moment at hand, Ben Hardin Helm found himself literally and figuratively between a rock and a hard place. Two of his advancing regiments stalled at the enemy's log defenses while his remaining Kentuckians, leavened by the Forty-first Alabama, bravely charged but were held in check by the ferocious musket fire from unprotected portions of the hardscrabble Union line. Caught in an intense crossfire, the Confederates attacked again and again in an attempt to simply overwhelm the Federals. Third time was not the charm for Helm or his soldiers. In the course of an hour, the Orphan Brigade lost more than one-third of its men, numerous officers and their brigade commander. Struck on his right side and bleeding profusely, Helm swayed but remained in the saddle and tried to stay in command before finally allowing himself to be carried litter-bound to the rear. Mortally wounded, he lingered in great pain and died the next day, September 21, 1863. His final word was reportedly, either as a question or a statement, "Victory."

Given the Victorian and Confederate proclivity for sanctifying deathbed utterances, this attributed last statement might be taken with some doubt but, whatever the truth or the inflection, could also be used as a measure of Helm's life as a most representative Kentuckian. Fortunately born and reared, Helm seems blessed and cursed by family position and connection, while his military career remains a curious enterprise marked by good service and bad luck in a pursuit of elusive victory.

Benjamin Hardin Helm was born in Bardstown, Kentucky, on June 2, 1831, into a gentrified but not aristocratic family of wealth, power, and privilege. His state and town, kith and kin, all contributed to the context and content of his character in a sadly short but comfortably distinguished life. For all the consensus interpretations of the name, "Kentucky" proved for Helm more a place of significant resources and golden opportunities than as any "dark and bloody ground." A geographically rich and historically crucial frontier community and border state, Kentucky looked back to an Old Virginian Southland and forward to an Ohioan Midwest. Bardstown, the second-oldest city in the state and the county seat of Nelson County, had been settled in the early 1770s and could boast of an evolved and diverse civic history. It was a cathedral town and the center of western American Catholicism until 1841.

Helm's father was Kentucky native John LaRue Helm. Born on the Fourth of July of 1802 and outliving his Confederate-general son by five years, the father knew firsthand the hard times on frontier homesteads and deftly turned to the law and politics that elevated the family financially and socially. Appointed county attorney for Meade County in 1823, John met Lucinda Barbour Hardin, then a fourteen-year-old girl from nearby Bardstown. He courted her for seven years and married her on August 10, 1830. First elected to the Kentucky House of Representatives as a Whig in 1825, the twenty-three-year-old Helm was chosen for six more consecutive terms and selected as Speaker for five. Although he failed to win his only contest for the U.S. House of Representatives, he served one term (1844–1848) as state senator and as Speaker of that upper chamber, became lieutenant governor in 1848, governor in 1850, and would be elected to a second term as Kentucky's chief executive in 1867. From the statehouse, John Helm promoted internal improvements, especially turnpikes and railroads. He labored assiduously if controversially as president of the Louisville and Nashville Railroad Company from 1854 until 1860. Politically no Fire-Eater, he doubted that states had the right to secede but simultaneously asserted that the national government didn't have the power of coercion to make them stay, a belief system mirroring much of Kentucky's fence-sitting sentiments. His power and prosperity went hand-in-hand and he was able to provide the good prewar life for his six daughters and five sons.

Named for a maternal grandfather, Benjamin Hardin Helm was born to young and up-and-coming parents, attended the local military institute and graduated from West Point in 1851, ranking ninth in a class of forty-two cadets. His one-year service with the Second U.S. Dragoons in Pennsylvania and Texas hardly made Second Lieutenant Helm a professional officer, and, given the sparse martial nature of West Point's curriculum, he should be rightly considered a citizen-soldier more properly educated for his subsequent civilian life. Refuting the standard war-vintage photograph of a balding and owlish thirty-something officer, his West Point photograph shows a handsome young Helm with a full head of hair and a fine pair of romantic eyes. Well-heeled, well-educated (at public expense), and well-connected as the governor's son, Helm studied law at Harvard and the University of Louisville, becoming by turns a onetime state legislator and the state's attorney. After four years of public service combined with family partnerships in private practice, he grew prosperous enough to marry into another well-placed, slaveholding Kentucky family when he wed the arrestingly beautiful Emilie Todd, younger half sister of Mary Todd Lincoln, in 1856.

By all accounts quick-witted, he got along famously with his rising in-law Abraham and was able to keep up with Lincoln's jokes, storytelling, and repartee. Kentuckians all, the Lincolns, Todds, and Helms exemplify the complex national, regional, and familial tragedy of the American Civil War. Although differing philosophically and politically, Ben Hardin remained a favorite and Emilie the pet of both Lincolns before and during the conflict, with the president initially offering Helm a commission as major/paymaster in the Union army. The position was refused and Helm stayed south to raise the First Kentucky Cavalry.

His rapid advancement in rank certainly owed more to his extensive personal connections (and the South's intense need for trained officers) than to any apparent soldierly qualifications. Promoted to colonel in October of 1861, Helm served under fellow Kentuckian Simon Bolivar Buckner during the occupation of Bowling Green but missed the surrender of Fort Donelson and the Shiloh campaign by being assigned to northern Alabama. Appointed brigadier general in March of 1862, he rather muddied up his service record by reporting incorrectly that Union major general Don Carlos Buell was not moving to Ulysses S. Grant's aid at Pittsburg Landing, Tennessee. After the battle of Shiloh, Confederate commander P. G. T. Beauregard claimed to have received but doubted the message, as did the captured but skeptical Hornet's Nest hero Benjamin Prentiss when shown Helm's telegram during the battle.

Ordered to Vicksburg under Kentuckian Maj. Gen. John C. Breckinridge, Helm was assigned to protect the CSS *Arkansas* at Yazoo, Mississippi, and participated in Earl Van Dorn's ill-planned campaign against Baton Rouge in the late summer of 1862. Van Dorn, who had also missed Shiloh but was as inclined as Beauregard to conceive overly grand strategies, hoped to reverse the Federal advances in his theater of operation by knocking Union forces out of Louisiana's river capital, possibly as an adventurous and threatening preemptive strike against New Orleans. He ordered Breckinridge to select four thousand men from Vicksburg's defenders and quickly move them eastward over the railroad to Jackson, Mississippi, and entrain them south to Camp Moore, a Confederate training base deep in Louisiana's piney woods north of Lake Pontchartrain and eighty miles above New Orleans.

On July 27, 1862, Breckinridge, Helm, and portions of the Orphan Brigade began a nightmarish ride down the rickety New Orleans, Jackson and Great Northern Railroad. A shortage of railroad cars forced all supplies save arms and ammunition to remain behind in Vicksburg. Officers and men alike suffered mightily as they rode unprotected in the Deep South's merciless sun and driving rain. There had been fever back in their Mississippi camps, and more fever and measles were waiting at their Louisiana destination. Despite an infusion of some 1,000 soldiers at Camp

Moore, bad weather, bad health, and bad luck soon reduced the force to some 3,600 effectives.

Breckinridge doggedly began a two-day forced march westward across the southeastern Louisiana backcountry but dutifully reported his diffi-culties commanding and applying a force of men weakened by the heat, a lack of good water, and an absence of shoes. This ever-decreasing army had been divided into two separate divisions, with Helm serving as one of two brigade commanders under Brig. Gen. Charles Clark. As an officer in the first division, Ben Hardin Helm certainly rode booted and spurred, but he led by example, suffering all the slings and arrows of outrageously bad planning to arrive tired and edgy within striking distance of Union-occupied Baton Rouge.

The Confederates employed two hundred poorly armed and undisci-plined partisan rangers as cover for their faltering advance on enemy out-posts. While the Confederates waited in the early morning darkness of August 5 for enough light to launch an attack, these irregulars moved too far ahead and tangled with alert Union pickets. After a brief exchange of hostile fire, the rangers raced back to the security of their cautiously de-ploying army and crashed into leading units. In the general confusion and amid a flurry of friendly fire, several men were killed or wounded. Helm was dangerously injured, shattering his right leg in the fall of his ruined horse, and his aide-de-camp, Capt. Alexander H. Todd, the twenty-three-year-old half brother of Mary Todd Lincoln, was killed.

Crashing down with or being thrown from a horse may not seem like a romantically earned wound suffered while doing your duty in the face of the enemy, but the damage was severe enough to disorder and disable Helm and keep him out of the unfolding battle. Meeting stiff opposition from the Union army garrisoning Baton Rouge and the Union navy steaming up and down the riverfront, Breckinridge's logistically incapaci-tated army was unable to capture the city, pulled back, and marched away to fight another day. With Breckinridge's subsequent return to division commander, the Orphan Brigade, which might have gone to Helm, now fell to Roger W. Hanson until that Kentucky officer fell at Murfreesboro on January 2, 1863. As Breckinridge rallied the leaderless brigade, he re-portedly lamented, "My poor orphans! My poor orphans!"

Between August of 1862 and January of 1863, Helm performed main-ly administrative and depot duties while slowly recovering from his fall. With Hanson's death, Helm became commander of the Orphan Brigade, served honorably in that capacity through the steady retreats of an outmaneuvered Gen. Braxton Bragg in the Tullahoma campaign of June 1863 and continued to do so until fatally wounded at Chickamauga on September 20. Fully three weeks passed before the grievous but unquestionable news of his death reached his family. Helm's body had been removed to Atlanta and Emilie came up from Alabama for her husband's funeral in St. Paul's Episcopal Church. Bragg promised to request from Grant permission for the widowed Mrs. Helm to return to her family in the still-Union state of Kentucky, but her mother obtained a pass from President Lincoln so her daughter could return home.

Unknown to Lincoln, Emilie was denied entry unless she took an oath of allegiance to the United States, an act she adamantly refused as an affront to the memory of her fallen husband. The Lincolns, who had lost a son to illness and a number of their Southern kinsmen in the war, took the news of Helm's death hard. The president, upon being notified of the complications by some kindly Federal officers, summoned Emilie, sans oath, to the White House where she was met with the warmest of affection and the deepest of sympathy.

Lincoln was observed to be never so moved as when he heard of Helm's death, saying "I feel as David did of old when he was told of the death of Absalom." But the First Family's obvious grief did much to harden Northern hearts against Mary Todd Lincoln, and the president soon had to defend Emilie's presence at the White House against political and personal attacks. Widow Helm never remarried, staying in perpetual mourning and raising their children alone. In 1884, survivors of the Orphan Brigade oversaw the disinterment of Helm's remains and his reburial in the family cemetery in Elizabethtown, Kentucky.

Assessing his career remains problematic. His combat experiences, ineffectively ending before Baton Rouge was lost or Chickamauga won, were rather minimal and show no particular military brilliance, but he commanded and fought well when he could. Respected before, during and after the war, Helm did his duty for his people and place. That he is remembered more as a Lincoln anecdote than as a Confederate officer is due as much to "the fortunes of war" as are his various and final wounds. None of his campaigns, save the last, can be considered Southern victories, but he appears to have escaped the obscurity to which Confederate generals in the western theater were consigned. Benjamin Hardin Helm rode, fought, and fell with and for Kentucky, rendering good service and enduring bad luck in pursuit of an elusive victory as an orphan in the Lost Cause of a lost state and nation.

BIBLIOGRAPHY

Davis, William C., ed. *The Confederate General.* 6 vols. Harrisburg, PA: National Historical Society, 1991.

McMurtry, Gerald. *Ben Hardin Helm: "Rebel" Brother-in-Law of Abraham Lincoln.* Chicago: Civil War Round Table of Chicago, 1943.

U.S. War Department. *The War of the Rebellion: A Compilation of the Official Records of the Union and Confederate Armies.* 70 vols. in 128 pts. Washington, DC: Government Printing Office, 1880–1901.

—CHARLES ELLIOTT

Brig. Gen. George Baird Hodge

THE SON OF WILLIAM and Sarah Baird Hodge, George B. Hodge was born in Fleming County, Kentucky, on April 18, 1828. After attending Maysville Seminary, he entered the U.S. Naval Academy and graduated in 1845. The young midshipman saw active duty during the Mexican War as an aide to Capt. David Connor, commodore of the fleet at the siege of Vera Cruz. He resigned his naval commission in 1851 and settled in Newport, Kentucky, where he began the practice of law. During the same year he married Keturah M. Tibbatts, who bore him six children. In 1853 he made an unsuccessful run for Congress on the Whig ticket. With the collapse of the Whig Party, Hodge cast his fortunes with the Democratic Party and was elected to the Kentucky House of Representatives in 1859. During the critical 1860 presidential contest he served as an elector at large on the ticket of native Kentuckian John C. Breckinridge.

Hodge continued to serve in the legislature throughout the secession crisis and on January 16, 1861, submitted a series of resolutions that included support for Kentucky senator John J. Crittenden's compromise resolutions. A conditional unionist, Hodge deplored secession but could not support a Union held together by military force. The failure of the pro-Southern faction to win the majority needed to call a sovereignty convention after Fort Sumter led Hodge to facilitate a change in tactics. As chair of the key Committee on Federal Relations, he helped guide the state toward adopting an official policy of neutrality on May 16. It should be noted that he later admitted that neutrality did not symbolize Kentucky's reluctance to enter the conflict. Rather the measure was regarded by pro-Southern legislators as the means to create a protective zone that would prevent the Lincoln administration from using Kentucky as an invasion route.

The Confederate seizure of Columbus, Kentucky, led the Union Party–dominated legislature to abandon neutrality on September 18, and many prominent Southern State Rights leaders were indicted for treason and marked for arrest. Hodge fled Kentucky on September 23 and made his way through the rugged mountains of eastern Kentucky to Virginia with George W. Johnson, who was destined to serve as Kentucky's first Confederate governor. Making his way to Bowling Green, Kentucky, he subsequently enlisted as a private in Brig. Gen. Simon B. Buckner's command. With the arrival of Brig. Gen. John C. Breckinridge in early November, Hodge was promoted to the rank of captain and assistant adjutant general on his staff.

Captain Hodge ably wielded both pen and sword from the fall of 1861 to the spring of 1862. He served as a delegate to the Russellville Convention held November 18–20, which established the provisional government of Kentucky. He served on Gov. George W. Johnson's executive council until he was elected as a Kentucky representative to the Provisional Congress of the Confederacy.

Hodge took his seat in Richmond on January 11, 1862. When the final session concluded on February 17, the Kentuckian resumed active duty on Breckinridge's staff and distinguished himself at the battle of Shiloh on April 6–7, 1862. Indeed, his horse was killed under him during the height of the first day's fighting. Another close call on the second day was recalled with some amusement nearly fifty years later by a veteran of the Orphan Brigade. Breckinridge and his staff had halted beneath a huge, spreading oak when a shell from a Union gunpoint exploded high in the branches above them. Breckinridge and his escort immediately scattered. However Hodge, whose poor hearing was no doubt further impaired by the din of battle, failed to apprehend the danger until he looked up. He swiftly "electrified his charger with both spurs" and barely escaped death from the falling limbs and branches.

Hodge resigned his commission on May 2, 1862, after his election as Kentucky representative for the Eighth District to the First Confederate Congress. Taking his seat on August 18, Hodge, no doubt as a result of his Mexican War service, was subsequently appointed to the committees for Naval Affairs and Ordnance and Ordnance Stores. His tenure in office was marked by efforts to enlarge and fully supply the Confederacy's armed forces. When the forces of Braxton Bragg and E. Kirby Smith prepared to enter Kentucky in August 1862, Hodge joined the Kentucky delegation in urging President Jefferson Davis to permit John C. Breckinridge's command to participate in the great offensive.

Although he longed to return to active duty, Hodge continued to serve in Congress until May 8, 1863. Prior to that date, on April 6, he received authority from the secretary of war to raise a mounted command in Kentucky. Promoted to the rank of colonel, he was sent to Maj. Gen. Simon B. Buckner's Department of East Tennessee, where he briefly served as inspector-general of the garrison at Cumberland Gap.

On July 6 he was assigned to the command of a small mounted brigade in Brig. Gen. William Preston's command based in the District of Southwestern Virginia. Service with Preston's command, which defended the Kentucky-Virginia border, provided Hodge with the opportunity for active service on his native soil. By late July, Hodge was prepared to cooperate with Confederate cavalry based in East Tennessee on a joint raid into central Kentucky. However a Union cavalry strike against the crucial Virginia and Tennessee Railroad at Wytheville, Virginia, on July 18 prevented Hodge's departure. Hodge's Kentucky and Virginia mounted infantry joined Brig. Gen. John S. Williams's cavalry in driving the raiders back into present-day West Virginia.

Any further hopes of entering Kentucky were dashed in August when Buckner's force, including most of Preston's border command, was ordered southward to reinforce Braxton Bragg's hard-pressed Army of Tennessee. Hodge's Brigade was accordingly transferred to Brig. Gen. John Pegram's Division of Forrest's Cavalry Corps. The Kentuckian's command held the extreme right of Forrest's line at the battle of Chickamauga and was not actively engaged in the great Confederate victory. In the aftermath of the Confederate victory, however, Hodge participated in Forrest's advance beyond the Hiawassee River that drove Maj. Gen. Ambrose Burnside's mounted forces from Charleston, Athens, and Calhoun, Tennessee. As part of Brig. Gen. Henry B. Davidson's division, Hodge's troopers subsequently participated in Maj. Gen. Joseph Wheeler's First Tennessee Raid (September 29–October 9, 1863) and were heavily engaged at Farmington, Tennessee, on October 7. Virtually unsupported, his single brigade covered the Confederate retreat. Hodge afterwards reported that he lost nearly a third of his command in five and a half hours of continuous fighting against overwhelming odds.

Hodge was temporarily relieved of command on October 15 and ordered to report to Richmond. On November 21, 1863, he was appointed brigadier general. On November 23, he was ordered to return to Bragg's Army of Tennessee and resume command of his old brigade, which had been assigned to Brig. Gen. Frank C. Armstrong's division of Wheeler's Cavalry Corps. Like many Kentuckians Hodge detested Braxton Bragg and immediately petitioned for a transfer. Accordingly, in January 1864 Hodge's Brigade was ordered to return to southwestern Virginia. During his northward march through the Carolinas, he requested permission to lead a cavalry raid into Kentucky that would sweep northward toward Cincinnati and then strike the heart of the Bluegrass. A second request to enter Kentucky was made when he reached Wytheville, Virginia, on February 3. However, his plan was not approved, and on February 10 he was ordered to report to Lt. Gen. James Longstreet for duty in East Tennessee.

His frustrated hopes were compounded by the news that his recent promotion was not confirmed by Congress. Hodge had openly expressed doubt about the wisdom of secession before leaving that body in the spring of 1863. During his tenure in Congress, Hodge had made powerful political enemies in Richmond by warmly defending his old commander, John C. Breckinridge, during the course of the latter's controversy with Bragg following the battle of Murfreesboro. The proud Kentuckian tendered his resignation but withdrew it on February 29, 1864.

Relinquishing command of his brigade, Hodge was appointed a colonel and adjutant and inspector general in the Confederate army on March 17, 1864. Ordered to report for duty in Lt. Gen. Leonidas Polk's Department of Alabama, Mississippi and East Louisiana, he conducted an extensive inspection tour of all troops within the department during April and May. Always eager for action, Hodge also urged his superiors to grant permission to coordinate a secret mission that would destroy the immense store of enemy supplies at Nashville. Instead, on June 4 he was ordered to conduct an inspection tour of the thinly defended region in western Mississippi and east Louisiana. President Davis personally instructed him on June 29 to investigate the role of Confederate officials in the illegal cotton trade with the enemy. On July 14, Hodge reported to Davis that many in the region had lost faith in the Confederate cause and that the illegal cotton trade was endemic to the region.

Ironically, on August 4 Hodge was appointed brigadier general for a second time and placed in command of the troubled District of Southwest Mississippi and East Louisiana with headquarters at Clinton, Louisiana. With a mere handful of troops at his disposal Hodge was ordered to obtain intelligence from New Orleans, observe enemy movements on the Mississippi, and suppress the illegal cotton trade.

Hodge took formal command on August 26 and in the months that followed raised the number of his effective troops from four hundred to well over a thousand. Nevertheless, Hodge's scattered forces barely repulsed a Union advance from Natchez in fighting around Woodville,

Mississippi, October 3–6, 1864. However, his chief struggle centered on efforts to suppress the illegal cotton trade, which by his own admission made him extremely unpopular with the civilian population. In a dispatch dated November 7, 1864, from his headquarters at Liberty, Mississippi, he lamented to fellow Kentuckian Col. William P. Johnston, "My life is a very lonely one."

On November 14, 1864, Union brigadier general Albert L. Lee launched a major cavalry raid from Baton Rouge and swiftly overran Hodge's district. Hodge's headquarters at Liberty was captured on the night of the sixteenth, and the Kentuckian was forced to flee alone on foot for twenty-four miles. He rallied elements of his command and organized what proved to be a futile pursuit. The failure of certain subordinates to picket key positions and send warning of the enemy advance led Hodge to suspect that the raiders were considerably aided by "cotton thieves" from within his own command. He requested a court of inquiry, which on March 9, 1865, absolved him of all blame for the humiliating defeat.

Despite the fact that the Confederate Senate rejected his promotion again on February 8, 1865, Hodge never relinquished his rank. However, his district was dissolved earlier that month, and he subsequently reported to Brig. Gen. Wirt Adams, who commanded the new District of South Mississippi and East Louisiana. Still operating in his former territory, Hodge checked a Union advance from Baton Rouge on March 7, 1865. He was nominated to be second auditor of the Confederate Treasury Department on March 13, but the Senate rejected it the next day. Consequently, Hodge remained in the field and established his headquarters at Jackson, Mississippi. On March 25, he reported to President Davis that his force had been entirely stripped of regular troops and he could no longer guarantee the safety of the region with poorly organized reserves.

On April 26, 1865, Hodge, at the direction of his superiors, negotiated a suspension of hostilities between the Union forces at Vicksburg and Confederate forces in Mississippi and East Louisiana. A Union veteran recalled, "On the occasion General Hodge was in full dress uniform and was as imposing a military figure as I ever saw. He was a Chesterfield in manners and made a pleasing impression upon the Federal officers." The Kentuckian was among the forces surrendered by Lt. Gen. Richard Taylor at Meridian, Mississippi, on May 10, 1865.

On the day he surrendered, Hodge petitioned the Union authorities for permission to return briefly to his Kentucky home. Under the impression that Kentucky Confederates would never be permitted to resume their former residence in their native state, he wished to visit his family in

Newport before he took up residence in Tuskegee, Alabama. Hodge, who had been indicted for treason in the Kentucky Federal courts, had enough political enemies in Newport to protest a movement to obtain a formal pardon from President Andrew Johnson on July 21, 1865. However, exile would not be his fate, and he was able to return to his former home in September 1865.

By 1866 he had resumed both his former residence and the practice of law. Although he also resumed his political career, Hodge did not blindly follow Kentucky's former Confederates into the Democratic Party. Indeed, in the 1872 presidential election he was chosen elector-at-large for the moderate Liberal Republican ticket headed by Horace Greeley. He subsequently presided over Kentucky's electoral college, which convened in Frankfort on December 4. In 1873 he was elected to a four-year term as state senator from Campbell County on the Democratic ticket. Hodge was nominated as a Democratic candidate for governor in 1875, only to be one of three respected Confederate veterans to be defeated in the primaries by the youthful James B. McCreary, who had served as a field officer in John Hunt Morgan's command.

The same period saw Hodge devote his talents to history. He not only wrote a brief account of his association with Breckinridge's legendary Orphan Brigade but also assisted Richard H. Collins in preparing an updated version of his father's classic *History of Kentucky* in 1874. Although the practice of dueling was fading in the postwar years, Hodge balanced his scholarly and political pursuits by agreeing to deliver a challenge from Judge Patrick U. Major to John A. Cockerill, the editor of the *Cincinnati Enquirer,* who had publicly attacked the Kentucky jurist in the columns of his paper. The journalist brushed the challenge aside, and the matter ended without bloodshed.

Failing health, complicated by increasing deafness, forced Hodge into retirement after his term in the General Assembly ended in 1877. He purchased a plantation at Longwood, Orange County, Florida, and spent the remainder of his years as a gentleman farmer. In 1889 he successfully applied for a veteran's pension on the basis of his Mexican War service. On August 1, 1892, he suffered a fatal stroke while out walking near his Florida residence. His body was discovered later that night by a passerby. After a temporary burial, his remains were brought to Newport in September and interred in Evergreen Cemetery.

Hodge was fondly remembered by Kentuckians of his generation as "an able lawyer, a shrewd politician, a handsome writer [and] a ready and enthusiastic popular speaker." Following his death, a former Union veteran recalled that the "social element was strong in him and his spirit was knightly."

BIBLIOGRAPHY

Davis, William C., ed. *The Confederate General.* 6 vols. Harrisburg, PA: National Historical Society, 1991.

Hodge, George B. *Sketch of the First Kentucky Brigade.* Frankfort: Kentucky Yeoman Office, 1874.

U.S. War Department. *The War of the Rebellion: A Compilation of the Official Records of the Union and Confederate Armies.* 70 vols. in 128 pts. Washington, DC: Government Printing Office, 1880–1901.

—JAMES M. PRICHARD

Gen. John Bell Hood

GEN. JOHN BELL HOOD was the second-highest-ranking Confederate officer from Kentucky, after Albert Sidney Johnston. His record in the Civil War is a disparate combination of early, brilliant success as brigadier in the Army of Northern Virginia, 1862; tragic and debilitating wounds in the summer of 1863 that caused him to be hailed in the South as a martyred hero; promotion to corps command, for which he had shown no talent beyond battlefield gallantry; and promotion higher still to army command, for which he was probably not entitled, save for the Confederacy's need for promotable officers in its shrinking talent pool, in the summer of 1864. Promoted at the age of thirty-three, he was the youngest of the Confederacy's eight full general officers. Hood is also the only Confederate raised to full general but later demoted to lieutenant general by act of Congress.

On June 29, 1831, Hood was born in Owingsville, forty miles east of Lexington. His parents, Dr. John and Theodosia French Hood, were land- and slave-owners in the eastern Bluegrass. Young John attended school there, without any noteworthy record. With aid from an uncle in Congress, he secured appointment to the Military Academy. He entered West Point in July 1849 and graduated four years later, forty-fourth in his class of fifty-two, with 374 demerits. After two years of duty on the West Coast, Hood served with the Second Cavalry on the Texas frontier. While on extended furlough from September 1860, Hood submitted his resignation from the army on April 16, 1861.

Four days later Hood received his Confederate commission as first lieutenant of cavalry. After recruiting in Kentucky, he was sent to Virginia and promoted to major on May 31. On October 1, he assumed the colonelcy of the Fourth Texas Infantry. On March 6, 1862, he was pro-

moted to brigadier general and given command of the Texas Brigade—
three regiments of Texans plus the Eighteenth Georgia. Already engaged
in several small fights, Hood cemented his reputation for battlefield courage at Gaines' Mill, June 27, 1862, when he led his men on foot in a
charge that broke the Yankee line. The young brigadier won more laurels
two months later at Second Manassas. Placed in command of a small division, Hood took part in Maj. Gen. James Longstreet's crushing flank attack on Maj. Gen. John Pope's army, August 30. "The gallant Hood," as
some began to call him, had become a shining star in the Army of Northern Virginia.

Hood's star shone brightly at Antietam on September 17. Again,
though still brigadier, Hood commanded a demidivision of Evander Law's
and his own Texas Brigade on the left of Lee's line. Hood's Division not
only stopped the attack of Joseph Hooker's corps but also drove the Yankees back in a fierce counterattack that helped stabilize Gen. Robert E.
Lee's threatened flank. Hood lost half his men, but for the third time that
summer the young Kentuckian—now thought of as a Texan—saw how a
bold infantry attack could turn the tide of battle.

After Antietam, Stonewall Jackson recommended Hood for promotion to major general. Lee endorsed Jackson's suggestion, and Hood was
promoted, effective October 10. In the army reorganization announced
in November 1862, Hood took charge of a four-brigade division in
Longstreet's corps. The newly promoted Kentuckian's future looked
bright indeed. "Anyone who had followed the operations of the Army
after Gaines' Mill," writes Douglas Southall Freeman, "would have said
that of all the officers under Longstreet, the most likely to be a great
soldier was Hood."

Yet for virtually the next year Hood had no real opportunity to demonstrate the one trait—combat courage—that had won him promotion
from first lieutenant to major general, all in eighteen months. At Fredericksburg Hood's Division did not come under attack. Five months later, at
Chancellorsville in May 1863, his command was detached from the army.
At Gettysburg, Hood's Division did not arrive in time to take part in the
first day's fight, July 1. On the second, just as Longstreet's attack on the
Union left was getting under way, Hood was taken out almost before the
battle began when Union shell fragments struck him in the left arm. Sent
to the rear, he was spared amputation, but his arm hung useless for the rest
of his life. Two and a half months later, Hood was transferred to Georgia
with his division, arriving in time for the battle of Chickamauga. In the
Confederates' breakthrough attack against Rosecrans's center on Septem-

ber 20, Hood was riding in the rear of his troops when a Yankee bullet struck his right leg. That night surgeons amputated at the thigh, rendering Hood even more a cripple.

At the same time, these tragic wounds added to Hood's persona a new element, that of wounded knight, the sacrificial hero, a martyr for the cause. Recovering in Richmond during the winter of 1863–1864, Hood became a hero. Soon came calls for his promotion. After Chickamauga, Longstreet recommended Hood's elevation to lieutenant general "for distinguished conduct and ability" in the recent battle. Secretary of War James Seddon endorsed the promotion, if for no other reason than to reward "a true hero," a "Paladin of the fight," and to express the "gratitude of the Confederacy." As early as October 29, President Jefferson Davis informed Braxton Bragg, "I will promote Major-General Hood to be a lieutenant-general." On February 11, 1864, the Senate confirmed Hood as lieutenant general.

In the Army of Tennessee Gen. Joseph E. Johnston, who succeeded Bragg after the humiliation at Missionary Ridge, had an opening for an infantry corps commander. The secretary of war accordingly ordered Hood back to Georgia; he arrived on February 25. Sherman opened the Atlanta campaign on May 5 with his advance on the Confederate position at Dalton. In the following weeks Johnston gave Hood key battlefield assignments. At Resaca on the second day, May 15, Hood's Corps charged the Union left and overran the enemy line before Federal artillery drove the Southerners back. At Cassville, May 19, Hood's Corps was given responsibility for the attack by which Johnston hoped to crush part of Sherman's army as it advanced in multiple, unsupported columns. Sweeping out to strike Hooker's corps, Hood's videttes came into unexpected contact with enemy cavalry that suggested another Union column approaching his flank. Hood canceled the assault, a decision with which Johnston could only regretfully concur. A week later Sherman's advance brought the two armies around New Hope Church. On May 28 Johnston called for Hood to lead a flank assault on the enemy position. But in advancing, Hood found the Federals fortified. He reported this to Johnston, who again was forced to call off the attack.

A month later, before Kennesaw Mountain, Johnston ordered Hood's Corps from the Confederate right to the left in order to block the enemy's turning movement against that flank. On June 22 at Kolb's Farm Hood ordered an assault without notifying Johnston's headquarters; the charge was bloodily repulsed and Hood was criticized for ordering it. A week later Federal turning marches forced Johnston to retreat to Smyrna, then to the north bank of the Chattahoochee. Enemy crossings upstream at Roswell compelled the army's withdrawal south of the river on the night of July 9–10, into the outer defenses of Atlanta. An alarmed Davis concluded that Johnston would have to be removed if Atlanta were to have a chance of being saved.

At Lee's suggestion, the president and his cabinet considered William J. Hardee, senior corps commander in the army. But Hardee had already turned down command of the army in late 1863, and Hood had told Bragg, now the president's adviser, that he wanted it. More importantly, Hood was a proven fighter, just what the crisis before Atlanta needed. By telegram of July 17, Johnston was relieved, and Hood, promoted to temporary rank of full general, took command of the army.

Hood inherited a bad situation. He was outnumbered almost two-to-one, maybe 52,000 Confederate effectives against Sherman's 90,000 men (organized in a group of three armies). Federal infantry were converging north and east of Atlanta, just a few miles outside of town, already cutting two of the three railroads feeding the Confederate army. Atlanta by this point may have been doomed to fall, but Hood (with the backing of Davis) was determined that it would not without a fight. In three attacking battles he tried to damage separate elements of Sherman's army group. On July 20, as George H. Thomas's Army of the Cumberland crossed Peachtree Creek north of the city, Hood sent Hardee's and A. P. Stewart's corps to attack the Yankees before they could dig in. Despite heavy fighting, the Southerners were repulsed, suffering approximately 2,500 casualties to Thomas's 1,900.

In Hood's second battle, Hardee's Corps delivered a Jacksonian flanking attack east of Atlanta. After an all-night march to strike James B. McPherson's Army of the Tennessee in flank and rear on July 22, Hardee achieved initial success. But the Yankees fought back, and by the end of the day the exhausted Southerners were forced to withdraw to their original positions. Casualties in this "battle of Atlanta" numbered 4,000 U.S. troops (including McPherson, who was killed in action) and 5,500 Confederates. Sherman then sent McPherson's, now Oliver O. Howard's, army west of Atlanta, aiming to cut the rebels' last railway to Macon. On July 28 Hood countered this move by sending Stephen D. Lee's and Stewart's corps out to strike Howard's flank at Ezra Church. But the Federals were dug in, and Lee ordered a piecemeal frontal assault with predictable repulse and lopsided losses (3,000 Confederates killed, wounded, and missing, to 600 Federals).

Throughout August Sherman extended his lines southward toward the railroad. Hood lengthened his lines, too, protecting the rails with a line of fortifications extending well southwest of the city. Following Secretary of War James Seddon's suggestion to launch a cavalry raid to cut Sherman's railroad back to Chattanooga, Hood sent Joseph Wheeler and half the army's cavalry well into the Federal rear in mid-August. But Wheeler never seriously damaged the Western and Atlantic Railroad in north Georgia before entering Tennessee and riding himself out of the campaign.

Finally, in late August Sherman gave up his investment of Atlanta. Leaving an infantry corps at the Chattahoochee threatening the city, Sherman took the rest of his men in a wide march southward, then east, aiming to cut Hood's last rail link well below Atlanta. Hood was unable to stretch his lines far enough as Sherman's right headed for Jonesboro. Hood's belated response, an unsuccessful attack on Howard's army at Jonesboro on August 31, became irrelevant when other Federal units cut the Macon and Western several miles to the north. On the night of September 1, Hood ordered the evacuation of Atlanta. Union troops entered the next day.

Having retreated southwest of Atlanta to Lovejoy's Station, on September 10 the Army of Tennessee counted just thirty-eight thousand officers and men present for duty. Sherman with his much larger force sat secure in the fortifications of Atlanta, and Hood could not attack him. On September 6 he wrote President Davis that he planned to march the army to the West Point Railroad and resupply, then march north, crossing the Chattahoochee, advancing into north Georgia to strike the Western and Atlantic and cut Sherman's lifeline, perhaps drawing him out of Atlanta. On September 19 he set his plan in motion, moving the army west to Palmetto and the West Point Railroad.

Hood's decision to assume the offensive was a desperate gamble. The hard summer's campaign and the loss of stores in Atlanta's evacuation had left many of Hood's men without shoes and clothing, or even small arms and ammunition. Nevertheless, when Davis conferred with Hood at Palmetto, September 25–27, the president approved the general's plan as the best one available.

The army crossed the Chattahoochee on September 29. On October 12–13 Hood's men tore up the railroad north of Resaca, but hearing that Federals were approaching in force, Hood moved the army into northeast Alabama. At that point, apparently, Hood determined to march into Tennessee. Delayed by bad weather, the army crossed the Tennessee River November 18–20. Hood's objective was never clearly stated to his superiors, but it appears to have been Nashville. On November 24, the Confederates began skirmishing with contingents of Maj. Gen. John M. Schofield's small army at Columbia. At Spring Hill, November 29, Hood came within a hair of closing a destructive trap on the retreating Schofield. The next day Hood ordered a frontal assault on Schofield's entrenched position at Franklin. In the heroic Confederate charge there six thousand Southerners were killed, wounded, and captured; six generals were killed, including the renowned Pat Cleburne; another five generals were wounded, with one captured. Fifty-five regimental commanders were casualties. As historian Richard McMurry has written, "the leadership of the army had been shot away."

Following Schofield's retreating forces, Hood stubbornly ordered an advance to Nashville. On December 3 Hood's troops began digging in south of the state capital, too weak to assail the combined forces of Schofield and George Thomas, which numbered 50,000 strong to maybe 23,000 for Hood. After much preparation, Thomas attacked December 15–16, routing the Army of Tennessee. Its survivors limped with Hood back into north Mississippi. On December 31, their demoralized commander could only report 18,700 officers and men present.

On January 13, 1865, Hood asked to be relieved of command. Three days later Davis replaced him with Lt. Gen. Richard Taylor. On the twenty-third Hood formally transferred command of what was left of his army to Taylor and began making his way to Richmond. The Confederate Congress added a final humiliation. As called for in the law of May 1864 that gave Hood his temporary rank of general, the Senate should have confirmed Hood's pro tem status but never did. The body had adjourned in mid-June, a month before Davis made the promotion, and did not reconvene till early November. By that time Atlanta was lost and Hood's Tennessee campaign was under way; senators apparently opted to await the outcome. Technically, with his resignation from army command, Hood reverted to his previous rank as lieutenant general. But just to make sure, during its last days in session, March 16, 1865, the Senate passed a resolution: "Resolved, that General J. B. Hood, having been appointed General, with temporary rank and command, and having been relieved from duty as Commander of the Army of Tennessee, and not having been reappointed to any other command appropriate to the rank of General, he has lost the rank of General, and therefore cannot be confirmed as such." Hood was painfully aware of his demotion. When he applied for pardon from President Andrew Johnson, writing from Galveston in October 1865, Hood referred to himself as having held the Confederate rank of lieutenant general and temporary general.

Settling in New Orleans, Hood turned to the insurance business and in 1868 married Anna Marie Hennen; he was thirty-six, she six years younger. Her prominent family's wealth, though much reduced by the war, helped assure the Hoods a comfortable lifestyle. Through eleven years of marriage they had eleven children.

After the war Hood talked of writing a memoir to justify his actions in the campaigns of 1864 and began to gather archival materials. To counter accusations of Johnston's *Narrative of Military Operations* (1874), Hood set down a long "Reply." The release in 1875 of Sherman's *Memoirs,* also not flattering to Hood, prompted him to expand his "Reply" into a fuller reminiscence of his war service. Hood had completed his manuscript when yellow fever struck New Orleans in the summer of 1879. Anna died on August 24; a daughter passed away two days later. Hood died August 30. His memoir, *Advance and Retreat,* was published the next year and remains Hood's valiant effort to defend a war record that boasts great initial accomplishment but ultimate failure. He is buried in the Hennen family tomb in Metairie Cemetery, New Orleans.

Bibliography

Davis, William C., ed. *The Confederate General.* 6 vols. Harrisburg, PA: National Historical Society, 1991.

Freeman, Douglas Southall. *Lee's Lieutenants: A Study in Command.* 3 vols. New York: Charles Scribner's Sons, 1942–1944.

Hood, J. B. *Advance and Retreat: Personal Experiences in the United States and Confederate States Armies.* New Orleans: Published for the Hood orphan memorial fund, 1880.

McMurry, Richard M. *John Bell Hood and the War for Southern Independence.* Lexington: University Press of Kentucky, 1982.

—Stephen Davis

Brig. Gen. Adam Rankin Johnson

THREE PILLARS SUPPORTED the civic infrastructure of nineteenth-century Henderson County, Kentucky: tobacco, slavery, and steamboats. The economic potency of a valued commodity, a large pool of slave labor, and the steam transport to move product to consumer markets made Henderson a wealthy environment in the American antebellum period. It was into this setting that Adam Rankin Johnson was born on February 8, 1834, to Dr. Thomas Jefferson Johnson and Juliet Spencer Rankin.

At the age of eight, Adam Johnson was given the use of a gun. This was the beginning of his long association with the natural environs of his raw Ohio River surroundings. Johnson spent fully one-third of his early years embracing the natural gifts of outdoor life, and his burgeoning abilities as a young hunter and fisherman were legendary among his childhood gang. His physical wherewithal, combined with a penchant for daring schoolboy stunts, made him a long-remembered leader among his peers.

Johnson finished his formal education at the local Henderson schoolhouse at age twelve and, after a short apprenticeship, became an apothecary's assistant at a drugstore. The owner soon left the business workings in the capable hands of the young adolescent, and Johnson ran the store independently for several years. At sixteen, he became involved with the lifeblood of Henderson County and went to work at the tobacco stemmery of his uncle, John Henry Barrett. A keen student of human behavior, Johnson became a lead man for the stemmery and at one point managed eighty men, establishing new productivity records under his stewardship.

Adam Johnson possessed the innate self-confidence to cut his own path in life, but the fixed economic infrastructure of Henderson left little to satisfy his entrepreneurial spirit. In 1854, Johnson left his western Kentucky home for the unsettled frontier of west Texas. For the next six years, Johnson was employed as a surveyor, marking prime Texas lands for new homesteads and commercial expansion.

During that time, Johnson lived and worked in a small, isolated pioneer community in the far reaches of outpost territory where the tribes of the Comanche predominated. By his own admission, he was "more frequently engaged in battle with the Indians than was any other man upon the plains." During his years in Texas territory, Johnson successfully defended his remote commune by employing a gambler's guile, a winner's luck, and a well-aimed weapon. The Texas plains became a high-stakes laboratory for the development of Adam Johnson's combat credo of illusion and surprise. His reputation as a leader left him with the nickname "the Young Colonel."

After Abraham Lincoln's election, Johnson closed out his business affairs and ended his first chapter in Texas by marrying his sixteen-year-old sweetheart, Josephine Eastland, on January 1, 1861. Soon thereafter, he headed north toward Kentucky. Near Hopkinsville, Kentucky, he met the man who would formally accept him into Confederate service, Lt. Col. Nathan Bedford Forrest.

Johnson was part of Forrest's crack scouting team between December 1861 and May 1862. During that time, he participated in Forrest's first combat trial at the battle of Sacramento, Kentucky. He also penetrated Union lines several times to gather intelligence during the Fort Donelson campaign. When the decision was made to surrender Donelson to Federal forces, Forrest refused to capitulate. Instead, he put his entire command into Johnson's hands by giving him just a few hours to find an escape route for the troops before the formal surrender. Miraculously, Johnson located a safe transit through Union lines, and Forrest's Confederate cavalrymen were led to safety. Thereafter, Johnson was entrusted with escorting the escape of the fort's commanding officer, Brig. Gen. John B. Floyd, to Nashville.

In late May 1862, Johnson met with fellow Kentuckian Maj. Gen. John Breckinridge. As a result of this meeting, Johnson began his independent command in the Civil War. Breckinridge sent Johnson behind enemy lines to recruit a Confederate cavalry regiment from Union-held western Kentucky. Johnson was probably the only man in the West who had a chance to succeed with such a mission.

Back home in friendly territory, Johnson spent the early weeks of June 1862 attempting to cajole local Southern sympathizers into joining him in the formation of a new cavalry unit. Johnson, however, was an unknown quantity to the men he met in early summer, and most prospects demurred. Faced with returning to Breckinridge in disgrace, Johnson instead initiated one of the most successful military campaigns in the upper South. He started by attacking Union garrisons in Henderson and Madisonville, Kentucky, which quickly brought him publicity, credibility, and recruits. By the end of the summer, he had captured Henderson; Hopkinsville, Kentucky; Clarksville, Tennessee; Uniontown, Kentucky; and Newburgh, Indiana.

Johnson's capture of Newburgh, a town of almost 1,200 citizens, was accomplished by the use of grand ruse with only twenty-seven recruits. Johnson fabricated a faux cannon battery made of a stovepipe and a charred log, each resting upon an old set of wagon wheels. Crossing the Ohio River from Kentucky to Indiana by surprise, he was able to convince a stunned Newburgh home guard captain that the cannons resting on Kentucky soil directly across from the town were real and ready for action. Newburgh quickly surrendered. Johnson spent the afternoon collecting weapons and paroling convalescing Union soldiers before making a safe getaway back to Kentucky.

Now a folk hero in western Kentucky, "Stovepipe" Johnson's exploits allowed him to fill the ranks of the Tenth Kentucky Cavalry, later known as partisan rangers. Toward the end of 1862, Johnson's regiment became attached to Morgan's raiders and participated in the destruction of the great Muldraugh's Hill trestle works during Brig. Gen. John Hunt Morgan's Christmas Raid through central Kentucky.

In the summer of 1863, General Morgan asked Johnson to be a brigade commander in what would become the Great Raid through the Northern homelands of Indiana and Ohio. While the mission appealed to Johnson, his objective was to return to western Kentucky, where his notoriety provided him with his best chances for success. In order to bridge these conflicting aims, Johnson and Morgan cut a deal that was to lead to controversy as Morgan's Great Raid unfolded. Colonel Johnson agreed to become Morgan's Second Brigade commander during the Kentucky leg of the operation as Morgan approached the Ohio River. Upon arriving at the river, Johnson would leave Morgan and have his own brigade detached westward by steamer to attack Henderson, Kentucky, and Evansville, Indiana. With both Morgan and Johnson seemingly settled on their conditions, the Great Raid began.

Johnson's advance guard captured two steamboats at Brandenburg, Kentucky, on July 8, 1863. For the rest of the day, Morgan's raiders shuttled north across the Ohio River on the captured steamers. At the point when most of the men had passed over to Indiana soil, Morgan bluntly told the youthful brigade commander that he had changed his mind about releasing Johnson's men westward downstream. As proof of his decision, Morgan pointed to a burning steamer just used to transit the river, leaving no doubt that Col. Adam Johnson would be with Morgan for the duration of the raid. Saddened but dutiful, Johnson accepted the situation like a soldier. It was ironic that one of the few times Johnson was tricked during the war was by his own commanding officer.

Morgan ordered Johnson to engage in the first serious combat action on Indiana soil by directing him to attack the assembled home guardsmen at Corydon. Johnson's coordinated assault defeated the Corydon garrison, opening the way eastward across southern Indiana and into Ohio. After creating a civilian panic by skirting close to Cincinnati, Morgan's raiders moved toward the Ohio River with the intention of returning to the safety of Southern soil. On July 19, the climactic showdown between Confederate and pursuing Union forces occurred at Buffington Island, Ohio. As the morning mist burned off, the raiders started constructing makeshift rafts in which to cross the Ohio River. Union forces, closing from two directions on land and by gunboat on the river, stopped the rebel migration. Encircled for the next several hours, the outnumbered Confederates were pressed into combat and eventually broke. General Morgan and Colonel Johnson escaped the battlefield with about a thousand Confederate cavaliers, while First Brigade commander Col. Basil Duke and approximately six hundred soldiers were surrounded and captured.

Moving upstream approximately fourteen miles, Morgan again tried to cross the Ohio River. His men formed in lines, and Adam Johnson led the men across the swollen river, at one point rescuing two of his men from drowning. Approximately three hundred of Morgan's raiders had crossed the river when a Union gunboat once again interrupted the exodus. Dodging gunshots and cannon shells, Johnson quickly led his men away from the Ohio River into West Virginia. Morgan remained with the Southern soldiers who were unable to cross the river and continued the retreat from Union forces for another six days before his capture.

Col. Adam Johnson was the highest-ranking officer to escape federal clutches during Morgan's Great Raid. Safely on Virginia soil, Johnson made his way to Richmond to make the first detailed report of Morgan's ride through Indiana and Ohio. As soon as he arrived in Richmond, he was descended upon by the Confederate congressional delegation from Kentucky. To the military establishment of the Confederacy, Morgan's raid was an apparent disaster. Johnson's testimony would either seal Morgan's fate as an insubordinate renegade or cast him as an unfortunate, but daring, cavalier. The day before Johnson's interview with President Jefferson Davis, the Kentucky congressmen urgently pleaded with Johnson to reconstitute the remainder of Morgan's command in order to keep the soldiers together for the moment when their leader returned. Even though Johnson believed he could be most effective in western Kentucky and felt no special connection to Morgan, he nevertheless agreed to reconstitute Morgan's cavalry. He spent the next several months collecting elements of Morgan's old command at Morristown, Tennessee, and Decatur, Georgia.

In mid-1864, Johnson got his wish to return to western Kentucky, a move that would portend his final chapter as a battlefield warrior. Unlike his first unassuming arrival in western Kentucky, this time he returned to his department as a legendary and revered Confederate officer carrying bigger plans than ever. Johnson was entrusted with one of the most far-fetched missions in the Civil War. After announcing a Confederate conscription order applying to all able men in western Kentucky, Johnson entered into a set of clandestine communications with an Indiana representative of the Sons of Liberty and conspired to participate in what is now called the "Northwest Conspiracy."

The Sons of Liberty was a secret society that comprised elements dedicated to aiding Confederate units in a grand scheme to invade and conquer southern Indiana. Ten thousand armed Southern sympathizers from Indiana, Illinois, and Ohio were to rendezvous at Newburgh, Indiana, as Johnson transported his 1,500 Confederate regulars north across the Ohio River. The combined force envisioned the capture of a series of northern towns in the lower Ohio valley, creating confusion and forcing Federal troops to break away from Virginia.

The ephemeral plot was foiled before it ever got under way. Johnson was thwarted in executing his part of the scheme by the movements of Union brigadier general Edward Hobson. On August 21, 1864, Johnson was leading a squadron of Federal captives back to his lines when he was shot in the temple by a round mistakenly fired by one of his own men. The bullet did not penetrate his brain, but he was blinded for life.

After the accident, Johnson was taken to several homes in western Kentucky to recover, but his mother eventually brought him back to Henderson. Upon his recovery, he was arrested, became a prisoner of war, and was sent to Fort Warren in Boston Harbor, Massachusetts. While there, Federal authorities tried to get Johnson to sign a petition requesting his exchange, but he refused and remained in prison for several months. In February 1865, Johnson was finally exchanged and conveyed to Richmond, Virginia.

At Richmond, Johnson proved he was capable of confounding his friends as well as his enemies. Despite personal entreaties from former Texas governor Francis Lubbock, Confederate president Jefferson Davis, and Maj. Gen. John Breckinridge (by then the Confederate secretary of war), Johnson steadfastly refused to retire from the Confederate army. A vexed Breckinridge finally acceded to Johnson's wishes to return to western Kentucky as a combat commander. Having been appointed brigadier general in September 1864, he was about to become the only blind field general of the American Civil War.

With the help of his subordinates, Johnson made his way to Macon, Mississippi, where he began to assemble his old command. Just as he was preparing to trek northward to his old department, he received the news that Robert E. Lee had surrendered. Johnson understood that meant that the war was over.

The rigors of service and Johnson's unfortunate blinding left him physically devastated and mentally exhausted. Refusing offers of assistance, Johnson and his wife made their way back to Texas and settled on a frontier homestead in Honey Creek Cove. Outwardly bereft of subsistence, Adam Johnson drew on the only resources left to him, his own inner determination and the knowledge he had gained during his first episode in Texas before the Civil War. Johnson called on his surveying experience to open a land office and worked for thirteen years relying on his memory to sell land he had previously surveyed.

In time, Adam Johnson became a development leader for central Texas. In 1887 his decades-old dream of a thriving town near the falls of the Colorado River was brought to life when he founded, platted, and began to sell lots for the town of Marble Falls, Texas. General Johnson's business acumen and legendary cachet became valuable assets, and a consortium led by Johnson built a large cotton factory on the Colorado River, a factory that became a source of economic stability and a defining landmark for more than half a century. Johnson also founded the Texas Mining and Improvement Company, donated land to bring the railroad into the region, and built a small college. His mining company donated the granite to build the Texas state capitol building. The blind man with the characteristic green lenses successfully pursued a grand vision for central Texas.

Adam Johnson had been sharing his incredible life story with friends and family in Texas for many years, and, toward the twilight of his life, he decided that his saga was worthy of sharing. In 1902, Johnson made one concluding pilgrimage to the heroic battlefields of his youth. He journeyed from Texas through New Orleans and up the Mississippi River, joyfully reuniting with his former comrades-in-arms throughout western Kentucky. Johnson soon pushed his final campaign on to Louisville, where he met with his publisher to discuss plans for his now famous autobiography, *Partisan Rangers of the Confederate States Army*. His life story and the stories of his fabled men were published in 1904.

Adam Rankin Johnson died on October 20, 1922, in Burnet, Texas. As befitted an irreplaceable Texas hero, Johnson's body was taken to the state capitol at Austin where it was displayed for viewing before the funeral services. The governor of Texas, Pat Morris Neff, paid his respects at the services. Adam Johnson—Kentucky rabble-rouser, Texas frontiersman, Confederate general, town founder, author, and successful businessman —was buried in the Texas State Cemetery at Austin. He was survived by his wife and six children.

BIBLIOGRAPHY

Davis, William C., ed. *The Confederate General*. 6 vols. Harrisburg, PA: National Historical Society, 1991.

Johnson, Adam Rankin. *The Partisan Rangers of the Confederate States Army: Memoirs of General Adam R. Johnson*. Louisville, KY: G. G. Fetter, 1904.

Mulesky, Ray. *Thunder from a Clear Sky: Stovepipe Johnson's Confederate Raid on Newburgh, Indiana*. Lincoln, Nebraska: Universe Star, 2005, 2006.

—RAYMOND MULESKY

Gen. Albert Sidney Johnston

THE FIFTH CHILD of John and
Abigail Harris Johnston, Albert
Sidney Johnston was born on
February 2, 1803, in Washington, Kentucky. He attended
Transylvania College in Lexington, Kentucky, for a year then in
1822 entered the U.S. Military
Academy. He graduated eighth
in the class of 1826, served as adjutant of the corps of cadets his
senior year, and entered active
duty with the army as a lieutenant of infantry. He served with
distinction in the Black Hawk
War and seemed destined for
high command. But in 1834 he
resigned his commission at the wish of his invalid wife, Henrietta Preston, and, following her death a year later, he migrated to the infant Republic of Texas, where he served first as commanding general of the army
and later as secretary of war. In 1843 he married Eliza Griffin of Louisville, Kentucky. In 1846 he volunteered for brief but gallant service in the
U.S. Army in the Mexican War. For almost ten years following this conflict he languished, first as an unsuccessful planter in Texas, then, back in
the army with the rank of major, as paymaster of the troops stationed in
the forts along the Texas frontier.

In 1855, largely through the agency of his fellow cadet of West Point
and admirer from the Mexican War, U.S. secretary of war Jefferson Davis,
he became the commanding colonel of the newly created Second Cavalry
Regiment guarding the Texas frontier against the Indians, a highly favored position, with Lt. Col. Robert E. Lee as second in command.

Shortly, when the command of the entire Texas Department fell vacant, Johnston was appointed temporarily to this position. In the summer
of 1857 Secretary of War John Floyd selected him to lead an expedition to
Utah Territory to quell the so-called Mormon Rebellion, an especially
delicate and difficult mission. The skill, resoluteness, and tact with which

he executed the job gained him further recognition and admiration and a promotion to brevet brigadier general. Bvt. Lt. Gen. Winfield Scott, commanding general of the U.S. Army, wrote of him during this assignment, "[Johnston] is more than a good officer. He is a God send to the country through the army."

After the Utah action Johnston was ordered to San Francisco as commanding general of the Department of the Pacific. He was there when the secession of the states of the lower South occurred. Though always a strong American nationalist, his most powerful loyalty turned out to be for his adopted state, Texas. When that state withdrew, he tendered his resignation from the U.S. Army. Though his announced intention at the time was to remain neutral, he changed his mind when hostilities began. Saying, "It looks like fate that Texas has made me a Rebel twice," he joined a group of dedicated pro-Confederates who made a grueling march across the Southwest to offer their services to the Confederacy.

Overjoyed over Johnston's appearance at the Confederate White House, President Jefferson Davis on September 10, 1861, placed him in command of the vast western theater of the Confederacy, designated Department No. 2. He immediately traveled to Nashville, where he temporarily located his headquarters, and there he made a momentous decision: to secure more of Kentucky, which was attempting to remain neutral, for the Confederacy. He established the center of his attenuated Kentucky line along with his headquarters at Bowling Green; the left flank of the Kentucky line rested on the Mississippi River at Columbus, where Maj. Gen. Leonidas Polk, his onetime West Point roommate, had already developed a position; his right flank, commanded by Brig. Gen. Felix Zollicoffer, lay at Cumberland Ford in the eastern reach of the state. West of the Mississippi, Johnston's department included Missouri, which, like Kentucky, was a divided state. The department also included Arkansas, northern Louisiana, and the Indian Territory (now Oklahoma).

Heavily outnumbered, and commanding a porous front penetrated by three major rivers—the Mississippi, Tennessee, and Cumberland—Johnston faltered in dealing with what proved to be the most vulnerable part of his line, that where the Tennessee and Cumberland intersected it. In early February 1862, Union brigadier general Ulysses S. Grant led a joint army-navy force that captured Confederate Fort Henry on the Tennessee and ten days later Fort Donelson on the Cumberland.

Johnston's most grievous error in attempting to defend the forts lay in ordering an additional twelve thousand troops into Donelson at the last minute, thereby losing them with the fort. His department was now open to Union invasion by transports and gunboats along the Cumberland to Nashville and along the Tennessee all the way into northern Alabama. Thus the state of Kentucky and most of Tennessee were at the moment lost to the Confederacy.

Ignoring an outburst of popular denunciation, Johnston went about the task of concentrating his scattered forces for a counterstroke against his opponents. His strategy was to withdraw his forces and unite them at a point below the great curve of the Tennessee River, thus placing them out of danger of entrapment by a Union movement up that stream combined with another movement overland from Kentucky. He placed the western segment of his army—mainly Polk's troops from Columbus—under the command of Gen. P. G. T. Beauregard, who had been sent west by President Davis to serve as Johnston's second in command.

Johnston personally led the troops from Bowling Green and eastern Kentucky and joined the wing under Beauregard at the town of Corinth, Mississippi, which lay at the junction of the two major railroads of the western Confederacy, the Memphis and Charleston running east and west and the Mobile and Ohio running north and south.

Johnston's poise and determination throughout this extraordinarily strenuous operation was exemplary and largely accounted for the success of it. He was bolstered by the support of President Davis, who steadfastly refused either to relieve or censure him, saying to a delegation demanding his removal, "If [Johnston] is not a general we had better give up the war, for we have no general." Johnston wrote Davis that he had remained silent during the commotion because he believed it best for the cause to do so. He said if he could successfully unite the wings of his army, the clamor against him would abate. "The test of merit in my profession with the people is success," he added, "it is a hard rule but I think it right."

When Johnston reached Corinth on March 23, he found there reinforcements sent by the Confederate authorities: Maj. Gen. Braxton Bragg with a contingent of troops from Mobile and Brig. Gen. Daniel Ruggles with troops from New Orleans. Ordering Maj. Gen. Earl Van Dorn with another small force in Arkansas to come to Corinth, Johnston and his subordinates immediately began planning a blow at the Union army commanded by Maj. Gen. Ulysses S. Grant, which was now encamped at Pittsburg Landing on the Tennessee River somewhat over twenty miles from Corinth. An epic battle was about to occur.

Shortly after midnight of April 2, after receiving intelligence that the overland Union force from Kentucky, via Nashville, led by Maj. Gen. Don Carlos Buell was about to join Grant, Johnston ordered his attack. He explained the situation in a telegram to Davis and indicated to him that he planned to strike with his three main corps abreast (William J. Hardee's, Polk's, and Bragg's) and with his reserve commanded by John C. Breckinridge. Unfortunately for his plans, he delegated the preparation of the march and attack order to Beauregard, who designed a formation with the two lead corps (Hardee's and Bragg's) in tandem, each spread across the entire front. Seemingly unaware of this configuration until the troops were on the march, Johnston felt it was too late to alter it.

Beset by every imaginable entanglement to be expected of a body of green troops led by green officers, drenched by a torrential downpour, and marching in water and mud almost to the soldiers' knees, the army was finally deployed for the attack. The date was late afternoon of April 5.

Another problem now arose: Beauregard lost his nerve and wanted to cancel the attack and return to Corinth. He said all hope of a surprise was lost; that the enemy would "be entrenched to the eyes" and the Confederates would be massacred. He convinced all the corps commanders except Polk of his point of view. Johnston faced the "moment of truth" so movingly described by the great philosopher on war, Karl von Clausewitz, who said that as the will of one subordinate after another collapses, the inertia of the entire mass rests on the commander. Only through his will and character could the undertaking go forward: only if he withstood all objections and protests "as the rock resists the beating of the waves."

Johnston listened courteously to Beauregard and the others then said he still expected to find the enemy unprepared. Then, quietly, he announced the supreme command decision of the campaign, "Gentlemen, we will attack at dawn tomorrow."

He was right; the attack took the Federals by surprise and in no defensive posture. They were initially driven back in confusion, many in panic. By midmorning masses of them—estimated by the renowned Civil War scholar Bruce Catton as perhaps a fourth of Grant's army—had abandoned the front and were huddled under the bluff at the edge of the Tennessee River. But the remainder rallied and fought tenaciously. Beauregard's attack formation with its initial assault by a single corps had squandered much of the advantage of the surprise. Also, thousands of the relatively undisciplined and hungry Confederates had dropped out of the charge to pillage the rich Union camps.

The combat was astonishingly fierce. Across a front of three miles it raged. Both Grant and his top division commander William T. Sherman wrote after the war that they had experienced no more severe fighting throughout the conflict. Confederates who were in the battle and who served the entire war said the same. The battle of Shiloh (as they called it, or Pittsburg Landing as the Federals called it) was the first truly great battle of the war. With its more than twenty-three thousand dead, wounded, and captured, it offered a grim harbinger of what was to come.

Johnston chose to command at the front, leaving Beauregard to coordinate movements from the rear. During the morning of April 6 Johnston rode across the front from left to right, observing the terrain and the fighting, conferring with corps and division commanders, occasionally adjusting the direction of their attacks. With the Federals in withdrawal, he appeared to be winning the battle. But the right wing of his attack, the main effort, which was supposed to shear the Federals away from their base at the landing, was stopped in a wooded area the Confederates named the Hornet's Nest, a tribute to the stubbornness of the resistance. Determined to break through to the landing, Johnston committed his reserve here.

At about two o'clock in the afternoon, when one of the reserve regiments faltered, he placed himself at its front, addressed the soldiers, and led the unit forward, at least part of the way. Delighted to witness the success of the charge, he kicked up one foot to show one of his staff members, Gov. Isham Harris of Tennessee, where a bullet had cut the sole of his boot. "Governor," he said gaily, "they came very near putting me *hors de combat* in that charge."

He may have grossly underestimated what had occurred. A few minutes later when Harris returned from delivering an order to a brigade commander, he found Johnston reeling unsteadily in his saddle. Told by Johnston that he feared he was severely wounded, Harris led the general on his horse down into a wooded ravine where he and other staff members attempted vainly to revive him. By about 2:30 Johnston was dead from loss of blood through a torn artery in his right leg. Whether he had been struck during the charge of the regiment, or by a stray bullet afterward, cannot be determined.

His grieving staff transported the general's remains to Corinth. From there, they were shipped by rail for burial in New Orleans. After the war Johnston was reburied in State Cemetery, Austin, in his adopted state of Texas.

Beauregard succeeded to the command. Late in the afternoon, believing his troops were too exhausted to continue fighting, and that Buell's reinforcing army could not reach the landing in time to alter the outcome of the battle, Beauregard ordered the attack halted. His intention was to finish the victory the next day. It was a fatal miscalculation. That night

Buell reinforced Grant with more than twenty thousand fresh troops; the following day the Federals won the battle and drove the Confederates from the field. They managed to get back to Corinth, but they could have been destroyed by a determined pursuit.

Johnston's death at the peak of the battle leaves two unanswered, doubtless unanswerable, questions. The first: Would he have won the battle before Buell's arrival if he had not been wounded? Many students of the war believe not, but many disagree. Any judgment on the matter is conjecture. His troops were advancing when he died. Possibly his leadership on the field could have gained victory.

The second question: How great a general was Johnston? Unquestionably, he made many errors during his brief period of command. But he demonstrated a distinct capacity to grow. His decisiveness and resoluteness in the Shiloh campaign contrasted sharply with his earlier hesitation and miscalculation. His death at Shiloh deprived him of the opportunity to develop his talents as Lee, Grant, Sherman, and Beauregard developed theirs. Had any of them been killed the afternoon of April 6, he would not enjoy much reputation today. Johnston lived long enough to show that he possessed the broad strategic vision and the high moral qualities that are essential to great military leadership.

Many of today's students of the Civil War strongly criticize him for placing himself on the front line where, they contend, he was out of touch with the battle as a whole, leaving its general direction to Beauregard, and where he needlessly exposed himself to hostile fire. This conclusion ignores his use of his staff to obtain information and issue orders throughout the battle as well as his personal contacts with subordinates; it also ignores a venerable military dictum: that the only decision by which a commander can alter the outcome of a battle once it has begun is to employ his reserve at the time and place of his choice. Johnston unquestionably did this at Shiloh.

This criticism also ignores the role of the commander in motivating his troops. Many great commanders in history, including Wolfe, Napoleon, and Wellington did this by commanding at the front. Bruce Catton wrote that to lead their troops successfully, Civil War officers, from army commander down to lieutenant, had to show conspicuous physical courage in battle. "If they could not do this," he concluded, "they could not do anything."

A British military commission after World War II decided that Gen. Erwin Rommel was the most effective field commander of that conflict because he commanded at the front where his "electric presence" added a weapon to his army's attack. The British military historian John Keegan, perhaps the most distinguished living scholar in his field today, writes: "The first and greatest imperative in command is to be present in person. It is the spectacle of heroism, or its immediate report, that fires the soldiers' blood." Every Confederate who witnessed Johnston's conduct at Shiloh testified that his galvanizing presence on the field fired his soldiers' blood and added a potent weapon to the Confederate attack.

Would a Johnston alive have exerted this effect on the western Confederate forces throughout the war?

BIBLIOGRAPHY

Davis, William C., ed. *The Confederate General.* 6 vols. Harrisburg, PA: National Historical Society, 1991.

Johnston, William Preston. *The Life of General Albert Sidney Johnston.* New York: D. Appleton, 1878.

Roland, Charles P. *Albert Sidney Johnston: Soldier of Three Republics.* Austin: University of Texas Press, 1964.

U.S. War Department. *The War of the Rebellion: A Compilation of the Official Records of the Union and Confederate Armies.* 70 vols. in 128 pts. Washington, DC: Government Printing Office, 1880–1901.

—CHARLES P. ROLAND

Brig. Gen. Joseph Horace Lewis

THE RUSSELLVILLE ORDINANCE of Secession aside, Kentucky's failure to officially secede from the Union, combined with Confederate inability to successfully occupy the Bluegrass State, should not be taken as a dependable measure of national loyalty. Borders, unlike Robert Frost's famously poetic fences, sometimes make combative neighbors, and the commonwealth remained contested territory during the War of the Rebellion. Kentucky's Southern sentiments are evidenced by more than just its symbolic presence as the central star in the rebel battle flag but might also be assessed by considering the quality of Kentuckians in gray and complemented by evaluating contemporary local judgments of their services. A brief examination of the antebellum, bellum, and postbellum careers of Joseph Horace Lewis perhaps allows some cautious appraisal of those benchmarks.

Lewis was born on October 29, 1824, near Rocky Hill, midway between Glasgow and Bowling Green, in the southern part of Barren County, itself in the south of the state and relatively close to the Tennessee border. His parents, John and Elizabeth Reed Lewis, were respectable farm folk and well-to-do enough to educate their son locally and to send him to Centre College in Danville.

Graduating in 1843, the nineteen-year-old read law for two years before opening an office in Glasgow, a country town known then as now for its Scottish antecedents. Studiously attentive to minute detail and possessing an analytical mind, Lewis showed promise as an attorney who could logically get to the heart of a legal matter in all its connective subtleties and then ardently hammer his case to a successful conclusion. Ambitious and hopeful, the young lawyer married Sarah Roberts in 1845 and entered politics that same year.

Serving three consecutive terms in the state legislature, Lewis began as a typical Kentucky Whig, though when later stung by Know-Nothing politics and attracted to states' rights philosophies, he became a Democrat. Self-identified in the 1850 Census as a "farmer," Lewis presented himself perhaps too solidly as a Southern nationalist and lost both his 1857 and 1861 bids for the U.S. Congress to more localist and unionist opponents.

Widowed in 1858, he possibly had fewer pressing personal concerns about putting his secessionist talk into action. With the outbreak of hostilities following an evolving rebellion in several other Southern states, Lewis used his local prestige to raise a regiment for Confederate service. Eschewing the romantically elite cavalry to raise a pedestrian infantry regiment may reflect more Lewis's rather phlegmatic nature than his comfortable financial means. He could be sanguine too and was credited with firing the first angry shots in Kentucky when his still-amorphous unit blazed away at Union sympathizers threatening the home of Confederate sympathizers on October 10, 1861.

Neighbors and clients, friends and family (including his fourteen-year-old son and grandfather's namesake, Jack) formed the Rocky Hill Guards and Barren County Musketmen before merging with other small detachments to become the Sixth Kentucky Infantry, Col. Joseph H. Lewis commanding. Formally organized at Bowling Green on November 19, they made a somewhat awkward showing by being initially armed with odd home-guard smooth-bore muskets and turned out in homemade and dangerously dark uniforms topped off by foolishly French kepis.

Lewis's patient and deliberate nature, combining with his careful attention to detail and discipline, helped transform clerks and farm boys into soldiers trusting and obeying a man who would soon prove as much a fighter as that other southern Joe Louis of different time. In early April of 1862, by now better armed with brand-new, blockade-run English Enfield rifles, the Sixth served as part of the 2,600-man First Brigade in John C. Breckinridge's Reserve Corps during the Shiloh campaign. "Reserve" and their positioning at the rear of Sidney Johnston's army in no way imply inactive or unengaged duties, and Lewis's regiment moved aggressively against the enemy. The Sixth attacked the Federal forces of Irwin McDowell's brigade, inflicting severe casualties and then with a bayonet charge drove them in great confusion from the field. Lewis's Kentuckians passed through, and probably plundered, Union camps before moving toward the sound of continued fighting at the later appropriately named Hornet's Nest, where they contributed to the final collapse of the Yankee line.

Certainly Shiloh provided Lewis with his greatest experience as a soldier, but Albert Sidney Johnston's death, P. G. T. Beauregard's indecisiveness, Ulysses S. Grant's tenacity, and Don Carlos Buell's arrival all conspired to deny a Confederate victory, and the Sixth ended its baptism of fire with a fighting retreat. The troops' citizen-soldier colonel had proved his mettle, commanding from the front and in the saddle, so actively engaged that, while unscathed, he had two horses killed and one wounded under him. His subsequent history essentially parallels that of his brigade, hand-in-glove, sword-in-scabbard.

A prewar supporter and presidential elector for Breckinridge, Colonel Lewis followed the former American vice president and now Confederate general south to reassignment in Vicksburg but, owing to ill health, missed serving with him in the poorly planned Baton Rouge campaign in the summer of 1862. At Murfreesboro, Tennessee, on January 2, 1863, Lewis and his regiment performed manfully under the intense Federal artillery bombardment punishing Breckinridge's perilous advance and retreat across a ford in the west fork of Stones River.

The First Kentucky Brigade passed to Robert W. Hanson's control when Breckinridge had been promoted to divisional commander, but when Hanson was killed at Murfreesboro, Benjamin Hardin Helm assumed command of what was now known as the "Orphan Brigade." When Helm fell on September 20 in the savage fighting at Chickamauga, Breckinridge instantly ordered Lewis to assume command in what was essentially a battlefield brevet to general. Lewis's successful fulfillment of that trust contributed to the spectacular Confederate victory and to his official promotion to brigadier general as of September 30.

Those heady days of Chickamauga were spoiled by bitter moments at Chattanooga when the new general's brigade was mauled and pushed back by the audacious Union assaults at Missionary Ridge on November 25. In early 1864, Lewis joined with fellow homesick Kentucky generals Breckinridge, John Hunt Morgan, and Simon B. Buckner in petitioning President Jefferson Davis for approval of their invasion plan to redeem Kentucky from its allegedly unpopular Union occupation. Bad memories of the Chattanooga campaign and the eventually disproved promises of popular Bluegrass Confederate sentiment combined with the hard reality of chronic troop shortages to consign their wistful hope to oblivion.

Lewis displayed courage and ability throughout the near constant combat in the major and minor battles of the Atlanta campaign of 1864. For all the conventional modern sneering characterizations of Joe Johnston as some haplessly delaying Fabius Maximus Cunctator, Joe Lewis's

Orphan Brigade fought while retreating. The hard combat that specifically thrills armchair generals generally kills the troops engaged, as evidenced by the casualty lists of Lewis's command showing the loss of fully half its men in the Dallas attack of May 28. Skirmishing before, but not directly engaged at, Kennesaw Mountain, his Kentuckians valiantly if unsuccessfully participated at Peachtree Creek and begrudgingly tangled with Kentucky Federals near Utoy Creek. Lewis's Brigade made a doomed stand at Jonesboro, hoping to defend the last rail line connecting Atlanta to the South, the raison d'être of the whole campaign, but was simply overrun and many were captured. Lewis's old Sixth Kentucky lost their battle flag here while their former regimental and current brigade commander unluckily suffered his only war wound, a shrapnel blow to his left side, but luckily avoided the capture common to many comrades in that particular defeat of September 1.

The Atlanta campaign's grueling retreat and massive casualties resulted in Lewis's Brigade being ruinously reduced to a near nonfunctioning level of 240 men. True "orphans" in the sense that they were continually and consistently depleted while being unable to resupply and recruit from either their Yankee-controlled home state or the pervasively faltering Confederate government, the brigade was eventually reformed as a mule-mounted force of old-fashioned dragoons. The former strawfooting-hayfooting infantry quickly mastered (or more probably remembered) the gee-haws of their fondly recalled Kentucky past while their forty-year-old commander recovered from his wounds and readjusted to the new tactical and strategic realities of their Georgia present.

Victory and defeat can prove equally exhausting, and after Atlanta a strange pause appeared in the fighting as both sides adjusted their lines and scrutinized their next moves. In that interim, Lewis's newly mounted infantrymen scouted about their location and scouted out the locals, spending some time visiting and socializing. Yankee depredations occasionally disrupted these curious pleasantries, and General Lewis, too sick, too distracted, or simply too battle coarsened, failed to prevent the hanging of captured Union marauders in what appears to be a warm-up for the infamous "March to the Sea."

Sherman's campaigns certainly proved his famous maxim "War is terrible; you cannot refine it," but when the grievously downsized but still disciplined brigade was attached to Wheeler's Cavalry Corps, the Kentuckians began experimenting with new ways to counter the oncoming Yankee leviathan of men and materiel. Not surprisingly, they were rather unsuccessful in halting the brilliant if equally cruel Georgia campaigns of the fall of 1864, but they were learning and adapting. Under Lewis's tutelage, the Kentuckians seemed to mimic the cunning tactics of Southern commander Nathan Bedford Forrest. If they were utterly unable to obey Forrest's famous maxim of "getting there first with the most men," they adopted some of his other methods when and where they could. Riding hard and dismounting to fight like infantry just as Forrest preached and practiced, the Orphan Brigade forced the invaders to fight for nearly every mile of hotly contested Southern territory. There seems to be no readily perceivable personal Forrest-Lewis connection, and while incidents of simultaneous creation are certainly provable and "necessity is (proverbially) the mother of invention," these new ways and means may simply reflect Lewis's analytical mind and his ability to get to the heart of a military matter in all its connective subtleties and then hammer away to a bloody conclusion. Imitating Forrest or not, Lewis surprisingly performed rather successfully, keeping the remainder of his brigade intact and aggressive in the Carolinas campaign of early 1865.

If this campaign appears today just one monotonously embattled retreat, its final fury is punctuated by two curious anecdotes. On February 11, members of the brigade drew up the remarkable "Resolutions of Lewis' Brigade," which democratically asserted their determined devotion to a cause they thought still winnable. Stating "We see nothing in the present aspect of affairs to justify a fear of our ultimate triumph, or any excuse for relaxing our efforts to conquer independence and peace," these Kentuckians argued that "the Minnie rifle [is] our best peace commissioner" and suggested that regional newspaper naysayers should join them in the saddle and on the firing line rather than subvert Southern optimism and will-to-power. As another aside, in April a detached element of Lewis's command fought a now famous black-and-blue regiment, the Fifty-fourth Massachusetts, but was forced to retreat before them.

While the Kentuckians still skirmished, rumors of an armistice between Sherman and Johnston ominously merged with vague reports of Robert E. Lee's surrender, but the confused nature of the times, combining with detached duties for most of the brigade in not-so-vain attempts to protect the local populace and infrastructure, helped keep the Kentuckians true to their vowed resolutions to resist even considering capitulation. Although theoretically included in Johnston's official April 26 surrender, they were actively fighting on April 29. Sherman's terms were neither parsimonious nor insulting, but perhaps the Orphans still resolutely held to their whistling-in-the-dark resolutions. Perhaps surrender seemed too abrupt, too terminal; perhaps they were just Kentucky-stubborn.

By now, the fighting had slowed down to a dangerous annoyance where no one in blue or in what now passed for gray wanted to be the last man killed for any cause, North or South. There appears little evidence of much talk among the brigade supporting armed resistance, in taking to the hills of Georgia, in returning to the Kentucky mountains to launch some guerrilla war, or in delaying the inevitable much longer. Yet having formed part of Jefferson Davis's desperately retreating presidential escort, General Lewis possibly feared more guilt by association but, ever the astute lawyer, began carefully negotiating with Yankee counterparts. Actual or not, secession, abetted by raising your hand (and worse, a regiment) against the national government (and losing) meant treason, might even mean death and actually meeting the devil in the details of incautious surrender. As possibly the second-most-wanted man after Davis himself, the brigade's old commander Breckinridge, triple damned now by being a traitorous American vice president, Confederate general and secretary of war, needed some guidance in rescuing what he could from his personally precarious position. Lewis's lawyering-up almost resulted in a preemptive capture, since at the same time that Union officers arrived to clarify the surrender terms for Lewis, Breckinridge incautiously rode into what he thought was a safe haven. He escaped detection and certain capture then and there, allowing Lewis time to logically assess conditions and to formally surrender with the remnants of the brigade at Washington, Georgia, on May 6, 1865. Rather than relinquish their remaining battle flags, the men reverentially cut the banners into pieces and carried them and their failed cause home to Kentucky.

By any military measure, Joe Lewis proved a brave and accomplished officer, leading and fighting with a brigade of brave and accomplished soldiers. Contemporary local private and public judgments of his wartime services to the Confederacy might be revealed by his postwar political career. Returning to a Kentucky, which, unlike most of the South, remained a loyal state in the Union, Lewis went back to his legal practice, and, still a Democrat, was again elected to the Kentucky House of Representatives in 1869 and 1870. In that latter year, the former Confederate officer was chosen to fill an unexpired term in the U.S. Congress. Elected to a full term in 1871, he served through 1873 before returning to private practice. In 1880, Lewis became his district's circuit judge but resigned to become a candidate for the court of appeals. He was duly elected and served until 1898. Lewis was chief justice for three terms beginning in 1882 and continuing through his 1888 and 1897 terms. Obviously popular, publicly trusted, and vaguely reconstructed, he remarried as well, taking Mrs. Cassandra Johnson, a widow eight years his junior, as his second wife in 1887. Married for seventeen years, they had no children.

Perhaps his postwar elections provide dependable benchmarks measuring Lewis's qualities and reflect favorably on Kentucky's sentiments of understanding and forgiveness, or at least prove a continued neutrality in matters of causes honorably and ably fought, won or lost. Possibly disproving any lingering Cain-and-Abel Bluegrass legacy as well as denying the adage that "the good die young," Lewis, having put aside his gray coat in 1865, took off his black robe in 1898, retired to his Scott County farm, remembering, as old men do, his service in war and on the bench, until he died there on July 6, 1904. Gen. Joseph Horace Lewis, Sixth Kentucky Infantry and First Kentucky Brigade, lies buried in Glasgow's City Cemetery.

BIBLIOGRAPHY

Davis, William C., ed. *The Confederate General.* 6 vols. Harrisburg, PA: National Historical Society, 1991.
Thompson, Ed Porter. *History of the Orphan Brigade.* Louisville, KY: Lewis N. Thompson, 1898.
U.S. War Department. *The War of the Rebellion: A Compilation of the Official Records of the Union and Confederate Armies.* 70 vols. in 128 pts. Washington, DC: Government Printing Office, 1880–1901.

—CHARLES ELLIOTT

Brig. Gen. Hylan Benton Lyon

HYLAN BENTON LYON was a native of Caldwell County, later Lyon County, in Kentucky, the son of Matthew Lyon (a state senator) and Elizabeth M. Martin. Born on the family farm, River View, on February 22, 1836, the youth lost both parents at an early age and was raised by a kinsman. At fourteen, he enrolled in Masonic University, located in La Grange, Kentucky, and also Cumberland College in Princeton, Kentucky. In 1852, Lyon accepted an appointment to the U.S. Military Academy at West Point, from which he graduated four years later, ranked nineteenth in his class.

The newly minted junior officer received a posting as a brevet second lieutenant of artillery at Fort Myers in Florida. He participated in activities against the Seminole Indians and received promotion to second lieutenant in the Third Artillery. Lyon transferred to Fort Yuma, California, before moving to San Bernardino for a brief period in early 1858. After a year in California, Second Lieutenant Lyon transferred with his command to Washington Territory, where he participated in active campaigning under Col. George Wright. Lyon was one of a number of young officers and future Civil War generals who gained valuable experience during this period in the field. Colonel Wright cited the Kentuckian in his reports on the battles of Four Lakes and Spokane Plains.

The lieutenant engaged in various activities in the Northwest before obtaining a leave of absence and a brief furlough to Kentucky. During this period, he received promotion to first lieutenant, but with the outbreak of the Civil War, felt his course was clear. Lyon resigned his commission from the old army on April 30, 1861, and pledged his sword to the Confederate States of America.

Helping to organize an infantry company, which attached itself to the

Third Kentucky under Lloyd Tilghman, he won election as captain. Then, on September 20, 1861, the detached unit formed an artillery command, in what became known as the First Kentucky or Cobb's battery, with Lyon as its captain. His new commander, Simon B. Buckner, tapped him as chief of artillery for the division, but Lyon shortly accepted promotion to lieutenant colonel of the Eighth Kentucky on February 3, 1862.

Lyon's command joined in the defense of Fort Donelson in Tennessee, participating in an assault on the Union lines on February 15. He set his losses on that day at 17 killed and 46 wounded, with one man missing. For the entire Fort Donelson campaign, the Eighth Kentucky suffered more casualties than any of the brigade's other regiments, with 27 killed and 72 wounded out of 312 combatants.

Compelled to surrender with his command on February 16, Lyon spent the next seven months in various prisoner-of-war facilities before being exchanged. He was promoted to colonel of the Eighth in September 1862. His regiment once again came under the command of now brigadier general Lloyd Tilghman and proceeded to the defense of the river citadel of Vicksburg, Mississippi.

In 1863, Lyon's Eighth, now mounted, covered Pemberton's retreat from the Big Black River into Vicksburg. Refusing to be invested, Lyon slipped out of Vicksburg with a force of approximately six hundred mounted men, ostensibly for the purpose of harassing Union operations and destroying valuable property that might otherwise fall into Federal hands. In early June, the Kentuckian received orders from Gen. Joseph E. Johnston to secure the countryside near the Big Black River, offering protection to local residents by thwarting Union patrols into the area.

The ink on these orders was hardly dry when Lyon received new instructions to move to Port Hudson, Louisiana, and bring whatever relief he could to the besieged Confederate defenders. The Kentuckian would find little to work with outside Port Hudson and ultimately left for Jackson, Mississippi, where he engaged in fighting before retreating with the rest of Johnston's command to Meridian, Mississippi.

In November, Gen. Braxton Bragg assigned Lyon to Maj. Gen. Joseph Wheeler, who promptly dispatched him to Kingston, Tennessee. He assumed command of a small force of cavalry with the responsibility for scouting and screening for Confederate troops in the region. Still listed on the returns for Brig. Gen. Abraham Buford's infantry brigade at the end of November, Lyon remained with Wheeler. He followed the diminutive horseman to Chattanooga, Tennessee, and for a brief time, in the wake of Bragg's disastrous defeat at Missionary Ridge, assumed the role of chief of artillery. The Kentuckian did his part in transporting the ordnance to Dalton, Georgia, before relinquishing that command. He also acted as Wheeler's chief of staff until transferred to Mississippi to command mounted troops under Nathan Bedford Forrest.

At the end of May 1864, Lyon assumed command of a brigade of Kentuckians. Federal efforts to march from Memphis into Mississippi soon dictated his next course of action as Forrest moved to thwart the advance of Brig. Gen. Samuel L. Sturgis and a formidable mixed force of 8,300 cavalry and infantry, twenty-two pieces of artillery, and 250 wagons.

As part of Forrest's defensive dispositions, Lyon's troops set out from Booneville before dawn on June 10, 1864, to intercept Sturgis's column near Brices Cross Roads. Forrest knew that he would have to buy time to concentrate his scattered commands if he were going to be successful in preventing Sturgis from reaching deeper into Mississippi. He planned to use Lyon's men to slow the Federals until the rest could reach the field.

In doing so, Forrest employed terrain, psychology, and other factors to the fullest. He ordered Lyon to dismount his men and push them through the thick underbrush toward the Union troopers, creating the impression of a sizable force, which added to the opponents' uncertainty. Next, he fed his men into the fight as they arrived, extending his lines and maintaining pressure on the exhausted bluecoat horsemen.

Early in the afternoon, the remainder of the Confederates and artillery reached the battlefield. The Federal infantry also finally arrived, with the men winded and worn from double-quicking as their cavalry colleagues called for help. The Union troopers gratefully gave way to their comrades, and the fight lapsed into a brief lull as both sides recouped their strength. The final push came in midafternoon, again with Hylan Lyon's men providing much of the impetus as the Union lines gave way.

Lyon received promotion to brigadier general June 14, four days after the stunning defeat inflicted upon Samuel Sturgis. General Forrest had witnessed the Kentuckian's worth on the battlefield firsthand. He wanted Lyon's services to remain in his employ and lobbied hard for that outcome. The retention of Lyon in Forrest's command made imminent sense. The cavalry general was desperately short of "experienced" field officers, particularly at the brigade level. The success of Lyon's role at Brices Cross Roads may also have prompted the War Department to respond favorably with orders that would keep him under Forrest.

General Forrest moved swiftly to solidify a place for the Kentuckian in his command. He issued a directive designating that "Lyon's Brigade" be composed of "Third Kentucky Cavalry, Colonel Gustavus A. C. Holt;

Eighth Kentucky Cavalry, Lieut. Col. A. R. Shacklett; Seventh Kentucky Cavalry, Colonel Edward Crossland; [and] Twelfth Kentucky Cavalry, Col. W. W. Faulkner." Yet, whatever the Kentuckian thought of the re-union with his chief, the posting once more proved short-lived. On September 26, the secretary of war directed Lyon to take command of a department in Kentucky.

Lyon was thus in position to support Forrest's ambitious operation to threaten the Federals' Tennessee River supply lines in November 1864. In the raid on Johnsonville, he augmented Forrest's forces with several hundred men. Although Lyon would not enjoy the kind of fast-paced, free-wheeling action he might have anticipated, he offered other important skills as an artillerist to the expedition. This was particularly true regarding the placement and support of some of the artillery pieces that would pummel the Union supply base at Johnsonville, Tennessee, and turn the depot, storage facilities, and several boats into a raging inferno.

Subsequently, Lyon would have a strategic impact on the situation developing in Middle Tennessee in late 1864, when he compelled Union major general George H. Thomas to dispatch sufficient cavalry forces to protect his line of communications and supply. As Confederate general John Bell Hood marched toward the Tennessee capital, he expected Lyon's troops to provide a diversion by raiding deep into Kentucky to disrupt Union transportation and communication lines.

Initially, Hood planned for Lyon to threaten Clarksville, Tennessee, and then move upon and destroy or disable the railroad and telegraph lines running through Kentucky into Nashville. To this end, Lyon left the area of Paris, Tennessee, on December 6, with approximately eight hundred men and two howitzers. His movement across the Cumberland River near Clarksville necessitated a response by General Thomas, who dispatched two brigades of Edward M. McCook's cavalry in pursuit. This shift in the vital cavalry support that would normally be available to him rendered Thomas's tendency toward caution all the more pronounced as he confronted Hood's main force.

Lyon's operation got off to an auspicious beginning. His raiding party reached the area of Cumberland City on the Cumberland River on December 9, seizing the town and fifty prisoners in the process. He hastily set his men to torching public property that included several steamers and barges. The estimated total of destruction in this opening phase tallied approximately $1 million. The move also placed the Confederates on the river between Dover and Clarksville, Tennessee, Lyon's next destination.

As the Confederates approached the river town, they found Clarksville well defended with earthworks that would have likely produced heavy casualties in the Southern ranks without offering the guarantee of victory. Lyon and his men could do little more than demonstrate against the Union post and damage such railroad and telegraph lines as they could safely reach. Hood had hoped for the capture of the town, but reality dictated that any success Lyon might obtain would have to be found elsewhere.

Lyon then put his men on the road toward Hopkinsville, Kentucky. When his troops arrived there, they found the garrison had evacuated and left the town open to the raiders. Many of these poorly armed and trained men were also inconsistently clothed and equipped. Lyon took the opportunity to secure badly needed supplies, especially shoes and clothing, which would come in particularly handy given the December weather conditions in which they were operating.

At Hopkinsville, Lyon also established something of a reputation for himself when he burned the courthouse, a feat he would revisit repeatedly as his men roamed through the region. Altogether, he and his men were responsible for the destruction of at least eight county courthouses, prompting a later historian to dub Lyon "the courthouse burnin'est general" in the Confederacy. After the war, Lyon would justify these actions as military necessities based upon their use by his opponents. The Southern raiders also garnered some four hundred recruits in the conscription dragnet they spread throughout the area.

Lyon's successes were also producing additional attention from his Federal pursuers. McCook shifted his focus toward Hopkinsville with the notion of catching the Southerners. He hoped to trap them by dispatching blocking forces to prevent the Confederates from escaping. To make the main assault, McCook employed the brigade of Oscar H. La Grange. Although the attack proved successful in striking a telling blow, the Confederates foiled the attempt to ensnare the entire command by slipping past the blocking force, who mistook the Southerners, many of whom were clad in captured Union apparel, for Federals and did not realize the mistake until it was too late.

In the meantime, Lyon pushed his men toward the Green River, pausing only to add to his torched-courthouse total at Madisonville. Once again, La Grange and his men caught up with the Southerners as they were in the vulnerable position of crossing the river. Lyon dealt with the matter aggressively, demonstrating against the threat with a handful of men while the rest effected a passage. Lyon lost some nineteen men and an undetermined number of horses and wagons in the delicate operation but managed to manhandle his remaining artillery piece across to the opposite side.

The Confederate continued to do such damage as he could, while attempting to elude or delay his Union pursuers. At Hartford he captured sixty-eight men guarding the town and burned another courthouse. Then moving on to Elizabethtown and Nolin Station, he captured approximately two hundred additional troops and disabled or destroyed property on the Louisville and Nashville Railroad. The Federal pursuit also continued, although the Confederates left little more than smoldering ruins in their wake.

In one sense, Lyon had succeeded in extricating his command from the vise of the Union pursuit, but the relentless pressure, the constant movement, and the harrowing weather conditions were having a severe toll on his unit's integrity. Rumor of Hood's defeat at Nashville compounded the situation and prompted considerable desertion in the wearied Southern ranks.

Even as elements of his command dissolved around him, Lyon held the rest together and continued his raiding through sheer determination. More courthouses went up in flames in Campbellsville and Burkesville. At the latter place he put the Cumberland River between his command and the enemy. As he approached the relatively isolated terrain of north central Tennessee, Lyon and his men could finally pause to regroup. They still remained beyond the security of Confederate territory, now sharply reduced by Hood's departure from Middle Tennessee into northern Alabama. The troops also faced the formidable barrier of the Tennessee River to cross, a crossing made all the more difficult by heavy rains, flooding conditions, and the ubiquitous presence of Union patrols and gunboats.

By now Lyon's command was reduced to barely three hundred effectives. Even so, he sought to strike once more against the Federals, targeting the town of Scottsboro on the Memphis and Charleston Railroad. The Confederates reached the town on the night of January 8 but could not pry the fifty or so African American defenders from their positions before the arrival of reinforcements necessitated a retreat. Except for the opportunity to destroy a few outlying buildings, inflict a handful of wounds, and cause the expenditure of ammunition, the Scottsboro investment proved largely ineffectual. Lyon's losses were unclear, although the defenders insisted that they had killed one of his officers and seventeen of his men in addition to wounding numerous others.

Lyon spent the next couple of days trying to get his men across the Tennessee River by any means that came to hand. One hundred fifty Pennsylvania cavalry under Col. William J. Palmer maintained the pressure, succeeding in launching a surprise attack against the Confederates as they slept in the hamlet of Red Hill at daybreak on January 15. General Lyon was one of the initial captives, placed under a Union sergeant's supervision. But the prisoner saw an opportunity when the guard acquiesced to his request for warmer clothing and in the confusion and darkness secured a weapon, shot the Union sergeant, and disappeared into the darkness. Sgt. Arthur P. Lyon was the only casualty the Federals sustained in the lightning operation. Even so, the Union tally was significant, and the dramatic series of events left Lyon's command scattered and demoralized.

In the spring of 1865, General Lyon held only a token force in the field. He rejoined Forrest in the closing days of the war but refused to surrender when the latter did at Gainesville, Alabama. Instead, the Kentuckian sought refuge in Mexico for a brief time before returning to his native state in 1866. His first wife, Laura O'Hara, having died, he married Grace Machen in 1869 and Ruth Wolfe in 1887, raising a numerous family. He remained engaged in farming and civic activities for the rest of his life. He dabbled briefly in politics when he served in the Kentucky House of Representatives from 1899 to 1901. Lyon died on his Eddyville farm on April 25, 1907, and was interred there.

Throughout his wartime career, Hylan B. Lyon had served the Confederate States of America effectively in a variety of capacities. His impact mirrored that of the cavalry arm generally. Tactically, he enjoyed success frequently, most notably under Bedford Forrest's watchful eye at Brices Cross Roads. Strategically, his accomplishments were less certain or significant. In either case, few could match his determination to contribute to the Confederate war effort, even in the face of staggering odds.

BIBLIOGRAPHY

Bearss, Edwin C. *Forrest at Brice's Cross Roads and in North Mississippi in 1864.* Dayton, OH: Press of Morningside Bookshop, 1979.

Davis, William C., ed. *The Confederate General.* 6 vols. Harrisburg, PA: National Historical Society, 1991.

Lyon, Hylan B. "Memoirs of Hylan B. Lyon, Brigadier General, C.S.A." Edited by Edward M. Coffman. *Tennessee Historical Quarterly* 18 (March 1959): 35–53.

Roberson, B. L. "The Courthouse Burnin'est General." *Tennessee Historical Quarterly* 23 (December 1964): 372–78.

—BRIAN STEEL WILLS

Brig. Gen. Humphrey Marshall

HUMPHREY MARSHALL, attorney, politician, and Confederate general, was born to John J. and Anna Birney Marshall on January 13, 1812, in Frankfort, Kentucky. He was the grandnephew of U.S. Supreme Court Chief Justice John Marshall and nephew of antislavery leader James G. Birney.

Due in part to family connections, Marshall received an appointment to the U.S. Military Academy at West Point, where he graduated forty-second out of forty-five cadets in 1832. Eschewing a military career, Marshall resigned his commission, married Frances McAlister, and began a legal practice in Louisville the following year. Eventually the couple would have five children, three boys and two girls. Marshall enhanced his standing in the community when he served on the Louisville City Council in the late 1830s, whetting his taste for politics. The Mexican War provided a perfect springboard for such a career.

Marshall volunteered in 1846 and held the rank of colonel in the First Kentucky Cavalry. The highlight of his service occurred at the battle of Buena Vista in February 1847. In Maj. Gen. Zachary Taylor's official report, he noted that Marshall's men held their ground "handsomely against a greatly superior force . . . using their weapons with deadly effect."

Returning to Louisville to great acclaim, Marshall entered national politics as a Whig member of the U.S. House of Representatives from 1849–1853. President Millard Fillmore named Marshall as U.S. minister to China, 1853–1854, before Marshall returned to the House for another two terms, 1855–1859, as a member of the Know-Nothing Party.

As sectional tension increased, Marshall threw his support to John C. Breckinridge in the election of 1860 but then, following Abraham Lincoln's election and the onset of civil war, sided with his state and adopted the precarious position of neutrality, as did many Kentuckians. Kentucky was vital to both the Union and the Confederacy, with both sides respecting its status until September 1861 when Confederate major general Leonidas Polk occupied Columbus, Kentucky. As both sides raced to gain strategic positions in the commonwealth, Marshall cast his lot with the Confederacy.

Standing five feet eleven inches and weighing nearly three hundred pounds, Marshall was physically unfit for active military command as a cavalry officer. But as a politician, he had developed strong ties with prominent Southern leaders, and during the fall of 1861, he traveled to Richmond in an attempt to secure a personal command. He was appointed a brigadier general, to rank from October 30.

One month later, however, Marshall tendered his resignation to Confederate secretary of war Judah P. Benjamin. While in Richmond, Marshall had received a guarantee from President Jefferson Davis that his command would be independent of any others in the region, with Marshall reporting only to Gen. Albert Sidney Johnston. But when Marshall learned that Maj. Gen. George B. Crittenden had been appointed to command the Eastern District of Kentucky, he believed his independent status was in jeopardy and, as a matter of personal pride, tendered his resignation. In December, an old political ally, Confederate vice president Alexander Stephens, wrote that he had persuaded the War Department not to act on the letter of resignation and that Marshall's two thousand men would remain an independent force.

During the winter of 1861–1862, Federal troops under the command of Col. James A. Garfield moved into eastern Kentucky at Louisa, forty-five miles north of Prestonsburg. Marshall saw the potential threat these troops posed and decided to move his nearly equal force to meet them. He also received reports that another Union force was moving eastward from Mount Sterling to join Garfield. Although he wanted to achieve a great victory in eastern Kentucky, Marshall could hardly afford to battle a vastly superior army, and his options were few. He could either attack Garfield before the combination occurred and then face the other force, or withdraw to a more defensible position in the Cumberland Mountains and wait for a better opportunity to strike. Garfield made Marshall's decision for him.

On the morning of January 7, 1862, the Union commander sent small detachments of infantry forward to confront and outflank Marshall, hoping to lure the Confederates into a fight. But Marshall opted for an immediate withdrawal southward to a better defensive position. Garfield pressed his men forward to overtake the Confederates, moving along a narrow, winding road by Middle Creek, when gunfire rained down from the mountains above. Marshall's men had not retreated; instead, they had fortified a position in the ridges above the creek. Marshall had set a deadly trap for Garfield, since the only passable road in the area was the one that Garfield's troops used to advance. But the Confederates were overly anxious to spring it and premature gunfire disclosed the ambush.

Sporadic gunfire continued throughout the morning. Marshall fired on the Union forces from an artillery battery and dismounted cavalry positioned in a gorge above the road along which the Federals had advanced. Across the creek, Marshall placed his remaining troops, supported by two additional guns. To ascertain the location and strength of Marshall's men, Garfield ordered a cavalry and infantry charge, but the terrain afforded the Confederates excellent cover and Marshall's men poured several volleys into Union ranks, forcing them to retreat.

In midafternoon, Garfield ordered another cavalry charge up the road to draw the Confederates' fire, while sending four hundred men around the base of the hills to the left, hoping to encircle Marshall. But darkness fell before the move was completed, with its success or failure remaining in doubt. Prior to dusk, Marshall observed another movement of men to the north, the earlier anticipated reinforcements for Garfield. Uncertain of their strength, Marshall decided not to risk another engagement, and he withdrew to Piketon and later to Pound Gap. Garfield did not pursue because his troops were fatigued, hungry, and suffering from exposure.

Both Union and Confederate forces suffered few casualties in the skirmish at Middle Creek. Official reports indicate that the Confederates lost eleven killed and fifteen wounded, while Union casualties were two killed and twenty-five wounded. The outcome of the skirmish was indecisive. The entire day had been a standoff, yet each side claimed victory. The result was perhaps best summed up by a local resident: "The South claims victory, the North admits no defeat."

By early March 1862, Garfield was once again ready to take the offensive against Marshall's forces. Despite a late-season snowfall, Garfield ordered a frontal attack on Pound Gap by two hundred cavalry while six hundred infantry crept along a steep mountainside path on the Confederate right. After several Union volleys, Marshall withdrew into western Virginia. The entire action took less than an hour. Garfield lost no men in the rout while the Confederates lost seven killed and wounded.

From his headquarters in Abington, Virginia, Marshall wrote Gen. Robert E. Lee and Jefferson Davis concerning the possibility of another advance into Kentucky. Both Confederate leaders agreed that a successful advance would bring about very desirable results but added that Marshall would have to recruit his own men. Marshall then issued an urgent call for militia from the counties of western Virginia, but after several weeks of recruiting, only five hundred men enlisted, far short of the number he needed to battle Garfield.

In the spring of 1862, Garfield received orders to combine his troops with units of the Army of the Ohio, commanded by Brig. Gen. George Morgan, with an eye toward dislodging the Confederates from Cumberland Gap. Confederate major general Edmund Kirby Smith realized that he needed more men in order to hold this strategic position, but he wouldn't be receiving any help from Marshall. In early May, Marshall wrote Kirby Smith that his effective force was less than one thousand men, whose condition was deplorable. Not only did Marshall balk at joining Kirby Smith's command, but also his preoccupation with an independent army dictated his own maneuvers. Less than a week after this telegram, Marshall marched his "deplorable" men and engaged Union brigadier general Jacob Cox at Princeton, Virginia. In a small but intense skirmish, the Confederates forced a Union retreat at day's end, the first clear-cut victory for Marshall.

Despite this moment of success, Marshall announced to his troops in mid-June that circumstances beyond his control compelled his resignation. Undoubtedly, the issues surrounding his second resignation stemmed from the same as his first: his obsession with an independent command and an invasion of Kentucky. With Kirby Smith on the defensive and in desperate need of men, Marshall realized that his army would probably be sent to join Kirby Smith, ending Marshall's independent status.

Marshall had expected to be the dominant Confederate leader in eastern Kentucky. Following his retreat into Virginia, however, Marshall's small independent army simply did not figure prominently in Confederate strategy. Marshall was, in the eyes of many Richmond officials, an obese, egotistical politician, whose value lay in securing eastern Kentucky for the Confederacy at the outbreak of war. In that he had failed. By the summer of 1862, Marshall's lengthy letters requesting additional men and equipment had grown intolerable. His resignation was accepted without hesitation.

By the end of June, Morgan had taken Cumberland Gap, prompting Confederate leaders to devise a summer campaign that would combine the armies of Kirby Smith in Knoxville with Gen. Braxton Bragg's force moving eastward from Tupelo, Mississippi, for an invasion of Kentucky. Jefferson Davis requested that Marshall reconsider his resignation, with the only stipulation being that Marshall's army would be subject to Kirby Smith's orders when they combined in Kentucky.

By early August, the Confederate invasion of Kentucky had begun, with Marshall once again leading Kentuckians, Tennesseans, and Virginians through Pound Gap. They occupied Pikeville, Prestonsburg, Salyersville, West Liberty, and other towns along the Mount Sterling–Pound Gap Road. Kirby Smith ordered Marshall to stop at Piketon, which would cut off Morgan's line of retreat from Cumberland Gap, while he moved toward Lexington. Marshall hoped to play a large role in the Confederate invasion of Kentucky, however, and when Kirby Smith ordered him to halt his force, Marshall did not comply. Reasoning that Kirby Smith had no authority to issue orders since a combination of the armies had not yet occurred, Marshall continued his march toward Lexington. When Morgan did indeed retreat from Cumberland Gap, Marshall did not intercept the Union army. Such noncooperation was an omen of things to come.

Bragg moved slowly into the heartland of the state and decided to install a provisional government in the recently captured state capital of Frankfort. The ceremony took place on October 4, 1862, with Marshall delivering the opening remarks, prior to the introduction of the new Confederate governor of Kentucky, Richard Hawes. This act was intended to garner thousands of enlistments, with Hawes promising that his government would have a permanent presence in the state. Unknown to Hawes, however, Federals were bearing down upon Frankfort, and their artillery bombardment brought his speech to a hasty conclusion. Marshall, indeed all of the dignitaries, fled the capital, and the Hawes administration spent the remainder of the war in exile.

October 8, 1862, brought much bloodshed to the Bluegrass State, as Bragg mistakenly believed he faced only a portion of the 50,000 men in Union major general Don Carlos Buell's Army of the Ohio. Bragg ordered Maj. Gen. Leonidas Polk, who had fewer than half that number, to attack without the support of troops from Kirby Smith and Marshall. After a hard day of fighting, with combined casualties approaching 7,500, Bragg withdrew from Perryville to the northeast toward Harrodsburg, to join Kirby Smith. Marshall's 3,000 troops were nearby, within supporting distance, if the battle resumed. In fact, Kirby Smith encouraged Bragg to resume the offensive, but Bragg feared that Buell could move eastward toward Danville and cut off his line of retreat. On the heels of the defeat at Perryville, with reports of an additional Union force moving from Cincinnati to join with Buell, with few supplies in the area, and, perhaps most disappointing, the lack of recruits joining his ranks, Bragg decided to withdraw from the commonwealth. As Bragg and Kirby Smith fell back into Tennessee, Marshall asked for and received permission to follow his own route back into western Virginia.

It would have been very difficult to put together a trio of Confederate commanders less likely to cooperate than Bragg, Kirby Smith, and Marshall. A major characteristic they shared was their unwillingness to serve under anyone else. To deliver Kentucky to the Confederacy, a concerted effort on their part was crucial, yet each eventually went his own separate way, following self-serving plans, dooming the invasion. The failure of the Confederate invasion of 1862 forced Bragg, Kirby Smith, and Marshall to withdraw from Kentucky and, with the exception of a few minor raids into the state, left Unionists in firm control of the state for the duration of the war.

Marshall considered himself to be the leader of a Confederate eastern Kentucky and he envisioned his army liberating the state. From the beginning, his command was a farce. Hampered by his weight, Marshall proved incapable of a rigorous field campaign in the eastern Kentucky mountains. He did not win a single victory in Kentucky, and when his army retreated into western Virginia following Perryville, eastern Kentucky was clear of Confederate forces.

His final wartime action occurred during the spring of 1863, when he led nearly two thousand men through Pound Gap once again and engaged Federal cavalry at Salyersville. Marshall continued to Louisa and rode through Breathitt, Wolfe, and Owsley counties before retreating to his base of operations in southwestern Virginia. Marshall's spring raid is credited with the destruction of over forty Union homesteads in eastern Kentucky. For the remainder of the year, Marshall's small band of men remained in the mountains, independent but also insignificant.

By June 1863, Marshall had grown weary of his inactivity, and for a third and final time tendered his resignation. He moved to Richmond to practice law until early the next year when he was elected to the Second Confederate Congress representing the Eighth District of Kentucky. Taking his seat on May 2, 1864, he became a member of the Committee on Military Affairs. He favored increased governmental action, including control over railroads and the use of slaves in the army, but balked at the suspension of habeas corpus. He also engaged in a verbal feud with Bragg over the failed invasion of Kentucky. Bragg remarked that Marshall's men in both the Mexican War and the Civil War had a penchant for running rather than fighting. But some of Marshall's men painted a far different picture: "Humphrey Marshall, he's our boss, big as hell, brave as a hoss."

Marshall held his seat until the conclusion of the war and then fled to Texas, but returned to Louisville in 1866 and practiced law there until his death on March 28, 1872. Marshall was laid to rest in the State Cemetery, Frankfort.

BIBLIOGRAPHY

Brown, Kent Masterson, ed. *The Civil War in Kentucky: Battle for the Bluegrass State*. Mason City, IA: Savas Publishing, 2000.

Guerrant, Edward O. "Marshall and Garfield in Eastern Kentucky." In *Battles and Leaders of the Civil War*, ed. Robert U. Johnson and Clarence C. Buel. Vol. 1. New York: Century, 1884.

Harrison, Lowell H. *The Civil War in Kentucky*. Lexington: University Press of Kentucky, 1975.

McKnight, Brian D. *Contested Borderland: The Civil War in Appalachian Kentucky and Virginia*. Lexington: University Press of Kentucky, 2006.

—C. DAVID DALTON

Maj. Gen. William Thompson Martin

INEXPERIENCE SHADOWED Confederate general and Kentucky native William Thompson Martin. Although he performed ably under capable cavalry leaders like J. E. B. Stuart, promotion and a move to the western theater damaged his career. Martin was too much of a neophyte, according to Lt. Gen. James Longstreet, to handle corps command. In addition, he became tangled in the cutthroat political climate of the western army, where bickering with fellow officers sometimes outshone military operations. Had Martin remained a regimental or brigade commander in Virginia, his career would have taken a different, more positive turn.

Martin was born in Glasgow, Kentucky, on March 25, 1823, to John Henderson Martin and Emily Moore Kerr Martin. He attended school in nearby Bowling Green before graduating from Danville's Centre College in 1840. Martin studied law with his father in Vicksburg, Mississippi, before moving to Natchez. There, he taught at a "classical school" and became district attorney. Martin was a well-respected private lawyer and, despite being a slave owner, acted as counselor for William Johnson, a free African American businessman. Johnson recorded Natchez's rough-and-tumble side in his diary, including Martin's having his finger bitten in a street fight as well as his caning a man in the street.

His life in Natchez included more than court days and fisticuffs. On January 5, 1854, Martin, the debonair attorney with William Faulkner good looks, married Margaret Dunlap Conner, the daughter of a wealthy planter. Four sons and five of their daughters lived to adulthood, and the Martins spent their antebellum years at Monteigne, a Natchez mansion built in 1855.

Politically, Martin was a unionist Whig who initially opposed secession. He later claimed that he made the last unionist speech in Mississippi before the Civil War and was "a cooperationist" who believed that slavery would eventually cause national conflict. He also supported colonization, claiming, "I never had any great fondness for the institution although I had been the owner of slaves from my youth up." By 1860 Martin owned ten slaves ranging in ages from fifteen to forty-two years.

In the spring of 1860, fear of a slave uprising spread, and Natchez citizens formed vigilante committees. Martin organized the groups to avoid chaos. "Being opposed to mob law," he testified, "and hoping that we would not have war . . . I proposed that a company of cavalry be armed and equipped." The men, all educated and "belonging to the best families," provided their own uniforms and horses while wealthy residents equipped the company. One "wealthy lady" even gave $600 for sabers.

In December, Martin went to Springfield, Massachusetts, to buy the swords. Hearing talk of war in the North changed Martin's views. He addressed the company on January 20, 1861, eleven days after Mississippi's secession. It was time to support their state, Martin argued. He later said that "there was no use of talking about a compromise any more: that the war was inevitable. . . . I proposed then to reorganize that company for war purposes, and told those who didn't want to take a part in it to step aside." Several officers, including one of Martin's best friends, made pro-Union speeches and resigned.

The company joined the Confederate army on May 18, 1861, and Martin became captain. In June the troopers were at the Memphis, Tennessee, fairgrounds. There, one Mississippian saw "a fine cavalry company from Natchez, commanded by Captain . . . William T. Martin. I had known and admired him when I lived in Jefferson county, as a fine lawyer." That month, they were sent to Richmond, Virginia.

On October 24, Martin took command of the Second Battalion Mississippi Cavalry with the rank of major, serving under the dashing Virginia cavalryman J. E. B. Stuart. Like Martin, the men were headstrong. As their commander, he was concerned about morale. He wrote his wife: "I am afraid there will be even worse complaints in the army than now exists. There is plenty already. The first flush of patriotism led many a man to join who now regrets it. . . . The prospect of winter here [in Virginia] is making the men very restive and they are beginning to resort to all sorts of means to get home." On October 27, 1861, one trooper declared that "if Martin does not meddle too much with us, we will get along very well."

On November 16, Martin led a reconnaissance to Doolan's farm, located southeast of Falls Church. The rebels encountered Federal pickets, charged, and defeated a Union foraging party. They killed and wounded several and bagged thirty prisoners. Martin, with no casualties, learned the advantage of surprise, while Stuart lauded "Martin's personal gallantry and prowess" and recommended him for promotion to lieutenant colonel of the newly formed Jeff Davis Legion into which his battalion had been merged. Martin was so commissioned on February 13, 1862.

After helping guard the Confederate withdrawal from the Peninsula, Stuart was sent in mid-June by Gen. Robert E. Lee to scout Union major general George McClellan's right flank and strike Union lines of supply and communication. Stuart chose 1,200 cavalrymen from the First, Fourth, and Ninth Virginia Cavalry regiments, as well as 250 men hand-picked by Martin from the Jeff Davis Legion. When they departed on June 13, Martin commanded the rear guard. Stuart had faith in the Kentuckian, stating his "entire confidence" in Martin's "judgment and skill."

Stuart's ride around McClellan was rapid, and Martin's cavalry demolished Union property, rounded up prisoners, seized horses and mules, and prevented straggling. Martin lamented that the fighting was taking place at the front of Stuart's column. After a 150-mile foray, the Confederates returned to Confederate lines. Stuart recommended Martin for promotion to colonel, "a grade which he had fairly won."

After Stuart's successful ride, Lee initiated the Seven Days' Battles, which lasted from June 25 to July 1. Martin skirmished, performed reconnaissance duties, and was present at the battle of Gaines' Mill and at Lee's repulse at Malvern Hill. As the Federals fell back, he rounded up arms and prisoners and skirmished.

When Lee invaded Maryland that autumn, Martin's command was active, skirmishing and guarding mountain gaps. At the September 17 battle of Antietam, Martin served on Lee's staff. Because of his performance during the Seven Days' Battles and in Maryland, Martin skipped the rank of colonel and was promoted to brigadier general on December 2, 1862, to rank from that date. His former brigade commander, Wade Hampton, wrote, "He is a first rate man, and I shall miss him greatly."

Martin departed the Army of Northern Virginia on January 7, 1863. President Jefferson Davis had promoted Martin to command a brigade of Mississippi cavalry in that state, but after Martin had been less than two weeks in that position, Maj. Gen. Earl Van Dorn put him in command of a division on February 2, 1863. In two months Martin had gone from a lieutenant colonel commanding a battalion in Virginia to a brigadier general commanding a division in Tennessee. After Martin fought under Van Dorn at the battle of Thompson's Station on March 6, Gen. Joseph E.

Johnston transferred him to Gen. Braxton Bragg's Army of Tennessee. Martin reported for duty at Tullahoma, Tennessee, on March 11, and three days later received orders from Bragg assigning him to Wheeler's Cavalry Corps. Maj. Gen. Joseph Wheeler had just divided his command into two divisions under John Hunt Morgan and John A. Wharton, and Martin was assigned to command Wharton's old brigade. Before the end of the month, Martin, Wheeler's third-highest-ranking subordinate, would assume command of a newly created third division.

Fighting and scouting from Nashville to Murfreesboro and around Chapel Hill and Liberty Gap kept Martin busy until mid-June. His toughest engagement during this period took place on June 27, when the Federals pushed Wheeler's cavalry through Shelbyville in a hand-to-hand fight. Wheeler, Martin, and fifty volunteers held a bridge and waited for reinforcements, but Federal troops swept over them. The officers plunged over a steep precipice into the Duck River to avoid capture.

Frequent skirmishing occupied Martin's Division during the Tullahoma campaign, as Bragg's army was pushed back beyond Chattanooga. Martin spent early September 1863 guarding mountain gaps in that region, and, on September 18, he reported a steady Federal advance, noting, "The enemy is keeping up a heavy dust." The next day, the troops clashed at the battle of Chickamauga. Martin led his division on the flanks of the Confederate army and helped drive the Northerners back to Chattanooga. From September 30 until October 17, Martin joined Wheeler in striking Federal lines of communication. Martin's performance during this period did not go unnoticed. The War Department promoted him to major general, to rank from November 10, 1863.

That month Martin reported at Knoxville to Lt. Gen. James Longstreet, who had been sent from the eastern theater prior to the battle of Chickamauga. Martin took over Wheeler's Cavalry Corps after Wheeler was ordered to Bragg's army in Georgia. Martin had served under Longstreet a year earlier, but neither their familiarity nor Martin's burgeoning responsibility would save Longstreet's opinion of Martin.

Longstreet had attacked Knoxville in late November and had been repulsed. As he later pulled back toward Virginia, Martin covered the withdrawal. It was evident that the commander thought Martin too inexperienced, giving him extremely detailed, meticulous dispatches that directed each brigade. Three days after Martin repulsed a Federal attack at Russellville, Longstreet, on December 13, attacked Federal infantry at Bean's Station.

Martin's cavalry struck the Union rear at May's Ford, crossed the

Holston River, and attacked the Federals' flank at Bean's Station. Martin took a hill and poured artillery into the Union breastworks while one of his divisions dismounted and attacked. Because of heavy rain, however, Martin's river crossing had been delayed, and he missed most of the fight. Longstreet quickly became frustrated with several subordinates, including Martin. The commander likely believed that Martin's late arrival contributed to the Confederates' failure to capture the Union force.

On December 23, Martin skirmished around Dandridge. The next day, the troops fought at Mossy Creek, where six hundred of Martin's men rode behind the Union troops, charged, and captured artillery before being driven off. Longstreet commended the troops but chastised Martin, stating, "It is hoped you may not have occasion to call upon our barefoot infantry to aid you. The commanding general regrets that you entertain the impression that your forces are fighting for the bread of the infantry. . . . The infantry forces of the army have fought too many desperate battles to be told that their bread is earned by the labor of the cavalry."

Martin's reputation was again bruised two days later, when Federal cavalry captured his camp. He took another hit on December 29, when he attacked Dandridge. There, the Northerners made a planned, tactical withdrawal to Mossy Creek before successfully counterattacking. Federal cavalry tactics and leadership were improving.

Longstreet had little faith in Martin, but he did try to compliment the cavalry officer. The commander told him, "You have already accomplished more than you or your command thought could be done." Because of Martin's recent failures, compliments were few and far between, and this one was weak at best.

By mid-January 1864, the enemy were "in full flight" toward Knoxville. Martin was told to "follow him and harass him until you are stopped only by the strongest necessity . . . give him no rest." The next day, Longstreet fumed when Martin burned bridges instead of chasing the Federals. He was told to continually press them and that "the commanding general expects to hear that you are in Knoxville soon." With Martin applying little pressure, an exasperated Longstreet told Martin that he "did not think you would wait to be ordered to pursue with your cavalry an enemy who was retreating, almost routed, from your front." During this campaign Martin was either too cautious, too fearful of superior cavalry, or too stubborn and refused to follow Longstreet's directions.

While operating near the Pigeon River on January 27, Federal cavalry drove Martin back, causing two hundred casualties. This was the final straw for Longstreet, who had lost all confidence in his cavalry commander. Longstreet complained to Gen. Samuel Cooper, the Confederate adjutant and inspector general: "Our cavalry is quite inefficient for want of a proper leader. General Martin has not had experience enough to give him confidence in himself or his men. Without confidence a cavalry leader can have no dash, and without either he cannot be the leader we need." Longstreet requested Wade Hampton from Virginia, adding, "Our cavalry is composed of very fine material, and only wants a good leader to render it very efficient."

Martin did not help his case when he complained to Longstreet about Joseph Wheeler. Martin blamed Wheeler for a rash of desertions, writing, "The course pursued by General Wheeler is gradually destroying my command." He lamented that Wheeler was withholding "wagons and supplies" as well as "officers and men" needed for his operations. Like his relationship with Longstreet, Martin's connections with Wheeler also deteriorated.

Longstreet's pleas to be rid of the Kentuckian were soon answered. President Jefferson Davis ordered Martin's cavalry transferred to Gen. Joseph E. Johnston's army at Dalton, Georgia. Longstreet told Martin that Davis gave "these orders with regret. He had hoped in retaining the services of your command to have helped the great cause by that good work which it is so well capable of performing." Martin likely bristled at this backhanded compliment, since Longstreet recognized the cavalry for their potential, not their actions. In addition, Longstreet hoped to keep "your command" but made little mention of keeping Martin. He wanted the men, but not the officer.

Before joining Johnston's army, Gen. Braxton Bragg, now serving as Jefferson Davis's military adviser in Richmond, warned Johnston about Martin's cavalry. Longstreet's complaints had not fallen on deaf ears. Bragg wrote Johnston that he could "well appreciate the embarrassment you feel in regard to your cavalry force. The Department is greatly disappointed in its expectations, based on Lieutenant-General Longstreet's reports of Major-General Martin's command. . . . [T]here is great neglect—nay, criminality—somewhere in that organization."

Longstreet was right. Lacking military experience, Martin was a lawyer, not a soldier. Untrained, he was a good regimental commander but was unsuccessful in leading a brigade or division. Corps command simply overwhelmed him. His promotion to general and his transfer into the poisonous command atmosphere of the western theater led to a tarnished reputation. Had he remained colonel, he could have flourished. Bragg, however, was wrong. There was no criminality, only inexperience. He would never command a corps again, and his inability—or refusal—to follow orders essentially ended his military career.

Leading a division in the Atlanta campaign, Martin scouted along the Oostenaula River, frequently skirmished, and, as Johnston retreated toward Atlanta, helped cover the withdrawal. With the constant campaigning came illness, and Martin took twenty days of sick leave ending on August 10. His absence, however, did not make Wheeler's heart grow fonder. On August 14, when Wheeler assaulted Dalton, their relationship shattered. Wheeler drove the Federals into their earthworks, but before resuming the attack he waited for Martin, who was supposedly rushing to Dalton. Martin never appeared, and that night the Federals were reinforced. Wheeler soon learned that Martin was camped several miles away. He immediately relieved Martin of command and placed him under arrest for disobeying orders. While "confusion in orders" may have kept Martin away, Wheeler believed that Martin deliberately disobeyed him.

Martin's service in Georgia was over, and he spent the remainder of the war commanding the District of Northwest Mississippi. He was inactive there, with the major event being a Union raid against the Mobile and Ohio Railroad. By May 4, Martin had learned that "an armistice" had been declared in other nearby departments. Within weeks, Martin's war ended.

Martin returned to Natchez and resumed his law practice. Late in 1865, he was a member of Mississippi's constitutional convention, which repealed the state's act of secession and re-wrote the constitution. Federal authorities, however, ignored the proceedings and placed Mississippi under military rule. Three years later, Martin was elected to the U.S. Congress as a Democrat, but the U.S. Congress prevented him from taking his seat.

By 1869, he was tired of Federal control. In a speech to local Democrats he said that they should give disingenuous support to "Conservative Republican nominees" as well as the new constitution. Appearing to reconcile, they could then "rid ourselves of Yankee-paid hireling office-holders" before securing "control of the State government, then we can strip this odious constitution of every objectionable feature, and we can mould and form it to suit ourselves."

Martin rebuilt his fortune as a lawyer and railroad executive. He also served as a delegate to the 1890 Constitutional Convention, where his views appeared to have mellowed. He pushed to publish the convention proceedings, to show that Mississippi knew the war had failed and that Mississippians "are now honestly disposed to return to our allegiance, and to make out of the disasters that have befallen us the best we can." Perhaps, in reprising his 1869 opinions, Martin played the role of reconstructed rebel so the Federals would leave Mississippi alone.

Martin remained politically active, attended many Democratic national conventions, and served in the state senate. He was a trustee for several universities and the state hospital in Natchez. In addition, Martin was Mississippi's vice president for the Southern Historical Society and postmaster of Natchez.

Martin died at Monteigne on March 16, 1910, and was buried in the Natchez City Cemetery. At the time of his death, the world of Martin's youth had completely changed. He recognized this fact in March 1867, stating, "Ours is no Constitution government now. It is a fierce democracy, & the will of the Majority Stands for Law." The Janus-faced Martin, however, survived and flourished no matter how his world evolved.

BIBLIOGRAPHY

Davis, William C., ed. *The Confederate General.* 6 vols. Harrisburg, PA: National Historical Society, 1991.

Hopkins, Donald A. *The Little Jeff: The Jeff Davis Legion, Cavalry, Army of Northern Virginia.* Shippensburg, PA: White Mane Books, 2000.

U.S. War Department. *The War of the Rebellion: A Compilation of the Official Records of the Union and Confederate Armies.* 70 vols. in 128 pts. Washington, DC: Government Printing Office, 1880–1901.

—STUART W. SANDERS

Brig. Gen. Samuel Bell Maxey

ONE OF THE most adverse and unusual careers in the Civil War belonged to Samuel Bell Maxey. Enlisting early in the war, Maxey initially wanted to fight in the western theater to protect his childhood home in Kentucky and win honor and laurels, only to be disappointed. As the war continued into 1863, Maxey requested a transfer to the Trans-Mississippi theater to defend his adopted state and was given command of the Indian Territory, one of the most troubled regions of the war. Though faced with demoralized soldiers, few supplies, and a displaced population, Maxey persevered and found resolutions to all those problems. Through these achievements Maxey found his battlefield glory and accolades, making him one of the most honored officers west of the Mississippi.

Born to Lucetta Pope Bell and Rice Maxey on March 30, 1825, in Tompkinsville, Kentucky, Sam moved with his family to Albany, Kentucky, before his tenth birthday. There they established what Maxey considered his childhood home. Growing up Maxey enjoyed the lifestyle of an upper-class Kentucky family, which included house servants. His father, a prominent attorney in the state, was well acquainted with most of the influential people of Kentucky including, but not limited to, Henry Clay, Robert Letcher, William Owsley, and Bryan Owsley. Maxey also grew up and befriended future prominent Kentuckians from his neighborhood, such as Thomas Bramlette, William Bramlette, and Preston H. Leslie. His father's wealth and prominence created many opportunities for young Maxey, such as a personal library, private tutors, and his appointment to the U.S. Military Academy at West Point.

Maxey, however, did not impress many people at West Point. In 1846, he graduated near the bottom of his class, beating out only George Pickett of Gettysburg fame. Maxey performed poorly in his mathematical, engineering, artillery, and cavalry studies but excelled in language lessons. Lack of discipline, especially the desire to sleep late, which his roommate Thomas J. "Stonewall" Jackson regarded unsympathetically, further contributed to his poor performance at West Point. Though not a standout he was classmates with cadets who later gained prominence in the Civil War, such as Ulysses S. Grant, Winfield Scott Hancock, Edmund Kirby Smith, James Longstreet, and Ambrose Burnside.

Soon after graduation the United States was at war with Mexico. During the Mexican War, Maxey proved to be a better soldier than student. He fought bravely in several engagements, including the battles at Cerro Gordo, Contreras, Churubusco, and Molino del Rey. When the war ended, he served as commander of one of the five companies assigned as city guards for Mexico City. Though graduating next to last in his class, Maxey proved himself an able leader in combat in Mexico, but more importantly he established some lifelong friendships that had a major impact on his later life, especially with Edmund Kirby Smith. After returning to the United States, Maxey did not find the peacetime army appealing and resigned his commission.

Done with the army, Maxey returned home and failed in his attempt to enter politics by running for the Kentucky House of Representatives. After his defeat Maxey decided to study law under his father. He passed the bar exam in 1851, joined his father's law firm, and was elected clerk of the circuit and county courts of Clinton County in 1852. A year later Maxey married Marilda Cass Denton, the daughter of a Baptist preacher. Though everything in Maxey's life appeared to promise success, the need for litigation in southern Kentucky declined, and the small wages of his clerkship forced Maxey to make a hard decision about the future of his family. After reading glowing accounts of Texas from a relative living there, Maxey and his father moved their families in October of 1857 to Paris, Texas.

In Texas, Maxey's political and professional ambitions improved when he received an appointment to fill a vacancy as district attorney in Lamar County. His political ambitions were further realized when he won reelection to the position in 1859 and 1860, eventually winning a seat in the Texas Senate in 1861. Though elected senator he never took his seat because of the secession crisis and his activities in the Confederate army. His father served in his place.

Following the Texas state secession convention in early 1861, Maxey raised a company of men from Lamar County, the Lamar Rifles, to accompany W. C. Young and his Texas cavalry into the Indian Territory. After briefly serving in the Indian Territory, Maxey returned to Texas and began to entertain the idea of raising a unit for service in the Confederate army in his native state of Kentucky. After obtaining permission to raise a regiment for Confederate service on September 3, 1861, he successfully organized a regiment of Texas infantry for service in the western theater.

By mid-October Maxey had his rosters full and mustered a regiment into Confederate service as the Ninth Texas Infantry. Maxey wanted to serve in Bowling Green, Kentucky, and telegraphed the Confederate commander there, Gen. Albert Sidney Johnston, requesting to be assigned to him. On February 13, 1862, Maxey received permission, and his regiment marched to Memphis, Tennessee, to join Johnston's army. He was promoted to brigadier general on March 7, to rank from March 4. His promotion to a general officer led to a change of command. He left the Ninth Texas Infantry to command a small garrison of 2,300 men defending Chattanooga, Tennessee.

The reassignment did not meet Maxey's expectations. He spent most of his time guarding bridges and clearing the railroad tracks in the Chattanooga region. Every attempt he made to get into a command that was actively engaged with the enemy failed. It troubled him that he missed the battles of Shiloh and Corinth and lost his opportunity to gain honor and laurels. Maxey's first real opportunity to confront the enemy came in August. In a small two-day engagement beginning on August 24, Maxey captured Union commissary supplies at Bridgeport, Alabama. On the last day of the same month, his troops stormed the strong fortifications at Stevenson, Alabama.

Less than a month later Maxey received orders to reinforce Maj. Gen. Edmund Kirby Smith in Kentucky with men and supplies. Kirby Smith was participating in Gen. Braxton Bragg's Kentucky campaign, an attempt to capture the Bluegrass State and recruit more soldiers for the Confederate army. Initially the prospects of returning to his childhood state excited Maxey, but it soon became dreadful. Feuding generals and the lack of cooperation of unionists surrounding Knoxville, Tennessee, kept Maxey's troops from moving north into Kentucky. By the time his men finally advanced, the campaign had already failed. Disheartened, Maxey retreated with Bragg to Murfreesboro, unable to participate in what proved to be his only opportunity to return and fight in his native state.

On December 14, 1862, two days after being assigned to duty in Hardee's Corps, Maxey was transferred to the Department of Mississippi and East Louisiana. Lt. Gen. John C. Pemberton, the departmental commander, assigned him to Port Hudson, Louisiana. Maxey commanded a brigade in the garrison there until May 1863, when Union general Ulysses S. Grant launched his final Vicksburg campaign.

Maxey and his men received orders to march to the New Orleans, Jackson and Great Northern Railroad. Boarding trains at Tangipahoa, they rode north to stop the Union advance at Brookhaven, Mississippi, twenty-five miles south of Jackson. Maxey's expectations of fighting the enemy in a large battle again were unfulfilled when his soldiers were relegated to shipping ordnance and supplies to the Confederates engaged with the enemy. Any of Maxey's hopes to engage the enemy quickly vanished when Grant encircled Vicksburg before the Kentuckian could get to the city. Vicksburg eventually surrendered to Grant on July 4, 1863.

The Confederate defeat at Vicksburg had a dramatic impact on the South's war efforts and left a deeper concern for Maxey. When the Gibraltar of the South fell to enemy hands, Maxey's goals for the war changed. Initially, Maxey fought to protect his native state and achieve military fame, but with the entire Mississippi River in Union control, his wife and family in Texas were now cut off from him and vulnerable to Union advances. Almost immediately after the capture of Vicksburg, Maxey wrote to his wife and to the Confederate government about returning to the Trans-Mississippi. On August 6, 1863, Maxey received orders to move his brigade to Mobile, Alabama, to help defend the port city. While en route to Mobile in mid-August Maxey finally obtained the orders transferring him to the Trans-Mississippi. Though anxious to get across the great river, he reported, with his troops, in Mobile before leaving his command.

Once across the Mississippi, he reported to his old friend Gen. Edmund Kirby Smith, now the commander of the Trans-Mississippi Department. After Maxey took a brief leave to visit his wife and family back in Paris, Kirby Smith appointed him commander of the Indian Territory in December 1863, one of the most complicated commands and conflicted regions in the Confederacy. At the outset of the war the Union army abandoned its posts in the region, which the Confederates occupied with little resistance. During this time Albert Pike entered the Indian Territory to establish an alliance with sympathetic Indians to defend the region. As the war progressed, Confederate hold on the territory waned slowly; two major forts were lost. By the time Maxey took command, he had three major problems in the Indian Territory: too few soldiers to fight the Union army in an attempt to defend the territory; the need to provide food and supplies not only for Confederate white and Indian soldiers but also for the families of their Indian allies displaced by the Union advance; and, most important to Maxey, the need to keep the encroaching enemy out of North Texas. Compounding these problems were the Indian soldiers under his command. The men were demoralized because of the major defeat they suffered at Honey Springs, Indian Territory, and feelings that the Confederate government had abandoned them. Additionally, disorganization ensued throughout the southern regions of the Indian Territory since the soldiers left their units to take care of their families suffering from their displacement.

The predicament of the Confederate Indians is attributed to the lack of an organized logistical system in the region. It was difficult for the Confederates to feed their own soldiers with supplies from North Texas, but providing for the families of their allies made the situation worse. Since the Indian troops felt the Confederacy was not honoring its side of the bargain, protecting and providing for their families, most Indian soldiers in the territory were on the verge of quitting the war, thus leaving North Texas exposed. Without the Confederate Indians, the only white force in the territory was Gano's Brigade, commanded by fellow Kentuckian Brig. Gen. Richard Montgomery Gano. That brigade, too, suffered from lack of food, supplies, and morale.

Maxey did not shy away from these problems. Instead he addressed many of the problems immediately with a meeting with the Indian leaders to build their confidence in his leadership. Little did Maxey know initially that Brig. Gen. Douglas H. Cooper challenged his leadership. Passed over for command of the Indian Territory twice, Cooper became a thorn in Maxey's side because he had a good rapport with the Indians and was good friends with President Jefferson Davis. Despite this challenge, Maxey proved his leadership quickly to the Indians through his flexibility, ability to build confidence, and support of Indian commanders.

When reorganizing the Indian soldiers, Maxey wanted to consolidate the regiments into two brigades. This quickly proved to be a major problem since the Indians enlisted as nations. The only way to satisfy the Indians, as Maxey eventually agreed, was to establish three brigades, one composed of the Cherokee regiments, another a combination of Choctaws and Chickasaws, and a third with Creeks and Seminoles. To build confidence among the reorganized Indian soldiers Maxey published all his orders, emphasizing that his goals were the same as theirs, to defend and protect all the land in the Indian Territory. To maintain the newly won confidence, Maxey showed more diplomacy than any commander of the

Indian Territory before him when he fought to promote Col. Stand Watie, who was three-quarters Native American, to brigadier general. After implementing these resolutions Maxey felt confident that his new command was ready to fight the enemy.

In April 1864, Maxey had his first opportunity to test his reorganized force against the Union army in Arkansas during the Camden campaign. Maxey arrived too late to fully participate in the Camden campaign but did assist Brig. Gen. John Marmaduke in capturing a Union supply train at Poison Spring. Though the senior commander, Maxey deferred to Marmaduke during the battle since the latter already had tactical knowledge of the enemy and terrain. The Confederates routed the enemy and forced them to abandon the train and much-needed supplies. After the battle ended, the killing of Union soldiers continued. Part of the Union force was the First Kansas Colored Volunteers, a unit composed of African American soldiers, which were not given quarter once the fighting ended. Maxey's men participated in the greatest massacre of African American soldiers west of the Mississippi River.

At the conclusion of the Camden campaign, Maxey returned to the Indian Territory feeling triumphant and ambitious. He quickly began planning for an offensive for the summer to take back Forts Gibson and Smith. Much to his dismay he realized that with his limited resources, it was improbable. All he could hope for was to isolate the Union soldiers at their forts and, if fortunate, force them to evacuate. Since most of the resources and men available to him were suited for guerrilla warfare, Maxey could starve them out of the fortifications by capturing or destroying their supply trains and attacking any foraging parties. He experienced successes with General Watie's capture and looting of a supply boat on the Arkansas River and General Gano's raid at Cabin Creek on a supply train containing $1.5 million worth of supplies. Though not entirely successful in forcing the Union army to evacuate, these activities boosted the morale of the people in the Indian Territory and North Texas because they received food and supplies from the raids while any Union attempt to encroach farther south was stunted.

Maxey arrived in the Indian Territory with the people hungry and the army demoralized and unorganized. He solved many of these problems while not allowing the enemy to gain any new territory, but this was not enough for him to keep his command. Problems with Cooper reemerged. Still upset about being passed over for command of the territory, Cooper called on his connections in Richmond to force Kirby Smith to replace Maxey with himself. Kirby Smith received the order but only enforced it after President Davis gave him a direct order to do so. Realizing the injustice of the situation, Kirby Smith did not leave Maxey without a command; he assigned him to a new division created especially for him. Maxey's removal upset the men in the territory. Cooper received a cold reception, especially from the white soldiers under Gano, who requested to leave the territory when Cooper took command.

Maxey spent the last few months of the war in command of his new division in Texas. After Kirby Smith surrendered the Trans-Mississippi, Maxey returned home to resume his law practice. Still interested in politics, Maxey was elected in 1875 as a Democratic senator from Texas. He served for two terms in the Senate, focusing on Indian Affairs. After leaving the Senate, he again practiced law and wrote a book on Texas history. On August 16, 1895, Maxey died in Eureka Springs, Arkansas, following a period of declining health and was buried in Evergreen Cemetery in his beloved city of Paris. Maxey's life spanned seventy years, during which he distinguished himself as a lawyer, soldier, and politician.

BIBLIOGRAPHY

Davis, William C., ed. *The Confederate General.* 6 vols. Harrisburg, PA: National Historical Society, 1991.

Hewitt, Lawrence Lee. *Port Hudson, Confederate Bastion on the Mississippi.* Baton Rouge: Louisiana State University Press, 1987.

Horton, Louise. *Samuel Bell Maxey: A Biography.* Austin: University of Texas Press, 1974.

Spencer, J. Elden. "Samuel Bell Maxey." In *Ten More Texans in Gray,* ed. W. C. Nunn. Hillsboro, TX: Hill Junior College Press, 1980.

Waugh, John C. *Sam Bell Maxey and the Confederate Indians.* Abilene, TX: McWhiney Foundation Press, 1995.

—CHARLES D. GREAR

Brig. Gen. John Hunt Morgan

JOHN HUNT MORGAN identified
with the military tradition of his
Morgan forebears and determined to serve in the military.
He was born the eldest son of
Calvin and Henrietta Hunt
Morgan on June 1, 1825, in
Huntsville, Alabama. When
John was five years old, his father, a lieutenant colonel in the
militia, closed his apothecary
business and moved the family
to Lexington, Kentucky, where
he worked as overseer of the
farm of Henrietta's father, prominent businessman John Wesley
Hunt. Slaves worked the farm

and performed the chores, and John Hunt Morgan enjoyed hunting and
horseback riding. He preferred the outdoors to studying, but, because of
family expectations, at the age of seventeen he enrolled in Transylvania
University. In his second year he dueled with a fellow student, and on July
4, 1844, the trustees suspended him, ending his formal education. The
next year, at the age of twenty, he applied for a commission in the U.S.
Marine Corps. Former vice president Richard M. Johnson recommended
him as a young man with an outstanding reputation for integrity, honor,
and chivalry.

Morgan's dream of active military service was temporarily fulfilled
when Congress declared war on Mexico. He was twenty-one when he
volunteered in Col. Humphrey Marshall's First Kentucky Cavalry. He
mustered in on June 9, 1846, in Louisville, and the seventy-eight men in
Company K elected him second lieutenant. He was immediately promoted
to first lieutenant and fought with the regiment under Maj. Gen. Zachary
Taylor in the battle of Buena Vista on February 23, 1847. Morgan loved
cavalry duty, but on June 7, 1847, his enlistment ended; with the other
forty-four survivors in his company, he returned to Lexington. Immediately, he organized a volunteer cavalry company and petitioned to unite it

with one of the new Kentucky infantry regiments. He also applied for a commission in the regular army, stating that he preferred an independent cavalry company but would take any position. He was still petitioning for an assignment when the war ended in 1848.

He went into business in Lexington breeding and training racehorses and conducting other ventures with his partner, Sanders Bruce. On November 21, 1848, he married Rebecca Bruce, his partner's sister. In 1853 he and his brother Calvin opened a partnership in hemp manufacturing, and in 1859 they entered partnership with brother Richard in wholesale wool and manufacture of militia uniforms. Earning the respect of his neighbors, Morgan became a Mason, captain of the Union Volunteer Fire Company, and member of the town council and school board. He organized a state militia artillery company and for two years drilled them in the school of the piece with a six-pound bronze cannon provided by the state. Then, in 1854 the Kentucky General Assembly deactivated the militia, and the company disbanded. Three years later, in 1857, he organized the Lexington Rifles volunteer infantry company, which later became part of the State Guard. Their stylish green uniforms included tall shako hats with bright green plumes and the seal of the state. Their motto was "Our laws the commands of our Captain."

When the Civil War began, Morgan supported Kentucky neutrality but raised a Confederate flag on the woolen factory and stopped manufacturing any color uniform other than gray. When the state legislature declared for the Union on September 18, 1861, and demanded that the Lexington Rifles and other units of the pro-Confederate State Guard turn in their arms, Morgan prepared to lead his men into the Confederacy. On the night of September 20 they delivered to the Lexington railroad depot boxes of bricks marked "Arms from Captain Morgan" and addressed to the state armory. Then they marched away toward Confederate lines on Green River with their weapons concealed in hay wagons.

Morgan had no formal military education, but he had one year of experience in the cavalry plus six years' militia service with the artillery and infantry. In the Civil War, he began by conducting guerrilla warfare on his own for twenty-seven days. Intuitively adopting hit-and-run tactics in the dark of night, he led a few mounted men behind enemy lines in western Kentucky and discovered that partisan raiding relieved the boredom of camp life and gave him an opportunity to use his leadership skills. On October 27, he enrolled his company in the Confederate cavalry and became famous as the "Francis Marion of the War" and the primary model for the Confederate Partisan Ranger Act. He fought at the battle of Shiloh and afterward was promoted to colonel to rank from April 4, 1862. After organizing the Second Kentucky Cavalry, he began raiding.

After meeting defeat in an action at Lebanon (the "Lebanon races"), Morgan and his men captured a southbound Louisville and Nashville (L & N) Railroad train at Cave City. While a detachment seized $6,000 from the express car, Morgan boarded the passenger cars. There were several wives of Union officers on board, going to Nashville to join their husbands. When Morgan greeted them, they asked him not to destroy their clothing packed in trunks in the luggage compartment. One young woman, seated beside her husband, who was wearing the uniform of a Union officer, told Morgan they were newly married and begged Morgan not to take him from her. Morgan politely agreed and allowed the train to return to Louisville, newlyweds, women, and baggage intact. Journalists exaggerated the story, and by the time it reached Richmond, Virginia, the $6,000 became $250,000 and the encounter with the newlyweds became a romantic saga of chivalry. According to the *Richmond Enquirer*, Morgan was an ideal Southern gentleman, protector of women, and "a humane warrior."

Early in the war the great fear of Union commanders in Kentucky was that the thousands of Kentuckian men of draft age who stayed home might rise en masse for the Confederacy. On Morgan's First Kentucky Raid, July 4–28, 1862, he heightened this fear by issuing a proclamation in Glasgow, Kentucky, challenging Kentuckians to join him and throw off the Federal yoke. Brig. Gen. Jeremiah T. Boyle, Union commander in the state with headquarters in Louisville, read the proclamation and assumed that Morgan's force was increasing. "All the rebels of the State will join him if there is not a demonstration of force and power sent in cavalry," he reported. Boyle concluded that Morgan was heading toward Louisville with 3,000 men, and when his cries for reinforcements reached Washington, President Abraham Lincoln telegraphed Gen. Henry Halleck in Corinth, Mississippi, "They are having a stampede in Kentucky. Please look to it." Morgan marched his 867-man brigade between Louisville and Lexington, captured Cynthiana, recruited 300 men, and turned back into Tennessee. Large crowds gathered to welcome Morgan, who confused curiosity to get a look at the famous raiders with secessionist sentiment and misled the Confederate high command into assuming that a regular army invasion would bring Kentucky into the Confederacy.

The *London Times* recognized Morgan as the pioneer in use of the telegraph for military intelligence, and history acknowledges him as the nemesis of the Union military telegraph in the western theater. Morgan recruited George A. "Lightning" Ellsworth as his personal telegraph operator. On raids Ellsworth would intercept Union army messages and send deceptive imitative communications. On August 12, 1862, when Morgan's men raided Gallatin, Tennessee, Ellsworth captured the telegraph office and, imitating J. N. Brooks, the Union operator, he assured the operator in Franklin to the north that it would be safe to send a southbound freight train to Gallatin. Ellsworth alerted Morgan that the train was on its way, and Morgan's men easily captured the train of twenty cars loaded with fifty horses, forage, and rations. The purpose of the raid was to destroy the twin L & N tunnels north of town, and after the freight train arrived, the raiders burned the tunnels. This closed Maj. Gen. Don Carlos Buell's supply line and caused Buell to suspend the Army of the Ohio's advance on Chattanooga for ninety-eight days. The raid was Morgan's greatest strategic accomplishment in the war because it gave the initiative to Confederate general Braxton Bragg for his invasion of Kentucky.

Morgan adapted to the revolution in arms by having his men throw away their sabers in favor of short Enfield rifles and Colt revolvers. In a fight, he had one-fourth of the men hold the horses, and those in action fought dismounted. On the defensive, he arranged the men in a semicircle that caught the attacking enemy in a cross fire that the raiders called Morgan's "jaws of death." After the Gallatin raid, General Buell massed his cavalry under Brig. Gen. Richard W. Johnson and ordered them to destroy Morgan. On August 21, 1862, Johnson attacked with a mounted saber charge near Gallatin. Morgan's men held their fire until the Union horsemen were within thirty yards, and on the first volley, two-thirds of the Union men and horses went down. The others fled in a panic, and Johnson condemned them for what he called a shameful retreat.

Morgan's men fought in Bragg's Kentucky invasion in September and October 1862, and when Bragg withdrew to Murfreesboro, Tennessee, the L & N Railroad was still closed from the Gallatin raid. Bragg showed his appreciation by supporting Morgan's December 7, 1862, Hartsville raid with infantry reinforcements and a diversion. Morgan's cavalry and infantry force marched through a snowstorm and surprised the Union brigade at Hartsville before breakfast, capturing 1,834 men. Maj. Gen. William S. Rosecrans, who had replaced Buell, responded: "It seems to me impossible that the entire brigade could have surrendered. Are there none left?" Six days later, Jefferson Davis—on a visit in Murfreesboro to quiet complaints against Bragg—signed Morgan's promotion to brigadier general.

Morgan entered the war as a widower. His first wife, Rebecca, gave birth to a stillborn son in 1853, five years into the marriage, and the delivery left her an invalid for the remainder of her life. Morgan took her to Hot Springs, Arkansas, and for years provided the most qualified medical attention available, but her condition worsened and she died on July 21, 1861. When Morgan had his headquarters near Murfreesboro in February 1862, Charles Ready, a prominent local attorney and former U.S. congressman, visited camp and sent a note home to his family that he was bringing Morgan for dinner. It included a message for his daughter Martha, or "Mattie": "Tell Mattie that Captain Morgan is a widower and a little sad. I want her to sing for him." Mattie and John fell in love and were married in Murfreesboro on December 14, 1862. After Morgan was killed, she gave birth to a daughter named Johnnie for her father.

Union major general Ulysses S. Grant wrote in his memoirs that every foot of road in the Union army rear in the western theater had to be guarded against Morgan. By the Christmas Raid, December 22, 1862–January 1, 1863, Morgan and others had forced the Union to post 20,357 men on guard duty behind Union lines. On the Christmas Raid, with 3,900 men, Morgan directly diverted 7,300 soldiers from Rosecrans's army on the eve of Murfreesboro who otherwise could have fought there. The Christmas Raid accomplished the mission of destroying the two L & N bridges at Muldraugh's Hill five miles north of Elizabethtown, closing the railroad for five weeks. L & N executives pleaded with the Union army for protection against Morgan, the railroad's number one enemy; he closed it during the war for a total of four and one-half months.

When Morgan was on the alert on a raid, he seemed invincible. Gen. George Patton of World War II wrote in the margin of one of his books that he admired Morgan for marching light and with lightning speed. The raiders had only their weapons; they carried no forage or rations, and the only wheels in the column were for the artillery. Morgan sent out scouts in all directions and used "rolling videttes" to guard crossroads and leapfrog to the front once the main body passed. However, on the Great Raid in Indiana and Ohio, July 1–26, 1863, once past Cincinnati, Morgan became overconfident and neglected to deploy scouts or conduct feints, enabling the Union cavalry in pursuit to surprise him at Buffington Island on July 19. Morgan escaped with most of the men but was captured one week later near West Point, Ohio. In violation of international law Union authorities incarcerated him in the Ohio State Penitentiary in Columbus. He escaped on November 27, 1863, and the reward of $6,000 for his recapture was never collected.

Assigned to southwestern Virginia, with many of his former men still in Union prison camps, Morgan's new command included several men more interested in plunder than sacrificing for the Confederacy. His second in command and brother-in-law, Col. Basil Duke, was still imprisoned and not available to render wise counsel and enforce discipline. From May 30 to June 12, 1864, Morgan conducted his last raid into Kentucky. He captured valuable horses in Lexington and captured a Union garrison at Cynthiana on June 11 but failed to deploy scouts to determine the location of Brig. Gen. Stephen G. Burbridge's strong cavalry brigade defending the state. Burbridge surprised and routed Morgan at Cynthiana on June 12, and several of the Confederate raiders remained in Kentucky to participate in the unauthorized guerrilla warfare that plagued the civilians. During the raid, some of Morgan's men robbed a branch of the Farmer's Bank of Kentucky in Mount Sterling as well as other banks. Morgan was not involved in the illegal robberies, but Confederate authorities charged him with neglect for allowing "excesses and irregularities." He was suspended on August 30, 1864, and a court of inquiry was scheduled for September 10 in Abingdon, Virginia.

Ignoring his suspension, Morgan marched his command into eastern Tennessee to attack a Union cavalry force under Brig. Gen. Alvan C. Gillem. On the night of September 3, 1864, he camped in Greeneville, intending to attack Gillem the next day at Bulls Gap, eighteen miles away. Gillem received inaccurate intelligence that a small detachment of Morgan's men was in Greeneville without Morgan. He advanced through the night in a thunderstorm, planning to capture the detachment. A few miles from Greeneville he received several reports that Morgan himself was in town with his main body of men camped outside of town, toward Bulls Gap. Gillem ordered Capt. C. C. Wilcox to take two companies, flank Morgan's camp on the Union right, and move into town and capture Morgan. When Wilcox's men surrounded Morgan's headquarters house, Morgan attempted to escape. Union private Andrew J. Campbell twice ordered Morgan to halt, but he kept running and Campbell killed him. Campbell did not know who it was until one of Morgan's staff identified the general's body.

As a heroic symbol of the Confederacy, Morgan had three funerals and three burials. The first funeral, in Abingdon, was attended by his wife, Mattie, and his men, and burial was in an above-ground vault in Sinking Spring Cemetery. Nine days later the body was taken to Richmond and honored with a procession to the Confederate House of Representatives where he lay in state. A graveside service and burial followed in Hollywood Cemetery. On April 17, 1868, Morgan's body returned to Lexington, and after a funeral in Christ Church Episcopal and an elaborate procession through the streets with sidewalks, windows, and doorways crowded with mourning citizens, he was buried in Lexington Cemetery.

BIBLIOGRAPHY

Davis, William C., ed. *The Confederate General.* 6 vols. Harrisburg, PA: National Historical Society, 1991.

Duke, Basil W. *A History of Morgan's Cavalry.* Cincinnati: Miami, 1867. Reprint, West Jefferson, OH: Genesis, 1997.

Ramage, James A. *Rebel Raider: The Life of General John Hunt Morgan.* Lexington: University Press of Kentucky, 1986.

Thomas, Edison. *John Hunt Morgan and His Raiders.* Lexington: University Press of Kentucky, 1975.

—JAMES A. RAMAGE

Brig. Gen. William Preston

BASED ON HIS family background, beliefs, and economic standing, William Preston was an advocate of the interests of wealthy southern landowners throughout his adult life. In the decades of the mid-nineteenth century, he defended the interests of the slaveholding South as a legislator, diplomat, and military officer. Ultimately, his successes and failures in these endeavors were determined by the fate of the system and region he represented.

His father, Maj. William Preston, had served under Gen. Anthony Wayne and came from one of the first families of Virginia, as did his mother, Caroline Hancock. Son William was born October 16, 1816, on a plantation just outside Louisville on land granted the Prestons by Virginia governor Thomas Jefferson in 1780. Following studies at two Kentucky boarding schools and at Yale and Harvard, William returned to Louisville in 1839, and the following year he married Margaret Wickliffe of Lexington, daughter of the largest slaveholder in the commonwealth. The couple would be parents to five daughters and a son. In the Mexican War, Preston served as a lieutenant colonel, although he did not see combat. After the war he was elected to the Kentucky legislature and to Congress, gaining renown as a proponent of states' rights and slavery. President James Buchanan appointed him minister to Madrid in 1858, and for three years the Kentuckian sought to purchase Spain's Cuban colony. However, the growing strength of the abolitionists successfully opposed this attempt to annex additional slave lands to the Union.

On his return from Spain in 1861, Preston left his family in Lexington and took up arms for the Confederacy. While he saw slavery as "the most prominent cause" of the war, he insisted, "It is not to perpetuate slavery that I have taken up sides with the South." "Born in the South," the Louisville native asserted that he was fighting for the Confederacy "because I love my country."

While not a professional soldier, Preston gained recognition as both an able and a valiant leader and held successively more important commands. Commissioned a colonel on November 3, 1861, he was promoted to brigadier general April 14, 1862. From 1861 through 1863, he would command combat troops in Tennessee, Mississippi, Kentucky, Virginia, and Georgia. Following a diplomatic assignment in 1864, the next year the Kentuckian served as a major general in Texas, though no proof that he was ever officially nominated as been found.

Preston's first assignment was as aide-de-camp to his brother-in-law, Gen. Albert Sidney Johnston, the commander of Department No. 2. Until April 1862 the colonel remained busy communicating orders to subordinates as the Southern forces retreated from Bowling Green through Tennessee to the town of Corinth in northern Mississippi. Delayed for several days by rain and logistical problems, the gray army of forty thousand untried soldiers on the morning of April 6 made a surprise attack on Maj. Gen. Ulysses S. Grant's forces of about the same size encamped along the Tennessee River. The ensuing battle became one of the most brutal and fiercely contested in American military history. Near Shiloh Church, just north of the Mississippi-Tennessee line, the Southern warriors moved forward during the first hours of the conflict, and an optimistic Preston reported "loud cheers and handsome advances of our troops." But stubborn Yankee resistance at a bastion dubbed the Hornet's Nest kept the Confederates from routing the enemy.

After encouraging his men to continue their advance, General Johnston rode to the rear around two o'clock and was struck by a minié ball, which pierced an artery in his right leg. The commander was taken to a small ravine and expired in the arms of his brother-in-law. Never in American military annals had such a high-ranking officer been killed at the head of his troops. Preston notified Gen. Pierre G. T. Beauregard, the next in command, that "the completion of the victory would fall upon him." Although the Confederates did take the Hornet's Nest in the late afternoon, fierce Union fighting frustrated their attempts to sweep toward the river. At six o'clock, Beauregard stopped the attack by his exhausted and depleted troops. That night 17,000 fresh Northern reinforcements arrived, and the following day Grant's army advanced, forcing Beauregard to withdraw his men to Corinth. After two days of conflict, 3,500 lay dead and another 16,000 wounded.

The South's closeness to complete victory at Shiloh has made the battle a controversial subject for generations of historians. For Preston, "when Beauregard missed the opportunity . . . to attack, all was lost," but defenders of the Creole general argued that the arrival of additional Northern troops signaled certain defeat. Debate aside, at Shiloh the South lost the most important battle of the Civil War for control of West Tennessee and the lower Mississippi Valley.

For his service to General Johnston, Preston was made brigadier general and assigned to Maj. Gen. John C. Breckinridge, William's Lexington cousin and former vice president under Buchanan. Breckinridge was reorganizing the First Kentucky Brigade, later affectionately known as the Orphan Brigade, as the men fought far from their Bluegrass homes. Preston took charge of a new brigade, composed of three regiments of the Kentucky Orphans and an Alabama battery. In June he led his men and wagon trains with supplies to Vicksburg, where the Confederate stronghold was threatened by enemy gunboats.

Beauregard was replaced as commander in the west by Gen. Braxton Bragg. Soon the new leader gained the enmity of many of his officers. Preston complained that he was "a stern and imperious soldier and [was] endeavoring by aggressive severity to establish discipline, but the men are indignant, and I fear trouble." The brigadier's complaints about Bragg would only increase as the war progressed. Nevertheless, Preston and Breckinridge were among the officers who convinced their commander to plan an invasion of Kentucky that summer. "I wish to help secure Kentucky forever for the South," Preston wrote, adding, "I wish on returning to get the men of influence to espouse our cause and enlist their children in our own ranks."

September 1862 marked the apex of Confederate success in Kentucky. Bragg's Army of the Mississippi invaded the commonwealth from the south, while Maj. Gen. Edmund Kirby Smith's Army of East Tennessee entered from the southeast, giving them control of a line stretching from Bardstown in the west through Frankfort to Lexington. Preston joined Kirby Smith's command and hosted "brilliant festivities" for him and Bragg at his wife's family home in Lexington. Bragg welcomed Preston's presence and noted that the brigadier "has great influence here." Outside of Perryville, near Danville, Confederate and Union forces met to determine the fate of Kentucky. The battle ended without victory for either side, but the outmanned Confederates retreated to Tennessee. Preston was not at Perryville but near Frankfort with troops defending the capital.

In December President Jefferson Davis ordered the formation of a new division under Breckinridge's command, and Preston was placed in charge of one of its four brigades. On December 31, 1862, and January 2, 1863, at Murfreesboro, Bragg's 38,000 men attempted to stop 43,000 Union troops marching south from Nashville under Maj. Gen. William S. Rosecrans. On New Year's Eve, Preston's brigade took a Federal position by deploying one unit far to his right, thus forcing the enemy to aim their fire both to the left and straight ahead. This allowed his men to charge across an open field and take their objective. En route some "fell into confusion under a crushing fire," until Preston "seized the colors and rode before the line toward the enemy," thus reanimating his troops' advance. During this charge, a shell fragment pierced his cap. By nightfall, 54 of his 1,951 men were dead and another 384 wounded.

Despite heavy losses, Rosecrans did not retreat on New Year's Day, and on January 2 the battle resumed. Bragg ordered Breckinridge's men to take a ridge on the other side of the river occupied by a Federal division and defended by artillery located on high ground. Breckinridge protested that such action could only end in defeat. When Bragg remained unmoved, Breckinridge agreed to follow orders but insisted that the unwise plan was his commander's responsibility. To support Breckinridge's assault, Preston's troops gave up the position they had taken two days earlier. When some of his soldiers panicked under heavy fire, the brigadier later wrote, "I beat all fugitive men and officers over the head with my saber until I got a handful of men around me," and they formed a new defensive line. By the end of the contest the brigade counted another 41 dead and 245 wounded. The next day the Confederates once again headed southward, this time to Tullahoma, Tennessee, where they spent the remaining winter months.

Following the fight at Murfreesboro, Generals Breckinridge and Preston, by now leaders of the "Kentucky bloc" opposing Bragg, asked President Davis to remove him as their commander. Davis did not do this, but in April 1863 he reassigned Breckinridge to Mississippi and Preston to Abingdon, in southwestern Virginia. There he commanded 2,416 men defending a vital saltworks and the Tennessee and Virginia Railroad from Union raiders.

By late summer Rosecrans's troops were advancing toward Chattanooga, so the Confederates planned a major offensive to stop him. In August, Preston was ordered to take his soldiers south to unite with Bragg's army and was placed in charge of a division of 4,000 men in three brigades. His was one of two divisions commanded by Maj. Gen. Simon Bolivar Buckner, a fellow Kentuckian. From Virginia Lt. Gen. James Longstreet brought another 12,000 reinforcements from Gen. Robert E.

Lee's army. By mid-September 125,000 Union and Confederate troops were facing each other along Chickamauga Creek in Georgia, a dozen miles south of the Tennessee line.

On September 19 the battle began, and both sides put up stout defenses. Only one of Preston's brigades was engaged that day, but it suffered about 150 killed or wounded. The following morning Longstreet's men charged through a gap in enemy lines and sent much of Rosecrans's army fleeing northward toward Chattanooga. However, Union major general George Thomas formed a new line atop Snodgrass Hill, a two-hundred-foot outcropping of the Missionary Ridge chain, and protected the Federals' retreat. Numerous Confederate assaults against this bastion resulted only in bloodshed and death. At the end of that day, Preston gained his greatest military success. Using a soldier whose farm bordered Snodgrass Hill to lead them, the brigadier took a reserve brigade in a flanking maneuver up a wooded ravine to the top of the ridge, where they surprised three regiments from Ohio and Michigan. While the Federals were occupied in battling the Confederates in their front, Preston directed a bayonet charge against the enemy's rear. Exhausted and low on ammunition, many of the brave Federals immediately surrendered, while others soon were captured. This was the last skirmish of the battle. One thousand fourteen men in Preston's Division were wounded and 202 killed, but his troops captured two colonels commanding brigades, more than six hundred prisoners, five standards, one artillery piece, and some two thousand arms. As General Longstreet observed, the Army of Tennessee finally had won its "first grand victory."

Chickamauga marked the high point of General Preston's military career. "The gallant manner in which he conducted his division," General Buckner insisted, "contributed in a manner second to none in winning the key point of the field and thus deciding the fate of the day." "Preston dashed gallantly at the hills," General Longstreet asserted, and "crippled the enemy so badly that his ranks were broken." A correspondent for the *London Times* claimed that Preston's "bearing on the slope of Missionary Ridge will rank with any other famous deeds of arms ever witnessed on the earth."

After Chickamauga, Preston's criticisms of Bragg caused Preston to lose his divisional command. That October, General Buckner reassigned Preston to his former district in southwestern Virginia.

On January 7, 1864, President Davis named Preston minister to the court of Emperor Maximilian in Mexico. The Confederacy had failed in its major diplomatic aim, the recognition of Southern independence by foreign nations. In 1863 the French emperor Napoleon III and conservative Mexicans made the Habsburg archduke Maximilian emperor, and the Richmond government believed he would recognize the Confederacy. The archduke encouraged the South to expect his support in interviews that he granted Confederate agents in Europe before he left for Mexico. However, France—strongly urged by Britain to reject Confederate recognition—remained opposed to establishing relations and thus forced her Mexican vassal not to take this step. Unaware of the impossibility of his undertaking, Preston waited in vain in Cuba for Maximilian to invite him to Mexico City for an audience, and then he traveled to London and Paris to speak with Southern agents about the prospects of recognition. Finally in December the Kentuckian realized that his mission was doomed, and he decided to return to the Confederacy.

Prevented by the Union blockade from reaching Wilmington, North Carolina, in January 1865, Preston sailed to Matamoros, Mexico. In April he made it to Texas, where he joined General Kirby Smith's forces defending the Trans-Mississippi Department. His friend Kirby Smith placed him in charge of a division and made him a major general. But by then the conflict was almost over, and there was no government left in Richmond to approve his promotion. On June 2 Kirby Smith's troops surrendered, and the war ended at last.

Preston's life following the war was not a happy one. After travels to Mexico, the Caribbean, England, and Canada, he returned to Lexington in December 1865, living in his wife's family home. In politics, Preston served two years in the Kentucky legislature. He also assisted his congressman friend from Louisville, Henry Watterson, in reaching an accord with Republicans beneficial for Southern Democrats in the disputed presidential election of 1876 between Samuel J. Tilden and Rutherford B. Hayes. Preston was a founder of the first company to supply water to Lexington, and he was involved in a host of civic groups. However, despite his activities, health and family problems overwhelmed him in his final years. While visits from grandchildren brought pleasure, Preston's only son, Robert, proved a major disappointment, living off his family name and fortune instead of taking advantage of the many other possibilities open to him. Margaret Preston's unfounded charges of marital infidelity and the couple's constant disputes over finances almost led to divorce but finally ended with the two living apart. Serious health problems, especially deteriorating vision, which deprived him of the pleasure of reading, also contributed to his frequent bouts of depression.

Preston died September 21, 1887, in Lexington and is buried in Cave

Hill Cemetery in Louisville on land adjacent to his boyhood home. After his death, he remained a heroic figure for Kentuckians for whom the Old South and the Civil War had become the subject of legend.

BIBLIOGRAPHY

Sehlinger, Peter J. "'At the Moment of Victory . . .': The Battle of Shiloh and General A. S. Johnston's Death as Recounted in William Preston's Diary." *Filson Club History Quarterly* 61 (1987): 315–45.

———. "General William Preston: Kentucky's Last Cavalier Fights for Southern Independence." *Register of the Kentucky Historical Society* 93 (1996): 257–85.

———. *Kentucky's Last Cavalier: General William Preston, 1816–1887.* Frankfort: Kentucky Historical Society, 2004.

———. "William Preston, Kentucky's Diplomat of Lost Causes." In *Kentucky Profiles: Biographical Essays in Honor of Holman Hamilton,* ed. James C. Klotter and Peter Sehlinger. Frankfort: Kentucky Historical Society, 1982, 72–98.

—PETER J. SEHLINGER

Brig. Gen. Jerome Bonaparte Robertson

JEROME BONAPARTE Robertson was a brigadier general in the Confederate army during the American Civil War, doctor, Indian fighter, politician, and railroad executive. Robertson gained prominence by commanding the Texas Brigade in the Army of Northern Virginia from 1862 to 1863.

Jerome Bonaparte Robertson was born to Cornelius and Clarissa Hill Robertson in Christian County, Kentucky, on March 14, 1815, the fourth and youngest son of five children. The elder Robertson, a Scottish immigrant, accumulated considerable wealth in Union County, Kentucky, but suffered significant losses in the Panic of 1819. That same year, he passed away, leaving the Robertson clan almost destitute. Consequently, the older boys served as apprentices with local tradesmen. When Jerome was eight, he too was apprenticed to a hatter. After about five years, the young boy moved with his master to St. Louis, the center of the fur and hat industry in the West. By the time he was eighteen, Robertson was able to buy the remaining years of his contract and returned to the Bluegrass State. After moving to Owensboro, Robertson worked as an office assistant for a local doctor who also provided an informal education in medicine and literary subjects. In 1834, Jerome B. Robertson attended the Medical School at Transylvania College. Graduating a year later, he returned to Owensboro to practice medicine.

In the summer of 1836, Robertson responded to the call from Texas seeking help in its revolutionary struggle against the Mexican government. He was elected second lieutenant in the Daviess County Company, First Regiment of Kentucky Volunteers, and later received a promotion to captain. Robertson and his fellow Kentuckians did not reach Texas until September due to unavoidable logistical delays. The war was all but over, but Robertson and his company served the newfound Republic of Texas for the remainder of 1836 and part of 1837. In the fall of that year, Robertson returned to Kentucky to convince his kinsmen to return to Texas with him. By December, Robertson, accompanied by his brother, James, and Moses Cummins, a respected civil engineer and lawyer in Kentucky, and his daughter, Mary, settled at Washington-on-the-Brazos. Robertson resumed his medical practice. On March 4, 1838, he married his travel companion and fellow Kentuckian, Mary Elizabeth Cummins. The couple had three children: Felix Huston; Julia Ann; and Henry Bell, who died in infancy.

For the next seven years, Robertson continued to practice medicine while delving into farming in eastern Texas. He also became a devoted public official, serving as county coroner as well as postmaster and mayor of Washington-on-the-Brazos. Soon thereafter, the doctor's health began to fail, and the Robertsons moved to Washington County, Texas, in 1845. In his new home, the Kentucky native joined the local militia and engaged in various campaigns against neighboring Native American tribes. In the 1840s, Robertson also served in several campaigns against Mexicans who resisted the notion that Texas was an independent republic. In Washington County, Robertson continued his dedication to public service, serving in the Texas House of Representatives from 1847 to 1849. Upon completing his term, Robertson was elected to the state senate, representing Washington, Burleson, Milam, and Williamson counties. During his term as state senator, Robertson served on various committees and voted against accepting the provision that settled the boundary dispute between Texas and New Mexico that had been incorporated into the Compromise of 1850. After fulfilling his senate term, Robertson returned to Washington County and refrained from public service until 1861, when he was elected to the secession convention in January. On February 1, Robertson voted with the majority of delegates to secede from the Union.

After the firing on Fort Sumter on April 12, 1861, President Abraham Lincoln called for troops to quell the rebellion, and four additional states seceded from the Union. In response to Lincoln's call, in June, Confederate secretary of war Leroy Pope Walker requested that two thousand Texas infantry be raised for service in Virginia. Robertson immediately volunteered, raising a company known as the Texas Aids in Washington County. Robertson was elected captain on August 3. Upon arriving in Richmond, Robertson's unit was designated Company I in the Fifth Texas Regiment and mustered into the Confederate army on September 7, 1861. On October 10, Robertson received a promotion to lieutenant colonel of the Fifth Texas. The War Department then assigned the regiment, along with the First and Fourth Texas and units from other states, to a brigade led by Brig. Gen. Louis T. Wigfall. His command became known as the Texas Brigade.

After spending some time in drill and exercise, the brigade received orders in November to report to the Potomac River line in Northern Virginia, where they remained for the next several months in winter's quarters. At this time, the Eighteenth Georgia replaced the Louisiana regiment in the Texas Brigade. In March, the brigade, now under the command of Brig. Gen. John Bell Hood, abandoned the Potomac line and moved south, toward Richmond. On June 3, 1862, Robertson received a promotion to colonel and command of the Fifth Texas. Later that month, the Texans fought with distinction in the Seven Days' Battles, from June 25 to July 1, leading Gen. Robert E. Lee's Army of Northern Virginia in its defense of the Confederate capital. On June 27, Robertson was wounded in the shoulder while leading the Fifth Texas in its assault against the Union lines at the battle of Gaines' Mill. The colonel recovered from his wound and participated in the Second Manassas campaign. At the battle of Second Manassas, on August 30, Robertson was wounded in the groin. In the subsequent Antietam campaign, Robertson insisted on leading the Fifth Texas as it invaded the North. The long march and the unhealed wounds proved too difficult for Robertson, however, and he was confined to an ambulance on September 14. Even though Robertson missed the battle of Antietam, he received a promotion to brigadier general on November 1, 1862, and command of the Texas Brigade, when Hood was promoted to major general.

In November 1862, as the brigades of the Army of Northern Virginia were reorganized by states, Robertson's Texas Brigade, which was assigned to Lt. Gen. James Longstreet's First Corps, lost the Eighteenth Georgia regiment and gained the Third Arkansas Infantry. In the subsequent battle of Fredericksburg on December 13, the Texas Brigade saw little action. In the following months, Robertson's men spent their time drilling, building breastworks, and foraging. Robertson was affectionately called "Aunt Pollie" and "Old Bob" by his men for his devout concern for their welfare. The Texans spent the spring of 1863 foraging and skirmishing near Suffolk before returning to Lee's army in May to participate in the Confederate invasion of Pennsylvania. Missing the first day at the battle of Gettysburg, Robertson led his brigade in the pivotal flanking maneuver of July 2. In the assault on Little Round Top, Robertson was wounded a third time when he received an injury to his right knee. The

Texas Brigade and the rest of Lee's army retreated to Virginia with depleted ranks after an unsuccessful third-day assault.

In September 1863, the War Department ordered two divisions of Longstreet's corps to reinforce Gen. Braxton Bragg's Army of Tennessee. Traveling more than eight hundred miles on a circuitous journey, Robertson's Texas Brigade was one of the first units to arrive in northern Georgia on the eve of battle. In the battle of Chickamauga, September 19–20, the Texans fought with distinction in the Confederacy's most significant victory in the West. The First Corps contingent participated in Bragg's subsequent siege of the Federal army at Chattanooga. In the battle of Wauhatchie on October 29, 1863, Robertson drew the ire of his corps commander when he appeared to retreat in a disorderly fashion. Longstreet relieved Robertson of command while Bragg convened a board of inquiry to examine the case. As Robertson prepared to defend himself against all charges, the board adjourned when Longstreet's corps prepared to advance against Knoxville on November 4. Robertson returned to duty on the eighth.

In the subsequent Knoxville and East Tennessee campaigns, Robertson continued to draw Longstreet's indignation with his critical commentary. The Kentuckian had complained to his regimental commanders about the lack of food, the mail, and the destitute condition of his men. Robertson essentially lacked confidence in the campaign. He insisted on only receiving written orders but declared he would follow them "under protest." After the battle of Bean's Station on December 14, 1863, Longstreet arrested Robertson for "conduct highly prejudicial to good order and military discipline" for failing to follow orders. Robertson's trial took place on March 12, 1864. The court found him guilty, but the War Department overturned the court's decision later that spring. Sometime after receiving word of the trial's outcome, Robertson requested and received a transfer to the Lone Star State. On April 9, Robertson bade farewell to his old brigade. The following month, he received instructions to report to Maj. Gen. John B. Magruder, the commander of the District of Texas. By June, the secretary of war ordered Robertson to assume command of the Lone Star State's reserve forces, with the task of recruiting soldiers for the Confederacy. After completing his task, Robertson received orders, in March 1865, to report to General Magruder for active field command. But by the time preparations were made, the eastern armies were surrendering and the Civil War was coming to a close. General Robertson was eventually paroled in Houston, Texas, on July 12, 1865.

Robertson's service to the Confederacy was a great source of pride. His oldest son, Felix Huston Robertson, also served as a brigadier general in the Army of Tennessee, the only native Texan to achieve that rank. After the Civil War, Robertson returned to his home in Independence and resumed his medical practice. His wife passed away from a throat affliction on April 7, 1868. Following her death, Robertson gave up the full-time practice of medicine for a few years. Nevertheless, he resumed his politically influential place in Texas society. In 1874, he was appointed as the state superintendent of the Bureau of Immigration, a position he held until 1876. He also continued his work with the Texas Medical Association and the Masonic Order during the Reconstruction era. Subsequently, he was employed by the Houston and Texas Central Railroad in 1877, and in 1878 as an immigration agent, helping settle thousands of immigrants in Texas. While working for the railroad, he married for the second time. In January 1878, he wed Hattie Hendley Hook, a native Virginian.

Robertson was also quite active in veterans' affairs, helping organize Hood's Texas Brigade Association in 1872 and serving as its first vice president before being elected president in 1875, a position he held eleven times. In 1887, he was elected the association's lifetime president. Two years later, the United Confederate Veterans (UCV) emerged as a national veterans' organization to serve as a benevolent, social, and historical association for former Confederate soldiers. A Texas camp was named the General Jerome Bonaparte Robertson Camp in honor of the former commander of the Texas Brigade, who led the brigade longer than any officer. It was one of the few UCV camps in the Lone Star State to be named for a living person.

In 1879, Robertson left his home in Independence and moved to Waco to be near his oldest son, Felix. Even though Robertson continued his affiliation with the local, regional, and state medical associations, he did not practice medicine in Waco. Instead, he ventured into private business with his son, investing in railroad promotion in West Texas and acting as a land and general agent in McLennan County. When not engaged in business, he devoted his time to attending Confederate veterans' reunions.

After a few years of declining health, Jerome Robertson passed away from cancer of the face on January 7, 1890, at the age of seventy-four. After an elaborate funeral in Waco on January 9, he was buried in Independence, next to his first wife and his mother. Four years later, however, Felix Robertson had the body of his father, mother, and grandmother reinterred at the Oakwood Cemetery in Waco.

BIBLIOGRAPHY

Brooks, Charles E. "The Social and Cultural Dynamics of Soldiering in Hood's Texas Brigade." *Journal of Southern History* 67, no. 3 (August 2001): 535–72.

Polley, J. B. *Hood's Texas Brigade: Its Marches, Its Battles, Its Achievements.* Dayton, OH: Morningside Press, 1976.

Robertson, Jerome B. *Touched with Valor: Civil War Papers and Casualty Reports of Hood's Texas Brigade.* Ed. Harold B. Simpson. Hillsboro, TX: Hill Junior College Press, 1964.

Simpson, Harold B. *Hood's Texas Brigade: Lee's Grenadier Guard.* Fort Worth: Texian Press, 1970.

—ALEXANDER MENDOZA

Brig. Gen. Joseph Orville Shelby

THE CONFEDERATE SOLDIERS who stood on the muddy banks of the Rio Grande were gaunt, their captured Union uniforms frayed and tattered. Their horses, scant survivors of a tortuous, privation-filled ride from Arkansas to Missouri and, finally, to Texas, were famished, their ribs showing beneath cracked saddles. Their commander, a Kentucky-born Missourian wearing a black plume in his dusty hat, had vowed never to surrender. Five hundred of his men, veterans of the fiercest fighting in Missouri and Arkansas, agreed. They would follow their leader, Joseph Orville Shelby, anywhere. Before they crossed into Mexico, the Southerners plunged their bullet-marked battle flag into the Rio Grande, burying the banner under the swirling, murky river. One wonders if these former Confederate soldiers, soon to be exiled south of the border, noted the irony that it was Independence Day, 1865.

Shelby's men were known for daring hit-and-run tactics and their ability to cover a retreating army, a much-needed trait when fighting on the prairies of Missouri or the mountains of Arkansas. Known as the Iron Brigade of the West, they wore red sumac in their hats, even when clad in captured Federal uniforms. Shelby, no doubt, appreciated this flair. His Kentucky charm, tenacity, wealth, and reputed love of quoting Sir Walter Scott made him Missouri's most chivalric figure during the Civil War. Most often compared to his childhood friend John Hunt Morgan because both made slashing raids into Union-occupied border-state territory, Federal major general Alfred Pleasanton, who fought Confederate cavalry (including J. E. B. Stuart) from Virginia to Missouri, said that "Shelby was the best cavalry general of the South. Under other conditions, he would have been one of the best in the world."

Shelby was born in Lexington, Kentucky, on December 12, 1830. He was part of a prominent family, his grandfather being a cousin to Kentucky's first governor. Joseph's father, Orville, died in 1835 and left his son a sizable trust. Joseph's widowed mother, Anna Boswell Shelby, eventually remarried Benjamin Gratz, a wealthy hemp-rope manufacturer whose friends included Henry Clay. The marriage gave Jo a set of noted cousins: Montgomery Blair, Francis P. Blair Jr., and Benjamin Gratz Brown, all of whom became influential pro-Union politicians. In addition, John Hunt Morgan lived two doors down from the Gratz home. Joseph and John became friends, and their wartime careers, in many instances, mirrored each other.

Shelby was homeschooled until 1845, when he attended Lexington's Transylvania University. After three years there, he finished school in his stepfather's hometown of Philadelphia. Upon his return to Lexington, Shelby joined the family hemp business.

In 1851, Shelby turned twenty-one years old, inherited his $80,000 trust fund, and followed two cousins, Frank Blair and Gratz Brown, to Missouri. There, he opened a hemp ropewalk in Waverly in Lafayette County, farmed, and owned a steamboat. He quickly became one of the wealthiest slave owners in Missouri.

When the Kansas Territory erupted into chaos after the Kansas-Nebraska Act of 1854, Shelby led pro-slavery fighters there. In the border struggle he gained both combat and leadership experience. After the Civil War, Shelby told author William E. Connelley: "I was in Kansas at the head of an armed force about that time. I was there to kill Free-State men. I did kill them. I am now ashamed of myself for having done so, but then times were different from what they are now, and that is what I went there for. . . . [T]he trouble we started on the border bore fruit for ten years."

Shelby found more than violence during this period. In 1858, he married a distant cousin, Elizabeth N. Shelby. Throughout their marriage they were blessed with seven children, but they were frequently separated after Shelby cast his lot with the Confederacy.

Although Shelby embraced the Southern cause, he was initially courted by both sides. In early 1861, Shelby met Francis Blair Jr. in St. Louis. Blair offered Shelby a Federal commission, but Shelby refused. He was already supporting the Confederacy, having sent one hundred thousand percussion caps, hidden in flowerpots, to his Confederate boyhood friend in Kentucky, John Hunt Morgan.

Returning to Lafayette County, Shelby raised, equipped, and mounted a Missouri State Guard cavalry company, of which he was elected captain. On July 5, 1861, his troops fought at Carthage, Missouri. Shelby's men won acclaim for their discipline and work scouting enemy lines. Casualties were nearly equal in number, and the Union commander, Brig. Gen. Franz Sigel, fell back to Springfield.

Siegel linked with Brig. Gen. Nathaniel Lyon, and, on August 10, the Federals struck the Confederates at Wilson's Creek. Shelby learned a valuable lesson when his horsemen charged infantry and were easily repulsed. In the future, unless he was leading a rearguard action, he fought dismounted. The battle of Wilson's Creek was also a family affair; his stepbrother, Union captain Cary Gratz, was shot five times and killed. Shelby spent much of the remaining year skirmishing in western Missouri.

In early February 1862, Union troops under Brig. Gen. Samuel Curtis advanced on Springfield to strike Maj. Gen. Sterling Price's Missouri troops. Price fell back into northwest Arkansas, where Shelby's men participated in the battle of Pea Ridge in early March. After fighting there, Shelby's troops again distinguished themselves while guarding the Confederate rear, a job they accomplished after many engagements.

Shelby's state commission expired that June, so he recruited in Lafayette County, raising one thousand men in four days. Upon his return to Confederate lines, he was elected colonel of the Lafayette County Regiment on September 12. Maj. Gen. Thomas C. Hindman then gave him a brigade consisting of the Fifth, Sixth, and Twelfth Missouri cavalry regiments and Capt. Richard Collins's artillery battery. These 2,500 men, who became known as Shelby's Iron Brigade, were placed in Brig. Gen. John S. Marmaduke's cavalry division. They became the most competent Confederate cavalry brigade to fight in Missouri and Arkansas.

After several months skirmishing in Arkansas and Missouri, on September 30, Federal brigadier general Frederick Salomon struck the Confederates at Newtonia. Shelby was initially kept in reserve, but when the Southerners were nearly outflanked, he drove the Union troops away, chasing them for more than twelve miles. Shelby simply reported that "we fought General Salomon at Newtonia, defeating him badly."

By late November, the brigade, bolstered by William Quantrill's guerrillas, was with Marmaduke at Cane Hill, Arkansas. On November 26, Union major general James Blunt, hoping to strike Marmaduke before rebel reinforcements arrived, attacked. Shelby met the enemy advance on the Fayetteville Road. After an artillery duel, Blunt's infantry deployed, assailing Shelby's lines three times. Outflanked, the Confederates pulled back to the Boston Mountains, and, as usual, the Iron Brigade covered the withdrawal. Guerrilla John McCorkle remarked that this was the most dangerous part of the battle. A captain riding next to Shelby was shot, and the officer's blood splattered Shelby's face. In addition, Shelby's black plume was severed by a bullet and three horses were killed under him.

Blunt gave chase, later proclaiming that "every foot of the ground was fought over and hotly contested." Again the Southerners retreated, and Shelby's Brigade protected the rear. His men counterattacked, but the action ultimately failed. Before night ended the battle, Shelby lost his fourth horse of the day. Blunt wrote that the enemy army had "fought desperately."

The Confederates withdrew to Van Buren, Arkansas. Although Hindman was ordered to send troops to Vicksburg, he demurred, hoping to destroy Blunt. In early December, Hindman drove between Blunt's division and Union brigadier general Francis Herron. In the battle of Prairie Grove, Shelby's men broke Herron's line of battle and chased the Federals across the prairie. Marmaduke remarked that "Shelby was wherever duty and danger called him, and rendered most distinguished service." Before Herron could be destroyed, however, Blunt arrived and struck the Confederate left. The battle ended in a stalemate, and Hindman returned to Van Buren, losing northwest Arkansas and western Missouri to the Federals.

There would be little respite that winter. On December 31, 1862, Shelby's 2,300 troops, including Quantrill's guerrillas, joined Marmaduke for a raid into Missouri. The Confederates rushed toward Springfield to strike Union supply bases and to cut Federal lines of communication.

On January 8, 1863, after several skirmishes, the Confederates reached Springfield, where they fought Union troops outside of town. Shelby followed a familiar tactic; he advanced with three dismounted regiments, keeping his scouts and the guerrillas in reserve. The Federals fell back into their works and repulsed three attacks. After eight hours, the Southerners withdrew to Hartville, burning forts and a bridge near Sand Spring along the way.

Hartville was empty, but after the Confederates passed through town, Shelby reported, they "received a terrible and well-directed fire." Shelby was nearly killed when a bullet struck a "gold badge he wore on his hat." Although the Federal troops were driven off, Shelby lost two horses and all but four of his captains were killed. His adjutant wrote that "Hartville was a stubborn, sudden, bloody fight."

Federal pressure mounted, and Marmaduke returned to Arkansas. Shelby soon joined him for a second Missouri raid, and he commanded a division in several actions. On April 26, his men were repulsed while attacking entrenched Union troops at Cape Girardeau, leaving their dead lying "thick and in clusters" in a nearby peach orchard. After enduring a night attack near Jackson, the Confederates left the state.

That summer, Union-occupied Helena was weakened to support the siege of Vicksburg, Mississippi. The Confederates struck on July 4, with Shelby's Brigade attacking Rightor's Hill. The assault was ill coordinated and unsupported. Caught in a cross fire, one Confederate wrote that "the slaughter around [Shelby's artillery] was awful." Shelby was shot in the upper arm, and his wrist "was shattered." The Confederates returned to Little Rock, and Shelby went to Batesville, Arkansas, to recover.

He would not remain in his sickbed. Instead, he devised another raid into Missouri. With Federal troops marching into Arkansas, Shelby planned to strike key sites to pull Union troops out of that state. He also hoped to recruit and bolster the morale of Confederate sympathizers. Supplied with six hundred cavalry and two artillery pieces, Shelby departed, his arm in a sling.

Shelby crossed the Arkansas River on September 27. After fighting in the Boston Mountains, he secured additional recruits and rode to Neosho. On October 4, his men drove the town's Union garrison into the brick courthouse. The Federals surrendered, one officer reported, after the Confederates "knocked the court-house down with their artillery."

During the raid, Shelby encountered dozens of families who had been displaced by Brig. Gen. Thomas Ewing's General Orders, No. 11. This edict cleaned Southern sympathizers out of several western Missouri counties following the Lawrence, Kansas, massacre. Shelby's wife and young son were evicted, and Shelby's stepfather took the family to Lexington, Kentucky. Although Elizabeth lived in the pro-Union Gratz residence, the Federals ordered her to leave. Gratz wrote to President Abraham Lincoln, a local teenage diarist recorded, "to get the order rescinded. Mr. Lincoln replied she might stay if Mr. Gratz would hold himself responsible for her good behavior."

Elizabeth remained in Lexington, and Shelby's cavalry continued their raid, fighting in several towns. The men struck Tipton, destroyed miles of telegraph wire and railroad track, and then drove off Col. Thomas T. Crittenden's Union horsemen. Like Shelby, Crittenden was a member of a prominent Bluegrass family and had been a guest at Shelby's wedding. Union forces under generals Thomas Ewing and E. B. Brown concentrated, striking Shelby at Boonville and pushing him to Marshall. Brown's forces continually assailed the Confederate rear, but, on October 12, Shelby ambushed Brown at the LaMine River. Hit hard, Brown slowed the chase.

Although Shelby staggered Brown, he encountered Ewing at Marshall and decided to cut through Ewing's line. The Confederates charged, and, after two hours, the Union left flank broke. As the fighting spilled into the streets, Brown's soldiers appeared and joined the fray. Their rear guard plagued by Union cavalry, the outnumbered Confederates endured a fighting retreat out of Missouri. One Federal wrote that Shelby's men were now "running like wild hogs." Upon crossing the Arkansas line, three thousand Union infantry moved from Fayetteville to block Shelby, but he escaped, reaching Confederate lines in Washington, Arkansas, on November 3. He and his men were greeted by local civilians as returning heroes.

Shelby had ridden nearly 1,500 miles in forty-one days, averaging an incredible 36 miles per day. His men killed and wounded 600 Union troops, paroled 500 soldiers, destroyed ten forts, demolished $800,000 worth of railroad property, and seized hundreds of weapons and forty stands of colors. Shelby also claimed that he captured six thousand horses and mules; destroyed $1 million in supplies, $50,000 in ordnance, and three hundred wagons; and garnered 800 recruits. He also boasted that he diverted 10,000 Union soldiers from reinforcing Maj. Gen. William Rosecrans's army at Chattanooga. Despite forty-seven battles and skirmishes, he lost only 125 casualties. On December 15, 1863, Shelby was promoted to brigadier general.

Shelby spent early 1864 skirmishing around Camden, Arkadelphia, and Little Rock. He was then ordered to "occupy the valley of White River" to block railroad and river transportation. On June 23, he turned his sights on Clarendon, a town on the White River, fourteen miles from Union-occupied Devall's Bluff.

The Federal tinclad gunboat *Queen City* was docked at Clarendon. This nine-gun ship protected local river navigation; as Shelby was ordered to wreak havoc along this route, removing the *Queen City* would make his job much easier. At midnight, Shelby's men captured the town and dragged their four Parrott rifles "up to within 50 feet of the boat." At dawn, the artillery erupted, and, Shelby reported, "in ten minutes the Queen City was a helpless wreck upon the water." Soon, three other Federal gunboats arrived. Although outmatched, Shelby damaged these vessels, but the roar of artillery caught the attention of Union troops fourteen miles away at Devall's Bluff. The next day, four thousand of them, led by Brig. Gen. Eugene Carr, with whom Shelby was acquainted, marched to Clarendon. Shelby withdrew.

Maj. Gen. Sterling Price was planning an invasion of Missouri. At one point, Shelby was considered to lead the raid, but Confederate authorities determined his rank was too low to command an army. Shelby joined Price at Pocahontas, Arkansas, on September 15. When he arrived, Price gave him a division.

Upon entering Missouri, Shelby's Division took several towns but missed the battle at Pilot Knob on September 27, which resulted in 1,500 Confederate casualties and 200 Union losses. After several fights across western Missouri, Price's men fought Blunt at the Little Blue River on October 21. The Union storm, however, was gathering. Blunt retreated past Independence, and Gen. Alfred Pleasanton's Federals moved on the Confederates' rear.

Price withdrew to avoid being trapped, and, on October 23, Shelby struck Westport, which his adjutant called "the hardest battle of the campaign." The Confederates initially drove the Federals back, but Pleasanton rolled over Marmaduke's Division at Byram's Ford on the Big Blue River. Shelby arrived to help, but the Federals counterattacked, breaking Fagan's two brigades on Shelby's right flank. The Confederates retreated. Casualties were so heavy that guerrilla Allen Parmer later wrote, "After the battle of Westport . . . the old crowd was pretty well shot to pieces."

By late October, the Confederates were south of Newtonia. Low on provisions, they considered retreating into Arkansas, but Shelby advised staying. "It is much better to lose an army in actual battle," he counseled, "than to starve the men and kill the horses." The Federals struck Newtonia on October 28. Price's army withdrew toward the Indian Territory as the Iron Brigade rode forward and dismounted, blocking Blunt. Again, Shelby's rearguard actions saved a Confederate army.

After a privation-filled march that indeed killed men and horses, Price's army reached Clarksville, Texas. His army was broken and the survivors were far from Missouri, but Price called his raid a success. They had marched 1,400 miles and fought forty-three battles and skirmishes, paroled more than three thousand Union soldiers, and pulled up miles of railroad track. But Price's army was destroyed by the raid, and Confederate officials excoriated him for losing the army.

As other Confederate armies surrendered, Shelby refused and led five hundred troops to Mexico. These men voted to support the Emperor Maximilian, who gave the former Confederates land. Shelby settled down to business pursuits, and when Maximilian was overthrown and executed, the Kentuckian returned to the United States.

In 1867, Shelby reached western Missouri, where he became a planter, built railroads, owned coal mines, and was active in Confederate veterans' affairs. In 1893, President Grover Cleveland appointed him U.S. marshal for the District of Western Missouri. Shelby died from pneumonia at Adrian, Missouri, on February 13, 1897. He was buried in Forest Hill Cemetery in Kansas City, Missouri.

BIBLIOGRAPHY

Davis, William C., ed. *The Confederate General.* 6 vols. Harrisburg, PA: National Historical Society, 1991.

Edwards, John N. *Shelby and His Men.* Cincinnati: Miami Printing and Publishing, 1867.

Leslie, Edward E. *The Devil Knows How to Ride.* New York: Random House, 1996.

O'Flaherty, Daniel. *General Jo Shelby, Undefeated Rebel.* Chapel Hill: University of North Carolina Press, 1954.

—STUART W. SANDERS

Brig. Gen. William Yarnel Slack

WILLIAM YARNEL SLACK was born in Mason County, Kentucky, on August 1, 1816, to John and Mary J. "Polly" Caldwell Slack. William was the fourth among seven children. Slack's parents were easterners, his mother a Quaker from Virginia and his father a Pennsylvanian, and the family settled in Mason County, where John Slack worked as a potter and farmer. In 1819, farming opportunities in Missouri Territory prompted a move to Columbia, and the Slacks settled in Boone County (then called Howard County). The senior Slack worked as a tobacco farmer but soon became the justice of the peace in Columbia, and young William developed an interest in the law. In 1837, the twenty-one-year-old Slack moved back to Kentucky to pursue a career in law, returning to Columbia in 1839 to continue his studies. That year he passed the bar and opened a practice in Chillicothe, in Livingston County.

Slack developed a reputation across the district circuit for his coolness under pressure as well as for his honesty and integrity. In 1842, he embarked upon a political career and won election to the state legislature as a Democrat. That same year, he married twenty-two-year-old Mary E. Woodward. The couple had two children, John W., born in 1844, and Emma I., born in 1849. Mary died in 1858, and the following year Slack married twenty-eight-year-old Isabella R. Bower of Monroe County. The couple had two sons, William Yarnel Jr., born in 1860, and Gustavus Bower, born in 1861.

Through the mid-1840s, Slack maintained his law practice but found himself drawn to the political arena, and in 1845 he served as a delegate to the state's constitutional convention. With the outbreak of the Mexican War in 1846, Slack volunteered for military service and helped organize a company from Livingston County. An outspoken opponent of war, he nevertheless proclaimed, "It is too late now to discuss the question whether or not the war could have been avoided. . . . I am for my country, gentlemen, first, last, and all the time." Slack won election as captain of Company L, Second Missouri Mounted Volunteers and quickly established a reputation among his men for discipline. He served for fourteen months under Missouri colonel Sterling Price and saw action during operations around Santa Fe. In January 1847, Price reported that Slack "rendered excellent service" at the battle of Embudo Pass, and on February 4 Slack's troopers cut off the enemy escape at Pueblo de Taos to secure victory.

After the Mexican War, Slack returned to Chillicothe to resume his law career. In the process, he advanced his public status as a man with great insight and influence. Throughout the 1850s, Slack established himself politically as a strict constitutional constructionist in support of states' rights. He argued against secession, however, and insisted that such a measure would lead to war, something he opposed vehemently. Yet, by 1860 his position had shifted somewhat, and, while still a proponent of compromise and conciliation, he served as a John C. Breckinridge elector. Although the Constitutional Union candidate, John Bell, carried the county by a narrow margin, and Stephen Douglas carried Missouri, Breckinridge supporters won control of the state legislature.

With Abraham Lincoln's election to the presidency, Slack acknowledged the likelihood of secession and war. Although the state legislature failed to enact an ordinance of secession, pro-secessionist governor Claiborne F. Jackson called up the militia to oppose a pro-Union home guard organized by Missouri congressman Frank Blair. In May, a bloody showdown between the forces near St. Louis prompted the legislature to grant Jackson the authority to convert the militia into the Missouri State Guard. Jackson appointed Sterling Price to command the troops, and on May 18 Slack received a commission as a brigadier in the State Guard. Price directed him to raise a force in the state's Fifth Congressional District, an area encompassing Chillicothe, and Slack established a recruitment center and training camp along the Chariton River. A Missouri volunteer asserted, "Slack was an officer of energy and dedication." In June, Slack marched his men southwest to Lexington. By the time they reached the vicinity, Union forces had already driven pro-Southern politicians from the capital at Jefferson City and defeated a State Guard force at Boonville. Accordingly, Slack guided his men toward Cowskin Prairie, in the southwest corner of the state, where the State Guard hoped to unite with Confederate troops from Arkansas.

During this time, Slack's command received the designation as Fourth Division of the Missouri State Guard. The division consisted of John T. Hughes's infantry and Benjamin A. Rives's cavalry, an aggregate of some 1,200 men. Slack's division saw action on July 5 in an engagement near Carthage when 1,200 Union troops under Franz Sigel closed on the State Guard ten miles north of town. The State Guard had nearly 4,000 men, but only 2,000 were armed, many of the latter with only shotguns and muskets used for hunting. With Slack's infantry holding the center of the line, the State Guard repulsed the Union advance. Meanwhile, Slack's cavalry was among the troopers sent to attack the enemy flanks and rear. Sigel's men fell back through the town, covering their retreat with artillery. The State Guard pushed their advantage, and Slack's command played a conspicuous role in the pursuit. Nightfall brought an end to the fighting with the State Guard suffering 77 casualties and inflicting 45. Slack reported that his men "displayed all the energy and endurance of veterans, giving abundant evidence that they can be relied on in any emergency."

Following the skirmish at Carthage, approximately six thousand Union troops, dispersed across southwest Missouri, rendezvoused at Springfield while the rebels, totaling nearly twice that number, concentrated fifty miles to the southwest near Cassville. In August, the Confederates, led by Benjamin McCulloch, advanced toward Springfield. On August 7, McCulloch's army paused at Wilson's Creek, ten miles southwest of Springfield, on Telegraph Road. Slack's command camped on the Edwards farm, along the creek just east of the road. At Springfield, the outnumbered Federal Army of the West, under Nathaniel Lyon, hoped to stop the Confederates before they could reach the town. Lyon seized the offensive and, at dawn on August 10, launched an attack that caught the Confederates by surprise.

Before the Confederates could organize a defensive line, Slack threw his men in front of the Union assault and, with artillery support, staggered the enemy advance. Slack's initiative gave Price time to deploy 2,800 Missourians into line of battle and mount a counterattack. Slack's troops took a position near the center, and the Confederates pitched into the Union line along high ground known as Oak Hill, later called Bloody Hill. After three assaults, the Federals withdrew from the field and commenced a retreat to Rolla. Both sides sustained heavy casualties, Slack among them, having suffered a severe wound below the right hip while leading a late-morning assault on Oak Hill. In his official report, McCulloch noted the "gallant conduct" displayed by Slack and the Missourians, while Price affirmed that the Kentuckian fell while "at the head of his column."

Slack's wife traveled to Springfield to help nurse the general back to health. In addition, his family doctor, Dr. William Keith, was in service with the State Guard and helped in Slack's treatment and recovery. Slack's wound prevented him from participating in the September campaign at Lexington, but by October he had regained his health and resumed command of his division, then stationed at Cassville.

In the interim, Missouri's pro-secession politicians voted to take the state out of the Union and into the Confederacy and provided the opportunity for Missouri State Guard units to volunteer for Confederate service. When Slack offered his services to the Provisional Army of the Confederate States, Price apparently—and without authority—made him a colonel. The Confederates restructured the newly monikered Army of the West, and Price received command of the Missouri troops with Slack leading the Second Brigade of Missouri Confederate Volunteers. The brigade consisted of infantry battalions under John T. Hughes, Robert S. Bevier, and Thomas H. Rosser, as well as two artillery batteries, one under John C. Landis, the other under William Lucas, and a mixed cavalry battalion, led by Colton Green. The horsemen in Green's battalion included Confederate cavalry, mounted infantry, and mounted units that remained in the Missouri State Guard. In total, Slack commanded approximately 1,100 soldiers, including 750 Confederate volunteers and 350 members of the Missouri State Guard.

In January, pressure from Union brigadier general Samuel R. Curtis forced Price to abandon Missouri for northwest Arkansas and a junction with McCulloch's troops. The Confederates appointed Earl Van Dorn to overall command of all forces in the Trans-Mississippi District, and he set out promptly to regain Missouri. In early March, Van Dorn found Curtis dug in behind the Little Sugar Creek on Telegraph Road just below the Arkansas-Missouri border. Rather than launch a frontal attack, Van Dorn ordered a flank march in an attempt to turn Curtis.

Along with the rest of Price's troops, Slack's brigade undertook a grueling march along the Bentonville Detour, west of Curtis's position, and swung behind Sugar Loaf Mountain, hoping to gain Telegraph Road well in the rear of the Union army. The mountain is actually a series of interconnected ridges and plateaus known by several names, including Big Mountain, Sugar Mountain, Trott's Hill, and Pea Ridge. The thickly wooded hills provided concealment and cover for the Confederates but also presented a formidable obstacle for the army to negotiate.

Before the Confederates completed the maneuver, Curtis discovered their movement around his right flank and turned his army to face Van

Dorn. On March 7, the armies clashed across the valley below Sugar Loaf Mountain. The ensuing two-day battle of Pea Ridge, called Elkhorn Tavern by Confederates, was the largest fought in the Trans-Mississippi theater up to that time and sealed the fate of Missouri in the war.

At 8:00 A.M., Price's command marched south along Telegraph Road through Cross Timber Hollow toward Elkhorn Tavern. Slack had instructions to deploy his men into line of battle and advance to the right of the First Missouri Brigade. Slack's men pressed forward along the west side of the road across rugged terrain that carried them through Tanyard Ravine. Around noon, the Missourians started to face skirmish fire from the Third Illinois Cavalry. Slack's men quickly drove the enemy away and continued to push forward.

As the Confederates advanced along the steep and wooded hillside, they began to take fire from the Twenty-fifth Missouri (Union) and the Ninth Iowa. Slack rode ahead toward the front of the lines and took a position with Rosser's troops to direct the advance. James E. Payne, a Missourian in Slack's brigade, described ensuing events in an article written in 1929 for *Confederate Veteran* magazine: "General Slack [sat] on his horse, conversing with Colonel Rosser . . . and watching the battle over on our left. A stray bullet [struck] a dead elm limb, ricochet[ed], glancing downward, and penetrate[d] Slack's groin." Slack reeled in the saddle and nearly fell from his horse, an aide-de-camp catching him and easing him to the ground. A Missouri officer described the wound as "fearful," and it left Slack partially paralyzed. Slack immediately turned over command of the brigade to Colonel Rosser, and stretcher bearers carried the wounded officer to the rear. An ambulance soon took Slack to a nearby house, where the Second Missouri surgeon, Dr. Peter Austin, treated the wound. Reportedly, the ball struck Slack inches from the site of the wound suffered at Wilson's Creek.

Twenty-four hours later, the Confederates began a retreat from Pea Ridge, and in the face of Union pursuit, aides moved Slack to the Roller house, east of Elkhorn Tavern, near Gateway. Dr. Keith remained with Slack until March 16, when they again fled to avoid Union troops, this time to Moore's Mill northwest of Gateway. Initially, Slack showed some improvement, but when he reached Moore's Mill, infection set in, and he died in the early morning of March 21. On April 12, Confederate command issued Slack a posthumous promotion to brigadier general. Of the original eight brigadiers in the Missouri State Guard, only one other, Mosby Monroe Parsons, attained comparable rank in Confederate service. Van Dorn's official report commended the general for "gallantry" at

Pea Ridge and Price noted in his report that Slack's men faced "heavy odds and the most stubborn resistance" during their attack. He called Slack one of his "best and bravest officers" and, praising the Kentuckian's leadership, characterized the general as having displayed "marked gallantry and energy" during the battle.

Slack was buried in the Roller Ridge Cemetery, but in 1872 the Southern Memorial Association of Washington County, Arkansas, secured three acres of land east of Fayetteville for the "gathering of our sacred dead." Early in 1880, a local newspaper began a crusade to have Slack reinterred in the new Confederate Cemetery and enlisted the general's wife as a part of the campaign. In the spring, Slack's body was exhumed and taken to Fayetteville for burial. On May 27, 1880, with Isabella Slack as the guest of honor, the general was reinterred at the Confederate Cemetery. Of the 622 soldiers laid to rest there, William Yarnel Slack is the highest-ranking officer.

In 1887, Confederate veterans of the battle of Pea Ridge erected a monument on the battlefield to honor their fallen comrades. The monument is located along Telegraph Road near Elkhorn Tavern, several hundred yards south of the site where Slack fell mortally wounded. Slack is one of three Confederate officers whose names are inscribed on the obelisk. Earlier, Colonel Rosser, who was present when the general suffered his mortal wound at Pea Ridge, reflected the view held by many veterans of Slack's brigade. The colonel wrote that Slack was "a man of much more than ordinary ability, cool and clear-headed." He emphasized that the soldiers under Slack's command "were devotedly attached to him and to them he was a model of soldierly bearing."

Those who knew Slack and served with him shared this common thread in their remembrances of the general. Veterans continually characterized him as a person of courage and integrity, beloved by his men. After the war, a Missouri Confederate offered the following description of Slack: "Simple and unostentatious in his life and manners, he was the soldier's friend, and the soldiers to a man were his friends." In an article published in *Century Magazine,* Thomas L. Snead, one of Price's lieutenants, wrote of Slack, "his men idolized [him] and . . . the whole army held [him] in honor." Accordingly, Slack's greatest contribution to the Confederate war effort came, not through his martial accomplishments on the field of battle, but rather in his ability to inspire and motivate his men. Slack's willingness to put himself at risk in order to direct his troops ultimately cost him his life. His death served to deepen the commitment of many Missourians to the Confederate cause.

Bibliography

Payne, James E. "The Test of Missourians." *Confederate Veteran* 37 (1929): 64–65.

Piston, William Garrett, and Richard W. Hatcher III. *Wilson's Creek: The Second Battle of the Civil War and the Men Who Fought It.* Chapel Hill: University of North Carolina Press, 2000.

Shea, William L., and Earl J. Hess. *Pea Ridge: Civil War Campaign in the West.* Chapel Hill: University of North Carolina Press, 1992.

Snead, Thomas L. "The First Year of the War in Missouri." In *Battles and Leaders of the Civil War,* ed. Robert U. Johnson and Clarence C. Buel, 1:278–88. New York: Century, 1884.

—Jeffery S. Prushankin

Maj. Gen. Gustavus Woodson Smith

GUSTAVUS W. SMITH entered the Confederate army as a major general at the beginning of the conflict, second in command of the major Confederate army in Virginia, and he left it as a major general in the Georgia state militia. And therein lies the tale that illuminates much of his Confederate career. A West Pointer with an admirable record in the Mexican War, Smith failed to live up to the promise this record might have suggested. Moreover, early on he began squabbling with President Jefferson Davis over various matters, activity that more or less guaranteed his consignment to the less-than-illustrious group of Confederate generals.

Smith was born at Georgetown, Kentucky, on January 1, 1822, the son of Byrd, a tanner and farmer, and Sarah Hatcher Woodson Smith of Cumberland, Virginia. As a beneficiary of decent schooling in Scott County and the patronage of Richard M. Johnson, the vice president of the United States, the sixteen-year-old lad obtained an appointment to West Point in June 1838. He graduated eighth in his class in July 1842. His high academic achievement earned him appointment as a lieutenant in the Corps of Engineers.

He was first assigned to the port city of New London, Connecticut, as an assistant engineer constructing Fort Trumbull. There he met his future bride, Lucretia Basset, the daughter of a sea captain. They married in October 1844, shortly before Smith received an appointment to teach engineering at West Point. When the war broke out with Mexico in May of 1846, he assumed second in command of a company in the Corps of Engineers, which arrived in Mexico in November. After initial work in road building and bridge repair, the company formed part of the twelve-thousand-strong force under Maj. Gen. Winfield Scott that landed at Vera

Cruz the following March. At this point Smith had assumed command of the unit following the illness and death of the original commander. Smith's engineers were responsible for constructing works during the three-week investment of Vera Cruz, and shortly thereafter they came to the attention of General Scott when they exchanged picks and shovels for muskets at the battle of Cerro Gordo. The company continued to serve creditably through the balance of Scott's campaign, and Smith was twice brevetted for gallantry: to first lieutenant following Cerro Gordo, and to captain after the battle of Contreras.

After Mexico, Smith returned to his position at West Point, where he remained until his resignation from the army in December 1854. Several reasons prompted this action: Smith was bored with teaching and disgusted at the slow rate of promotion—his promotion to first lieutenant in December 1853, eleven years after his commissioning, was his first. He also wanted to participate in John A. Quitman's filibustering scheme to invade Cuba. When these plans failed, Smith worked as a construction engineer on jobs in New Orleans and as chief engineer for construction of the Treasury Building in Washington, D.C., and the Cooper and Hewitt Iron Works in Trenton, New Jersey. Politically well connected, Edward Cooper became street commissioner for New York City upon election of a reform mayor in 1857, and he appointed Smith as his deputy. Six months later, Smith took over the position when Cooper resigned.

Smith's pro-Southern views were no secret. But he chose to view secession and the outbreak of war from his municipal post, not leaving New York until the end of July 1861. He had suffered an attack of paralysis shortly after the firing on Fort Sumter and on doctor's advice was traveling to Hot Springs, Arkansas, when he learned that U.S. authorities sought to arrest him. Smith officially resigned his position in New York in early September, and two weeks later, in Richmond, he offered his services to the Confederacy. Not coincidentally, Smith's final move to associate with the South came shortly after Kentucky's neutrality ended with the entrance of Confederate troops into the state.

On September 19, Davis accepted Smith's offer and bestowed upon him the rank of major general with a date of rank sufficient for him to outrank almost everyone else. Shortly thereafter, Joseph Eggleston Johnston, commander of the Confederate army in Virginia, installed Smith as commander of the army's second corps and his own second in command. Given Smith's paltry military experience—he had never held field command—his immediate elevation to these heights remains puzzling.

The Kentuckian had made an auspicious entry into Confederate service. Within months, he was participating in high-level strategy conferences attended by President Davis, his military adviser Gen. Robert E. Lee, and Secretary of War George W. Randolph. His star would never again be as ascendant. (By all accounts, Smith entertained an exalted opinion of himself and was not shy about advertising it. Lt. Gen. James Longstreet derisively referred to him as "big name.")

"Big name," however, remained relatively inconspicuous until the first day of the battle of Seven Pines on May 31, 1862, during George B. McClellan's Peninsula campaign. He surfaces sporadically in accounts of the action, but when Johnston was seriously wounded, command of the entire army quite unexpectedly devolved upon Smith. That evening, the general met with President Davis, who naturally wanted to know Smith's plans for the next day's battle. Nervous and fatigued, Smith seemed tentative, anything but confident, and he said he would not know what needed to be done until he had further information on the condition of the army. The conversation convinced Davis that the army needed a new commander. The next day Confederate forces renewed their attacks, but the effort was fainthearted; by noon the attacks had fizzled, and the battle ended. Two hours later, to the general's shock, Davis personally relieved him of command and appointed Lee in his stead. Without delay, Lee unceremoniously broke up Smith's wing of the army and redistributed the units. Thus ended General Smith's active service with the Army of Northern Virginia, although he remained nominally assigned to it until his resignation from the army the following year; he had been its commander for eighteen hours.

Smith had quickly proven himself unsuitable for high command, physically and mentally. Later on June 1, he suffered a physical and mental breakdown brought about by strain. His condition, which he described as paralysis, and which others have termed variously "an apoplectic condition" or "traumatic shock," persisted for several weeks. Upon his return to duty, after a few weeks of interim duties, Smith was given command of the Department of North Carolina and Southern Virginia, which included command in Richmond. Primarily administrative, this was a middling assignment for an officer of Smith's rank.

In mid-October, Smith learned that he had been passed over for promotion to lieutenant general by five officers junior to him. This slight on his abilities only confirmed in his mind the malevolence of the president. He obsessed about it for months and never forgot it. He was only slightly mollified when asked to serve as interim secretary of war (November 17–21, 1862) when Randolph ran afoul of Davis and resigned. The following month, on December 17, Thomas Clingman's brigade of about 1,200 Confederate troops engaged the Federals at Goldsboro, North Carolina, under Smith's watchful eye. The Union raiders succeeded in their objective of burning a key railroad bridge and retired back to New Bern, from whence they had come. Smith chose not to pursue them.

Although the Federal raid was but a momentary annoyance, Smith's conduct in North Carolina engendered criticism that reached the ears of first Lee, then the president. So in late January, Smith was recalled to Richmond amid rumors that he would next be posted to the hinterlands of Louisiana or Texas. A personal interview with Davis on January 28, 1863, did not assuage Smith's anger or convince him that he had any future with the army. He still burned with resentment for not being promoted. Consequently, he submitted his letter of resignation on February 7; it was accepted by the War Department ten days later, after an unseemly and acerbic exchange of correspondence with Davis.

Smith might have abandoned the army but not the Southern cause. He soon volunteered as aide-de-camp to his friend General P. G. T. Beauregard in Charleston. He offered valuable engineering expertise on his inspection of fortifications there but soon left for Georgia to serve as aide to Governor Joseph E. Brown. Impressed by the Kentuckian, Brown recommended Smith as president of the Etowah Manufacturing and Mining Company, a post he accepted in May 1863. He remained there for a year. He achieved great success during this time, rescuing the company from financial distress and maintaining its output of crucial iron products despite steadily growing problems in obtaining coal for smelting.

With the Federal force under Maj. Gen. William T. Sherman advancing inexorably toward Atlanta, the Georgia militia chose Smith as field commander, to his delight. On June 1, 1864, Governor Brown confirmed the selection and ordered him to Atlanta to assume command. Although ridiculed by the regular military, the militia made up in pluck what they lacked in skill. During the ensuing bitter fighting around Atlanta, Smith and his militia acquitted themselves well, both outside the city on July 4 at Nickajack Ridge against a superior force and again at the battle of Atlanta on July 22. During the ensuing weeks of the siege, the militia shifted from one part of the line to the other and was often engaged in fierce fighting.

After the fall of the city, the governor, a champion of states' rights who had been almost constantly embroiled in controversy with Richmond, granted the militia a thirty-day furlough, a shrewd move that allowed the troops to gather the autumn crops as well as kept them from being enrolled into Confederate service. With the main Confederate force, the Army of Tennessee, on its ill-fated march north into Tennessee, the Georgia militia endeavored to impede Sherman's march to the sea. The Georgians saved a substantial quantity of supplies in a clash with Federal cavalry at Forsyth on November 17, and they repelled a strong Federal demonstration at Macon the following day.

Ordered to Augusta by Lt. Gen. William J. Hardee, who had assumed overall command of the Confederate forces in Georgia, Smith remained in Macon procuring supplies and transport while the militia force departed under the command of Brig. Gen. Pleasant J. Phillips. Smith ordered the militia to halt at the village of Griswoldville, ten miles northeast of Macon, and wait for him there. If attacked, Smith had stipulated that the force fall back onto the Macon fortifications. Despite these orders, an inebriated Phillips marched past Griswoldville and attacked a brigade of Sherman's rear guard, took heavy casualties, and was forced back to Macon. The fruitless effort did nothing to slow Sherman's steady march toward Savannah.

Now needed for the defense of that port city, on November 25 Smith's militia left Macon and, via a roundabout journey by rail to Albany and on foot from there, arrived at Savannah early on November 30. Hardee had to convince Smith, and Smith had to convince his men, that their services were urgently required out of state in South Carolina near the Charleston and Savannah Railroad at Honey Hill. It was imperative that this crucial rail lifeline between the two cities remain open. So it was that a small Confederate force of about 1,500 effectives repulsed several attacks there by an amphibious Union force that had disembarked at Boyd's Landing, about nine miles to the east. Keeping the line of retreat open for Hardee's garrison in Savannah was General Smith's last significant action of the war. The Georgia militia were the last troops to depart Savannah on December 20. They spent the balance of the war in Macon, where they surrendered, along with their commander, on April 20, 1865. As a general officer, Smith had to apply personally to President Andrew Johnson for a pardon; it was not granted until November 1867.

Smith's engineering and administrative skills proved beneficial to the severely crippled Etowah Manufacturing and Mining Company, to which he returned after the war. He did not stay there long. In early 1866, he left Georgia to assume general management of the Southwestern Iron Company in Chattanooga. He had obtained this position through the influence of Abram S. Hewitt, his former employer in Trenton. The company did well until business took a downturn in 1868. It merged with another company two years later.

In the meantime, Smith had moved on to better employment, accepting an appointment as the first insurance commissioner of Kentucky in June 1870. By dint of his intelligence and fair-mindedness, Smith became a respected figure in the life insurance business nationwide. During this time, he wrote *Notes on Life Insurance,* which examined theory and practice in the business; it was the first of several works that flowed from his pen after the war. He remained in this position in Frankfort, Kentucky, until 1876, when he returned to New York City.

Smith lived a tranquil life in New York. Officially listed as a surveyor and engineer in city directories, he no longer spent any time in these pursuits. He was active in the Confederate Veterans Camp, a benevolent association founded in 1890 to assist former soldiers ineligible for pensions, and in the Masons. Apparently he spent a good deal of his time writing articles—three for the *Century Magazine*'s famous series—and booklength manuscripts. The first of these to be published was *Confederate War Papers* (1884). Inevitably, this book, critical of Jefferson Davis on several counts, and *The Battle of Seven Pines* (1890), which blamed Longstreet for the defeat, launched Smith into the continuing imbroglio of charges, countercharges, and self-justifications among former Confederates about events during the war. Smith also wrote *Generals J. E. Johnston and G. T. Beauregard at the Battle of Manassas, July 1861* (1892). His final book, *Company "A" Corps of Engineers* (1896), proved his most valuable, an examination of the recruitment, training, and activities of the unit during the Mexican War.

A chronic victim of sickness, Gustavus Smith died peacefully at his home in New York City on June 23, 1896, after an illness of several months. Lucretia, his wife of thirty-seven years, had preceded him in death in 1881. The couple had no children; one of Smith's nephews served as administrator of the general's meager estate. Smith was buried beside his wife in an unmarked grave in her family's section of Cedar Grove Cemetery in New London, Connecticut.

A man of unquestionably high character and strict probity, Gustavus Smith, a good and honest man, must be adjudged a failure as a general. He achieved a modicum of success as small-unit leader, but he never lived up to his reputation otherwise. Civil life, where he succeeded in several occupations, was far more congenial to him than military leadership. And his contributions to the literature of the Mexican and Civil Wars, lucid and based on careful research, remain his most lasting legacy. Smith the writer far exceeded Smith the general in both skill and usefulness.

BIBLIOGRAPHY

Davis, William C., ed. *The Confederate General.* 6 vols. Harrisburg, PA: National Historical Society, 1991.

Hudson, Leonne M. *The Odyssey of a Southerner: The Life and Times of Gustavus Woodson Smith.* Macon, GA: Mercer University Press, 1998.

Smith, Gustavus W. *Confederate War Papers.* New York: Atlantic Publishing and Engraving, 1884.

—THOMAS E. SCHOTT

Lt. Gen. Richard Taylor

RICHARD TAYLOR WAS the only son of President Zachary Taylor and Margaret Mackall "Peggy" Smith Taylor. He was born at Springfield, a three-hundred-acre plantation near Louisville, Kentucky, on January 27, 1826. Known to family and friends as Dick, he attended various frontier schools until about 1839. In September 1840, he entered a distinguished preparatory school in Lancaster, Massachusetts. He entered Yale University in 1843 and graduated on August 21, 1845. During the Mexican War he briefly served as secretary for his father, the latter a major general at the time. From an early age, Taylor suffered from several illnesses, particularly rheumatism and arthritis. Unable to decide on a vocation, Taylor began to manage his father's plantation, Cypress Grove, in Jefferson County, Mississippi. Then in 1850, he purchased Fashion, a large sugar cane plantation in St. Charles Parish, Louisiana. By 1860, the plantation had grown to a total of four thousand acres and had on it 197 slaves. The people of St. Charles and Jefferson parishes elected him to the Louisiana state senate in November 1855, and he served in that body until 1861. Originally a member of the Whig Party, Taylor later became a Know-Nothing (American Party) and eventually a Democrat. After the Democratic National Convention of 1860, he served as one of Louisiana's delegates to the Southern Democratic conventions held in Richmond and Baltimore. At the Louisiana secession convention in January 1861, he became chairman of the Military and Naval Affairs Committee. He assisted in the passage of two ordinances, one calling for the raising of two regiments to defend Louisiana and a second authorizing the purchase of arms and ammunition by Gov. Thomas O. Moore. Taylor then returned to Fashion to await the war he saw as inevitable.

Brig. Gen. Braxton Bragg, commanding Confederate forces at Pensacola, Florida, named Taylor an extra and acting or volunteer aide-de-camp on his staff on May 20, 1861. Taylor did not arrive at Bragg's headquarters until about five days later and left in early June for a short visit home. He returned to Pensacola by July 4. That same day, Taylor learned of his election as colonel of the Ninth Louisiana Infantry Regiment on July 2, and he left for its training camp north of New Orleans. He saw his new command off for the Confederate capital in Richmond, Virginia, on July 11. He went to the Crescent City to secure ammunition and field equipment and joined his regiment on July 20. Taylor and his men left Richmond and reached Manassas Junction at dark on July 21, too late to participate in the first battle of Manassas.

The Ninth Louisiana Infantry was assigned on July 25, 1861, to a brigade also composed of the Sixth, Seventh, and Eighth Louisiana regiments. Brig. Gen. William H. T. Walker of Georgia assumed command of the brigade. Taylor was named commander of the brigade on October 22, 1861. His promotion to the rank of brigadier general was effective as of October 21. He was absent sick at the time. Because he was the junior colonel, many officers and men of the brigade expressed dissatisfaction with his promotion. He feared charges of favoritism as Jefferson Davis's former brother-in-law (Davis's first wife, long deceased by this time, was Sara Knox Taylor, Richard's older sister) and went to Richmond to request a revocation of the promotion. Davis refused, and Taylor assumed command on November 4.

Taylor's brigade served as the army's rear guard during the movement from Manassas to Orange Court House in March 1862. Now a part of the division commanded by Maj. Gen. Richard S. Ewell, Taylor often conversed with his new superior in an attempt to learn more about the art of command. Receiving orders to report to Maj. Gen. Thomas J. "Stonewall" Jackson's army in the Shenandoah Valley, Taylor took his brigade on a twenty-six-mile march in one day. This so impressed Jackson that he chose the Louisiana brigade to lead his advance the following day. From this time onward, Taylor's brigade set the pace for the long marches in the Shenandoah Valley. During the succeeding operations, Taylor and his brigade played major roles in Confederate victories at the battles of Front Royal, Winchester, and Port Republic. At the end of the Shenandoah Valley campaign, Taylor took his brigade with Jackson's army to Richmond to assist in defending it against Maj. Gen. George B. McClellan's Union army. He became so ill shortly after reaching the city that he had to relinquish command of the brigade to its senior colonel. Taylor accompanied his men throughout the Seven Days' Battles in an ambulance. At the recommendation of Stonewall Jackson, Taylor received promotion to the rank of major general on July 28, 1862. The War Department assigned him to command of Confederate forces in western Louisiana.

Taylor established his headquarters at Opelousas on August 18, 1862. Two days later his command was officially designated as the District of West Louisiana. The state was in an almost helpless condition following the fall of New Orleans and Baton Rouge. One of Taylor's first goals was to protect the rich agricultural region between Bayou Lafourche and the Mississippi River from Union incursions out of New Orleans. Taylor began organizing independent battalions and companies into regiments, and he succeeded in having several battle-tested regiments and artillery batteries transferred to his district from east of the Mississippi River.

Initially, things did not go well for Taylor's army. In late October, while Taylor was away at Vicksburg, Mississippi, conferring with Lt. Gen. John C. Pemberton, a Union force moved into the Lafourche region and defeated the Confederate forces in the battle of Labadieville. The defeat forced Taylor's troops to evacuate the Lafourche. They began erecting earthwork fortifications on Bisland Plantation along Bayou Teche below Franklin. In the spring of 1863, Maj. Gen. Nathaniel P. Banks, new commander of the Department of the Gulf, began a campaign to drive Taylor's forces out of south Louisiana. Banks's goal was to destroy or severely weaken Taylor's army so that he could conduct an attack on the Confederate stronghold at Port Hudson on the Mississippi River north of Baton Rouge. Taylor's outnumbered army successfully defended their earthworks on April 12 and 13, 1863. A portion of Banks's army moved by steamers through a lake east of Fort Bisland and landed at a point in Taylor's rear. This forced him to evacuate his position. He supervised an attack on this flanking force in the battle of Irish Bend on April 14, defeating it and allowing his men to get to safety with most of their supplies.

Taylor's army conducted a slow retreat through Vermillionville (now Lafayette) and Opelousas to Alexandria as Banks's Federals pursued. Because a Union naval squadron had entered Red River from the Mississippi and was approaching Alexandria, Taylor had to continue his retreat to Natchitoches. Banks's men reached Alexandria, remained there for a few days, and then turned southward to go after Port Hudson. Maj. Gen. Ulysses S. Grant's army had crossed the Mississippi River below Vicksburg and was slowly placing a stranglehold on that fortress city. Taylor's superior, Lt. Gen. Edmund Kirby Smith, ordered Taylor to take command of a division of Texas infantrymen and some scattered cavalry units and to attack Grant's lines of communication along the Mississippi River above Vicksburg. Taylor sent his forces against Union garrisons at Milliken's Bend and Young's Point on June 7, 1863, but could not overrun the Federal positions because Union gunboats helped defend them. Then with a small force consisting largely of cavalrymen, Taylor moved into south Louisiana, captured the important Union base at Brashear (now Morgan) City on June 23, and began moving eastward toward New Orleans. Before he completed his plans for attacking Union shipping on the Mississippi River, Taylor learned of the surrender of the Vicksburg and Port Hudson garrisons on July 4 and 9, respectively. Knowing that Banks would soon transfer much of his army against his smaller force, Taylor again abandoned the Lafourche district. During the fall and winter of 1863, Taylor's force remained in south Louisiana and fought several successful battles against Union forces advancing into the region. At Sterling's Farm on September 29 and Bayou Bourbeau on November 3, the Confederates inflicted heavy losses on their opponents and captured more than a thousand prisoners, several artillery pieces, and much equipment.

In March 1864, Banks led about twenty-eight thousand men in what became the Red River campaign. Banks's goal was to destroy Taylor's army, capture the town of Shreveport with its supply depots and munitions shops, and push into east Texas. With only about six thousand troops under him, Taylor had to retreat from Alexandria through Natchitoches and toward Shreveport. He urged Kirby Smith to send reinforcements from Texas and Arkansas, and he ultimately received two cavalry divisions from the former and two infantry divisions from the latter. Taylor finally felt confident of facing Banks's army in open battle and begged Kirby Smith to allow him to stop the Federal advance before it could reach Shreveport.

Kirby Smith ignored Taylor's frequent pleas. Finally, on April 8, Taylor aligned his forces south of the town of Mansfield and awaited Banks's army. By late afternoon, he had heard nothing from Kirby Smith so he conducted an assault on the leading elements of the Union column. Taylor's men crushed two Federal divisions, captured twenty artillery pieces, two hundred supply wagons, and thousands of small arms. Only darkness and a stout defense by a third Union division halted the Confederate attack. Banks retreated to the town of Pleasant Hill. He sent the remnants of his forces that had fought at Mansfield back toward the Red River. Some twelve thousand troops were camped around the village. Taylor wanted to keep up the momentum his army had gained, so he ordered an attack on Banks's men on the afternoon of April 9. His plans to outflank the Union positions failed, and the battle turned into a stalemate. Taylor ordered his troops back to a place where they could find water. During the night, Banks conducted a retreat back toward the safety of a Union fleet in the river near Grand Ecore. Taylor thus gained a strategic victory.

Here things began to fall apart for Taylor, however. He met with Kirby Smith and urged a strong pursuit of the defeated Federals. Taylor felt confident of destroying Banks's army and forcing the destruction of the Union fleet. Kirby Smith instead decided to take three of Taylor's infantry divisions and go on a campaign against a small Union army in Arkansas. Though greatly outnumbered, Taylor determined to do everything he could to prevent the escape of the Union army and navy. In the end, he was unable to stop Banks's retreat. After several engagements and a few skirmishes, the Federals finally reached the Atchafalaya River at Simsport and safely crossed it, ending the campaign.

On June 5, 1864, Taylor submitted a blistering letter of criticism to Kirby Smith and asked to be released from duty under his command. Incensed by this and other missives he had received from Taylor, Kirby Smith quickly obliged. He relieved Taylor from command and ordered him to Natchitoches on June 10. Kirby Smith also forwarded to Jefferson Davis all the pertinent correspondence concerning the controversy. He probably hoped that Taylor would receive censure from the president or War Department. Several days later, word reached the Trans-Mississippi Department that Taylor had received a promotion to the rank of lieutenant general on May 18. Davis and the War Department named him as commander of the Department of Alabama, Mississippi, and East Louisiana.

After an unsuccessful attempt to cross two of his infantry divisions over the Mississippi River that summer, Taylor crossed the river in early September near Woodville, Mississippi. He reached Meridian, Mississippi, the department headquarters, on September 5 and assumed command the following day. Taylor's main concerns at this time were to attempt to interrupt the supply lines to Maj. Gen. William T. Sherman's Union armies at Atlanta and to protect the important city of Mobile, Alabama. He ordered Maj. Gen. Nathan Bedford Forrest to move his cavalry command north of the Tennessee River to attack Sherman's communications. Following the defeat of the Army of Tennessee at Franklin and Nashville in late 1864, the remnants of that force marched to Tupelo, Mississippi. On January 17, 1865, Taylor received orders to take command of the army. In a short time, the army was in good enough condition that it began making its way to North Carolina to oppose Sherman's march into that state. In late March, Taylor found his department threatened from two directions. A large Federal cavalry force under Brig. Gen. James

H. Wilson moved into northern Alabama on a raid aimed at Montgomery and Selma. About the same time, Maj. Gen. Edward R. S. Canby led a Union army against Confederate defenses on the eastern shore of Mobile Bay opposite the city of Mobile. Canby planned to capture these earthworks and then move to link up with Wilson. When the latter's cavalrymen attacked Forrest at Selma on April 2, Taylor was in the town and barely escaped capture as the Confederate forces were routed. Canby completed his attacks on April 9, capturing Spanish Fort and Fort Blakely, and his army entered Mobile three days later.

Taylor soon learned of the surrender of Gen. Robert E. Lee's army. Then word reached him that Gen. Joseph E. Johnston had asked Sherman for an armistice in North Carolina. On April 23, Taylor wrote to Canby asking for a truce. The two generals met six days later north of Mobile. Taylor expressed a desire to negotiate a surrender of his small army. On May 2, he accepted the terms offered by Canby, but the capitulation did not become official until two days later when Taylor and Canby met at Citronelle. Taylor would always claim May 8 as the date of the surrender because that was the date of the acceptance of his men's paroles. Canby took Taylor to New Orleans from Mobile. On May 25, he witnessed the formal surrender of the Trans-Mississippi Department to Canby.

In July 1865, Taylor traveled to Washington, D.C., to meet with President Andrew Johnson and to seek the release from prison of Jefferson Davis and other Confederate officials. While he was eventually allowed to visit his former brother-in-law at Fortress Monroe, Taylor failed to see him released or brought to trial. Davis would not be freed until May 1867. With his plantation and fortune gone, Taylor attempted several means of making a living but did not enjoy much success at any of them. Eventually, he became friends with Samuel L. Barlow, a wealthy attorney in New York City, and received some financial support from him. Barlow was also influential in the Democratic Party and assisted Taylor in working with Presidents Johnson and Ulysses S. Grant and with members of Congress to achieve better treatment for the former Confederate states. In 1876, he supported the presidential campaign of Democrat Samuel J. Tilden. When the election returns were disputed, Taylor worked to help achieve the Compromise of 1877, which brought an end to Radical Reconstruction. He wrote his memoirs and succeeded in having them published under the title *Destruction and Reconstruction: Personal Experiences in the Late War* the week before his death.

Taylor married Myrthe Louise "Mimi" Bringier in February 1851 at the Bringier family house, Melpomene, in New Orleans. They had three daughters—Louise Margaret, Elizabeth "Betty," and Myrthe Bianca—and two sons: Zachary "Zach" and Richard "Dixie" Jr. The two boys died of scarlet fever during the Red River campaign.

On April 12, 1879, Taylor died at the home of his friend Barlow in New York City. Severe intestinal congestion caused his death. His body was taken to New Orleans and placed in a family crypt in Metairie Cemetery.

BIBLIOGRAPHY

Bergeron, Arthur W., Jr. "General Richard Taylor: A Study in Command." Master's thesis, Louisiana State University, 1972.

Parrish, T. Michael. *Richard Taylor: Soldier Prince of Dixie*. Chapel Hill: University of North Carolina Press, 1992.

Prushankin, Jeffery S. *A Crisis in Confederate Command: Edmund Kirby Smith, Richard Taylor, and the Army of the Trans-Mississippi*. Baton Rouge: Louisiana State University Press, 2005.

Taylor, Richard. *Destruction and Reconstruction: Personal Experiences in the Late War*. Ed. Richard B. Harwell. New York: Longmans, Green, 1955.

—ARTHUR W. BERGERON JR.

Brig. Gen. Thomas Hart Taylor

THOMAS HART TAYLOR was born in Frankfort, Kentucky, on July 31, 1825, the son of Edmund H. Taylor and Louisa Hart Taylor. He received his education at Kenyon College in Ohio and Centre College in Danville, Kentucky, and graduated from the latter school in 1843. Taylor studied law and practiced that profession briefly. At the outbreak of war with Mexico, he enlisted as a private in the Third Kentucky Infantry Regiment. His service during the conflict led to his promotion to the rank of first lieutenant, and he sometimes exercised command of his company. Taylor made two trips across the plains to California in 1852 and 1853, driving cattle herds to the new state. After his return to Kentucky, he operated a farm and lumber business in Hickman County. A flood wiped him out, and he became a businessman in Memphis.

Taylor entered the Confederate army as a captain of cavalry in the regular service. On April 13, 1861, Adj. Gen. Samuel Cooper ordered him to go through Memphis and Nashville to Kentucky and examine the possibility of establishing recruiting stations at those points. He eventually made his way to Louisville and began enlisting men. Lts. John Bell Hood and George B. Cosby assisted Taylor in this effort. Cooper issued orders on May 24 recalling Taylor to Nashville to assume charge of the depot there.

By late June or early July, Taylor had relocated to Richmond, Virginia. There he served as a mustering officer for infantry and cavalry companies. On July 7, Jefferson Davis sent Taylor through the lines with a message to Abraham Lincoln concerning the treatment of the crew of the privateer *Savannah*, which had been captured by a Union blockading vessel. Brig. Gen. Pierre G. T. Beauregard at Manassas provided a small cavalry escort for Taylor. Arriving at Arlington, Taylor was taken by one of Bvt. Lt. Gen. Winfield Scott's staff officers to Scott's headquarters. Scott took the message and promised to deliver it to Lincoln. Taylor then returned to Manassas with a small Union cavalry escort. He submitted a brief report to Davis on July 10 concerning his mission.

Under orders from the War Department, Gen. Joseph E. Johnston organized two separate Kentucky battalions into the First Kentucky Infantry Regiment on August 7. As a lieutenant colonel, Taylor received orders to go to Manassas and assume command of the new unit. His appointment as colonel of the unit did not come until October 14. The regiment established a camp at Centreville and performed picket duty in the area. Taylor and his men saw their first action against enemy troops on September 28 at Mason's Hill, about four miles from Alexandria. Their mission was to recover some items abandoned there by other Confederate troops. Forming his regiment across the road and with skirmishers out in front, Taylor ordered an advance on the hill only to find that Union troops thought to be there had retreated. One company did engage in a brief skirmish with a small enemy force, killing three or four of the enemy. After holding the hill for half an hour, Taylor ordered his regiment back to its camp.

Taylor's men became involved in a more serious engagement at Dranesville on December 20. Brig. Gen. James E. B. Stuart led a force of cavalry, infantry, and artillery toward that town to protect a foraging expedition. Union troops under Brig. Gen. Edward O. C. Ord had marched toward Dranesville in an attempt to capture the foragers, and an engagement ensued as the troops from both sides arrived on the field. Stuart had intended to use the First Kentucky as a reserve but sent it to the left of his line. There it became engaged with the Ninth Pennsylvania. Once Stuart saw that the wagons had reached safety, he ordered a withdrawal from the field about three o'clock. Taylor's role was less than glamorous and demonstrates the confusion that existed on many Civil War battlefields. Stuart reported, "Colonel Taylor became separated from his regiment in passing from its left to its right and found himself beyond the enemy's lines, but by great coolness and presence of mind he extricated himself and joined his regiment that night." The First Kentucky lost one man killed, twenty-one wounded, and two missing in the fighting.

Taylor's regiment became a part of Brig. Gen. David R. Jones's Georgia brigade, of Maj. Gen. Gustavus W. Smith's division, in early 1862. The men continued to perform picket duty. In response to an increased enemy presence on his front, General Johnston ordered his army to abandon its positions near Manassas Junction and withdraw to the Rappahannock River. The movement began on March 7, and Taylor's men left their winter quarters the following day. On March 17, 1862, Taylor was placed in command at Orange Court House and was named provost marshal for the vicinity. The First Kentucky subsequently moved with Jones's Brigade to the Peninsula. On April 16, Taylor and his troops participated in fighting with Union troops at Lee's Mill, or Dam No. 1. The regiment reorganized on April 30, but the War Department did not accept it as a wartime unit. When the Confederate army retreated from the Yorktown lines on May 4, Taylor and his men did not halt but continued on to Richmond. There it was mustered out on May 13 at Camp Winder.

The War Department soon ordered Taylor to report to Maj. Gen. Edmund Kirby Smith in eastern Tennessee. On June 10, the general organized a brigade for Taylor consisting of the Twenty-third Alabama, Fifty-second Georgia, and Third Tennessee (Provisional) infantry regiments. Several days later, Kirby Smith planned to send the brigade to Chattanooga in response to a threat against that city, but the movement of another Union force southward from Cumberland Gap caused him to retain Taylor's men near Knoxville. Taylor and his men finally took position at Blain's Crossroads northeast of Knoxville. As this Union threat failed to materialize, Taylor's brigade received orders to occupy the town of Clinton, northwest of Knoxville.

Kirby Smith reorganized his army in early July, and Taylor's brigade became a part of Brig. Gen. Carter L. Stevenson's division. Taylor lost the Fifty-second Georgia Infantry but gained the Forty-sixth Alabama and the Thirty-first and Fifty-ninth Tennessee regiments. When Kirby Smith's army marched into Kentucky in mid-August, Stevenson's division moved on August 16 to besiege Cumberland Gap. His troops invested the Union garrison from the east, south, and southeast. Kirby Smith sent more troops and soon had the Federals almost surrounded. Stevenson refused to attack the enemy, waiting to starve them out. Taylor's men participated in the month-long operation against that place and were the first troops into the post after the Federals evacuated it on September 17. Stevenson's division conducted an unsuccessful pursuit of the Union troops into Kentucky until October 1. The division then formed the right flank of Kirby Smith's army as it retreated from Lexington. Taylor and his men saw no fighting while the Confederates were in the state. The division retreated back into Tennessee after the battle of Perryville.

Shortly after the return to East Tennessee, Kirby Smith again reorganized his army. Confederate policy called for the brigading of units from the same state whenever possible. Taylor's new brigade consisted of the Thirty-fourth, Thirty-sixth, Thirty-ninth, Fifty-sixth, and Fifty-seventh Georgia infantry regiments. President Jefferson Davis appointed Taylor a brigadier general effective November 4, 1862, but never forwarded his nomination to that grade to the Confederate Senate. Historian Ezra J. Warner speculated in his study of Confederate generals that Davis failed to do so because Taylor did not command troops from his home state, saying that the latter policy was "a *sine qua non* with Davis."

The brigade accompanied Stevenson's division to Vicksburg in December 1862, arriving after the battle of Chickasaw Bluffs. After occupying a position along the center of the entrenchments there for a few days, Taylor and his men moved to Jackson for several weeks. Taylor brought his brigade back to Vicksburg toward the end of January 1863 and put them in camp south of the city. The troops did picket and guard duty for the next several months. On March 29, because Brig. Gen. Stephen D. Lee had left the city on other duties and as ranking officer, Taylor assumed command of the troops in the river batteries and on the Vicksburg waterfront in addition to his own brigade. When Maj. Gen. Ulysses S. Grant's army crossed the Mississippi River below Vicksburg, Taylor's brigade moved toward the Big Black River and joined other Confederate units gathering to oppose the Union advance. Because Taylor had never been confirmed as a brigadier, the War Department found another commander for his brigade. Brig. Gen. Alfred Cumming of Georgia received orders to go from Mobile to replace Taylor, which he did on May 13. Lt. Gen. John C. Pemberton was instructed to "make such other disposition of Colonel Taylor" as he thought proper. Later Gen. Joseph E. Johnston instructed Pemberton to retain Taylor on duty in his army.

Pemberton found a place for Taylor on his staff. During the pivotal battle of Champion Hill on May 16, Taylor carried orders from Pemberton to division commanders Stevenson, William W. Loring, and John S. Bowen. In the afternoon, as Confederate soldiers began straggling back from the fighting, Pemberton sent Taylor with some couriers to try to rally the men. Taylor reported later that he kept at this task "until it was useless to try any longer." Later, as the Confederate army was retreating in confusion, Taylor again attempted vainly to gather men together to continue the fight. The next day, Pemberton ordered Taylor to place four artillery pieces on the west side of Big Black River Bridge, which he did. He again tried to rally fleeing soldiers after the disaster in that battle but soon returned to the artillery position, where he remained until the army was ordered to fall back into the Vicksburg entrenchments. During the siege,

Taylor served as Pemberton's inspector general and as post commander. Pemberton reported that "in both capacities [he] rendered most valuable service." Taylor received his parole when the Confederate garrison surrendered on July 4, and went to Montgomery, Alabama.

After his exchange, Taylor saw duty at Mobile early in 1864. Lt. Gen. Leonidas Polk, commander of the Department of Alabama, Mississippi, and East Louisiana, picked Taylor to go to eastern Louisiana to raise and perhaps command cavalry units. Maj. Gen. William T. Sherman's Meridian raid in February delayed Taylor from taking his new post. On March 5, Polk assigned Taylor to command of the District of South Mississippi and East Louisiana. Taylor assumed command on March 30. In his new position, he had few troops to protect the region from enemy incursions and faced civilian discontent with government seizures of supplies. Col. John S. Scott, who had lived in that part of Louisiana prior to the war, relieved Taylor as district commander on April 28. Taylor then reported to department headquarters in Demopolis, Alabama.

On June 24, Maj. Gen. Stephen D. Lee named Taylor as provost marshal general of the department with headquarters at Meridian, Mississippi. He had moved to Mobile by November 1 and become post commander there. As post commander, Taylor had under his command only a few units of reserve and local defense troops to preserve order in the city. One of his last duties was to help organize all able-bodied men in Mobile into local defense units. This came in response to Union major general Edward R. S. Canby's campaign against Spanish Fort and Fort Blakely on the eastern shore of Mobile Bay in March 1865. Taylor joined the Confederate forces as they evacuated the city on April 11. As a part of that evacuation, he had charge of the destruction and removal of cotton located in Mobile. Lt. Gen. Richard Taylor named him as his commissioner to parole troops at Jackson, Mississippi, when he surrendered the Department of Alabama, Mississippi, and East Louisiana to Canby on May 4, 1865. Thomas Hart Taylor received his final parole as a part of that army.

Taylor ran a business in Mobile until 1870 and then returned to his native Kentucky. He served as a deputy U.S. marshal for five years. In 1881, he was elected police chief of Louisville and filled that office for eleven years. He received an appointment in February 1886 as superintendent of the Louisville and Portland Canal. The superintendent of the district claimed that Gov. Simon B. Buckner, a Democrat and former Confederate general, had insisted upon Taylor's appointment even though Taylor had no experience as an engineer. The return of the Republican

Party to power under President Benjamin Harrison in 1889 resulted in Taylor's replacement as superintendent. The chief engineer for the district claimed that Taylor "had upset the entire canal work force by creating the impression that he would replace them with his friends."

Taylor married three times during his lifetime. In 1844, he married Sarah Elizabeth Blanton, of Frankfort. They had one child, Edmund Haynes Taylor, born in 1845. Sarah died in 1858. While stationed at Mobile in 1864, Taylor married Sarah A. Moreland of that city. She died at an unknown date. Taylor's last marriage was to Eliza Adair Monroe in 1878 at Frankfort. Taylor and Eliza had four children: Mary Louise (1880), John Adair Monroe (1881), Thomas Hart Jr. (1883), and Adair Monroe (1885).

Taylor died of typhoid fever on April 12, 1901, in Louisville and is buried in the State Cemetery in Frankfort.

BIBLIOGRAPHY

Davis, William C., ed. *The Confederate General.* 6 vols. Harrisburg, PA: National Historical Society, 1991.

Johnson, Leland R. *The Falls City Engineers: A History of the Louisville District, Corps of Engineers, United States Army.* Louisville, KY: U.S. Army Engineer District, 1974.

Johnston, J. Stoddard. *Kentucky.* Vol. 11 in *Confederate Military History,* ed. Clement A. Evans. Atlanta: Confederate Publishing, 1899. Rev. ed. Wilmington, NC: Broadfoot Publishing, 1988.

Warner, Ezra J. *Confederate Generals in Gray: Lives of the Confederate Commanders.* Baton Rouge: Louisiana State University Press, 1959.

—ARTHUR W. BERGERON JR.

Brig. Gen. Lloyd Tilghman

BORN AT RICH Neck Manor near the village of Claiborne on Maryland's Eastern Shore in Talbot County, on January 26, 1816, Lloyd Tilghman was the fourth child and only son of James and Anne Caroline Shoemaker Tilghman. He was also the grandson of Col. Tench Tilghman, who had served as an aide to Gen. George Washington during the American Revolution and delivered the news of the British surrender at Yorktown to the Continental Congress. A member of one of Maryland's leading families, Tilghman was educated in private schools and, at the age of fifteen, entered the U.S. Military Academy at West Point. His record as a cadet was less than stellar and at time of graduation in 1836 he stood forty-sixth in a class of forty-nine who were commissioned that day. Among those with whom he graduated were future Civil War generals Montgomery Meigs, Thomas W. Sherman, and Joseph R. Anderson. Tilghman was assigned to duty with the First U.S. Dragoons but, three months later, resigned his commission and worked as a construction engineer on railroads and canals in Panama and across the American South until the outbreak of the Civil War.

Tilghman married Augusta Murray Boyd in Portland, Maine, on May 26, 1843. She was the daughter of Maj. Joseph Coffin Boyd, who served as the first state treasurer of Maine. Fellow West Pointer and future Union general Joseph Hooker reportedly stood as best man at the wedding. Little is known of their courtship or how they even met, but speculation is that they met while he was a cadet at West Point. The couple had eight children, one of whom, Lloyd Tilghman Jr., served as his father's aide during the Civil War and was killed in Canton, Mississippi, on August 6, 1863, when he was thrown from his horse and hit his head on a piece of rail iron.

When war with Mexico erupted, Tilghman briefly returned to military duty and served as aide-de-camp to Bvt. Maj. Gen. David Twiggs. He participated in the early actions of the war in northern Mexico and helped construct the fortifications around Matamoros. He later joined the forces under command of Bvt. Lt. Gen. Winfield Scott for the drive against Mexico City. Participating in the battle of Cerro Gordo and a number of lesser actions, Tilghman advanced inland to Puebla, where the army halted to await fresh troops for the final push on Mexico City. On August 14, 1847, as Scott's army closed on the Mexican capital, Tilghman was commissioned a captain in the Maryland and District of Columbia Volunteer Artillery and returned toward the coast to greet the arrival of his unit. Following disembarkation, his six-gun battery was stationed at Jalapa. Mustered out of service on July 13, 1848, Tilghman returned to the peaceful pursuits of a civil engineer and resumed his work on railroad construction.

In 1852, Tilghman moved his family to Paducah, Kentucky, and took up residence in a large, six-thousand-square-foot, two-story home. (The Tilghman home on the corner of Seventh and Kentucky Avenues is now operated as a Civil War museum.) For the remainder of the antebellum period he labored on railroads in Kentucky, Tennessee, Mississippi, Louisiana, and Arkansas. Among the railroads on which he worked were the New Orleans and Ohio, Mobile and Ohio, and the New Orleans, Jackson and Great Northern. These lines were destined to play an important role in the war that soon burst in fury across the American landscape.

Known for his pro-Southern sentiments, Tilghman watched with mounting anxiety as the nation drifted to the brink of civil war. Following the election of Abraham Lincoln, he helped to recruit men for the Kentucky State Guard, which was led by Simon Bolivar Buckner, a man with whom Tilghman later served in the Confederate army. Kentucky, however, did not secede, and many men, including Tilghman, entered Confederate service in neighboring Tennessee. On July 5, 1861, Tilghman was commissioned colonel of the Third Kentucky Infantry, which had organized at Camp Boone in Montgomery County, Tennessee. On October 18 he was promoted to brigadier general in the Confederate army and placed in command of troops that had advanced into Kentucky and occupied Hopkinsville. A more important assignment, however, soon followed.

On November 17, 1861, Tilghman was ordered to "repair to the Cumberland [River] and assume command of Forts Donelson and Henry and their defenses." These earth forts were then under construction. Once completed, they would block the natural pathways of Federal invasion formed by the Cumberland and Tennessee rivers. (Work on a third fort, Heiman, overlooking the Tennessee River opposite Fort Henry, was also under way.)

Early in 1862, Union naval and land forces led by Flag Officer Andrew H. Foote and Brig. Gen. Ulysses S. Grant moved against the forts. On February 6, Forts Heiman and Henry stood silent against the gray dawn as Federal warships came into view and prepared for battle. Unbeknownst to the Union commanders, the Confederates had abandoned Fort Heiman, which was incomplete, and thus posed no threat. Fort Henry, however, was a powerful bastion that mounted seventeen guns, twelve of which fronted the river. Due to faulty engineering for which Tilghman was not responsible, the fort was situated on low ground close to the river and was partially flooded at the time of the attack. Realizing that the fort was untenable, Tilghman sent most of his men to Fort Donelson and remained behind with a handful of gunners to contest the Union fleet. The small band of artillerists proved no match for the powerful gunboats, which disabled a number of Confederate cannon. "Dismembered bodies lay beside shattered guns, fires had kindled combustibles in the fort, and demoralized officers and men milled about," is how one Southerner described the scene inside the fort. At 1:50 P.M., Tilghman ordered the colors struck.

Foote ordered Cdr. Roger Stembel of the flagship *Cincinnati* to take possession of the fort. A detail from the ironclad lowered a rowboat and, gliding over the calming water, moved up to a sally port, rowed inside the fort, and came to rest on the parade ground. Returning with Tilghman to the gunboat, Stembel watched as the Confederate commander greeted Foote, saying, "I am glad to surrender to so gallant an officer." The crusty Foote was less gracious in his reply: "You do perfectly right, sir, in surrendering, but you should have blown my boat out of the water before I would have surrendered to you." (On February 16, Simon Bolivar Buckner surrendered Fort Donelson to Grant.)

Despite the loss of these forts, Confederate president Jefferson Davis later wrote that none

more heroically, more patriotically, more singly served his country than Tilghman at Fort Henry, [who] when approached by a large army, an army which rendered the permanent defense of the fort impossible, with a handful of devoted followers went into the fort and continued the defense until his brigade could retire in safety to Fort Donelson; then with that work finished, when it was impossible any longer to make a defense, when the wounded and dying lay all around him, he, with the surviving remnant of his little band, terminated the struggle and suffered in a manner thousands of you who have been prisoners of war know how to estimate. . . . All peace and honor to his ashes, for he was among those, not the most unhappy, who went hence before out bitterest trials came upon us.

The hapless Tilghman was taken to Fort Warren in Massachusetts. Located on Georges Island, at the entrance to Boston Harbor, Fort Warren was a massive pentagon made of stone and granite that had been constructed between 1833 and 1861. Tilghman and his fellow officers captured at Fort Donelson arrived on the island in early March. Included in the group were Simon Bolivar Buckner, John Gregg, Hiram Granbury, and George Cosby.

On July 31, Tilghman's imprisonment came to an end as he boarded the transport *Ocean Queen* for the voyage to Fortress Monroe in Virginia. In keeping with the terms of the Dix-Hill Cartel, he had been exchanged for Union brigadier general John F. Reynolds, who had been captured at Boatswain's Swamp, Virginia, on June 28, 1862. (Reynolds was later killed at Gettysburg on July 1, 1863.) Arriving there on August 5, Tilghman was transferred to a lighter vessel, which carried him up the James River to Aiken's Landing, fifteen miles below Richmond, where he once again set foot on Confederate soil. Much to their embarrassment, the authorities in Richmond had made no plans to meet the exchanged officers or provide for transportation to greet their arrival at Aiken's Landing. Tilghman and his comrades had to walk to Richmond to inquire of their future.

On August 7, Tilghman met with Secretary of War George Randolph, who ordered him to Mississippi. Placed in charge of rendezvous and instruction camps in Clinton, between Jackson and Vicksburg, he worked feverishly to reorganize exchanged prisoners and forwarded them to Maj. Gens. Earl Van Dorn and Sterling Price in north Mississippi. Most of these troops, however, did not arrive in time to participate in the battles of Iuka (September 19) and Corinth (October 3–4), both of which ended in failure for Confederate forces.

In October, Tilghman was assigned command of a division in the corps commanded by Maj. Gen. Mansfield Lovell, then part of Van Dorn's army. But to his dismay, Tilghman's first duty was to sit as a member of the court of inquiry that convened at Abbeville, Mississippi, on November 15, 1862, to evaluate charges of drunkenness and inefficiency leveled against Van Dorn following the debacle at Corinth. Although the court, which consisted of Generals Tilghman, Price, and Dabney Maury, exonerated Van Dorn, the flamboyant Mississippian was soon replaced by Lt. Gen. John C. Pemberton.

In late November, Maj. Gen. Ulysses S. Grant led his Union army south from Tennessee into Mississippi in his opening drive against Vicksburg. As Confederate troops fell back from Holly Springs, north of the Tallahatchie River, through Oxford to Grenada, south of the Yalobusha River, Tilghman's division was hotly engaged in a rearguard action at Coffeeville on December 5. In a furious running fight his command checked the Federal advance then drove Grant's vanguard back two miles. The Union campaign was eventually turned back when horsemen under Van Dorn sacked Grant's supply base at Holly Springs.

In the spring of 1863, the Vicksburg campaign began in earnest as Grant's army pushed south through Louisiana and crossed the Mississippi River below Vicksburg. Driving deep into the interior of Mississippi, Grant's forces captured Jackson then turned west toward Vicksburg. Pemberton moved out of the fortress city to contest the Federal advance and collided with Grant on May 16 at Champion Hill. In the largest, bloodiest, and most significant action of the campaign, Pemberton's army was routed and driven from the field.

To cover the Bakers Creek ford, the only avenue of escape left the Confederate army, Tilghman, now commanding a brigade, formed his men in a line on Cotton Hill. This was the highest ground between the ford and the enemy. If the Federals seized his position, Tilghman realized, enemy artillery would command the crossing, effectively cutting the Confederate escape route to Vicksburg. Knowing that he must hold his position at all hazards, the adopted Kentuckian was determined to sacrifice his command, if need be, to save the army. Fortunately, his position was naturally strong, as it commanded a wide sweep of open ground. Strengthened by the six guns of Capt. James J. Cowan's Company G, First Mississippi Light Artillery, and two guns of Company C, Fourteenth Mississippi Artillery Battalion led by Capt. Jacob Culbertson, Tilghman's position was difficult to turn and would prove costly to assault.

The redlegs from Mississippi opened with canister and sent the enemy scrambling for cover. Union artillery, however, quickly moved into position in front of the Coker house, five hundred yards to the east, dropped trail, and roared into action. The Federal guns pounded Tilghman's position with telling effect, yet the Mississippians remained at their posts and handled their guns with cool deliberation. Amid the crash of shot and shell, Captain Cowan was somewhat startled when Tilghman suddenly dismounted, walked over to one of the guns and said, "I will take a shot at those fellows myself." As he aimed the cannon, enemy shells screamed past Tilghman, who remarked to the delight of his men, "They are trying to spoil my new uniform." His jest was prophetic and a member of the battery recorded of Tilghman, "He then sighted the gun again & as he stepped back to order fire, a Parrott shell struck him in the side, nearly cutting him in twain." The general's badly mangled body, escorted by his son and aide Lloyd Tilghman Jr., was taken to the Yeiser house, where the brigadier was pronounced dead. Tilghman thus became the second Confederate general to die in the campaign, following Brig. Gen. Edward D. Tracy, who had been killed at Port Gibson on May 1, 1863. Two others would follow before the fortress city surrendered on July 4, 1863.

Col. Arthur E. Reynolds of the Twenty-sixth Mississippi Infantry, who succeeded Tilghman in command, lamented: "As a man, a soldier, and a general, he had few superiors. Always at his post, he devoted himself, day and night, to the interests of his command. Upon the battlefield, collected and observant, he commanded the respect and entire confidence of every officer and soldier under him, and the only censure ever cast upon him was that he always exposed himself too recklessly."

That evening, under a flag of truce, the remains of Lloyd Tilghman were sent into Confederate lines and taken back to Vicksburg, where the general was interred in Cedar Hill Cemetery. In 1902, the general's surviving sons, Frederick and Sidell, visited Vicksburg and had their father disinterred. His remains were taken to New York City and buried next to his wife in Woodlawn Cemetery in the Bronx. On the anniversary of the general's death in 1909, Frederick and Sidell unveiled a monument to their father in Lang Park in Paducah. The standing statue was the work of the renowned sculptor Henry H. Kitson. A few days later, his sons, assisted by kinsman Oswald Tilghman, former secretary of state of Maryland, placed a monument in Tilghman's honor on Champion Hill battlefield to mark the site where he had been mortally wounded. They also later commissioned Frederick William Sievers to sculpt a heroic-size equestrian statue to their father, which was dedicated on the grounds of Vicksburg National Military Park in 1926.

Bibliography

Bush, Bryan S. *Lloyd Tilghman: Confederate General in the Western Theater.* Morley, MO: Acclaim Press, 2006.

Davis, William C., ed. *The Confederate General.* 6 vols. Harrisburg, PA: National Historical Society, 1991.

Rabb, James W. *Confederate General Lloyd Tilghman: A Biography.* Jefferson, NC: McFarland, 2006.

—Terrence J. Winschel

Brig. Gen. John Stuart Williams

BORN NEAR MOUNT Sterling, Kentucky, on July 10, 1818 (according to most sources), July 18, 1820 (his Mexican War pension application), or June 29, 1818 (from his tombstone), John S. Williams was the son of Samuel L. Williams and Fanny Cluke. The elder Williams distinguished himself during the War of 1812 as a captain in the Fifth Kentucky Regiment and was taken prisoner at the battle of Raisin River. He subsequently served one term in the Kentucky House and three terms in the Kentucky Senate. Young John was educated in the local common schools and the Winchester Academy before attending Miami University in Oxford, Ohio. He graduated in 1838 and two years later was admitted to the bar. He practiced law under Maj. Thomas Elliott in Paris until 1845. Williams married Mary Harrison on April 19, 1842, and removed to Clark County, where he added farming and stock raising to his legal pursuits. Two years later Williams's wife died after giving birth to a daughter.

With the outbreak of the Mexican War, Williams raised a rifle company in Clark County only to have his unit accidentally excluded from Kentucky's volunteer quota. Williams's Independent Kentucky Rifles was subsequently accepted into the regular U.S. Army by an order from the War Department in June 1846. The Kentuckians were initially attached to the Sixth U.S. Infantry during Bvt. Lt. Gen. Winfield Scott's advance on Mexico City. However, at the battle of Cerro Gordo on April 18, 1847, Williams's company was attached to the Second Tennessee Infantry of Brig. Gen. Gideon Pillow's brigade.

Pillow's command was repulsed after a desperate charge under murderous fire. However, the Americans won the day, and the Kentuckian, who distinguished himself in the fighting, would be known as "Cerro

Gordo" Williams for the rest of his days. After his independent company was mustered out in May 1847, Williams returned to Kentucky and was appointed colonel of the newly raised Fourth Kentucky Volunteer Infantry on September 20, 1847. Williams's regiment reached Mexico after the fighting concluded and served as part of the American occupation forces before returning to Louisville to be mustered out on July 25, 1848.

Williams's reputation as a bold fighter led Cuban exiles to offer him a commission in Gen. Narciso Lopez's army of American adventurers seeking to liberate the troubled island from Spanish control. Hundreds of Kentuckians fought and died with Lopez during his ill-fated "filibuster" expeditions between 1849 and 1851. However, Williams refused to join the ranks of the would-be liberator.

A staunch Whig like his father, Williams entered politics and narrowly defeated his Democratic rival, and future Confederate general, Roger W. Hanson, in the 1851 race for Clark County representative in the Kentucky House. Ironically, Hanson had served as his first lieutenant at Cerro Gordo. A close friend of Sam Houston, Williams entertained the noted Texan when he attended Henry Clay's funeral in 1852. From 1855 to 1856 Williams, along with future Union general George B. McClellan, served as an American military observer during the Crimean War and reportedly traveled extensively in Europe, Asia, and Africa. Upon his return from Europe he left Kentucky and purchased a four-thousand-acre tract in Piatt County, Illinois. He was apparently working these lands when the 1860 presidential election propelled the nation toward war. After the death of the Whig Party he fought under the Native American or Know-Nothing banner. A Union man throughout the turbulent fifties, he supported the conservative John Bell and the Constitutional Union Party in 1860.

However, Williams was a conditional unionist whose loyalty to the old flag faded when the Lincoln administration adopted a policy of coercion against the newly formed Confederacy. Reportedly driven from Illinois for his anti-Lincoln stance, Williams returned to Kentucky and joined the Southern State Rights Party. On May 4, 1861, while Kentucky still reeled from the aftermath of Fort Sumter and Lincoln's call for troops, Williams delivered a stirring address in Mount Sterling in which he warned that Kentuckians faced ruin unless they "with brave hearts and stout arms" supported the Confederacy in what he termed a struggle between liberty and despotism.

Williams's stance cast him against his own family, as his father and brother, Richard, remained staunch Unionists. On May 17, while his aged father addressed a newly formed company of Union Home Guards in Mount Sterling, Williams was delivering a spirited states' rights speech at nearby Flat Rock. At a convention held in Owingsville on May 27, Williams was nominated as the Southern State Rights candidate for Kentucky's Ninth Congressional District. Williams was defeated at the polls on June 20, and when the final votes were counted Kentucky's Union Party had won an overwhelming victory.

The weakened Southern State Rights Party began to advocate "peace" while both sides warily supported the state's official policy of neutrality during the summer of 1861. On July 30, 1861, a Kentucky admirer urged the Confederate government to place Williams in command of the Kentucky volunteers who gathered south of the state line at Camp Boone, Tennessee. However, Williams was not chosen to command what later became the legendary Orphan Brigade.

The defeat of the Southern State Rights Party in the elections in August, coupled with the Confederate occupation of the Mississippi river town of Columbus, led the Union-controlled legislature to officially reject neutrality on September 18. With Kentucky firmly allied with the North, Williams and other Southern State Rights leaders fled their homes to avoid arrest. Passing through Mount Sterling, he rode up the Licking River valley to West Liberty, where he issued a call for volunteers. According to one report over two hundred men rallied to his standard. Williams proceeded to Prestonsburg, the home of John M. Elliott, a former Democratic member of Congress and the Kentucky legislature who was perhaps the most prominent Southern State Rights champion in the Big Sandy Valley. The small mountain town soon became a rallying point for hundreds of Confederate volunteers from Covington to the Virginia line.

On October 2 the leaders of the Prestonsburg encampment petitioned the Confederate government for a commander and sent four delegates to Richmond to expedite the process. At the same time, Williams was sent to the Confederate capital to procure arms and the authority to muster the mountain column into the Confederate service. He also attempted unsuccessfully to obtain the transfer of Col. John Bell Hood, a native of Bath County, to the Sandy Valley. By mid-October Williams returned to Kentucky with a colonel's commission and set out to forge his raw recruits into a fighting force. By October 19 he had over 2,500 men under his command. However only 500 were well armed, while an additional 1,000 carried only pistols and bowie knives.

With artillery, reinforcements, and adequate arms, Williams might have posed a serious threat to central Kentucky. However, men and arms

moved slowly over the primitive mountain roads that connected Prestonsburg with the nearest Confederate supply depots in southwestern Virginia.
When Union forces under Brig. Gen. William "Bull" Nelson advanced up
the Licking River Valley against Prestonsburg, Williams had no choice
but to fall back. Although a delaying action at Ivy Mountain on November 9, 1861, slowed Nelson's advance, Williams was forced to retreat to
Pound Gap on the Virginia line. "We had nothing on our side," he lamented, "except courage."

This reverse was followed by news that undoubtedly wounded Williams's pride. On November 1, a fellow Kentuckian, Humphrey Marshall, was commissioned a brigadier general and placed in command of
all Confederate forces on the Kentucky-Virginia border. On November
16, 1861, Williams became colonel of the Fifth Kentucky Infantry, a unit
composed entirely of mountaineers. Williams's command was so poorly
uniformed and equipped that it was soon christened the Ragamuffin
Regiment. Reinforced by a battery of artillery and two Virginia infantry
regiments, Marshall's little Army of Eastern Kentucky returned to the
Big Sandy Valley in the dead of winter and established a fortified camp at
Paintsville.

However, history soon repeated itself. Marshall's poorly armed and
supplied force formed the extremely isolated right flank of Gen. Albert S.
Johnston's line of defense in Kentucky. When another Federal column
under Col. James A. Garfield advanced from the mouth of the Big Sandy
River in December 1861, Marshall was forced to abandon his position
and fall back toward the Virginia line. On January 10, 1862, Marshall
fought a delaying action at Middle Creek near Prestonsburg, where Williams's Ragamuffins distinguished themselves. Nevertheless, like Williams before him, Marshall was forced to retreat through Pound Gap into
Virginia.

While Marshall's command passed the winter in southwestern Virginia,
Williams's star was about to rise. On March 27, 1862, several prominent
Kentuckians in Richmond petitioned President Jefferson Davis for Williams's promotion. Accordingly, on April 16, 1862, Williams was commissioned a brigadier general and ordered to report to Marshall. In this
capacity, Williams led the advance of Marshall's force at the battle of Princeton, (West) Virginia, on May 16 and 17, 1862. The Confederate victory
blunted one of the first major Federal thrusts against the strategic Virginia
and Tennessee Railroad, which ran through southwestern Virginia.

Marshall's failure to be promoted to major general created an awkward
situation, for his Army of Eastern Kentucky, no larger than a single bri-

gade, now had two brigadiers. Marshall submitted his resignation on June 16, 1862, and Williams no doubt expected to be his successor. However, President Davis refused to accept Marshall's resignation, and Williams was transferred to the neighboring Department of Western Virginia. Commanding an infantry brigade in Maj. Gen. W. W. Loring's Army of Western Virginia, Williams played an active role in the Confederate offensive that won control of the Kanawha Valley in September 1862. However, by the close of the year, the Confederates had been driven back to their former position along the present day Virginia–West Virginia line.

During the winter of 1862–1863 Williams added his voice to those of several prominent Kentuckians who, in the aftermath of Perryville, urged Richmond to support another invasion of Kentucky. On March 29, 1863, after Marshall launched a small-scale cavalry raid through eastern Kentucky, Williams obtained permission to visit the Confederate capital. On April 11, he set out on what he believed was a temporary leave of absence to raise recruits along the Kentucky-Virginia border. He hoped to rally enough men to enter Kentucky and advance to the Ohio River. However, while he was recruiting his border command at Saltville, Virginia, Maj. Gen. Sam Jones, Loring's successor, placed John Echols in command of Williams's old brigade. This left Williams in command of a skeleton force of raw recruits and marked the beginning of frequent clashes between the Kentuckian and his commanding officer.

As Ambrose Burnside's Union forces prepared for a major advance from Kentucky into East Tennessee, the Virginia and Tennessee Railroad became the target of three separate cavalry raids in June and July. Although repulsed on July 18, the enemy strike at Wytheville caused further friction between Williams and Jones. Despite the fact that Williams's troops struck the Federal raiders at every opportunity, the Kentuckian was blamed for failing to block their escape.

The dual advance of Burnside on Knoxville and William Rosecrans on Chattanooga led the Confederate high command to order Maj. Gen. Simon Buckner to abandon East Tennessee and reinforce the hard-pressed Army of Tennessee in north Georgia. After the fall of Knoxville to Burnside's forces, Sam Jones was ordered to assume responsibility for the defense of East Tennessee. On September 6, 1863, Jones ordered Williams to assume command of the skeleton force left by Buckner to defend the Virginia-Tennessee line. Williams's advance units met Burnside's cavalry in East Tennessee and fought a series of sharp delaying actions all along the railroad until the Federals fell back at Bristol.

Maj. Gen. Robert Ransom subsequently assumed command of the

forces along the Virginia border and prepared to attack the Union garrison at Cumberland Gap. Jones ordered Williams, now in command of a newly organized cavalry brigade, to support Ransom's movement by making a demonstration against Burnside's advance position at Bulls Gap, Tennessee. Williams's little force of 1,500 cavalry took up defensive positions at Blue Springs, but days passed with no word from Ransom. In the meantime, Burnside advanced with his entire force of 9,000 men, prompting Williams to telegraph Jones that his situation was critical. Jones tersely replied that Williams merely faced a demonstration in force and ordered the Kentuckian not to yield an inch of ground. Enraged by Jones's response, Williams fought Burnside's entire force to a standstill at Blue Springs on October 10, 1863. Although outnumbered six to one, Williams held his position until nightfall.

Incredibly, Williams refused to retreat. However, when he rode to Greeneville to telegraph Jones about his successful stand, his subordinates wisely retreated under the cover of darkness. Burnside's cavalry set out in pursuit on the eleventh and surrounded Williams's force at Henderson's Mill. However, the Kentuckian cut his way out, and one of his men recalled how "Cerro Gordo, like a veritable god of war, waved his sword on high as he led the van, cheering the boys and storming and raging." But the command was overtaken and encircled at Rheatown. To the amazement of his men, Williams inexplicably ordered the command to pitch camp as the Federals began to shell their position. One of his men exclaimed, "What the hell does all this mean, going into camp in the presence of the enemy?" A comrade jokingly replied, "Strategy my boy. Strategy!" Which brought the reply, "Strategy, hell!"

In 1875, when Williams sought the Democratic nomination for Kentucky governor, Col. Henry L. Giltner claimed that his old commander was too drunk at Rheatown to exercise command. Williams's force was scattered and retreated in complete disorder to Virginia. A Tennessee officer formally charged him with drunkenness, and on November 3 Williams requested to be temporarily relieved from command in order to clear his name through a court of inquiry. He rode to Saltville to await trial, but little is known of his activities during the winter of 1863–1864. Giltner assumed permanent command of Williams's Brigade, and Richmond ignored petitions from the officers of George B. Hodge's cavalry brigade to have Williams replace their former commander in early 1864.

Williams was eventually transferred to the Army of Tennessee and assumed command of Col. J. Warren Grigsby's Kentucky brigade of Wheeler's Cavalry Corps shortly after Sherman launched his drive on Atlanta in May 1864. Although not present at every engagement, Williams led his men through the hard fighting in Georgia throughout the summer. On August 10, as the Federals closed in on Atlanta, Wheeler was ordered to raid Sherman's lines of supply and communication. Williams's Brigade played an active role in destroying the railroad between Tunnel Hill and Grayville. Wheeler drove so deeply into East Tennessee that he was unable to rejoin the main army until October.

During the course of his lengthy raid Wheeler reluctantly gave Williams permission to attack the Union outpost at Strawberry Plains, near Knoxville. The Kentuckian was cut off from Wheeler's command and joined forces with Brig. Gen. John C. Vaughn's brigade for a proposed attack on Bulls Gap. Williams was unable to form a juncture with Vaughn which provided an unexpected blessing for the beleaguered Confederate forces in southwestern Virginia. A full Union cavalry division had crossed the mountains from Kentucky on a mission to destroy the crucial Confederate salt-production facilities at Saltville. Williams readily responded to a plea for reinforcements from Brig. Gen. John Echols, who temporarily commanded southwestern Virginia, and on October 2, 1864, "Old Cerro Gordo" arrived on the field just in time to repulse the Federal attack. It was said that his booming voice was clearly heard above the din of battle as he swore and barked orders all along the line. Although Williams was criticized for failing to pursue the retreating enemy, it should be noted that he was placed under arrest the day after his victory on orders from Wheeler, who charged the Kentuckian with failing to rejoin his command.

Williams led his troopers back through the Carolinas to Georgia only to find that John Bell Hood, now a general, had led the Army of Tennessee northward on its last, doomed offensive. Williams overtook Hood at Columbia, Tennessee, but was informed that headquarters had no knowledge of Wheeler's charges. Still considered under arrest, Williams was ordered to report to Gen. P. G. T. Beauregard in Charleston, South Carolina. Ironically, while he awaited a court of inquiry, Williams learned that on January 28, 1865, the Confederate Congress had passed a formal resolution of appreciation for his victory at Saltville. The intercession of the Confederate high command finally ended the farce. However, Williams did not resume command of his brigade until February.

Williams participated in the battle of Bentonville, North Carolina, March 19–21, 1865. Following the surrender of the Army of Tennessee on April 18, the remnants of Williams's Brigade formed part of the Confederate forlorn hope that rode southward with President Davis. Indeed, Davis himself later recalled that an ailing Williams offered Mrs. Davis the use of his personal carriage. Paroled with his command at Washington, Georgia, on May 9, 1865, Williams made his way back to Kentucky via Chattanooga and Nashville.

Williams relocated to New Orleans for a brief period but soon returned to Kentucky. Like many former Confederates, Williams became active in Kentucky politics. He made an unsuccessful bid for commonwealth attorney in the Tenth Judicial District in 1868 but was elected to a two-year term as state representative for Montgomery County in 1873. He lost his bid for the Democratic nomination for governor in a closely contested race between several prominent former Confederates in 1875. In 1876 he made an unsuccessful bid for the U.S. Senate. In 1878 he successfully campaigned for the vacant Senate seat of Thomas C. McCreery but failed to win reelection in 1884. After failing to secure the post of minister to Mexico, he became a land developer in Florida and helped found the town of Naples. He then retired to the life of a gentleman farmer with his second wife, Henrietta Hamilton, née Lindsey, whom he married in 1871. Shortly before his death in Mount Sterling on July 17, 1898, the old soldier keenly regretted that he was unable to bear arms in the conflict with Spain. He was laid to rest in the city cemetery in Winchester.

Brig. Gen. Basil Duke described Williams as "an extremely handsome man, tall, large, well proportioned . . . with many generous and manly qualities." Proud, profane, and utterly fearless in battle, "Cerro Gordo" Williams was unquestionably one of the most colorful Kentuckians to wear the gray.

BIBLIOGRAPHY

Davis, William C., ed. *The Confederate General.* 6 vols. Harrisburg, PA: National Historical Society, 1991.

Johnston, J. Stoddard. *Kentucky.* Vol. 11 in *Confederate Military History,* ed. Clement A. Evans. Atlanta: Confederate Publishing, 1899. Rev. ed. Wilmington, NC: Broadfoot Publishing, 1988.

U.S. War Department. *The War of the Rebellion: A Compilation of the Official Records of the Union and Confederate Armies.* 70 vols. in 128 pts. Washington, DC: Government Printing Office, 1880–1901.

—JAMES M. PRICHARD

FIELD OFFICERS OF
KENTUCKY CSA UNITS

ADAIR, JOHN ALEXANDER. Born May 28, 1827, Lawrence County, Alabama, son of Alexander and Elizabeth Monroe Adair. Grandson of Kentucky governor John Adair. Prewar druggist in Greensburg, Green County, Kentucky. Second lieutenant, Greensburg Guards, Kentucky State Guard, May 20, 1860. First lieutenant, January 8, 1861. Married Mary Bird Stockton. Captain, Company F, Fourth Kentucky, September 13, 1861. Wounded in the head at the battle of Shiloh and disabled. Major, February 13, 1863. Lieutenant colonel, February 28, 1863. Resigned August 31 1863, due to the effects of his Shiloh wound. Farmer in Hart County postwar. Died November 28, 1898, Hart County. Buried in Sims Cemetery, near Canmer, Kentucky.

ALLEN, JOHN. Born c. 1810, Kentucky, son of John and Margaret Hornsby Allen. Known as "Jack" Allen. Veteran of the Texas Revolution and the Mexican War. Filibusterer with Narciso Lopez and William Walker. Shelby County farmer prewar. Said to have killed a man in Shelby County when young and to have gone to Texas after that. Married three times in all, including Ruth M. Thomas. Captain, Company B, Morgan's Second Kentucky Cavalry, 1862, succeeding his brother Thomas. Promoted to lieutenant colonel, Third Kentucky Cavalry, date uncertain. Resigned his lieutenant colonel's commission January 30, 1863. Removed to Bright Star, Hopkins County, Texas, c. 1870. Died there November 5, 1871. "A tried and gallant soldier."

ALSTON, ROBERT AUGUSTUS. Born December 31, 1832, Macon, Georgia, son of Willis W. and Elizabeth Howard Alston. Prewar clerk, then lawyer, in Charleston, South Carolina. Married Mary Charlotte Magill. Private, Charleston Light Dragoons, South Carolina militia, 1861. Captain and assistant adjutant general to John Hunt Morgan by June 1, 1862, resigning November 23, 1862, to become major, Ninth Tennessee Cavalry. Lieutenant colonel, Ninth Tennessee Cavalry, December 23, 1862. Volunteer aide-de-camp to General Cheatham at the battle of Murfreesboro. Captured July 5, 1863, near Lebanon, Kentucky. Upon exchange in October 1863, made lieutenant colonel, First Kentucky Special Battalion Cavalry. Often led a brigade, 1864–1865. Postwar farmer in DeKalb County, Georgia, then partner with Henry Grady in the *Atlanta Herald*. Georgia state representative, 1878–1879. Murdered March 11, 1879, at the Georgia capitol building in Atlanta, by a man angered at Alston's selling property that had been promised to him. Buried Old Decatur Cemetery, Decatur, Georgia. While on Morgan's staff Alston published an army newspaper, the *Vidette*.

ANDERSON, BENJAMIN M. Born c. 1836, Kentucky, son of James and Mary Wigglesworth Anderson of Louisville. Captain in William Walker's filibusterer army, and wounded in Nicaragua before returning to Kentucky. Clerk for a pork packing firm in Louisville. Unmarried. Captain, Davis Guards, April 26, 1861, a Kentucky company (later Company I, Taylor's First Kentucky) that, since Kentucky had not seceded, joined the First Louisiana as Company H. Captain, Company I, First Kentucky, May 2, 1861. Major, July 12, 1861. Transferred to Third Kentucky July 20, 1861. Lieutenant colonel, Third Kentucky, October 18, 1861. Wounded in action at Shiloh. Resigned June 1, 1862, due to his wounds. Commissioned colonel, to raise a regiment of partisan rangers behind Union lines in Kentucky, and nominated to the Confederate Senate April 6, 1863. Nomination rejected, February 17, 1864. Discouraged, he returned to Louisville and took an oath of loyalty. Involved in the planning phase of the Northwest Conspiracy. Arrested in December 1864 for treason. In the midst of the trial, Anderson seized a gun from a guard and shot himself. He died two days later, on February 21, 1865. Buried in the family plot in Cave Hill Cemetery, Louisville. A newspaper report on the trial called Anderson "a young man of gentlemanly appearance and possessed of much ability."

AUSTIN, JOHN PRESTON. Born December 22, 1829, Norwich, Connecticut, son of Andrew Y. and Susan Tennant Rogers Austin. Relative of Texas founder Stephen Austin. Prewar clerk to his uncle, a Galveston merchant. Member of Galveston Artillery, a prewar militia unit. Married Amanda Wilson. With Galveston Artillery on the Rio Grande, March 1861. Discharged after six months' service. Left Texas to serve in the Army of Tennessee. Captain, Company I, Ninth Kentucky Cavalry, April 15, 1862. Captured at Lebanon, Tennessee, in 1862. Imprisoned at Camp Chase and Johnson's Island. Exchanged September 1862. Promoted major, probably December 15, 1862, at the regiment's organization. Real estate agent in Atlanta postwar. Died February 10, 1911, at his son's home in La Grange, Georgia. Buried Hill View Cemetery, La Grange. Austin wrote an interesting memoir titled *The Blue and the Gray* in 1899. An obituary described Austin as "a brave soldier and a dashing officer."

BARNETT, THOMAS THRELKELD. Born October 6, 1838, Crittenden County, son of Phineas C. and Jeannette Threlkeld Barnett. Prewar farmer in Crittenden County. Attended Cumberland College in Princeton, Kentucky. Married Jennie

L. Hibbs. Enlisted July 1, 1861, in Confederate army. Captain, Company K, Third Kentucky, July 19, 1861. Signer of Kentucky Ordinance of Secession. Major, September 22, 1863. Lieutenant colonel, 1863. Postwar farmer and stock raiser in Crittenden County. Died March 12, 1899, Paducah. "A typical Southern gentleman . . . brave and chivalrous, yet gentle, social, and kind-hearted."

BINGHAM, JABEZ. Born February 27, 1827, Athens County, Ohio, son of Silas and Martha (Cranston) Bingham. Parents moved to Trigg County, Kentucky, in 1843. Trigg County farmer, millwright, magistrate prewar. Married Sarah V. Daniel; Susan Norris. Captain, Company C, Eighth Kentucky, October 24, 1861. Major, October 24, 1861. Captured at Fort Donelson. After exchange, assigned to duty as commander of the divisional pioneer corps in 1863. Resigned commission in 1864. Postwar Trigg County farmer and contractor. Militia colonel. State representative, 1883–1884. Died October 13, 1884, Trigg County. Buried Wall Cemetery, Trigg County. "A man of strong convictions."

BOWLES, JAMES WILLIAM. Born May 21, 1837, Louisville, Kentucky, son of Joshua B. and Grace Shreve Bowles. Attended Yale University but left prior to graduation due to the impending war. Farmer near Louisville prewar. Married Ann Pope in 1866. First lieutenant, Kentucky State Guard, February 2, 1861. Second lieutenant, Confederate regular army, September 9, 1861. Captain, Company C, Second Kentucky Cavalry, September 21, 1861. Major, November 1862. Lieutenant colonel, January 24, 1863. Colonel, September 9, 1864. Wounded in action and captured at Cynthiana. To Johnson's Island prisoner-of-war camp, released June 1865. Real estate agent in Louisville postwar. Retired to Waynesville, North Carolina, in 1903. Died July 16, 1921, Waynesville. Buried Cave Hill Cemetery, Louisville.

BOWMAN, CURTIS C. Born 1834, Murray County, Kentucky, son of Nathan and Mary Holley Bowman. Columbus merchant in 1860. Married Sarah Jane Starr. Captain, Company F, First Kentucky, 1861–1862. Major, Seventh (First) Kentucky Cavalry, date uncertain. Captain, Company A, Twelfth Kentucky Cavalry, April 29, 1863. Captured August 26, 1863, near the Tennessee River. Died December 11, 1863, at the Johnson's Island prisoner-of-war camp. Body shipped to Paducah for burial. Brother-in-law of Col. A. P. Thompson.

BOWMAN, JAMES HOLLEY. Born c. 1835 Ballard or Murray County, Kentucky, son of Nathan and Mary Holley Bowman. Prewar merchant in Lovelaceville. Married Fanny A. Belcher. Captain, Company B, Third Kentucky, July 5, 1861. Severely wounded in action at Shiloh. Major, June 1, 1862. Resigned August 30, 1863, in order to raise a cavalry regiment in western Kentucky. Lived in Tennessee, Mississippi, and Kentucky postwar. Sawmill owner in Ballard County in 1907. Died May 14, 1908, at the Confederate Soldiers Home in Peewee Valley,

Kentucky. Buried Lovelaceville. Brother of Maj. C. C. Bowman. According to Congressman Henry Burnett, "no man is better qualified or more worthy."

BRADLEY, BENJAMIN FRANKLIN. Born October 5, 1825, near Georgetown, Kentucky, son of John and Sallie Suggett Bradley. Graduated from Georgetown College and Transylvania University. Officer in Mexican War. Prewar Scott County farmer. Married Emily Sanders. Captain, Kentucky State Guard, August 19, 1861. Captain and assistant adjutant general to Gen. Humphrey Marshall, November 26, 1861. Major, First Battalion Kentucky Mounted Rifles, elected May 10, 1862. Resigned September 10, 1862, due to a liver ailment. Member of Confederate Congress, 1864–1865, serving on the Ordnance Committee. Scott County circuit clerk and state senator postwar. Died January 22, 1897, Georgetown. Buried Georgetown Cemetery. A fellow staff officer found Bradley "a gentleman of fine attainments . . . a most rigid disciplinarian."

BRECKINRIDGE, ROBERT JEFFERSON, JR. Born September 14, 1834, Baltimore, Maryland, son of Rev. Robert J. Breckinridge, a prominent unionist spokesman, and his wife, Ann Preston. Cousin of Gen. John C. Breckinridge, brother of Col. W. C. P. Breckinridge. Attended Centre College and the University of Virginia. Lawyer in Danville and Lexington. Said to have been drummed out of college for drinking. In U.S. Coastal Survey. Married Kate Morrison; Lilla Morrison. Captain, Kentucky State Guard, May 11, 1861. Captain, Company B, Second Kentucky, July 5, 1861. Delegate to Kentucky secession convention. Confederate congressman, 1862–1863. Commissioned colonel of cavalry September 13, 1864, for a term of three months, in order to recruit behind Union lines in Kentucky. Captured Woodford County, Kentucky, February 22, 1865. To Johnson's Island prisoner-of-war camp. Released May 22, 1865. Postwar lawyer and judge in Lincoln County, Kentucky, New York City, and Danville. Died March 13, 1915, Danville. Buried Lexington Cemetery. Kentucky Confederate governor Richard Hawes called him "a gentleman of considerable political intelligence."

BRECKINRIDGE, WILLIAM CAMPBELL PRESTON. Born August 28, 1837, Baltimore, Maryland, son of Rev. Robert J. Breckinridge, a prominent unionist, and his wife, Ann Preston. Cousin of Gen. John C. Breckinridge. Raised in Kentucky. Graduated from Centre College and Louisville University Law School. Lawyer in Lexington, Kentucky, prewar. Married Lucretia Clay; Issa Desha; Louise Wing. Captain, Kentucky State Guard, May 18, 1861. Colonel, Ninth Kentucky Cavalry, December 17, 1862. Often led a brigade of Kentucky cavalry in the Army of Tennessee. Commanded Jefferson Davis's bodyguard at war's end. Surrendered at Augusta, Georgia, May 8, 1865. Lawyer in Lexington postwar. Newspaper editor. U.S. congressman, 1885–1895. Died November 19, 1904, Lexington. Buried Lexington Cemetery. In 1894 a woman sued Breckinridge for breach of promise. The publicity from that suit helped end his political career. Breckinridge's papers are at the Library of Congress.

BRENT, THOMAS YOUNG. Born 1835, Paris, Kentucky, son of Hugh and Margaret Chambers Brent. Prewar grocer in Bourbon County. Married Mary A. Moore. Private, Company B, Ninth Kentucky, October 2, 1861. Transferred to Basil Duke's Second Kentucky Cavalry, December 3, 1861. Major, Fifth Kentucky Cavalry, September 2, 1862. Killed July 4, 1863, during the battle of Green River Bridge, Kentucky. General Duke said he was "recklessly brave, and possessed a natural military aptitude."

BULLITT, WILLIAM GRIGSBY. Born May 16, 1833, Shelby County, Kentucky, son of Cuthbert C. and Harriet Willett Bullitt. Attended Shelby College. Lawyer in Paducah in 1860. Married Catherine Pilkington. McCracken County delegate to Kentucky Secession Convention. Raised a company of the Third Kentucky in 1861. On staff duty during the Fort Donelson campaign, escaping capture there. Major, Sixth Kentucky Cavalry, at the September 10, 1862, organization of that regiment. Captured at Cheshire, Ohio, July 20, 1863, during Morgan's Ohio raid. Paducah lawyer and judge postwar. Member, 1891 state constitutional convention. Moved to Frankfort in 1892. Died there February 6, 1901. Buried State Cemetery, Frankfort.

BULLOCK, ROBERT S. Born May 8, 1828, Fayette County, Kentucky, son of Waller and Mary Burch Bullock. Prewar Fayette County farmer. Captain, Lexington Cavalry, Kentucky State Guard, May 18, 1861. Married Mary Franklin. Major, Eighth Kentucky Cavalry, September 10, 1862. Said to have been promoted to lieutenant colonel. Captured July 19, 1863, at Buffington Island, during Morgan's Ohio raid. Imprisoned at Columbus, Ohio, penitentiary and at Fort Delaware for the rest of the war. Sheriff of Fayette County postwar. Cashier at a bank. Died March 6, 1912, Lexington. Buried Lexington Cemetery.

BURNETT, HENRY CORNELIUS. Born October 5, 1825, Essex County, Virginia, son of Dr. James and Martha Garnett Burnett. Raised in Kentucky. Educated at an academy in Hopkinsville. Lawyer in Cadiz, Kentucky, prewar. U.S. congressman, 1855–1861, taking a Southern-rights stance in Congress. Married Mary A. Terry. While in Congress in the spring and summer of 1861, opposed administration war efforts. Called by a hostile newspaper "a big, burly, loud-mouthed fellow who is forever raising points of order." President of the rump Kentucky secession convention, and commissioner from that convention to the Confederate government. Colonel, Eighth Kentucky, November 1, 1861. Resigned, February 3, 1862. Confederate congressman, 1861–1862. Confederate senator, 1862–1865. Served on the Finance and Military Affairs committees. Lawyer in

Cadiz postwar, dying there September 28, 1866. Buried East End Cemetery, Cadiz. Burnett never led the Eighth in the field, being in Congress at the time.

BUTLER, JOHN RUSSELL. Born December 18, 1823, Shelby County, Kentucky, son of Pierce and Eliza Allen Butler. Attended Centre College and University of Louisville Medical College. Prewar physician in Lexington and Frankfort. Aide-de-camp to his uncle, Gen. William O. Butler, in the Mexican War. Married Jane Short. Colonel, Third Kentucky Cavalry, September 2, 1862. Charged with misbehavior before the enemy, February 1863, as part of his long-standing feud with Gen. Abe Buford, but got off without punishment. Regiment consolidated with First Kentucky Cavalry in 1863, and the combined unit is often called the First. Sent to Canada in 1864 to work for the release of Confederate prisoners. Foreman in Louisville in 1880. Died June 11, 1884, Louisville, of Bright's disease. Buried Cave Hill Cemetery, Louisville.

CALDWELL, JOHN WILLIAM. Born January 15, 1836, Russellville, Kentucky, son of Austin and Louisa Harrison Caldwell. Grew up in Russellville and in Texas. Attended Bethany College and University of Louisville. Farmer and clerk. Surveyor in Texas. Lawyer after 1858. Married Sarah J. Barclay. Second lieutenant, Kentucky State Guard, early 1861. Captain, Company A, Ninth Kentucky, September 27, 1861. Major, Ninth Kentucky, January 29, 1862. Wounded in action at Shiloh (right arm broken). Lieutenant colonel, May 14, 1862. Colonel, April 22, 1863. Wounded in action at Chickamauga (left arm broken and disabled). Captured at Shelbyville, Tennessee, October 7, 1863. Exchanged August 3, 1864. On detached service during the Carolinas campaign. Paroled May 17, 1865, Nashville. Lawyer in Russellville postwar. Judge. U.S. congressman, 1877–1883. Died July 4, 1903, Russellville, of paralysis. Buried Maple Grove Cemetery, Russellville. Termed "the bravest of the brave" in an obituary.

CAMPBELL, CHURCHILL GIBBS. Born May 3, 1818, Culpeper, Virginia, son of John and Frances Green Campbell. Nephew of Revolutionary War hero Col. William Campbell. Dry goods merchant in Millersburg, Kentucky. Silk merchant in New York City and Philadelphia. To Versailles, Kentucky, in 1858, to start a retail dry goods store. Lieutenant of Kentucky Volunteers in the Mexican War. Unmarried. Raised Company A, Fifth Kentucky Cavalry, and became its captain September 2, 1862. Promoted to lieutenant colonel July 4, 1863. Captured during Morgan's Ohio raid. Imprisoned at Columbus Penitentiary, suffering from rheumatism. Exchanged October 1864. Paroled Washington, Georgia, in 1865. Dry goods merchant in Versailles postwar. Died there October 2, 1877. Buried Versailles Cemetery. "A brave soldier . . . a man of high and honorable principles."

CAMRON, ORVILLE GLASGOW. Born July 12, 1819, Kentontown, Robertson County, Kentucky, son of Andrew and Ann Glasgow Camron. Harrison County merchant prewar. Married Susan Ann Conn. Captain, Company A, First Battalion Kentucky Mounted Rifles, October 18, 1861. Major, September 10, 1862. Died March 11, 1872, Memphis, Tennessee. Buried Kentontown Cemetery, Robertson County.

CASSADAY, ALEXANDER. Born January 23, 1836, Kentucky, son of Samuel and Eliza McFarland Cassaday. Prewar attorney in Louisville. Lieutenant in the local militia. Captain, then major, Kentucky State Guard, 1860–1861. Married Nancy Craik. Assistant adjutant general on the staff of General Buckner with rank of major, October 4, 1861. Lieutenant colonel, Ninth Kentucky, October 3, 1861. Captured at Fort Donelson. Died March 21, 1862, at the Camp Chase prisoner-of-war camp in Ohio. Buried Cave Hill Cemetery, Louisville.

CASSELL, JACOB T. Born c. 1830, Kentucky, son of James T. and Jane Thorn Cassell. Trader in Louisville just prior to the war. Married Louisa Thurman. Private, Company A, Second Kentucky Cavalry, March 25, 1862. Promoted to captain, June 2, 1862. Wounded in action July 3, 1863, near Columbia, in the thigh, during Morgan's raid. Wounded again and captured July 19, 1863, at Buffington Island. Major, Second Special Battalion Kentucky Cavalry, 1864. Returned to Louisville after the war and ran a gambling house. Died there in 1872. Probably buried in Cave Hill Cemetery, Louisville, where his wife is buried. One battle report noted his "cool and determined manner."

CASTLEMAN, JOHN BRECKINRIDGE. Born June 30, 1841, at Castleton, near Lexington, Kentucky, son of David B. and Virginia Harrison Castleman. Relative of Gen. John C. Breckinridge. Studied at Transylvania University Law School prewar. Married Alice Barbee. Captain, Company D, Second Kentucky Cavalry, June 1, 1862. Promoted to major, date uncertain. Detached and sent to Canada with Thomas Hines to help free the Camp Douglas prisoners. Involved in the Northwest Conspiracy. Captured September 1864 in Indiana. Tried and sentenced to exile from the United States. Pardoned in 1866. Attended medical school in Paris, France. Graduated in 1868 from the University of Louisville Law School. Horse breeder. Adjutant general of Kentucky, 1883–1887. Brigadier general, U.S. Army, during the Spanish-American War. Died May 23, 1918, at his home in Louisville. Buried Cave Hill Cemetery, Louisville. Castleman's memoirs, titled *Active Service,* are among the more entertaining veteran's memoirs.

CAUDILL, BENJAMIN EVERAGE. Born February 11, 1830, Letcher County, Kentucky, son of John and Rachel Cornett Caudill. Farmer in Letcher Company prewar. Married Martha Asbury. Colonel, Thirteenth Kentucky Cavalry, to rank from September 1, 1863 (General Marshall had appointed him colonel, November 2, 1862, upon the organization of the regiment). Captured at Gladeville, Virginia, July 7, 1863. Exchanged August 3, 1864. Led the Thirteenth in Kentucky and Virginia, 1864–1865. Farmer and preacher postwar, living in Clay County. Died February 11, 1889, London, Kentucky. Buried Slate Hill Cemetery, Farriston, Kentucky.

CAUDILL, DAVID JESSE. Born March 9, 1839, Perry County, Kentucky, son of John and Rachel Cornett Caudill. Farmed in Perry County prewar. Married Margaret S. Frizel in 1867. Private, Company F, Eighth Kentucky, no date. Captain, Company B, Thirteenth Kentucky Cavalry, 1862. Lieutenant colonel, September 1, 1864. Wounded in action at Big Leatherwood, October 19, 1862. Carter County farmer postwar. Committed suicide there April 9, 1907, by hanging himself in his smokehouse. Buried Lindsey Chapel Cemetery, Carter County. "A strong conviction and personality—a Baptist by profession, a democrat politically, and a good citizen socially." Brother of Col. Ben Caudill.

CHAMBLISS, NATHANIEL RIVES. Born March 31, 1834, Greenville, Virginia, son of John G. and Celia Cain Chambliss. Cousin of Gen. John Chambliss. Attended Cumberland University, 1855–1856. Graduated from West Point in 1861. Married Anna, daughter of Gen. William J. Hardee. Nominated second lieutenant of Artillery, Confederate regular army, August 27, 1861, to rank from March 16, 1861. Major, Helm's First Kentucky Cavalry, December 12, 1861. Transferred to staff duty. Captain, ordnance officer to Generals Buckner and Hardee. Major, ordnance officer to General Villepigue. Later commanded the Columbus, Selma, and Charleston arsenals. Farmer in Dallas County, Alabama, postwar. Died March 7, 1897, Baltimore, Maryland, where he and his wife had gone to visit their son. Buried Live Oak Cemetery, Selma, Alabama.

CHENAULT, DAVID WALLER. Born February 5, 1826, Richmond, Kentucky, son of Anderson and Emily Cameron Chenault. Farmer in Madison County prewar. Mexican War veteran. Active in local Whig Party politics. Married Ann T. Phelps. Colonel, Eleventh Kentucky Cavalry, September 10, 1862. Killed in action, Green River Bridge, July 4, 1863, during Morgan's Ohio raid. Buried on the battlefield, later reburied in Chenault Family Cemetery, and finally in Richmond Cemetery.

CHENOWETH, JAMES QUILBERT. Born February 9, 1841, Louisville, Kentucky, son of Thomas and Nancy Passmore Chenoweth. Graduated from Asbury University (now DePauw) in Indiana in 1860. Resided in Harrison County, Kentucky, prewar. Studied law in Montgomery, Alabama. Married Scota M. Inskeep. Lieutenant, Kentucky State Guard, June 18, 1861. Drillmaster, Bennett's Tennessee Cavalry Battalion, 1861–1862. Wounded in action at Shiloh. Major, First Kentucky Cavalry, September 2, 1862. Wounded in action at Murfreesboro, Chickamauga. Appointed colonel, September 6, 1864, and ordered to go behind Union lines in Kentucky and recruit a regiment. Raised Chenoweth's Kentucky

Cavalry, a unit in Gen. Adam Johnson's partisan brigade, and led this regiment to the end of the war. The original appointment was for three months only. After it expired, Chenoweth was reappointed colonel March 13, 1865. Lawyer postwar, in Montgomery, Alabama; Kentucky; and Bonham, Texas. State senator in Kentucky. State representative in Texas. Judge. Auditor of the U.S. Treasury, 1885–1888. Publisher, *Bonham Daily Favorite*. Superintendent of the Texas Confederate Home for Veterans in Austin. Died June 2, 1909, at the Elks home in Bedford, Virginia. Buried Harrodsburg (Kentucky) City Cemetery. Colonel Bennett called him "a gentleman of fine attainments . . . fitted by nature for a military man."

CHENOWETH, THOMAS JOHN. Born April 10, 1834, Mercer County, Kentucky, son of John S. and Elizabeth Ross Chenoweth. Merchant in New Orleans pre-war. Married Mary E. Pearce in 1867. Second lieutenant, Company B, Fifth Kentucky, October 16, 1861. Promoted to first lieutenant the same day. Captain, date uncertain. Captured at Gladeville, Virginia, July 7, 1863. Major, Thirteenth Kentucky Cavalry, September 1, 1864. Druggist in Maysville, Kentucky, postwar. Died there July 16, 1915. Buried Maysville Cemetery.

CLANTON, GEORGE WESLEY. Born October 18, 1831, Maury County, Tennessee, son of John W. and Ann Thompson Clanton. Farmer in Graves County, Kentucky, in 1860. Also ran a tannery. Married Sarah Amanda Mickle. Enlisted April 11, 1862, in West Tennessee. Elected captain, Company C, Twelfth Kentucky Cavalry, September 15, 1863. Detached June 19, 1864, by order of General Lyon, to go into Kentucky. Made major, probably at the February 1865 consolidation of the Eighth and Twelfth Kentucky. Paroled as major Eighth/Twelfth Kentucky Cavalry, May 16, 1865. Farmer and dry goods merchant in Graves County postwar. Died there August 7, 1872. Buried Old Bethlehem Cemetery, Graves County.

CLARKE, WILLIAM LOGAN. Born June 26, 1839, Louisville, Kentucky, son of Charles J. and Eliza Logan Clarke. Deputy surveyor of the customhouse in Louisville prior to the war. Married Sallie Helm. Captain, Kentucky State Guard, May 8, 1860. First lieutenant Company D, Sixth Kentucky, November 19, 1861. Regimental adjutant, February 14, 1862. Major, elected at May 10, 1862, regimental reorganization. Wounded in action at the battle of Baton Rouge. Lieutenant colonel, September 30, 1863. Left arm shattered during an action at Dallas, Georgia, in May 1864, and disabled for the rest of the war. Hardware businessman in Louisville and Nashville postwar. Died January 19, 1895, Nashville. Buried Evergreen Cemetery, Murfreesboro, Tennessee. "A brave and efficient officer . . . a man of fine, attractive person."

CLAY, EZEKIEL FIELD. Born December 1, 1840, Runnymede, Bourbon County, Kentucky, son of U.S. Congressman Brutus J. and Amelia Field Clay. Attended

Kentucky University. Married Maria Letitia Woodford. Private, First Battalion Kentucky Mounted Rifles, 1861. Captain, Company C, October 21, 1861. Elected lieutenant colonel, Third Battalion Mounted Rifles, November 29, 1862. Wounded in action Shelbyville, Tennessee, in 1863. Wounded in the eye April 13, 1864, in a skirmish at Puncheon Creek, Kentucky, and captured there. Prisoner at Johnson's Island until January 1865. Returned to Runneymede after the war. Noted horse breeder. Twice won the Kentucky Derby. President of the Kentucky Racing Association. Died July 26, 1920, Bourbon County. Buried Paris (Kentucky) City Cemetery. "No truer or more valiant soldier entered the Confederate service."

CLUKE, LEROY STUART. Born December 30, 1824, Montgomery County, Kentucky, son of Waller and Maria Williams Cluke. Commonly known as "Roy" Cluke. Graduated from St. Joseph's College in Bardstown. Wealthy farmer in Clark County prewar. Mexican War veteran. Traded horses throughout the South. Married Kate Kerr. Staff officer, Kentucky State Guard, 1861. Colonel, Eighth Kentucky Cavalry, September 10, 1862. "Extremely bold and tenacious." Captured July 26, 1863, Sabinsville, Ohio, during Morgan's Ohio raid. Sent to Johnson's Island Prison. Died there of diphtheria, December 31, 1863. Buried first in a family cemetery in Clark County; reinterred in Lexington Cemetery in 1891. A state marker is at the site of his Clark County home.

COFER, MARTIN HARDIN. Born April 1, 1832, Elizabethtown, Kentucky, son of Thomas and Mary Hardin Cofer. Prewar lawyer in Elizabethtown and (1853–1856) Illinois. Newspaper editor. Captain, Kentucky State Guard, 1860–1861. Married Mary Bush. Lieutenant colonel, Cofer's Kentucky Infantry Battalion, November 1, 1861. Severely wounded in action at Shiloh. Lieutenant colonel, Sixth Kentucky (formed from his battalion), May 10, 1862. Wounded in action December 29, 1862. Lost race for Confederate Congress in 1863. Colonel, September 30, 1863. Provost marshal, Army of Tennessee, winter of 1863–1864 and from August 30, 1864. During Hood's retreat from Nashville, Cofer organized the crossing of the Tennessee River. Paroled May 1, 1865, Greensboro, North Carolina. Attorney in Elizabethtown postwar. Associate justice and later chief justice, Kentucky Supreme Court. Died May 22, 1881, in Frankfort. Buried Elizabethtown Cemetery. A fellow soldier called Cofer "an officer of extraordinary merit. . . . His sense of order was remarkable."

COLEMAN, CICERO. Born October 7, 1833, Fayette County, Kentucky, son of Horace and Nancy Ellis Thompson Coleman. Farmer in Fayette County prewar. Went to Missouri during the Kansas "border troubles" and joined the pro-slavery raiders. Married Eva Field. Lieutenant colonel, Eighth Kentucky Cavalry, September 10, 1862. Wounded December 7, 1862, at the battle of Hartsville. Captured at Cheshire, Ohio, July 19, 1863, during Morgan's Ohio raid. Imprisoned at Columbus Penitentiary and at Fort Delaware. Paroled c. March 1865. Raised cattle and sheep near Chilesburg postwar. Died January 24, 1915, Fayette County. Buried Lexington Cemetery. "The men in his regiment were warmly attached to him; had great confidence in his courage and judgment."

CONNOR, GEORGE W. Born May 28, 1830, Kentucky, son of Harrison and Elizabeth Nickells Connor. Bath County merchant prewar. Unmarried. Captain, Company H, Fifth Kentucky, October 31, 1861. Taken prisoner January 11, 1862, near Prestonsburg. Exchanged autumn 1862. While in prison, promoted to major, April 18, 1862. Lieutenant colonel, November 14, 1862. Wounded at the battle of Jonesboro, August 31, 1864. Druggist in Owingsville and state senator postwar. Died in Owingsville March 21, 1894.

CROSSLAND, EDWARD. Born June 30, 1827, Hickman County, Kentucky, son of Samuel and Elizabeth Harry Crossland. Farmer and lawyer in Clinton, Hickman County, prewar. County sheriff. State representative. Married Mary Hess. Captain, Company E, First Kentucky (a twelve-months unit), April 23, 1861. Major, December 1, 1861. Lieutenant colonel, April 19, 1862. Colonel, Seventh Kentucky, May 25, 1862. Regiment mounted in 1864. Led brigade in Forrest's cavalry, with great distinction. Wounded in action at Paducah, Tupelo, and Butler's Creek (November 21, 1864). Paroled May 26, 1865, Columbus, Mississippi. Attorney in Mayfield, Graves County, Kentucky, postwar. Judge. U.S. congressman. Died September 11, 1881, Mayfield. Buried Maplewood Cemetery, Mayfield. The historian of the Orphan Brigade found Crossland "as plain as the proverbial 'old shoe' and an accomplished gentleman."

CUNNINGHAM, SIDNEY P. Born October 9, 1836, Bourbon County, Kentucky, son of Abner and Parmelia (Clarkson) Cunningham. Family moved to St. Joseph, Missouri. Attorney. Married Lou Hoskins. Second lieutenant, Company A, Chenoweth's Eleventh Kentucky Cavalry, September 10, 1862. Captain and assistant adjutant general to Gens. John H. Morgan and Adam R. Johnson, December 9, 1863. Appointed lieutenant colonel, Chenoweth's Regiment of Partisan Rangers (aka Sixteenth Kentucky Cavalry), September 6, 1864. Surrendered May 9, 1865, Meridian, Mississippi. Teacher in Bath County postwar. Moved to Texas. Taylor County and Fort Worth attorney. Died April 11, 1887, Fort Worth. Buried Oakwood Cemetery, Fort Worth.

DESHA, BENJAMIN. Born January 16, 1837, Cynthiana, Kentucky, son of Gen. Lucius and Julia Ann Moore Desha. Harrison County farmer. Captain, Kentucky State Guard, May–September 1861. Married Mary M. Cromwell. Captain, Company D, Fifth Kentucky, October 18, 1861. Wounded at the battle of Shiloh and long disabled. Promoted to major, April 22, 1863. Collarbone shattered at the battle of Jonesboro; he was disabled for the rest of the war. Said in some sources to have been promoted to lieutenant colonel. Harrison County farmer postwar. Died November 8, 1885, Cynthiana. Buried Battle Grove Cemetery, Cynthiana. "One of the handsomest men ever reared in [Harrison County]."

DIAMOND, GEORGE R. Born July 2, 1837, Giles, Virginia (now West Virginia), son of Charles and Susannah Lucas Diamond. Farmer in Lawrence County, Kentucky, prewar. Married Mary Graham. Captain, Company D, Fifth Kentucky, October 26, 1861. Mustered out October 26, 1862. Major, Tenth Kentucky Cavalry, October 9, 1863. Lieutenant colonel, August 3, 1864. Colonel, October 2, 1864. Paroled May 8, 1865, Athens, Georgia (as lieutenant colonel). Farmer and logger in Lawrence County postwar. State legislator. Moved to Scott County, Missouri. Died Sandy Woods, Scott County, December 6, 1919. Buried Hickory Grove Cemetery, Scott County. Diamond's service record does not show his promotion to colonel, though it records that he was "entitled to be Colonel since [Colonel Edwin] Trimble's death [on October 2, 1864]," and other evidence has him receiving the promotion.

DUNCAN, HENRY BLANTON. Born July 2, 1827, Louisville, Kentucky, son of William G. and Patricia Martin Duncan. Attended Jefferson College in Mississippi and the University of Louisiana. Prewar lawyer and politician. Owned a plantation in Mississippi. Dropped his first name and went by "Blanton." Married Mary T. Atkinson. Lieutenant colonel of a Kentucky battalion in 1861 that merged to form Taylor's First Kentucky, a twelve-months unit. Formally commissioned as lieutenant colonel, October 14, 1861. Delegate to Kentucky Secession Convention. After the First's term of service ended, he got a contract for printing the Confederacy's currency. His high-handed efforts to monopolize government printing, including the appropriation of printing supplies owned by other firms, led to his losing his government contract in 1863. Moved to Texas, then California, postwar. Owned a ranch near Los Angeles. Died April 8, 1902, Los Angeles. Buried Cave Hill Cemetery, Louisville. According to one friend, Duncan was "the most entertaining man I ever saw, but not one bit of common sense. . . . [H]e ha[d] more political opinions than any one I ever saw." One rumor had him secreting Confederate gold in tunnels on his ranch.

EVERETT, PETER M. Born c. 1839, Mount Sterling, Kentucky, son of Samuel D. and Henrietta Richardson Everett. Attended Centre College. Farmer in Victoria County, Texas, in 1860. Unmarried. Private, Company E, First Battalion Kentucky Mounted Rifles, c. October 12, 1861. Captain, Company B, Third Battalion Kentucky Mounted Rifles, September 1, 1862. Promoted to major at a later date. Led several daring raids into northern Kentucky. Known as "little Pete." Put in command of Col. Tom Johnson's brigade late in the war. Postwar farmer in Montgomery County. Bitten by a rabid dog in 1874, losing his reason.

Spent the remainder of his life in the state asylum in Lexington. Died there November 20, 1900. Buried Machpelah Cemetery, Mount Sterling.

FAULKNER, WILLIAM WALLACE. Born c. 1836, Christian County, Kentucky, son of Richard C. and Frances Lee Faulkner. Merchant in Woodville, Kentucky, prewar. Married Ann E. Walden. First lieutenant, "Woodville Cavalry," Kentucky State Guard, April 23, 1861. Captain of scouts / partisan rangers operating in Kentucky and West Tennessee. Captured October 16, 1862, near Island No. 10. Escaped while en route to Johnson's Island prisoner-of-war camp. Authorized March 12, 1863, to raise a battalion of partisan rangers. Lieutenant colonel of the battalion, 1863. Colonel, Twelfth Kentucky Cavalry, January 28, 1864 (appointed by Gen. Nathan Bedford Forrest under authority of the president). Severely wounded in action at the battle of Tupelo. Killed in Dresden, Tennessee, February 1865, by some guerrillas he was trying to arrest. Buried Herring Cemetery, Ballard County, Kentucky. "A courageous, dashing soldier" but not "popular with his men."

FICKLIN, JOHN. Born July 1, 1822, Bath County, Kentucky, son of Thomas and Mary Goodloe Ficklin. Bath County farmer prewar. Mexican War veteran. State representative, 1857–1859. Married Sarah A. Graham. Private, Company H, Fifth Kentucky, October 21, 1861. Detached in that winter to raise a new regiment around Bath County. Major, Ficklin's Battalion Kentucky Infantry. The unit reported to Gen. Humphrey Marshall's camp in eastern Kentucky in late 1862, but most deserted and the remainder were merged into other units. Further service unknown. Returned to his Bath County farm after the war. Elected county sheriff in 1868. Moved to Clinton County, Missouri, in 1882. Died February 20, 1893, King City, Gentry County, Missouri. Buried King City Cemetery.

FREEMAN, DANDRIDGE CLAIBORNE. Born November 3, 1827, Frankfort, Kentucky, son of Dandridge C. and Martha Fox Freeman. Graduated from Georgetown College in 1849. Lawyer in Austin, Texas, in 1860. Married Mary A. Walker; Mary E. Robinson. In late 1861 he raised a battalion of infantry, of which he was chosen major. The companies were merged into the Fifth Kentucky. Later, volunteer aide-de-camp to General Pegram. Farmer in Milam County, Texas, postwar. Died in Austin July 15, 1895, after being shot on a train near Holland, Texas. Buried Oakwood Cemetery, Austin.

GILTNER, HENRY LYTER. Born June 5, 1829, Carrollton, Kentucky, son of Michael and Mary Lyter Giltner. Attended Hanover College in Indiana. Owned ferry in Carrollton prewar. County sheriff. Married Martha R. Young. Captain, Kentucky State Guard, June 15, 1861. Delegate to Kentucky Secession Convention. Captain and aide-de-camp to Gen. Humphrey Marshall, 1861. Captain,

Company F, Fourth Kentucky Cavalry, September 2, 1862. Colonel, October 6, 1862. Led brigade in Virginia and Kentucky, 1864–1865. Surrendered at Mount Sterling April 29, 1865. Farmer in Carrollton postwar. Died August 19, 1892, Murfreesboro, Tennessee. Buried Independent Order of Odd Fellows Cemetery, Carrollton. A fellow staff officer called Giltner "a lithe, graceful man, of dignified mien."

GRAYSON, WILLIAM POWHATAN BOLLING. Born September 9, 1810, Greenup County, Kentucky, son of Robert H. and Sophonisba Cabell Grayson. Cousin of Gens. John C. Breckinridge and John B. Grayson. Wealthy farmer in Henderson County prewar. Married Susan Dixon. Commissioned colonel, October 10, 1864, under an act of the Confederate Congress, to raise a regiment behind enemy lines in Kentucky. It is difficult to determine why Congress, this late in the war, commissioned the inexperienced Grayson for such a difficult mission. Captured in Hardinsburg, Kentucky, while recruiting, January 24, 1865. Imprisoned at Johnson's Island, released July 25, 1865. Died 1872. Buried Fernwood Cemetery, Henderson. His brief service record is as colonel, Thirteenth Kentucky Cavalry, but his regiment never formally organized. On Grayson's postwar pardon application, the unionist governor of Kentucky called him "more sinned against than sinning."

GRIFFITH, JACOB WARK. Born October 13, 1819, Jefferson County, Virginia, son of Daniel W. and Margaret Wark Griffith. Moved to Oldham County, Kentucky. Planter. State representative, Mexican War veteran. In California gold rush. Married Mary P. Oglesby. Captain, Company E, First Kentucky Cavalry. Wounded in action at Hewey's Bridge (May 9, 1862) and Sequatchie Valley (October 2, 1863). Lieutenant colonel, Third Kentucky Cavalry (which had been consolidated with the First), March 1, 1863. Farmed in Oldham County postwar. Died there March 3, 1885. Buried Mount Tabor Methodist Church, near Crestwood. Father of noted movie director D. W. Griffith.

GRIGSBY, JOHN WARREN. Born September 11, 1818, Rockbridge County, Virginia, son of Joseph and Mary Scott Grigsby. Brother of Col. A .J. Grigsby of the Twenty-seventh Virginia. Attended William & Mary College and the University of Virginia. Newspaper editor in Rockbridge County. U.S. consul at Bordeaux, France, 1841–1849. Lawyer in New Orleans. Farmer in Lincoln County, Kentucky. Married Susan Shelby. Staff officer, Kentucky State Guard, 1861. Colonel, Sixth Kentucky Cavalry, September 2, 1862. Wounded in action at Milton, Tennessee, March 20, 1863. Often led a cavalry brigade in Joseph Wheeler's Corps. Appointed inspector general of cavalry, Army of Tennessee, 1864. Appointed chief of staff to General Wheeler, 1865. Paroled May 1865. Lived in Lincoln County and Danville postwar. Attorney. State representative, 1875–1877. Died January 12, 1877, Lexington, Kentucky. Buried Lexington

Cemetery. The "noble and pure" Grigsby was often listed postwar as a Confederate general, but he was paroled a colonel. Grigsby-Shelby family papers are at the Filson Club, Louisville.

HALE, HENRY STEPHENSON. Born May 4, 1836, near Bowling Green, Kentucky, son of Nicholas and Rhoda Crouch Hale. Raised in Graves County. Married Virginia A. Gregory. Captain, Company H, Seventh Kentucky, September 18, 1861. Elected major, May 10, 1862. Regiment mounted. Severely wounded in the left hip at the battle of Tupelo in 1864. Promoted to lieutenant colonel, by order of Gen. Nathan Bedford Forrest, when the Third and Seventh were consolidated in February 1865. Sheriff of Graves County, 1866–1870. State senator, bank president. State treasurer under Gov. Simon Buckner. Died Mayfield, Graves County, July 24, 1922. Buried Maplewood Cemetery, Mayfield. "Full of zeal and chivalry . . . a live, wide-awake officer."

HAMILTON, OLIVER PERRY. Born January 8, 1825, Celina, Tennessee, son of Dr. Adam and Sarah Atterbury Hamilton. Farmer in Jackson County, Tennessee, prior to the war. Married Helen Kirkpatrick. Captain of Tennessee Cavalry, late 1861. Lieutenant colonel of Hamilton's Battalion Tennessee Cavalry (the Fourth; a "guerrilla" unit), July 1, 1863. Lieutenant colonel, Second Special Battalion Kentucky Cavalry, late in the war. Captured at Celina March 4, 1864. Shot and killed by a guard July 22, 1864, at Lexington, Kentucky. Buried Lexington Cemetery. In 1864 Hamilton and his men were ordered to report to Col. Richard Morgan, who was organizing Kentucky cavalry, but refused.

HAWKINS, HIRAM. Born September 9, 1826, Bath County, Kentucky, son of Thomas and Mary Dean Hawkins. Farmer and merchant in Bath County prewar. Owned a sheep ranch in Texas. State senator. Militia colonel. Captain, Kentucky State Guard. Married Mary Workman; Mrs. Louisiana A. Boykin. Commanded camp of recruits in Prestonsburg, Kentucky, September 1861. Captain, Company C, Fifth Kentucky, October 21, 1861. Major, January 17, 1862. Lieutenant colonel, April 18, 1862. Colonel, November 14, 1862. Wounded in action at Atlanta. Moved to Eufaula, Alabama (his wife's home), after the war. Farmer. State legislator. President of Union Female College. Died July 27, 1913, Eufaula, of paralysis. Buried Fairview Cemetery, Eufaula. A fellow officer praised Hawkins's "zeal, intelligence, gallantry, and ability."

HAYS, THOMAS HERCULES. Born October 6, 1837, West Point, Kentucky, son of William H. and Nancy Neill Hays. Educated at St. Joseph College in Bardstown. Hardin County farmer and lawyer prewar. Married Sara Hardin Helm; Georgia Broughton. Captain and major, Kentucky State Guard, 1860–1861. Major, Sixth Kentucky, November 1, 1861. Assigned to duty to the staff of Gen. Ben Helm (his wife's brother) as adjutant and inspector general May 10, 1862.

Later served on staffs of Generals Preston and Lewis. After Hood's retreat from Tennessee, detached to serve in western Virginia. Paroled Savannah, Georgia, at war's end. Businessman and railroad executive postwar. Farmed in Jefferson County. State senator. Died November 9, 1909, Louisville. Buried Cave Hill Cemetery, Louisville.

HENRY, ROBERT WILLIAM. Born June 6, 1825, Kentucky, son of William and Cornelia Gano Henry. Christian County farmer. Mexican War veteran. Militia colonel. Married Martha Douglas Cocke; Fannie S. Bell. Delegate to Kentucky Secession Convention. First lieutenant, Company G, Eighth Kentucky, September 26, 1861. Major, November 1, 1861. Taken prisoner at Fort Donelson in February 1862. Died at the Camp Morton prisoner-of-war camp, Indianapolis, February 28, 1862. First buried at Crown Hill Cemetery, Indianapolis; later reburied in Cocke Cemetery, Christian County. Henry's daughter married Col. Lee Sypert.

HEWITT, JAMES W. Born August 27, 1827, Kanawha County, Virginia, son of James Hewitt, a cotton factor, and his wife Clarice Grant. Raised in Louisville. Attended Kentucky Military Institute. Commission merchant in St. Louis and New York City. Captain in New York's famed Seventh Militia. Married Belle Key. Major, Second Kentucky, July 17, 1861. Wounded at Fort Donelson but escaped capture. Assigned to staff duty under Generals Breckinridge and Preston until his regiment was exchanged. Promoted to lieutenant colonel, December 13, 1862. Wounded by a shell at the battle of Murfreesboro. Killed September 20, 1863, at the battle of Chickamauga. Buried Cave Hill Cemetery, Louisville. "A brave and skillful soldier, and a man of great force and worth of character."

HIGGINS, JOEL. Born c. 1834, Kentucky, son of Joel and Anna Gibson Higgins. Raised in Fayette County, Kentucky, his family being prominent Lexingtonians. Planter in Phillips County, Arkansas, in 1860. Married Ellen Curran. First lieutenant, Company B, Second Kentucky, July 5, 1861. Captain, February 4, 1862. Major, September 1864. Paroled Jackson, Mississippi, May 6, 1865. Farmed in Fayette County postwar. Died June 11, 1894, Lexington. Buried Lexington Cemetery.

HINKLE, JESSE FERNE. Born September 28, 1829, Shelby County, Kentucky, son of Casper and Mildred Oglesby Hinkle. Merchant and farmer in Shelby County and later in Hinkleville, Ballard County. Married Susan S. Hinkle; Katie C. Moylan. Enlisted September 15, 1861. First lieutenant, Company C, Seventh Kentucky, October 15, 1861. Captain, May 10, 1862. Relieved of duty with the Seventh in the 1863 consolidation of the regiment and placed on conscript duty. Regiment mounted later in the war. Paroled at Meridian, Mississippi, May 12, 1865, as major. Moved to Cairo, Illinois, in 1872. Tobacco merchant. Member of

Cairo City Council. Died May 1907, Porterville, California. Buried Old Porterville Cemetery.

HOLLADAY, JOHN BUCKNER. Born 1824, Bourbon County, Kentucky, son of Thomas and Charlotte Buckner Holladay. Officer in Mexican War. Sheriff of Nicholas County in 1860. Married Sallie Morgan. Captain, Company D, First Battalion Kentucky Mounted Rifles, October 22, 1861. Promoted to major, Third Battalion, sometime later in the war. Postwar, grocer in Bourbon County and state legislator. Died August 6, 1897, Paris, Kentucky. Buried Paris City Cemetery. "A most clever & affable gentleman."

HOLT, GUSTAVUS ADOLPHUS CHRISTIAN. Born March 2, 1840, Salem, Kentucky, son of Dr. James and Julia Hodge Holt. Graduated from University of Louisville Law School in 1859. Lawyer in Murray, Calloway County, Kentucky, prewar. Married Inez Berry. Inspector, Kentucky State Guard, early 1861. First lieutenant, Company H, Third Kentucky, 1861. Captain, July 22, 1861. Wounded in action at Jackson, Mississippi, resulting in the paralysis of his right hand and arm. Lieutenant colonel, August 30, 1863. Colonel, March 25, 1864. Lawyer in Kentucky and Memphis, Tennessee, postwar. State senator. Speaker of the Kentucky Senate. Lieutenant governor. Died June 1, 1910, Memphis. Buried Forest Hill Cemetery, Memphis. Holt's brigade commander recommended him for promotion as "a man of great character and qualifications."

HUEY, JAMES K. Born March 27, 1827, Livingston County, Kentucky, son of Robert and Eliza Calhoun Huey. Deputy sheriff of McCracken County. Sheriff of Livingston County. Lawyer. State representative. Married Alice Powell. Captain, Company K, First Kentucky Cavalry, October 17, 1861. Escaped from Fort Donelson prior to the surrender. Raised a battalion for Lyon's Cavalry Brigade and was appointed major of that unit. Surrendered at Paducah, May 1865, as colonel. Moved to New Orleans postwar and worked as a commission merchant. Returned to Livingston County in 1872. Lawyer and county judge. Died December 1, 1891, Smithland. Buried Smithland Cemetery, Lyon County. "Firm, outspoken, and a true friend. . . . [H]onor has always been dearer to him than life."

HUFFMAN, JOHN MILLER. Born February 6, 1832, Spencer County, Kentucky, son of Joseph and Catherine Smeltzer Huffman. Farmer in Collin County, Texas, in 1860. Married Zarilla Irene McDuffie. Captain Company B (a Texas unit), Gano's Cavalry Battalion, 1862. Elected lieutenant colonel, Seventh Kentucky Cavalry, at the September 2, 1862, organization of that regiment. Shot in the left arm at Gallatin, Tennessee, August 20, 1862. Wounded and captured during Morgan's Ohio raid. Assigned to duty in the Trans-Mississippi Department in 1864. Postwar planter in Texas and in Morehouse Parish, Louisiana. Died January 1, 1889, Oak Ridge, Morehouse Parish. Buried Oak Ridge Baptist Church

Cemetery. General Gano said, "Huffman is of a brave stock, and is an honor to the name."

HUNT, THOMAS HART. Born January 2, 1815, Lexington, Kentucky, son of John W. and Catherine Grosch Hunt. Uncle of Gen. John Hunt Morgan. Merchant in Lexington and (from 1848) Louisville. Major, then colonel, Kentucky State Guard, 1860–1861. Married Mary Tilford. In the spring of 1861, as colonel Second Regiment Kentucky State Guard, established a Kentucky State Guard camp of instruction near Louisville. Colonel, Ninth Kentucky, October 1, 1861. Wounded in action at Baton Rouge. Resigned April 22, 1863, "impelled by a sense of duty to his family." Lived in Augusta, Georgia, the remainder of the war. Merchant in New Orleans postwar. Secretary of the World's Fair Exposition of 1884. Died May 6, 1884, New Orleans. Buried in the Hunt-Morgan Lot, Lexington Cemetery. Hunt, with a "superior natural intellect" often led the Orphan Brigade and, if he had stayed in the army, would soon have been promoted to general.

HUTCHESON, JOHN BENNETT. Born c. 1838, Tennessee, son of John S. and Mary Hutcheson. Raised in Springfield, Robertson County, Tennessee. Attended Union College in Schenectady, New York. Unmarried. First lieutenant, Company K, First Kentucky, June 17, 1861. Captain, April 29, 1862. Served in Virginia. When the First Kentucky's twelve-month enlistments expired, the men headed west and under Hutcheson formed Company E, Second Kentucky Cavalry. Lieutenant colonel, Second Kentucky Cavalry, December 7, 1862. Shot in the temple and killed in a skirmish January 24, 1863, at Woodbury, Tennessee. Gen. Adam Johnson found Hutcheson "one of the most brilliant, efficient and beloved officers of the command."

HYNES, ANDREW ROSE. Born January 27, 1820, Kentucky, son of William Rose and Barbara Chenault Hynes. Raised in Nelson County. Moved to Louisiana. Officer in a Louisiana regiment during the Mexican War. Lawyer in Morehouse Parish. Married Martha Ann Kincaid. Lieutenant colonel, Fourth Kentucky, September 13, 1861. Wounded "slightly" at the battle of Shiloh. Resigned his commission December 18, 1862. To California postwar. Bookkeeper in San Francisco in 1880. Died there (committed suicide in a bathtub) February 2, 1881. Hynes's "self possession and ability" at Shiloh were noted in the reports of that battle.

JOHNSON, ROBERT ADAMS. Born May 3, 1817, near Lexington, Kentucky, son of Henry and Betsy Flournoy Johnson. Nephew of Vice President Richard M. Johnson and cousin to Sen. Robert W. Johnson of Arkansas. Graduated from the University of Virginia in 1839. Commission merchant in Louisville and New Orleans prewar. Attorney in Vicksburg, Mississippi. Married Cornelia Ruffin;

Mrs. Lucy Johnson; Ellen McMahon. Lieutenant colonel, Second Kentucky, July 12, 1861. Colonel, July 16, 1861. Wounded in action at Shiloh. Resigned October 19, 1863, due to dysentery. Appointed colonel and judge, military court of the Texas Corps, Trans-Mississippi Department, March 23, 1865. He lived in retirement postwar, in Louisville and (after 1880) Knoxville. Prominent horse breeder and racer. Died March 15, 1886, Knoxville. Buried Lexington Cemetery. Pvt. John S. Jackman of the Orphan Brigade found Johnson "a clever brave man but utterly ignorant of military tactics."

JOHNSON, THOMAS. Born July 4, 1812, Montgomery County, Kentucky, son of Jacob and Anna Masterson Johnson. Farmer and trader in Montgomery County prewar. Militia general. Mexican War veteran. State representative. Married Elizabeth Peters. Member, Confederate Congress, 1861–1862, serving on the Military Affairs Committee. Raised four companies in 1862 that became the Second Battalion Kentucky Mounted Rifles. Lieutenant colonel of the Second, March 12, 1862. Led a brigade during the Cynthiana campaign of 1864. Wealthy farmer in Montgomery County after the war. State representative and senator. Died in Montgomery County April 7, 1906, one of the last surviving members of the Confederate Congress. Buried Machpelah Cemetery, Mount Sterling. Staff officer Ed Guerrant hinted strongly that Johnson "like[d] his tea [alcohol] too well."

JOHNSTON, ALFRED. Born January 22, 1813, Caldwell County, Kentucky, son of Isaac and Charlotte Baker Johnston. Farmer in Calloway and Marshall counties prewar. State representative. Married Lucinda Howard. Private, Company A, Third Kentucky, July 5, 1861. Captain, October 25, 1861. Major, to rank from October 18, 1861. Wounded at the battle of Shiloh. Lieutenant colonel, June 1, 1862. Resigned, June 1, 1863. Settled in Paducah postwar and died there September 9, 1873. Buried Bethlehem Cemetery, Benton, Marshall County. According to an obituary, "Col. Johnston was one among the very few men of character we ever knew, who went through the world without making enemies."

JOHNSTON, WILLIAM PRESTON. Born January 5, 1831, Louisville, Kentucky. Son of Gen. Albert Sidney Johnston and his wife, Henrietta Preston. Attended Western Military Institute and Yale University. Prewar Louisville lawyer. Married Rose Duncan. Major, First Kentucky (mistakenly noted as the Second in some sources), July 16, 1861. Lieutenant colonel, First Kentucky, October 14, 1861. Colonel, April 19, 1862, to serve as President Davis's aide. Johnston made several inspection trips to the West during the war, essentially serving as Davis's informant on conditions in the West. To Canada postwar. Returning to United States, taught at Washington & Lee University. President of Louisiana State University and Tulane. Authored many historical articles and a biography of his father. Died July 16, 1899, Lexington, Virginia. Buried Cave Hill Cemetery,

Louisville. Johnston passionately defended his father's generalship in his postwar writings.

JONES, WILLIAM EDWARD. Born c. 1824, Kentucky, son of Gabriel S. and Esther Camp Jones. Steamboat clerk and policeman in Louisville. Officer in the Mexican War. Married Kate Franklin. First lieutenant, Company I, First Kentucky, July 12, 1861. Captain, Company A, Ninth Kentucky Cavalry, September 12, 1862. Promoted to major soon after. Killed while leading a charge December 24, 1862, in a skirmish at Glasgow, Kentucky. Probably buried in Glasgow Municipal Cemetery.

KING, HENRY CLAY. Born July 29, 1831, Burkesville, Kentucky, son of Alfred and Nancy Haggard King. Attended University of Alabama. Prewar, lawyer in Paducah, Kentucky, and Memphis. Married Sarah Haughton; Maria J. Dallum. Captain, Company K, Twenty-first Tennessee (a Kentucky company later transferred to King's Battalion), June 13, 1861. Appointed major, King's Battalion, Kentucky Cavalry, April 5, 1862. Elected colonel, First (aka Sixth, Twelfth) Confederate Cavalry, September 24, 1862. Captured Shelbyville, Tennessee, June 27, 1863. Imprisoned for one and a half years. After exchange, in March 1865, sent to the Trans-Mississippi Department on a secret mission. Postwar, lawyer in Memphis. In 1891 he murdered fellow lawyer David Poston in one of the most notorious murders in Memphis history. King had fallen in love with the widow of Gen. Gideon Pillow. Poston made insulting comments about the widow, whereupon King shot him. Tried and sentenced to the state penitentiary at Nashville. Died in prison, of stomach cancer, December 10, 1903. Buried Calvary Cemetery, Nashville. Union general David Stanley called King "one of the bravest and most fearless men" he had ever known.

LANNOM, WILLIAM D. Born 1823, Tennessee. Lawyer and state senator in Hickman County, Kentucky, prewar. Married Milbry J. McGregor. Captain, Company B, Seventh Kentucky Cavalry, September 26, 1861. Lieutenant colonel, November 1, 1861. Resigned commission after Shiloh on account of ill health. Appointed lieutenant colonel, Twelfth Kentucky Cavalry, October 13, 1863. Wounded in action at Union City, Tennessee, March 23, 1864. Wounded again May 24, 1864. Removed to Paris, Tennessee, postwar. Practiced law with Col. Ed Crossland. Murdered in Paris, March 4, 1872, by a client who owed Lannom money. Buried City Cemetery, Paris.

LEAVELL, HENRY C. Born February 23, 1824, Todd County, Kentucky, son of Benjamin and Elizabeth Willis Leavell. Christian County planter. Married Sarah Ann Clardy. Captain, Company H, First Kentucky Cavalry, 1861, a unit he raised. Lieutenant colonel, June 30, 1862. Died August 26, 1862, near Chattanooga, Tennessee, of typhoid fever. Buried Leavell Cemetery, Christian County.

"A brave and gallant soldier, an officer of more than ordinary ability, a thorough gentleman and a Christian."

LEE, PHILIP LIGHTFOOT. Born October 22, 1832, Bullitt County, Kentucky, son of Wilford and Margaret Hill Lee. Graduated from St. Joseph's College and the University of Louisville Law School. Prewar, attorney in Bullitt County. State representative. County attorney. Captain, Kentucky State Guard. Married Belle Bland Bridgeford. Captain, Company C, Second Kentucky, July 12, 1861. Captured at Fort Donelson. Exchanged September 1862. Major, September 30, 1863. Lieutenant colonel, October 19, 1863. Wounded at the battles of Resaca and Dallas. Surrendered in South Carolina in May 1865. Postwar lawyer in Bardstown. Commonwealth attorney in Louisville. Died July 12, 1875, Louisville. Buried Cave Hill Cemetery. "One of the best Commonwealth's attorneys in the country, the effect of his speeches before juries was remarkable."

LEE, WILLIAM RICHARD. Born April 1831, Spartanburg, South Carolina, son of William F. and Elizabeth Harman Lee. Storekeeper in McDowell County, Virginia (now West Virginia) in 1860. Married Martha "Patsy" Cline. Sergeant, Company C, Thirty-fourth Virginia Cavalry Battalion, June 1, 1862. Captain, Company E, Second Virginia State Line, August 27, 1862. State Line dissolved in April 1863. Major, Tenth Kentucky Cavalry, no date. Resigned October 31, 1863, due to ill health and to "restore harmony in the command." Farmer in McDowell and Wyoming counties postwar. Died May 13, 1888, while visiting his son in Buchanan County, Virginia.

LEWIS, THOMAS WILSON. Born September 10, 1840, Stewart County, Tennessee, son of Thomas and Sophronia Nolen Lewis. Farmer there prewar. Married Alice Thomas; Mrs. Eliza West. Private, Company E, Sixteenth Tennessee, July 20, 1861. Discharged April 10, 1862, to become third lieutenant of Company I, Fourth Tennessee Cavalry. Second lieutenant, May 26, 1862. Captured May 30, 1862, near Corinth, Mississippi. Imprisoned at Johnson's Island. Exchanged December 9, 1862. Captain, Company C, Woodward's Second Kentucky Cavalry, December 9, 1862. Promoted to major, probably August 28, 1863. Stewart County farmer postwar. State representative, 1885–1889. Store owner. Died June 27, 1915, Cumberland City. Buried in a family graveyard near Cumberland City. "One of the most beloved men of his regiment."

LOGAN, MATTHEW DAVID. Born January 8, 1822, Marion County, Kentucky, son of Beatty and Martha Everhart Logan. Attended University of Louisville Medical School. Graduated from Jefferson Medical College. Garrard County physician in 1860. Mexican War veteran. Unmarried. Captain, Company I, Third (Seventh) Kentucky Cavalry (originally Company G, Bedford Forrest's Cavalry Regiment), August 20, 1861. Captured at Fort Donelson and exchanged.

Captured June 20, 1863, Cheshire, Ohio, during Morgan's raid. One of the "Immortal 600." Exchanged December 1864. Appointed major, August 3, 1864, while still imprisoned. Boyle County farmer postwar. Died June 18, 1898, Boyle County. Buried Bellevue Cemetery, Danville. Logan was one of three brothers who served in the Third.

MALONE, JOHN W. Born April 29, 1838, Tippah County, Mississippi, son of William G. and Sarah Battle Malone. Merchant in Columbus, Kentucky, prewar. Never married. Private, Company A, Twelfth Kentucky Cavalry, April 28, 1863. Major, appointed September 26, 1863. Captured at Swallow Bluff, Tennessee, September 30, 1863, and confined on Johnson's Island the remainder of the war. Taught school in Hickman County postwar. Died August 8, 1871, at his mother's home just south of Columbus. Buried Columbus City Cemetery.

MARTIN, ROBERT MAXWELL. Born January 10, 1840, Greenville, Kentucky, son of Hugh and Elizabeth Roark Martin. Worked on his father's farm prewar. Married Caroline Wardlaw. Scout for Bedford Forrest, 1861–1862. Lieutenant colonel, Tenth Kentucky Cavalry, August 13, 1862. Colonel, at some unrecorded date. Served with Gen. Adam Johnson in partisan operations in Kentucky behind Union lines. Wounded in action at McMinnville, Tennessee, April 19, 1863. Wounded in action at Mount Sterling in 1864, and after recovering, sent to Canada on clandestine operations. Involved in the Confederate scheme to burn New York City, 1864. Paroled Augusta, Georgia, May 26, 1865. Martin was held in New York City 1865–1866 on arson charges stemming from the 1864 scheme. Tobacco warehouseman in Evansville, Indiana, 1866–1874. Warehouse inspector in Brooklyn, 1874–1887. Tobacco broker in Louisville after that. Made and lost several fortunes after the war. Died January 9, 1901, New York City, where he had gone for treatment of his lung disease. Buried first in Green-Wood Cemetery, Brooklyn. Reburied in Cave Hill Cemetery, Louisville. General Duke found Martin "a man of extraordinary dash and resolution."

MAXSON, GEORGE WASHINGTON. Born October 14, 1831, Friendship, New York, son of Abel and Abigail Lull Maxson. Raised in Wisconsin. Hardin County resident in 1860. Married Dorcas Williams; Ella G. Smith. Captain, Kentucky State Guard, 1861. Delegate to Kentucky Secession Convention. Enlisted in Confederate army September 26, 1861. Captain, Company B, Sixth Kentucky, October 28, 1861. Wounded at the battle of Murfreesboro. Promoted to major, December 5, 1863. Taken prisoner at the battle of Jonesboro in 1864. Presbyterian minister in Georgia postwar. Teacher at Auburn College in Alabama. Moved to southern California in 1887 for his health. Presbyterian minister and farmer in Riviera. Died April 28, 1904, at his Montebello home. Buried in Broadway Cemetery, Whittier. A man "of finely cultivated intellect."

May, Andrew Jackson. Born January 28, 1829, Prestonsburg, Kentucky, son of Samuel and Catherine Evans May. To California during the gold rush. Lawyer in Prestonsburg and West Liberty prewar. Married Matilda Davidson; Nell Davidson. Captain, Company A, Fifth Kentucky, October 21, 1861. Lieutenant colonel, November 17, 1861. Colonel, April 18, 1862. Resigned November 14, 1862, due to ill health and a wish to recruit a cavalry regiment. Colonel, Fourteenth Kentucky Cavalry, August 6, 1863. Resigned July 4, 1864, due to bladder inflammation, and went to live in Jeffersonville, Virginia. Commanded local defense troops in southwest Virginia in 1864. Commissary agent in Tazewell County, Virginia, in 1865. Lawyer in Tazewell, Virginia, postwar. Died May 3, 1903, Tazewell County. Buried Jeffersonville Cemetery. A "brave and daring soldier."

McCreary, James Bennett. Born July 8, 1838, Richmond, Kentucky, son of Edmond R. and Sabrina Bennett McCreary. Graduated from Centre College and from Cumberland University Law School. Prewar, lawyer in Richmond. Married Sarah Catherine Hughes. Enlisted in the Confederate army as a private. Major, Eleventh Kentucky Cavalry, September 10, 1862. Lieutenant colonel, July 4, 1863. Captured at Cheshire, Ohio, during Morgan's raid, and sent to Fort Delaware prisoner-of-war camp. One of the "Immortal 600." Exchanged, and returned to command the Eleventh. A long and brilliant postwar political career included election as state representative (1869–1875, serving as Speaker 1871–1875), two terms as governor of Kentucky (1875–1879 and 1912–1916), twelve years in the U.S. Congress (1885–1897) and one term in the U.S. Senate (1903–1909). Died October 8, 1918, at his Richmond home. Buried Richmond Cemetery. "Clear headed, comprehensive, just, conservative." His diary is at Duke University.

McDowell, Hervey. Born April 15, 1835, Fayette County, Kentucky, son of John L. and Nancy Scott McDowell. Raised in Owen County. Attended Kentucky Military Institute. Graduated from Missouri Medical College in 1858. Cynthiana physician prewar. Major, Kentucky State Guard. Married Louise I. McDowell, his second cousin. Captain, Company F, Second Kentucky, July 16, 1861. Wounded in head and side, and captured, at Fort Donelson. Exchanged September 1862. Wounded three times at the battle of Murfreesboro. Promoted to major October 9, 1863. Wounded again at Resaca and Atlanta. Promoted to lieutenant colonel after the battle of Jonesboro. After the war McDowell studied medicine at Transylvania University. Practiced medicine in Cynthiana and St. Louis, Missouri. Died November 6, 1901, Cynthiana. Buried Battle Grove Cemetery, Cynthiana. "Always uncomplaining, calm, energetic and daring." "His coolness and composure under the heaviest fire [w]as phenomenal."

McGoodwin, Albert Marion. Born c. 1835, Kentucky, son of David W. and Susan Wigginton McGoodwin. Graduated Cumberland (Kentucky) College in

1853. Dry goods merchant in Caldwell County prewar. Lieutenant in Kentucky State Guard, 1861. Married Elizabeth Crossland, a relative of Col. Ed Crossland. First lieutenant Company C, Third Kentucky, July 10, 1861. Regimental adjutant, early 1862. Captain, April 7, 1862. Wounded and captured in the attack on Paducah, March 25, 1864. Promoted to major, probably on March 25, 1864. Reporter of the Kentucky House of Representatives in 1880. Died 1889. Probably buried in Maplewood Cemetery, Mayfield.

MILLETT, JOSEPH H. Born c. 1836, Indiana, son of John and Mary Millett. Raised in Louisville, Kentucky. Clerk in Daviess County in 1860. Captain, Kentucky State Guard, 1861. Married Mary J. May. Captain, Company K, Fourth Kentucky, September 13, 1861. "Displayed conspicuous gallantry" in the 1862 battle of Baton Rouge. Wounded at the battles of Murfreesboro and Chickamauga. Major, November 19, 1863. Killed in action at Dallas, Georgia, May 28, 1864.

MONROE, THOMAS BELL. Born July 3, 1833, Frankfort, Kentucky, the son of Judge Thomas Monroe and his wife, Elizabeth Adair. Attended Kentucky Military Institute. Graduated from the University of Louisiana. Lexington lawyer. City attorney and later mayor of Lexington. Editor, *Kentucky Statesman*. Appointed Kentucky secretary of state by Gov. Beriah Magoffin. Lieutenant colonel, Kentucky State Guard. Married Elizabeth, daughter of Justice Robert Grier of the U.S. Supreme Court. Major, Fourth Kentucky, October 1861. Mortally wounded on the second day of the battle of Shiloh and died on the battlefield. First buried on the battlefield, later reburied in State Cemetery, Frankfort. "Warm, genial . . . fearless, honest, just."

MOREHEAD, JOSEPH CLAYTON. Born 1828, Butler County, Kentucky, son of U.S. Sen. James Morehead and his wife, Susan Roberts. Attended West Point. Lieutenant in Mexican War. Lawyer in California. State legislator. Filibusterer in Mexico in the 1850s. Returned to Kentucky, practicing law in Cloverport, then settled in Jackson, Mississippi. Married Nancy Hamilton; Sallie Thomas. In early 1861 Morehead applied for a captaincy in the Confederate regular army. Appointed colonel in 1861 by the provisional governor of Kentucky to raise a regiment. Authorized by Confederate military authorities on April 24, 1862, to recruit a Partisan Rangers regiment. Captured June 17, 1862, Hernando, Mississippi. Exchanged June 22, 1863. Volunteer aide-de-camp to General Helm. Died November 20, 1863, in a hospital in Troy, Alabama. Buried Oakwood Cemetery, Montgomery, Alabama. His very confusing service record is listed under Morehead's Kentucky Partisan Rangers Regiment, though the unit was never formally organized. Morehead's claims of recruiting success were greatly exaggerated.

MORGAN, GEORGE WASHINGTON. Born December 1, 1817, Calhoun, Tennessee, son of Gideon and Margaret Sevier Morgan. Mexican War veteran. Farmer in

Monroe County, Tennessee. Married Martha K. Mays. Major, Third Tennessee, May 3, 1861–May 1862. Major, Second Kentucky Cavalry, 1862. Mortally wounded in an action at Ashland, Kentucky, October 18, 1862. Died October 27. Buried Lexington Cemetery. Known as "Wash" Morgan, he was not a relative of Gen. John Hunt Morgan.

MORGAN, RICHARD CURD. Born September 13, 1836, Kentucky, son of Calvin C. and Henrietta Hunt Morgan. Brother of Gen. John Hunt Morgan. Attended Kentucky Military Institute. Worked in the family's general merchandise business in Lexington prewar. Adjutant, Kentucky State Guard, January 5, 1861. Married Alice Bright. Captain, staff, March 23, 1862. On A. P. Hill's staff (Hill was his brother-in-law). Major, assistant adjutant general, May 26, 1862. On March 24, 1863, Morgan was authorized to recruit a regiment of cavalry and to receive a colonel's commission to date from the completion of the muster rolls. Transferred to his brother's staff. Captured July 19, 1863, during the Ohio raid. Exchanged August 3, 1864, as colonel, Morgan's Kentucky Cavalry Regiment (sometimes called the Fourteenth Kentucky Cavalry). Assigned to his brother's staff again. Colonel, Second Special Battalion in Basil Duke's Brigade, late 1864. Captured again, December 1864 in East Tennessee, while commanding Duke's brigade. To Johnson's Island Prison. Hemp dealer in Lexington postwar. Died September 28, 1918, Lexington. Buried Lexington Cemetery. General Pender thought Morgan "weak," an assessment backed up by his numerous transfers.

MORRIS, JOHN DABNEY. Born January 28, 1813, Taylor's Creek, Hanover County, Virginia, son of Richard and Mary Watts Morris. Attended the University of Virginia. To San Antonio, Texas, in 1837. Lawyer, legislator there. Lieutenant colonel in Texas army during its wars with Mexico. Moved to Christian County, Kentucky, in 1844, to run a farm. Married Margaret L. Meriwether. In late 1861 appointed by the Confederate government to sequester the deposits of Kentucky banks. Enlisted as private, First Kentucky Cavalry, 1862. Volunteer aide-de-camp to Gen. John S. Williams, 1862–1863. Lost race for the Confederate Congress in 1864. Served (as a volunteer) with the Twenty-eighth Virginia in the Wilderness campaign. Appointed colonel, Provisional Army of the Confederate States, September 13, 1864, to raise a regiment in Kentucky, the commission to be issued if he raised it within three months. Captured in Kentucky in 1865 while recruiting. The Union troops put him in chains, but after protests by the Confederate government he was treated as a prisoner of war and exchanged. Farmer and lawyer in Hopkinsville, Christian County, postwar. Newspaper owner. Died July 30, 1896, Hopkinsville. A relative noted that Morris "led a wild and roving life."

MOSS, JAMES W. Born October 1822, Greensburg, Kentucky, son of Tom and Judith Bullock Moss. Captain in Mexican War. Trader in livestock and produce in Greensburg and later Columbus, Kentucky. Captain, Company A, Second Kentucky, July 5, 1861. Captured at Fort Donelson. Exchanged September 1862. Major, December 1, 1862. Lieutenant colonel, September 20, 1863. Colonel, October 19, 1863. Mortally wounded in action at Jonesboro, August 31, 1864 (arm shattered), and captured. Died September 19, 1864, Marietta, Georgia, while in Union hands. First buried in Marietta. Reburied in State Cemetery, Frankfort, Kentucky, in 1888. A "stern and quiet" man, said by a fellow soldier to be "wholly insensible to fear."

MYNHEIR, WILLIAM HENRY. Name also spelled Mynhier. Born October 13, 1821, Morgan County, Kentucky, son of John and Sally McKenzie Mynheir. Raised in Fleming County. Prewar, sheriff of Morgan County. Circuit clerk, 1856–1861. Married Sallie Cartmell. First lieutenant, Company A, Fifth Kentucky, October 21, 1861. Captain, November 17, 1861. Major, November 14, 1862. Wounded in the thigh at the battle of Chickamauga. Morgan County judge postwar. Commissioner of circuit court. Moved to Mount Sterling in 1884. State representative. Died July 26, 1892, Mount Sterling. Buried Machpelah Cemetery, Mount Sterling.

NAPIER, THOMAS WILSON. Born April 25, 1818, Kentucky, son of Benjamin W. and Margaret Wilson Napier. Farmer in Lincoln County. County judge and state representative. Officer in the Mexican War, and wounded at the battle of Buena Vista. Unmarried. Quartermaster, First Kentucky Cavalry, 1861. Lieutenant colonel, Sixth Kentucky Cavalry, September 2, 1862. Wounded in the thigh in an action at Milton, Tennessee, March 20, 1863. Most of his regiment captured during Morgan's Ohio raid. Transferred to Adam Johnson's command and appointed (by Johnson) colonel, Fourth Regiment of Johnson's Partisan Ranger Brigade, August 1864. Elected sheriff of Lincoln County postwar. Killed September 18, 1869, in Stanford, Lincoln County, by a drunk he was trying to arrest. Buried Buffalo Springs Cemetery, Stanford.

NUCKOLS, JOSEPH PREYER. Born April 28, 1826, Barren County, Kentucky, son of Hezekiah and Susan Foster Nuckols. Deputy sheriff in Glasgow, Barren County, prewar. Captain, Kentucky State Guard. Married Malinda Carr; Caron Donaldson. Captain, Company A, Fourth Kentucky, September 13, 1861. Major, April 7, 1862. Lieutenant colonel, December 8, 1862. Colonel, February 28, 1863. Wounded in action at Shiloh, Murfreesboro, Chickamauga. Retired c. February 1864 because of his wounds. Commanded post of Aberdeen, Mississippi in late 1864. Paroled May 15, 1865, Meridian, Mississippi. County clerk postwar. State representative. State adjutant general. Died August 30, 1896, Glasgow. Buried Glasgow Cemetery. His uniform coat, showing his Chickamauga wound, still exists.

OWEN, WASHINGTON GOLDSBOROUGH. Born July 12, 1839, Frederick, Maryland, son of Thomas and Matilda Chase Goldsborough. Attended University of Maryland and medical school in Baltimore. Moved to Henderson, Kentucky, c. 1859. Druggist there. Married Minnie Evans. Second lieutenant, Company B, Fourth Kentucky, September 9, 1861. Resigned August 13, 1862. Transferred to Cobb's Artillery Battery briefly. Major, Tenth Kentucky Partisan Rangers, August 13, 1862. Captured in Morgan's Ohio raid and confined to the Columbus Penitentiary. Wounded in the lung during the war. Moved to Atlanta postwar. Physician and surgeon there. Died September 30, 1887, Atlanta. Buried Oakland Cemetery, Atlanta. Gen. Adam Johnson found Owen "a young man of much brilliance . . . the best drill-master in the command."

PARKER, NATHANIEL. Born August 16, 1825, Trimble County, Kentucky, son of Noah and Nancy Hunter Parker. Trimble County farmer. Helped manage his father's spa at the Bedford Mineral Springs. Captain, Kentucky State Guard, 1860. Married Sophronia Lane. First lieutenant, Buckner Guards, Kentucky Cavalry company. Major, Fourth Kentucky Cavalry, September 27, 1862. Shot in the heart and killed May 10, 1864, in an action at Wytheville, Virginia. First buried in Wytheville, later reburied in his hometown of Bedford, Kentucky, in the Independent Order of Odd Fellows Cemetery. A fellow soldier remembered Parker's "attractive personality and superb martial bearing. . . . [The soldiers] loved Parker."

PATTON, OLIVER ANDREW. Born May 30, 1839, Fleming County, Kentucky, son of Robert and Nancy Bryan Patton. Lawyer in Mount Sterling in 1860. Married Rachel E. Tompkins, a relative of President Ulysses S. Grant. Captain, Company G, Ninth Kentucky Mounted Infantry, no date. Lieutenant colonel of the Ninth and of Patton's Battalion, Partisan Rangers. Captured October 1863 but later exchanged. Moved to Nashville, Tennessee, and later to Charleston, West Virginia, postwar, to practice law. Died July 3, 1901, Deepwater, West Virginia. Buried Spring Hill Cemetery, Charleston. Col. W. W. Ward, in his diary, suspected Patton of malingering after his exchange, and one Union major called Patton "the meanest white man living."

PRENTICE, CLARENCE JOSEPH. Born November 24, 1840, Kentucky, son of powerful Louisville newspaper publisher George Prentice and his wife, Harriet Benham. Educated at Kentucky Military Institute and in Germany. Captain of the Hunt Guards of Louisville, Kentucky State Guard, in 1861. Married Julia McWilliams. Volunteer aide with Jeff Thompson in southeast Missouri, 1861. Major, Second Kentucky Cavalry Battalion. Volunteer aide-de-camp to General Wheeler. Arrested in April 1862 while visiting his Louisville home. After exchange, commissioned (September 1862) lieutenant colonel, Seventh Confederate Cavalry Battalion. Unit operated as "guerrillas" in eastern Kentucky and Wise County, Virginia. Surrendered at Chattanooga at the end of April 1865. Operated a whorehouse in Louisville postwar. Killed November 15, 1873, in a buggy accident. Buried Cave Hill Cemetery. A fellow officer called Prentice "agreeable and smart—well qualified to do much better than he does." Prentice's unit ("a band of thieves," according to one staff officer) had a well-earned reputation for marauding, embarrassing both Confederate authorities and his father, a prominent unionist.

PRYOR, MOSES TANDY. Born February 4, 1832, Kentucky, son of Henry and Amelia Tandy Pryor. "Trader" in Carroll County in 1860. Lieutenant, Kentucky State Guard, 1861. Married Barbara, sister of Col. Henry Giltner. Captain, Company E, Fourth Kentucky Cavalry, October 28, 1862. Lieutenant colonel, November 5, 1862. Taken prisoner at the battle of Cynthiana, June 12, 1864, and imprisoned at Johnson's Island for the rest of the war. Moved to Woodruff County, Arkansas, postwar, and operated a livery stable there. Died in Woodruff County January 8, 1873, of "swamp fever." Buried Independent Order of Odd Fellows Cemetery, Carrollton. "Quick, decisive, intelligent . . . a favorite with the men."

RAY, WILLIAM D. Born c. 1826, Trimble County, Kentucky, son of George and Minerva Lacklane Ray. Hotel owner in Bedford, Kentucky. Married Nancy Bain. Private, Buckner Guards, October 10, 1861. Delegate to Kentucky Secession Convention. Captain, Company A, Fourth Kentucky Cavalry, September 1862. Major, May 10, 1864. Captured June 12, 1864, at Cynthiana. Exchanged in 1865. Died c. 1867–1870. "A brave, reliable officer."

ROBERTS, WILLIS SLAUGHTER. Born March 7, 1837, Owenton, Kentucky, son of Willis and Laetitia Green Roberts. Attended Centre College. Lawyer in Scott County. Married Sarah Dickens. Captain, Company D, Ninth Kentucky, September 12, 1861. Wounded in the battle of Baton Rouge. Major, December 18, 1862. Killed January 2, 1863, in the charge of Breckinridge's Division at the battle of Murfreesboro. Buried Cave Hill Cemetery, Louisville. "There was not a more gallant officer."

ROGERS, JOHN BYRD. Born January 11, 1835, on a farm near Goodknight, Barren County, Kentucky, son of William Byrd and Nancy Bagby Roberts. A "love of sport" led him to wander the West, exploring and hunting. Taught school in Holt County, Missouri, then returned to Barren County to study law. First lieutenant, Kentucky State Guard. Unmarried. First lieutenant, Company A, Fourth Kentucky, August 1, 1861. Wounded at the battle of Shiloh. Captain, April 7, 1862. Major, May 28, 1864. Killed June 20, 1864, in skirmishing near Kennesaw Mountain, Georgia. According to a fellow soldier, he disappeared while relieving a skirmish line and was never heard from again. He had vowed never to return home until the Confederacy won its independence.

SELLARS, ROBERT HENDERSON. Born c. 1818, Tennessee. Carpenter in Graves County, Kentucky. Married Annie Lewis Boaz. Private, Company A, Seventh Kentucky, September 12, 1861. Elected major April 22, 1862. Defeated for major at May 1862 reorganization election. Discharged July 14, 1862, Vicksburg. Wagon maker in Mayfield, Graves County in 1870. Died in the 1870s.

SHACKLETT, ABSALOM REDMOND. Born December 7, 1826, Brandenburg, Meade County, Kentucky, son of Blancit and Rachel Ashcraft Shacklett. Farmer in Meade and McLean counties prewar. Private in U.S. Army in Mexican War. Married Minerva Jane Humphrey. Captain, Company D, Eighth Kentucky, October 13, 1861. Captured at Fort Donelson, exchanged September 1862. Lieutenant colonel, September 25, 1862. Regiment mounted in 1864. Colonel, July 29, 1864. Paroled May 1865 at Columbus, Mississippi. Farmer near Island, McLean County, postwar. State representative. Postmaster. Died August 27, 1910, Island. Buried Island Baptist Cemetery. Shacklett (known as "little Ap") was great-granduncle of Hall of Fame baseball player "Pee Wee" Reese.

SHAWHAN, JOHN. Born April 2, 1811, Bourbon County, Kentucky, son of Joseph and Sarah Ewalt Shawhan. Worked in the family whiskey distilling business in Bourbon and Harrison counties. State representative. County sheriff. Captain in Mexican War. Wounded at the battle of Buena Vista. Married Tabitha Rush. Captain, Company A, First Kentucky Cavalry, October 1, 1861. Wounded in an action at Ivy Mountain, Kentucky, November 1861. Major, First Kentucky Cavalry Battalion, March 12, 1862. Served in eastern Kentucky. Killed October 3, 1862, about eight miles from Morehead, Kentucky, in a skirmish with bushwhackers. Buried Old Cemetery, then Battle Grove Cemetery, Cynthiana. "A dry, cracklin' looking little fellow."

SHERRILL, JACOB LEANDER. Born June 14, 1825, Christian County, Kentucky, son of Jacob and Jincy Stephenson Sherrill. Ballard County farmer, known as "Lee J." Sherrill. Prospected for gold in California and lived in Texas for a while. First lieutenant, Kentucky State Guard, 1861. Married Amanda M. Cooper. Captain, Company F, Seventh Kentucky, October 1, 1861. Elected lieutenant colonel May 10, 1862. Killed in the battle of Tupelo, Mississippi, July 15, 1864. Reports of that battle called Sherrill "lionhearted," "brave and lamented—a modest, retiring officer."

SIMMS, WILLIAM EMMETT. Born January 2, 1822, Harrison County, Kentucky, son of William and Julia Shropshire Simms. Graduated from Transylvania University in 1846 with a law degree. Paris, Kentucky, lawyer. Captain in Mexican

War. Editor, *Kentucky State Flag*. State representative. U.S. Congress, 1859–1861. Married Lucy Blythe. Lieutenant colonel, First Kentucky Cavalry Battalion, December 24, 1861. Resigned February 17, 1862. Confederate senator, 1862–1865, serving on the Foreign Affairs Committee. Fled to Canada after the war but soon returned to Paris. Attorney and farmer there. Died June 25, 1898, Mount Airy, near Paris. Buried Paris Cemetery. A states' rights proponent, "a gallant soldier, an able lawyer."

SMITH, DABNEY HOWARD. Born November 24, 1821, Georgetown, Kentucky, son of Nelson and Sarah Kerr Smith. Attended Georgetown College and Transylvania University Law School. Graduated from Miami University of Ohio. Lawyer in Georgetown prewar. State representative and senator. Married Josephine Lemon. Colonel, Fifth Kentucky Cavalry, September 2, 1862. Captured July 19, 1863, during Morgan's Ohio raid and imprisoned at the Columbus Penitentiary with Morgan. Exchanged March 6, 1864. In January 1865, he applied for transfer to staff duty in Texas, in order to better care for his family (then in Kentucky). He noted that his regiment numbered fewer than fifty effective men. Paroled May 15, 1865, Columbus, Mississippi. Lawyer in Georgetown postwar. Kentucky state auditor. Died July 15, 1889, Louisville. Buried Lexington Cemetery. Smith's papers are at the Kentucky Historical Society and the Filson Club in Louisville.

SOERY, ROBERT B. L. Born c. 1837, Kentucky, son of William Soery. Last name also spelled Sorey. Raised in Trigg County. Commission merchant in New Orleans in 1861. Enlisted as private, Company C, Third Kentucky, September 12, 1861. Promoted to lieutenant and regimental adjutant, May 21, 1862. Wounded at the battle of Baton Rouge. Resigned January 15, 1863. Joined up with Adam R. Johnson's partisans. Appointed lieutenant colonel, Sypert's Kentucky Cavalry, September 6, 1864. Killed in action October 11, 1864, in a skirmish near Fort Donelson.

STEELE, THEOPHILUS. Born July 17, 1835, Fayette County, Kentucky, son of Dr. Theophilus and Caroline Worthy Steele. Graduated from the Kentucky School of Medicine. Studied medicine in Germany. Lexington physician prewar. Married Sophonisba Breckinridge, sister of Col. W. C. P. Breckinridge. Surgeon, Second Kentucky. Captured at Fort Donelson and exchanged. Captain, Company B, Seventh Kentucky Cavalry. Major, upon November 6, 1862, organization of regiment. Wounded January 1863. Captured July 26, 1863, at Cheshire, Ohio, during Morgan's raid. Lieutenant colonel, August 3, 1864. Captured September 1864 in Kentucky, while recruiting behind enemy lines. Released February 20, 1865. General Duke said he promoted Steele to colonel, with President Davis's consent, during Davis's flight from Richmond. Physician in Lexington and New York City postwar. Prominent in veterans' affairs. Died August 24,

1911, at his daughter's home on Long Island. Buried Mount Hope Cemetery, near New York City. "A lovable man, kind, gentle, tender."

STONER, ROBERT GATEWOOD. Born January 22, 1838, Bath County, Kentucky, son of George W. and Nancy Tribble Stoner. Bath County farmer. Married Alice Rogers; Ida Hamilton. Enlisted September 1861. Captain, Company E, First Battalion Kentucky Mounted Rifles, October 12, 1861. Resigned June 10, 1862. Major, Stoner's Kentucky Cavalry Battalion, fall of 1862. Lieutenant colonel, Ninth Kentucky Cavalry, December 15, 1862. Surrendered at Augusta, Georgia, May 1865. Farmed and bred horses in Montgomery and Bourbon counties postwar. Died September 5, 1898, at his Bourbon County home. Buried Paris Cemetery. A fellow officer said, "He had an eye like an eagle, and knew no such word as fear."

SYPERT, LEONIDAS ARMISTEAD. Born December 15, 1832, Lebanon, Tennessee, son of Hardy and Ann Donalson Sypert. Attended Cumberland University. Lawyer in Christian County, Kentucky, prewar. Married Martha D., daughter of Maj. William Henry. Served with Green's Kentucky Battery at Fort Donelson, escaping before the surrender. Wounded in action at Shiloh as a volunteer with an Arkansas regiment. Returned to Kentucky and recruited a company for Woodward's Kentucky Cavalry, but the unit, recruited for one year's service, was not accepted by Confederate authorities. Returned to Kentucky in 1864 to recruit a regiment. Colonel, Sypert's Kentucky Cavalry (Third Regiment, Adam Johnson's Partisan Ranger Brigade), September 6, 1864. Lawyer in Hopkinsville postwar. Died March 23, 1893, Christian County. Buried Cocke Cemetery, Christian County. Called "a thoroughly brave man and a gentleman" by a local newspaper.

TATE, THOMAS SIMPSON. Born November 2, 1844, Somerville, Tennessee, son of Sam and May Carnes Tate. Raised in Memphis, where his father was a prominent railroad president. Married Mary De Jarnette. Private, Company A, Fourth Tennessee, May 15, 1861. Private, Company A, Seventh Tennessee Cavalry, October 15, 1861. Promoted to first lieutenant and aide-de-camp on the staff of Gen. Nathan Bedford Forrest. Appointed by Forrest major, Twelfth Kentucky Cavalry, March 7, 1864. Wounded at battle of Brices Cross Roads. War Department later voided Tate's appointment. Merchant in Winona, Mississippi, postwar. Railroad contractor in Birmingham, Alabama. Mayor of Birmingham. Died May 6, 1917, Birmingham. Buried Elmwood Cemetery, Birmingham. Forrest felt his former staffer had "energy, ability and gallantry."

TENNEY, OTIS SETH. Born December 4, 1822, Windsor County, New Hampshire, son of Seth and Esther Miller Tenney. Graduated from Norwich Military College in Vermont. Taught at military schools in Delaware and Kentucky. Lawyer in Mount Sterling, Kentucky. Married Junia M. Warner. Major, Second Battalion Kentucky Mounted Rifles, March 12, 1862. Appointed major and quartermaster to General Cosby, September 9, 1864. Postwar, lawyer in Mount Sterling and (after 1882) Lexington. Died March 31, 1916, Fayette County. Buried Lexington Cemetery.

THOMPSON, ALBERT PETTY. Born March 3, 1829, Green County, Kentucky, son of Samuel and Alice Petty Thompson. Raised in Calloway County. Lawyer in Murray and Paducah, Kentucky, prewar. Elected commonwealth attorney of McCracken County. Married Mary Jane Bowman; Harriet Harding; Mary Mayes. Lieutenant colonel, Third Kentucky, September 2, 1861. Colonel, October 18, 1861. Wounded in the neck at Baton Rouge, where he led a brigade. Regiment mounted in 1864. Led brigade in Bedford Forrest's cavalry. Killed by a cannon shot March 25, 1864, in an attack on Paducah, his home town. Buried first in Oak Grove Cemetery, Paducah. Reburied in Bowman Graveyard, near Murray, Calloway County. A state historical marker is at the site of his death. Often recommended for promotion to general. Gen. Abe Buford called Thompson "a man of strong mind, highly cultivated."

THOMPSON, PRESTON. Born October 24, 1815, Scott County, Kentucky, son of Charles and Sarah Paine Thompson. Owned a gristmill in Scott County prewar. Partner in a cotton business in New Orleans. Unmarried. Elected lieutenant colonel, Fifth Kentucky Cavalry, September 2, 1862. Failed to report for duty and dropped from the rolls. Farmer in Scott County postwar, dying there April 17, 1889. Buried Georgetown Cemetery.

THOMPSON, THOMAS WILLIAMS. Born January 13, 1840, Louisville, Kentucky. Orphaned at an early age and raised by his uncle Thomas Williams in Louisville. Worked in his uncle's plumbing business prewar. Married Ophelia Welch. Captain, Kentucky State Guard, June 7, 1861. Captain, Company I, Fourth Kentucky, September 13, 1861. Wounded in action at Shiloh. Major, March 27, 1863. Lieutenant colonel, August 31, 1863. Wounded in action at Chickamauga. Colonel, probably February 1864. Wounded in action three times in the Atlanta campaign. Recommended in 1865 for promotion to general. Paroled at Nashville May 15, 1865, as colonel. Owner of a wholesale stove and tinware business in Louisville postwar. Clerk of the circuit court in Louisville, 1874–1880. Died there August 6, 1882. Buried Cave Hill Cemetery. A sketch by a friend called Thompson "quiet, firm, reticent, and self-reliant" (the same sketch says he was born in Philadelphia, February 28, 1839).

TRABUE, ROBERT PAXTON. Born January 1, 1824, Columbia, Adair County, Kentucky, son of Daniel and Mary Paxton Trabue. Raised in Columbia. Moved to Natchez, Mississippi, in the 1850s. Lawyer. Officer in Mexican War. Married

Hibernia Inge of Natchez. Colonel, Fourth Kentucky, September 13, 1861. Led brigade at Shiloh and Murfreesboro (after General Hanson's death). Died February 12, 1863, of pneumonia, at Richmond, Virginia, while on a visit there to lobby for promotion to general. Buried Hollywood Cemetery, Richmond. Reburied later in Natchez City Cemetery. Often recommended for promotion, exhibiting "the courage of a true soldier, and the coolness of an able commander."

TRIMBLE, EDWIN. Born c. 1838, Kentucky, son of Edwin and Dorothy Graham Trimble. Raised in Floyd County. Attended Emory & Henry College, 1857–1858. Clerk in Floyd County in 1860. Joined his parents in Bexar County, Texas, just prior to the war. First lieutenant, Company E, Fifth Kentucky, January 9, 1862. Mustered out, October 1862. Captain, Company A, Tenth Kentucky Cavalry, September 25, 1862. Lieutenant colonel, 1864. Colonel, August 3, 1864. Killed in the October 2, 1864, battle of Saltville, shot through the head. Buried first in the James Witten Cemetery, later in Maplewood Cemetery, Tazewell, Virginia. A staff officer called Trimble "a true patriot, an accomplished soldier, . . . a braver man never fell." Trimble's service record has him promoted to colonel August 3, 1864, and the next month he signed a receipt using that rank, but the records on promotion of field officers in the Tenth are very contradictory.

TUCKER, JOSEPH THOMAS. Born August 31, 1833, Boston, Massachusetts, son of Dr. Eben and Hannah White Tucker. Graduated from Yale University and Transylvania University Law School. Lawyer in Winchester, Kentucky, prewar. Married Mariam W. Hood, cousin of Gen. John Bell Hood. Lieutenant colonel, Eleventh Kentucky Cavalry, September 10, 1862. Colonel, July 4, 1863. Captured at Cheshire, Ohio, July 20, 1863, during Morgan's Ohio raid. Exchanged August 3, 1864. Colonel, Third Special Battalion, Duke's Brigade, winter of 1864–1865. Surrendered April 29, 1865, Mount Sterling, Kentucky, while in command of a brigade. Mined in Georgia, 1865–1869. Lawyer in Winchester after that. County attorney. State legislator. Died September 28, 1906, Winchester. Buried Winchester Cemetery.

WARD, WILLIAM WALKER. Born October 5, 1825, Ward's Crossroads, Tennessee, son of Nathan and Lucy Hughes Ward. Graduated from Cumberland University. Lawyer in Carthage, Tennessee. State representative, 1855–1857. Married Elizabeth Rucks. Private, Company B, Seventh Tennessee, May 20, 1861. Discharged May 19, 1862, due to an old ankle injury. Lieutenant colonel, Ninth Tennessee Cavalry, September 1, 1862. Colonel, December 23, 1862. Captured at Buffington Island during Morgan's Ohio raid. Imprisoned at Columbus and Fort Delaware. Exchanged August 3, 1864. Appointed on September 5, 1864, commander of the First Kentucky Special Cavalry Battalion, made up in part of survivors of the raid. Wounded in leg in action at Bull's Gap, November 12, 1864. Paroled at Columbus, Georgia, May 8, 1865. Carthage lawyer postwar.

Chancellor of Smith County. Died April 10, 1871, Smith County. Buried Rucks Family Cemetery near Rome, Tennessee. Basil Duke called Ward "intelligent, zealous and firm." Ward's war diary has been published.

WEBBER, THOMAS B. Born c. 1834, Virginia, son of Matthew W. and Martha Walker Webber. Raised in Tennessee by his father, a prominent Baptist minister. Prewar, merchant and postmaster in Byhalia, Mississippi. Married Ann Bogan in 1866. Private, Company D, Ninth Mississippi, March 26, 1861. Captain, Company F, Second Kentucky Cavalry (a Mississippi company), May 14, 1862. Major, January 24, 1863. Captured at Portland, Ohio, July 17, 1863, during Morgan's raid. Later exchanged. Died in Jackson, Mississippi, August 1869, of "softening of the brain." Buried Hill Crest Cemetery, Holly Springs, Mississippi. Called the "Iron Man" by his troopers, Webber was a fervent slavery and secession advocate.

WELBORN, WILLIAM JOSEPH NELSON. Born November 23, 1821, Bedford County, Tennessee, son of Kinchen and Narcissa Hess Welborn. Ran a livery stable in Gibson County, Tennessee, in 1850. Later moved to Columbus, Kentucky. Married Bernetta Crossland; Rebecca E. McLemore. First lieutenant, Company B, Seventh Kentucky, September 26, 1861. Major, November 1, 1861. Mortally wounded April 6, 1862, at the battle of Shiloh. Died at Corinth, Mississippi, April 16, 1862.

WICKLIFFE, CHARLES ARTHUR. Born June, 1819, Bardstown, Kentucky, son of Nathaniel and Ann (Logan) Wickliffe and nephew of Gov. Charles A. Wickliffe. Graduated from West Point in 1839. Lieutenant, U.S. Army, 1839–1842. Major, Fourteenth U.S. Infantry in Mexican War. Lawyer in Ballard County, Kentucky. State legislator. County attorney, 1851–1855. Militia colonel. Married Martha Eugenia Moore. Assistant adjutant general on staff of Gen. Leonidas Polk, October 1861. Colonel, Seventh Kentucky, November 1, 1861. Mortally wounded in action the second day of Shiloh. Praised for "distinguished service and noble conduct" in a report on that battle. Died April 22, 1862, near Jackson, Tennessee, at the home of William Butler. Probably buried in an unmarked grave near Jackson. The city of Wickliffe, Kentucky, is named for him.

WICKLIFFE, JOHN CREPPS. Born July 1, 1830, Nelson County, Kentucky, son of Gov. Charles A. Wickliffe and his wife, Margaret Crepps. Graduated from Centre College. Attorney in Louisville and Bardstown. State representative, 1857–1859. Secretary of the state senate, 1859–1861. Captain, Kentucky State Guard. Married Ellen Hunt Curd. Captain, Company B, Ninth Kentucky, October 2, 1861. Major, May 15, 1862. Lieutenant colonel, April 22, 1863. Resumed law practice after the war. Judge. U.S. district attorney. State adjutant general 1893–

1894. Died January 3, 1913, Attala, Alabama. Buried Lexington Cemetery. A "tried and true soldier to the cause he espoused."

WITHERS, WILLIAM TEMPLE. Born January 8, 1825, Harrison County, Kentucky, son of William and Eliza Perrin Withers. Graduated from Bacon College in Kentucky. Lawyer in Cynthiana, Kentucky. Lawyer and planter in Jackson, Mississippi. Officer in Mexican War. Wounded in action at Buena Vista. Married Martha Sharkey. Acting general of Kentucky recruits in 1861, while commanding Camp Boone, a training camp on the Tennessee-Kentucky border. Requested by the secretary of war to raise an artillery regiment. Captain, Company A, First Mississippi Artillery, March 22, 1862. Colonel, May 14, 1862. Often on sick leave, due to his Mexican War wounds. Distinguished at Chickasaw Bluff, while leading the Confederate right. Captured at Vicksburg, while commanding artillery there. Later served in the Mobile defenses. Retired to Invalid Corps March 5, 1865. Lawyer in Jackson, Mississippi, postwar. Moved to near Lexington, Kentucky, in 1871, and bred horses. Died June 16, 1889, Lexington. Buried Lexington Cemetery. An obituary called Withers "a thorough Christian gentleman, a noble and honest man."

WOODWARD, THOMAS GRIFFITTS. Born July 30, 1827, New Haven, Connecticut, son of Thomas G. Woodward, an influential newspaper editor, and his wife, Abigail Montgomery. Attended Yale and West Point but was dismissed from both due to drunkenness. Moved to Christian County, Kentucky, c. 1847–1848. Teacher in Garrettsburg. Lawyer. Captain, Woodward's Company (a one-year unit, soon attached to the First Kentucky Cavalry), Tennessee Cavalry, June 25, 1861. Lieutenant colonel, First Kentucky Cavalry, 1861 (probably December 19). Colonel, March 14, 1862. Lieutenant colonel, Woodward's Kentucky Cavalry Battalion, 1862. Colonel, Woodward's Second Kentucky Cavalry, December 1862. Court-martialed four times during the war, once suspended from command and twice reprimanded. Led forces that captured the Union garrison at Clarksville, Tennessee, in 1862. Wounded in action in the attack on Dover in 1863. Detached on recruiting duty in Kentucky in 1864. Shot and killed while parading around the streets of Union-held Hopkinsville, Kentucky, August 19, 1864. Buried Riverside Cemetery, Hopkinsville. A short man (termed "an insignificant little cuss" by a Union colonel he captured at Clarksville), eccentric, extravagantly dressed, he is said to have ridden into Hopkinsville alone and intoxicated, proclaiming he could take the town single-handed.

CONTRIBUTORS

N.B.: The institution granting the contributor's highest degree is given in parentheses following his or her name.

BRUCE S. ALLARDICE (Illinois) is past president of the Civil War Round Table of Chicago. A lifelong Chicago-area resident and long-suffering White Sox fan, he is a graduate of the University of Illinois and the University of Illinois School of Law and teaches at South Suburban College. He has authored or coauthored three books and numerous articles on the Civil War. His *More Generals in Gray* (1995) was a selection of the History Book Club. A fourth book, *Confederate Colonels: A Biographical Register,* will be published in 2008.

LINDSEY APPLE (South Carolina) is emeritus professor of history at Georgetown College. The recipient of the Sears-Roebuck Teachers Award and the Cawthorne Excellence in Teaching Award, he served on the board of the Kentucky Historical Society. His publications include *Scott County, Kentucky: A History* (1993), *Cautious Rebel: A Biography of Susan Clay Sawitzky* (1997), and a number of articles in journals and historical and biographical encyclopedias. Another work, on the family legacy of Henry Clay, is in progress.

ARTHUR W. BERGERON JR. (Louisiana State) is a reference historian at the U.S. Army Military History Institute, Carlisle Barracks, Pennsylvania. He is a member of the Harrisburg Civil War Round Table and a past president of the Baton Rouge and Richmond Civil War Round Tables. His publications include *A Thrilling Narrative: The Memoir of a Southern Unionist* (2006); *The Civil War in Louisiana,* 2 vols. (2002, 2004); *Louisianans in the Civil War* (2002); *The Civil War Reminiscences of Major Silas*

T. Grisamore, CSA (1993); *Confederate Mobile, 1861–1865* (1991); and *Guide to Louisiana Confederate Military Units, 1861–1865* (1989).

C. David Dalton (Kentucky) is professor of history and holds the Elizabeth Hoyt Clark Chair of Humanities at College of the Ozarks. The recipient of the 2000 Missouri Governor's Award for Excellence in Teaching, he has been a frequent speaker before Civil War Round Tables in Kentucky, Indiana, and Missouri as well as having authored several publications related to Kentucky and the Civil War.

Stephen Davis (Emory) of Atlanta is the author of *Atlanta Will Fall: Sherman, Joe Johnston, and the Yankee Heavy Battalions* (2000). He has written numerous articles for such scholarly and popular magazines as *Civil War History* and *Civil War Times Illustrated*. For over twenty years he served as book editor for *Blue & Gray Magazine*.

William C. Davis (Sonoma State) is the author or editor of more than fifty books on Civil War and Southern history. He spent twenty-one years in executive management in the book and magazine publishing industry, including many years as editor and publisher of *Civil War Times Illustrated*, after which he devoted a decade to writing and consulting in the United States and England. Since 2000 he has been professor of history and director of programs for the Virginia Center for Civil War Studies at Virginia Tech, Blacksburg.

Charles Elliott (Southeastern Louisiana) is instructor of history at Southeastern Louisiana University. He won the 1997 William S. Coker Prize in Gulf South History for "Bienville's English Turn Incident: Anecdotes Influencing History." He is coeditor of *Carnivals and Conflicts: A Louisiana History Reader* (2000) and author of "A Geography of Power: French and Indians in Louisiana's Florida Parishes, 1699–1706," which was published in *A Fierce and Fractious Frontier: The Curious Development of Louisiana's Florida Parishes* (2004). He directed three documentary films: *Louisiana's Florida Parishes: Securing the Good Life from a Troubled Land* (2002), *Reluctant Americans: The West Florida Revolt* (2003), and *Manchac Swamp: Manmade Disaster in Search of Resolution* (2006).

John D. Fowler (Tennessee) is associate professor of history at Kennesaw State University. He teaches courses on the antebellum South, the

Civil War, U.S. military experience, World War II, and the Third Reich. His research focuses on the Western military heritage and the impact war has had on society. Among his recent publications are *Mountaineers in Gray: The Story of the Nineteenth Tennessee Volunteer Infantry Regiment, C.S.A.* (2004), which won the nationally recognized Mrs. Simon Baruch University Award for the best manuscript in Civil War history in 2002; and *The Confederate Experience*, which will be released in the fall of 2008.

ROBERT I. GIRARDI (Loyola of Chicago) is employed as a homicide detective for the Chicago Police Department. He is a past president of the Civil War Round Table of Chicago and a fellow of the Company of Military Historians. His publications include *The Soldier's View: The Civil War Art of Keith Rocco* (2004) and *The Memoirs of Brigadier General William Passmore Carlin, U.S.A.* (1999). Two of his works, *The Military Memoirs of General John Pope* (1998) and *The New Annals of the Civil War* (2004), were selections of the History Book Club. He is currently coauthoring a biography of Union general Gouverneur K. Warren.

CHARLES D. GREAR (Texas Christian) is assistant professor of history at Prairie View A & M University. The 2005 recipient of the Lawrence T. Jones III Research Fellowship in Civil War Texas History from the Texas State Historical Association, he is currently the book-review editor for the H-CivWar online discussion group. His publications include "For Land and Family: Local Attachments and the Grapevine Volunteers," *Military History of the West* (2003); and "Texans to the Home Front: Why Lone Star Soldiers Returned to Texas during the War," *East Texas Historical Journal* (2007).

LOWELL H. HARRISON (New York) taught at New York University, West Texas State University, and Western Kentucky University before retiring in 1988. Among his books are *The Civil War in Kentucky* (1975, 1988) and *Lincoln of Kentucky* (2000). He has published some two dozen articles on the Civil War in various journals.

LAWRENCE LEE HEWITT (Louisiana State), a native of Louisville and a graduate of the University of Kentucky (BA, 1974), was professor of history at Southeastern Louisiana University. The 1991 recipient of that university's President's Award for Excellence in Research and the Charles L. Dufour Award for "outstanding achievements in preserving the heritage of the American Civil War," he is a past president of the Baton Rouge Civil War

Round Table and former managing editor of *North & South*. His publications include *Port Hudson, Confederate Bastion on the Mississippi* (1987), *The Confederate High Command & Related Topics* (1990), *Leadership During the Civil War* (1992), and *Louisianians in the Civil War* (2002).

Nathaniel C. Hughes (North Carolina), a native Tennessean, has had two careers. One has been as a teacher, coach, and headmaster in Bell Buckle, Tennessee, at St. Mary's Episcopal School and at Girls Preparatory School in Memphis, and at the University of Memphis. His second career has been in writing history. He has published twenty-three books, from *General William J. Hardee: Old Reliable* (1965) to his latest, *In Taller Cotton* (2006), with Gary Gallagher and Bob Krick. He also served in the Marine Corps as leader of an armored amphibian platoon and takes great pride in his three sons' becoming Marine officers.

M. Jane Johansson (North Texas) is currently associate professor of history at Rogers State University in Oklahoma. A native Oklahoman, she has authored *Peculiar Honor: A History of the 28th Texas Cavalry, 1862–1865* (1998) and edited *Widows by the Thousand: The Civil War Correspondence of Theophilus and Harriet Perry, 1862–1864* (2000). In recent years, she also served as the coeditor of the Papers of Will Rogers Project. She is currently researching the history of the Adams-Gibson Louisiana brigade.

Marshall D. Krolick (Northwestern) is a retired attorney. A former president of the Civil War Round Table of Chicago, he was the 1990 recipient of its Nevins-Freeman Award for distinguished scholarship and dedication to Civil War study. He has addressed Civil War organizations and symposiums throughout the country, served as a guide for Civil War battlefield tours, and contributed a column to *Civil War Times Illustrated* for several years. Other published works include articles in *Blue & Gray Magazine*, *Virginia Country Magazine's Civil War Quarterly*, *Civil War Magazine*, and *Gettysburg Magazine*, and the introduction to the reprint edition of the *History of the Eighth Cavalry Regiment, Illinois Volunteers*.

Mary Gorton McBride (Louisiana State) was professor of English and dean of liberal arts at Louisiana State University at Shreveport and at Florida Atlantic University, where she also served as vice president of the Broward County campuses. She is the author (with Ann Mathison McLaurin) of *Randall Lee Gibson of Louisiana: Confederate General and New South Reformer* (2007). She lives in Fairhope, Alabama.

BRIAN D. MCKNIGHT (Mississippi State) is assistant professor of history at Angelo State University, San Angelo, Texas. He is a specialist in the American Civil War who focuses on the issue of loyalty; his publications include *Contested Borderland: The Civil War in Appalachian Kentucky and Virginia* (2006) and numerous scholarly articles. He is currently working on a biography of the infamous Confederate guerrilla Champ Ferguson.

ALEXANDER MENDOZA (Texas Tech) is assistant professor of history at the University of Texas at Tyler. His book, *The Struggle for Command: General James Longstreet and the First Corps in the West,* will be published in 2008.

RAYMOND MULESKY (New York at Stony Brook) is a member of the Southwestern Indiana Civil War Round Table. He specializes in the roles played by Indiana and Kentucky in the Civil War and is author of *Thunder from a Clear Sky: Stovepipe Johnson's Confederate Raid on Newburgh, Indiana* (2005). He is now writing his second book about Indiana's Civil War experience.

JAMES M. PRICHARD (Wayne State) has supervised the Kentucky State Archives research room since 1985. A native of Dayton, Ohio, and a member of the Lexington Civil War Round Table, he has traveled the state for over ten years frequently speaking on Civil War–era topics for the Kentucky Humanities Council. A contributor to the *Biographical Dictionary of the Union,* David S. Heidler and Jeanne T. Heidler's *Encyclopedia of the American Civil War, Encyclopedia of World Slavery, Civil War Times, Virginia Country Magazine,* and *North & South,* he has coauthored a history of the Tenth Kentucky Cavalry, CSA, and is currently working on a coauthored biography of Union general Stephen G. Burbridge. His essay on "Devil Anse" Hatfield appears in the 1863 volume of the *Virginia at War* series, published by the University Press of Kentucky.

JEFFERY S. PRUSHANKIN (Arkansas) is lecturer in American history at Penn State University's Abington College. His specialization is the military history of the Civil War, and he received the 2006 Penn State Abington Special Recognition Award for developing and implementing a Gettysburg Staff-Ride for students. Recent publications include *A Crisis in Confederate Command: Edmund Kirby Smith, Richard Taylor, and the Army of the Trans-Mississippi* (2005) and "They Came to Butcher Our People: The Civil War in the West," in *Struggle for a Vast Future: The American Civil War* (2006). He is currently writing a biography of Edmund Kirby Smith.

JAMES A. RAMAGE (Kentucky) is Regents Professor of History at Northern Kentucky University. He won the 2003 Kentucky Acorn Award for teaching excellence presented by the Kentucky Advocates for Higher Education. In 2005 the City of Fort Wright named the James A. Ramage Civil War Museum in recognition of his work in preserving Civil War Battery Hooper. His book *Rebel Raider: The Life of General John Hunt Morgan* (1986) won the Douglas Southall Freeman Award and was co-winner of the Kentucky Governor's Award. He also wrote *Gray Ghost: The Life of Col. John Singleton Mosby* (1999).

CHARLES P. ROLAND (Louisiana State) served as a combat infantry captain in Europe in World War II and as assistant to the chief historian of the U.S. Army 1951–1952. A member of the history department of Tulane University 1952–1970 and Alumni Professor of History at the University of Kentucky 1970–1988, he was also the Harold Keith Johnson Visiting Professor of Military History at the U.S. Army Military History Institute and Army War College 1981–1982, and visiting professor of military history at the U.S. Military Academy 1985–1986 and 1991–1992. He is the author of many books on the Civil War and the American South, including *Albert Sidney Johnston: Soldier of Three Republics* (1964, 2001) and *An American Iliad: The Story of the Civil War* (1991, 2001).

STUART W. SANDERS (Centre College) is Civil War heritage specialist and community services administrator for the Kentucky Historical Society. He is former executive director of the Perryville Battlefield Preservation Association and has written for *The U.S. Encyclopedia of Military History, Civil War History, Civil War Times Illustrated, Military History Quarterly, America's Civil War,* the *Journal of America's Military Past, Blue & Gray Magazine, Civil War: The Magazine of the Civil War Society,* and several other publications.

THOMAS E. SCHOTT (Louisiana State) served for many years as a historian for the U.S. Air Force and U.S. Special Operations Command. He is the author of *Alexander H. Stephens of Georgia: A Biography* (1988), which won both the Society of American Historians and the Jefferson Davis awards. He has also written numerous articles and reviews on subjects ranging from the Civil War to baseball to theology.

PETER J. SEHLINGER (Kentucky) was professor of Latin American history at Indiana University, Indianapolis, 1967–1997. A Louisville native, he has published articles on Chilean and Peruvian history and U.S. diplomatic history in journals in this country, Chile, and Peru, as well as a guide to archives and libraries in Chile. He is coauthor with Holman Hamilton of *Spokesman for Democracy: Claude G. Bowers, 1878–1958* (2000) and author of a biography and three articles on William Preston.

BRIAN STEEL WILLS (Georgia) is Kenneth Asbury Chair of History in the Department of History and Philosophy at the University of Virginia's College at Wise. He is the author of numerous works relating to the American Civil War, including *A Battle from the Start: The Life of Nathan Bedford Forrest* (1992), *The War Hits Home: The Civil War in Southeastern Virginia*, (2001), and *Gone with the Glory: The Civil War in Cinema* (2006). He received the Outstanding Faculty Award from the State of Virginia in 2000.

TERRENCE J. WINSCHEL (Mississippi College) serves as historian at Vicksburg National Military Park. He is author of *Triumph & Defeat: The Vicksburg Campaign, Vol. 2* (2006), *Vicksburg is the Key: The Struggle for the Mississippi River* (2003), *The Civil War Diary of a Common Soldier* (2001), *Vicksburg: Fall of the Confederate Gibraltar* (1999), and *Triumph & Defeat: The Vicksburg Campaign* (1998). He was the 2004 recipient of the Nevins-Freeman Award presented by the Civil War Round Table of Chicago and the 2006 Charles L. Dufour Award presented by the Civil War Round Table of New Orleans.

ILLUSTRATION CREDITS

INDEX